HARRY'S WAR

The Great War Diary of
HARRY DRINKWATER

Edited by Jon Cooksey and David Griffiths

EBURY
PRESS

1 3 5 7 9 10 8 6 4 2

This edition published 2014
First published in 2013 by Ebury Press, an imprint of Ebury Publishing
A Random House Group company

Introduction and additional text copyright © Jon Cooksey 2013
Original diaries copyright © David Griffiths and Jon Cooksey

Jon Cooksey has asserted his right to be identified as the author
of the introduction and additional text in accordance with the
Copyright, Designs and Patents Act 1988

The Random House Group Limited Reg. No. 954009

Addresses for companies within the Random House Group can be found at
www.randomhouse.co.uk

A CIP catalogue record for this book is available from the British Library

The Random House Group Limited supports the Forest Stewardship
Council® (FSC®), the leading international forest-certification organisation.
Our books carrying the FSC label are printed on FSC®-certified paper. FSC is
the only forest-certification scheme supported by the leading environmental
organisations, including Greenpeace. Our paper procurement policy can be
found at www.randomhouse.co.uk/environment

Printed and bound by CPI Group (UK) Ltd, Croydon, CR0 4YY

ISBN 9780091957223

To buy books by your favourite authors and register for offers visit
www.randomhouse.co.uk

CONTENTS

PREFACE

by David Griffiths

The Harry Drinkwater diary is unique. It is the only one, as far as I know, written day-by-day for five years by a private soldier who later became an officer in the British Army. As the owner of the diary and the many artefacts connected with it, I have often been asked how I acquired them.

By pure chance, that moment came on my birthday in 1980, at an auction in Stratford-upon-Avon. Amongst those bidding was the Imperial War Museum, which already held a copy donated by Harry prior to his death in 1978. This brave young man's Military Cross and other medals were also bought by me. Later, I acquired other related items from the family.

My interest in the Great War springs from the tales my father told me of his terrifying experiences as a Vickers machine gunner in the Machine Gun Corps. Then came the Second World War, and as a child, I remember only too clearly the searchlights, the guns and the bombing. Perhaps it was only natural that a lifetime interest in battlefields and militaria followed for me.

Many years ago, I spent a fascinating three weeks in France and Belgium driving to every village, building, field and forest which Harry mentions in his diary. It must have been an amusing sight to see this Englishman, parked at the edge of a field, rummaging through a library of Great War books, neatly arranged in the boot of his car. I climbed into attics where Harry had slept and explored stables where he had rested with his comrades, covered in mud, eating a slice of cold bacon and a piece of stale bread. A complete on-the-spot reading of his day-to-day diary made me realise what an utterly brave young man Harry was, and lucky too, as he admits that he should have died many times.

I hope you will enjoy it. You will certainly feel his presence as the diary works its way into your soul. You will hear his voice and be lost in a world of mud, blood and screaming shells. You will feel the futility of war, as Harry sometimes did, and profound admiration for the young man who did his duty and endured fighting on the Somme, at Arras, at Ypres, on the bank of the River Piave in Italy and finally in the Nieppe forest. Decorated for gallantry once, wounded twice, after five and a half years of Army service he was still indomitable. He was, and still is, an example to us all. When you have read this book, perhaps you will salute him, as I do now with the publication of his diary.

David Griffiths
Gerrards Cross
July 2013

INTRODUCTION

by Jon Cooksey

If the angry Egyptian who stepped from a carriage in the central station square in Cairo on the evening of 3 December 1919 had raised his sights just a fraction higher before pulling the trigger of his revolver, this book might never have been published. His target was Harold Victor Drinkwater, a 30-year-old major in the Royal Warwickshire Regiment, then serving as commandant of a leave camp for Indian troops on the outskirts of Cairo. Although one bullet struck the pavement and lodged in his foot, Harold Drinkwater – Harry – survived, along with his adjutant who was with him at the time. We know this because Harry later recorded the events in his diary, a diary he had kept faithfully for more than five years, ever since he had rushed to the local recruiting office in his home town of Stratford-upon-Avon in the heady days of the summer of 1914 in response to Lord Kitchener's steely gaze, pointing finger and patriotic appeal, 'Your Country Needs You'.

Harry Drinkwater first fought in the squalid trenches on the Western Front in France in December 1915, took part in the titanic struggles against the Germans on the Somme and the charnel house which was the Third Battle of Ypres – always Passchendaele to those who fought it – then moved south to take on the Austro-Hungarian Army in Italy before a final stint on the Western Front which culminated in a serious wound and the award of the Military Cross for gallantry. Harry had promised faithfully in 1914 to serve his king and country and he had steadfastly done just that, as both a lowly private and a bright, intelligent young officer, commissioned from the ranks to be a leader of men. Above all, Harry had survived the carnage which claimed the lives of so many of his contemporaries and robbed the world of untold promise and potential.

To have been murdered at the hand of a lone assassin in a Cairo square would have been an ignoble end to a tumultuous five years of this young man's life and Harry's diary, his remarkable record of those dark, dangerous times, may have been lost forever. That he survived was yet another remarkable piece of good fortune which allows his fascinating account of those years to be read at last by a wider audience.

Yet I almost allowed this exceptional diary to slip through my fingers.

The date 4 August 2014 marks the centenary of Britain's declaration of war on Germany and, for the British, the outbreak of the First World War. There are now no survivors left who served during the 1914–1918 war to tell their story in person on the centenary. The First World War has passed from living memory.

But a good many first-hand accounts remain. Several diaries and memoirs written during the war appeared in the 1920s, with other accounts published during the following five decades. But as the participants grew older, so the distance between what they had actually experienced and what they could remember grew greater. The link became more tenuous; the immediacy was lost and when, finally, they passed away with their stories untold, their memories were gone forever. As the centenary of the war approached, so it became increasingly difficult to find previously unheard, yet authentic voices of those who fought in the great battles of the 'Great War for Civilisation'. Harry Drinkwater's is such a voice, a rich, vibrant and powerful voice, yet one which would have gone unheeded by me except for a phone call in 2012.

The caller – David Griffiths – explained that he'd had Harry Drinkwater's war diary in his possession for decades, thought it very good – possibly unique – and wondered if somehow it might be published. Would I care to read it and offer an opinion? Over the years I have received many such requests. Keeping a wartime diary – although highly illegal due to possible breaches of security if it fell into the wrong hands – was not unusual. Many men kept some form of daily record but most consisted of just a few hastily scribbled lines; flimsy sketches of what a man had done on a particular day with only slight variations on the theme of 'went up the line', 'came out of the line', 'went into rest'. I had read several of those. Though valuable to the soldier in charting his progress through the great adventure of the war, or indeed to his family in the years that followed, such entries can rarely sustain a reader's interest for long or can be said to add significantly to the sum total of knowledge of the First World War. Did I want to make a long journey to read such a document? Yet Mr Griffiths was persuasive. Harry Drinkwater had joined as a Kitchener volunteer in 1914 and became an officer in 1917, he said; he had served on the Somme, at Ypres and in Italy and had received the Military Cross for bravery. Most important of all, he had survived. It was an interesting war record. I fixed a date in my own diary.

As I started to leaf through the pages of the huge, brown leather-bound war diary, and to read the entries, I began to hear Harry Drinkwater speak to me in a distinctive voice which carried across a distance of almost 100 years. The more I read, the more Harry's voice developed and became stronger, more insightful and more passionate as it matured. He began to draw me in and I realised that here was a very rare thing indeed; a Great War diary spanning almost five years of continuous service by a man who survived some of the worst fighting in which the British Army was involved. Here was a diary which chronicled Harry's experiences of life and death in the trenches, containing vivid personal descriptions of the brutal vagaries of war written in real time on the battlefields, charting, with a refreshing candour and honesty, the mixed fortunes which befell Harry and the men with whom he lived and served.

With Harry acting as my guide and interpreter, I was transported to the very heart of the action; I felt the cold, cloying mud oozing into boots and the quickening pulse before action, heard the terrifying crash of exploding shells, smelled the acrid fumes of cordite and mustard gas and the sharp, rusting-iron scent of spilled blood. I also felt the hurt at Harry's loss. I knew, long before I had finished reading it, that Harry's diary was truly something remarkable. But who was Harry Drinkwater and what shaped him?

Harry was born on 19 February 1889 in Stratford-upon-Avon. His father, David, was a boot dealer who ran his business from a shop in Henley Street – a short stroll from the house where William Shakespeare first drew breath in 1564. Harry's father worked in the boot and shoe trade all of his life. Originally from Corse, Gloucestershire, by his mid-thirties, David Drinkwater had worked his way up to be manager of a boot and shoe business on Worcester High Street, having married Harry's mother, Rachel Wilson, in 1874.

The couple already had three children, Harry's eldest brother Robert, and sisters Ella and Clara, when they moved east to Stratford-upon-Avon, and soon the family increased by two more sons: William, born in 1886, then Harry, the last and youngest of the Drinkwater children.

Harry's birth coincided with a period of prosperity for the Drinkwater family. Within a three-month period in 1898 David Drinkwater bought his business and two other properties outright. Harry would grow up in relative comfort as the son of a successful businessman, an upbringing which included the instilling of a strong moral compass. The members of the Drinkwater family were committed Wesleyan Methodists and prominent members of the local chapel. Harry attended the adjoining Sunday school regularly and was imbued with the core values which powered late Victorian and Edwardian society: those of duty and service to God, monarch, country and family.

Tragedy struck the Drinkwater family two days into the new year of 1898, with the death of Harry's sister, Clara. Death was no stranger to the families of Britain at the turn of the 19th century, irrespective of the social class from which they were drawn. Accidents occurred more frequently and disease was no respecter of privilege or position. Clara Drinkwater was just 16 and Harry, eight years younger, would have grieved and would then have had to get on with his life.

In September 1901, Harry followed in the footsteps of his eldest brother Robert as a boarder at the King Edward VI Grammar School in the heart of the old town. Here he developed his handwriting, grammar and punctuation and learned to organise his thoughts and ideas on paper.

Influenced by the ethos of muscular Christianity established in several leading English public schools, outdoor sports and team games were also features of Harry's schooling. He played cricket for the Second XI and by the spring of 1903 was playing for the 'Football' (Rugby) XV, sometimes as captain of the Second XV. 'This diminutive full-back should without doubt be heard of a good deal in the distant future,' commented the school magazine, *The Stratfordian*, in March 1903. 'Very plucky, quite willing to collar anyone and to stop any rush.' Harry would need every ounce of pluck he could muster a year later when, in February 1904, six years after the death of his sister Clara, his 28-year-old eldest brother Robert collapsed and died suddenly. Harry had now lost two close family members in the space of six years. He was learning to cope with loss.

With Robert's death, the mantle of assisting their father in the family firm fell on the shoulders of middle brother William, two years Harry's senior. With no niche for Harry, he had to go out and find his own way and, by 1911, was living at a lodging house and working as a shop assistant at an ironmongers in Banbury in Oxfordshire.

Whether he enjoyed his job, or felt it had prospects, we will never know, for three years later, in August 1914, Britain declared war on Germany and Harry travelled back to his home town to join the army. He was one of more than 343,000 men throughout Britain who volunteered for the army in the first five weeks of the war. However, when called for his medical, he was told he was half an inch too short and was duly turned down. Undeterred, Harry travelled to Birmingham the following Monday to try again. He wanted to join the Birmingham 'Pals'.

Like many industrial towns and cities, Birmingham was intent on raising, equipping and training its own battalion of Pals – a recruitment tool which drew men from the same towns, trades, occupations or backgrounds into local units – which were then offered to the War Office as a complete battalion.

The concept behind the raising of Pals battalions seemed to be a sensible solution to the burgeoning logistical problems created by the nationwide tsunami of young men desperate to get into uniform. Spurred on by the desire to ensure that their towns and cities were in the vanguard of those contributing the most at this testing time, civic leaders tapped into the core values of duty, service to king and country, honour and self-sacrifice which had been drilled into the nation's young men in schools, Sunday schools, chapels and churches.

Though the seeds of the idea were sown with the raising of a Stockbrokers' Battalion of men who worked in the City of London, it really took off in Liverpool where Lord Derby appealed directly to local businessmen, telling them they need not enlist alone and risk being posted to strange battalions in distant parts alongside men who spoke in strange dialects. They could live with their pals and eat, drill, shoot, crawl and charge with their pals. With their pals they would go to war and get a 'crack at the Hun'. And so the unique phenomenon of the Pals battalions was born. Swept along by the swirling currents of a great crusade, while clinging to those twin pillars of duty and honour, what everyone – both leaders and the led alike – had overlooked was that the logical corollary of 'join together, train together, fight together', might ultimately be 'die together'. The ultimate outcome in a big battle would mean whole streets, whole factories, stripped of their young men, leaving entire communities wracked with grief.

Successful in his second attempt to join up, Harry was given the regimental number 161 and placed in No. 2 Platoon, A Company of the 2nd Birmingham City Battalion – the 2nd Birmingham Pals – later to become the 15th Battalion of the Royal Warwickshire Regiment. Harry was now a proud addition to Kitchener's New Army with an insider's view of one of the most significant and, with hindsight, infamous socio-military phenomena of the First World War – the Pals battalions.

It is at this point that Harry starts to commit his thoughts to paper. His entries are at first concise. The battalion's early organisation and training followed a similar pattern to that of most of the Pals battalions which sprang up during the late summer and autumn of 1914. It is with his departure for the Western Front in November 1915 that Harry's war diary begins in earnest. Posted to the extreme southern limit of the entire British line on the Western Front, he enters the trenches for the first time just before Christmas in 1915. Conditions are truly atrocious and here the steady haemorrhage of casualties begins. Later, looking back on his war service, Harry regards that first month in the trenches on the Somme as 'one of the worst'.

In February 1916 he moves north to the front at Arras and helps dig beneath the German lines, experiencing the terrifying power and ferocity of prolonged bombardments and the sudden, violent shock and awe of mine explosions. His diary points to the implications of advances in science, technology and engineering when applied to waging war in the early 20th century, and through Harry we begin to understand the overwhelming power of modern artillery to deliver indiscriminate death and mutilation. We sense some of the nerve-shredding fear of living every moment knowing that the earth beneath his feet could erupt in sheets of flame. We hear of the machine gun, the rifle grenade and the trench mortar and their devastating effects as, through Harry's words, we witness the fatal final moments of many of his contemporaries of the original Birmingham Pals. We begin to wonder how the human heart can live under such an onslaught.

Yet there are also precious moments of relief away from the front line – and this too is part of Harry's war. He records the enjoyment of watching football matches played in real football jerseys. That single and almost mundane detail serves as a stark reminder of a normality left behind. Later he goes for a walk alone and basks in the warmth of the sun, an experience that fills him with life, reinvigorates his hope and seems to wake him, albeit fleetingly, from a nightmare.

After service during the infamously harsh winter of 1916–1917, Harry enquires about the possibility of a commission as an officer. Plucked from the ranks, he is whisked away from the battlefield to Ireland, to be trained as an officer cadet.

Harry returns to the Western Front in the autumn of 1917, but he is not the same man who left it eight months earlier. By accepting the King's Commission he moves from being an educated, perceptive private soldier to being an educated, perceptive junior officer. The day he moves from the ranks into the officer class he enters a different world; a world ordered according to a strict hierarchy and governed by an Edwardian paternalism. Whereas once, when he had been one of many in the ranks, he could sometimes be seen to fail, now, as a leader of men, he cannot, indeed will not, be allowed to do so. For almost two years Harry has been told where to go, what to do and at what time to do it. Now, he gives the orders and he knows exactly what he is asking of his men, for he has been on the receiving end of such orders many times.

Harry must have felt the burden of responsibility keenly. He would have been well aware that in following his orders the chances were that some of his charges would die. Now, instead of following an officer over the top it would be he who would be the first over. His men would look to him for leadership, and they would follow him into battle if he led them well.

His first opportunity to show his mettle could not have come in a harder school than that of Ypres in October 1917. The visceral description of his part in the disaster which was his battalion's attack on the German pillboxes around the atomised Polderhoek Château during the Third Battle of Ypres is jaw-dropping in its intensity.

Early in 1918 Harry and his men are shunted through southern France to the Italian Front. Journeying by rail via Lyons, Monte Carlo and Menton, Harry is struck by the delicious contrast to the squalid attrition of the trenches; for a time he forgets the war and drinks in the view.

But his southern sojourn is not to last. Returning to France immediately after the German onslaughts of 1918 have recaptured all the ground gained by the British at such a heavy cost, Harry leads his men in an audacious and dangerous night-time raid on the German trenches in which he is badly wounded and recommended for a gallantry award. After months of treatment and convalescence he is passed fit by a medical board, but freely admits to a sense of impending doom at the thought of returning to the fighting. In the event, he doesn't have to – he is still at a depot in Dover looking out to sea and the distant French coast at the 11th hour of the 11th month of 1918, the moment when the Armistice begins.

Harry's war is over but his journey, faithfully recorded in his diary, is a remarkable story indeed. His years of army service, full of thrills and adventures, take him finally to Egypt from where – with the exception of a few broken bones in his foot – he is delivered 'safe home at last'.

Harry saw his war service as a series of small 'scenes' in a vast production across several theatres of war. He had squeezed more into the five years between 1914 and 1919 than most men achieve in a lifetime and, somehow, he had come through it all.

This, then, is not a diary which terminates abruptly with the death of the author, raising lingering questions regarding the 'might have beens' of one of the Lost Generation of 1914–1918. Harry's record of one man's war reflects in microcosm almost the entire sweep of the experience of the British Army in its major engagements during this 'Great War'. Here, reflected in Harry's words, are the proud successes and the desperate failures, the ready wit and the interminable boredom, the crushing grief and the long, hard and bloody learning curve traced by the British Army over more than four years of hard fighting.

Most of the men who survived came home, buried their feelings and never talked of their experiences again but, unlike them, Harry reviewed his diary and recorded his feelings later. Perhaps it was his therapy; his means of processing all that he had seen and experienced. Whatever the motive, his words serve to illuminate the experience of war shared by so many men of his generation – unimaginable for us now – but carried for the rest of their lives by the survivors, along with physical or mental scars inflicted on the battlefields. As such, they add significantly to our knowledge and understanding of that great conflict.

After a century of silence, I believe that history will come to recognise Harry Drinkwater's voice as one of the most potent of all those that have yet emerged from the First World War. It will carry far into the next 100 years.

This, then, is Harry's War.

Jon Cooksey
Stratford-upon-Avon
August 2013

A NOTE ON THE TEXT

Harry Drinkwater began his diary in 1914 when he joined the army. He wrote in pencil in a series of six small notebooks which he named 'Books 1–6', several of which he purchased in France. He kept his diary throughout his training in Britain and carried his notebooks with him when he crossed to France, keeping the current book in his tunic pocket.

Harry was demobilised from the army in May 1920 and at some point in the mid-1920s he took a bold decision to revisit the entries in his original notebooks and embarked on what must have been a time-consuming process of copying the entries longhand into a foolscap, leather-bound book he had had embossed with the title, 'War Diary'. Having the unique benefit of being able to compare both sources side-by-side we know that he transcribed his entries faithfully, apart from correcting his own grammar and establishing greater clarity. At times he added notes and reflections on the pages opposite. Written so recently after the war's end – Harry was then in his mid-30s – these amplifications often indicate deep-seated feelings triggered by rereading certain diary entries and no doubt brought into focus as Harry's knowledge and understanding of the events of 1914–1918 gradually accumulated during the decade after the war.

This book reproduces the diary as Harry transcribed it, with a few exceptions. For example, the correction of the names of people and places he would only ever have heard rather than seen written down, inconsistencies in the format of recording dates and the amendment of some of the more archaic forms of expression which might appear clumsy to modern readers. Harry was writing for himself of course; he had never intended his diary to be read by a wider audience and so there have been judicious cuts in cases where obvious repetition slows the narrative.

Precisely because Harry was writing for himself it has been necessary to interweave editorial additions among Harry's diary entries. These editorial additions – indicated by the use of italic type, or within square brackets – are intended to provide social and historical context or to add clarification.

JOINING UP
AND TRAINING

August 1914 – November 1915

'Half an inch short in height was not going to stop me'

German troops crossed the neutral border into Belgium west of Aachen on the morning of 4 August 1914 with the intention of crushing the Belgian frontier defences and capturing the strategically vital, fortified city of Liège. Although the Belgian army put up a spirited resistance in the face of overwhelming force, it was clear that it would need assistance; the Belgian government called on Britain, France and Russia for help. Britain gave Germany until midnight in Berlin – 11pm in London – to comply with an ultimatum that Belgian neutrality would be assured and made it clear that if no assurance was given, then a state of war would exist between the two most powerful nations in Europe. There was no response.

In London, Downing Street, Whitehall and Parliament Square were thronged with people eager for news. An hour before midnight they listened in silence as Big Ben began to chime until the eleventh, and last, solemn note was struck. Many in the crowd burst into a spontaneous chorus of 'God Save the King'.

It was a date which would change the course of history; a day on which the very globe rocked on its axis and which led to unprecedented bloodshed and political and economic dislocation. Britain was at war with Germany. Nothing would ever be the same again.

August

The actual outbreak of war came as a shock to most folk in England. Leading politicians and some army men (notably Lord Roberts) told us that war with Germany was always possible, but no one took much notice; therefore on

4 August when war was declared, except for our small army, nothing was prepared and the country started to get itself into a state for war.

September

Large towns all over the country started to raise battalions of men for overseas service and for a time, so great was the rush that recruiting stations had to close down. Such was the state of affairs when I applied for enlistment. My name was taken but it was a month later before I was called up for medical examination only to find I was half an inch short of the required height and so for the time being was turned down.

October

Half an inch short in height was not going to stop me getting into the army. The following Monday morning I again applied to Birmingham hoping that this time I might find a different medical board. I was not disappointed and taking my turn I was passed fit for general service and so, on paper at least, I became a soldier.

Birmingham was at this time raising a battalion of infantry to be known as 'The City Battalion'. So great was the rush of city fellows to join, that first the one was completed, a second was formed and completed in a few days, and in less than a week a third thousand had flocked to the recruiting station. With the regimental number 161 I was placed in the Second Battalion. In the early days we were known as the 1st, 2nd and 3rd City Battalions, afterwards 14th, 15th and 16th Battalions, The Royal Warwickshire Regiment.

The war had been going on now for some seven or eight weeks. Germany, fully prepared for war at the outset, started to invade France through Belgium and each successive morning and evening paper brought us news of some advance on their part whilst we on our part were kicking our heels at home waiting whilst someone in authority was working day and night to try and fix up quarters and a drill ground.

The popular idea was that the war would be over long before we were in a condition to go overseas.

Definite orders were received on the 10th and on the 12th, in company with other Stratford fellows who had joined the same unit, I set out for Wylde Green, Birmingham where the battalions were assembling and were going into training.

It was Mop Day at Stratford [the ancient annual fair at which agricultural and domestic labour was hired] and the thought crossed my mind, as no doubt it crossed the mind of other fellows, as we walked down the street and saw the showmen uncovering their shows as we passed, how many more Mop Days we should see, for the rumours were somewhat startling to fellows who had not handled a rifle in their life; boys and young men in Belgium were being given about six hours' instruction in the use of the rifle and then rushed into the firing line to try and stop the German invasion. Buildings all over England, suitable and unsuitable, were being commandeered for the use of hospitals and concrete facts in the shape of the arrival of wounded and the publication of long casualty lists in the paper all gave colour to the thought. Things were going to be rapid, we thought.

On 10 October 1914 Harry received a postcard from Captain George Smith, the temporary commanding officer of the 2nd Birmingham Battalion, who had been the chief recruiting officer responsible for enlisting more than 8,000 men. Harry's orders had arrived:

> *You are hereby warned to entrain at Stratford-on-Avon at 7.0am on Monday the 12th… (G. W. Ry). On arrival at B'ham proceed to New St Station, No.2 platform by 8.45am. You will meet Pte P E Kennard at Stratford who holds the travelling warrant.*

Monday, 12 October 1914, Sutton Park, Wylde Green, Birmingham
Arriving in Birmingham we found specials waiting to carry us on to Wylde Green, a suburb about five miles from the city. We had been previously informed that we were to be billeted on the inhabitants pending the completion of huts which were in the course of construction. On Wylde Green platform we were given instructions regarding our movements for the immediate future and then made off, some thousand fellows, in varying directions to find our billets.

I was separated here from the other Stratford fellows and joined in with the general throng going in the direction where the majority of the billets appeared to lay. Getting in conversation with a fellow here and there as I passed along comparing addresses of billets I eventually found [Harold]

Drakeford who was going to the same house as me. Together we made our way to Jockey Road and introduced ourselves to Mr and Mrs Blackband, our billet people, till the huts were ready for use.

In the afternoon Drakeford and myself made our way to the parade ground. It was for all the world like going to a football match; men appeared to be coming from all directions. Punctually at 2pm, a bugle sounded and we fell in according to instructions in four companies A, B, C and D. The afternoon was spent in sorting ourselves out, finding who and what we were and what obligations we had assumed in becoming private soldiers.

When the Mayor of Birmingham, in concert with the mayors of other large towns, first started to raise these battalions, they had in mind the fact that there would be many thousands of fellows in the country not desirous of, or willing to wait for a commission, but providing they could join the ranks with their friends and remain with them, were keen to become private soldiers. These battalions came to be known as 'Pals Battalions' and afterwards partly formed Kitchener's Army.

We were an extraordinary collection of fellows. The commanding officer appointed to the battalion was an old regular army man; the adjutant was a regular and the remainder, for the most part, were officers who had had some military experience or training to a degree of sorts. The NCOs were without exception old army men long pensioned and roped in again for the purposes of this new army. There were barristers, solicitors, bank clerks, qualified engineers and men and boys who, by their looks at least, required some good square meals before they would ever be able to stand the conditions which we were beginning to understand existed in France. Later on I found out that the fellow next to me in the ranks had never done a day's work in his life but had had something in the nature of a valet to do it for him. He was barely 17. A boy of 16, who gave his age as 18 so that he could join up, later became our lance corporal and we learned that breeding and education do not always count.

It was evident that there were not sufficient NCOs to go round the battalion and that a lot more would have to be forthcoming before we could be anything like organised. We were told this on parade the following morning and that any fellow who liked to volunteer for a stripe would have his application considered. But we thought this was going to be a short, sharp

Comfortable billet: Harry (right) and fellow Birmingham Pal Private Harold Drakeford pose with Mr Thomas Blackband – holding a rifle and wearing cavalry boots – outside Mr Blackband's home on Jockey Road, Sutton Coldfield. The 2nd Birmingham Pals Battalion was so short of space for its recruits that many men were billeted in private houses until they could move into purpose-built huts in Sutton Park. Harry shared his billet with Harold Drakeford who, in October 1917, became an officer in the Somerset Light Infantry and was killed on 5 April 1918. (David Griffiths)

war – quick training, over to France and back again, and finished. With the foregoing in our minds and the fact that for the most part we were fellows with something in common, we decided in the main that as we had joined as privates we would remain privates. Therefore shortly afterwards, when our platoon officer Lieutenant Rubery asked any fellow desiring a stripe to step forward, we remained in the ranks. It was some moments before there stepped forward a pale, anaemic, undersized little fellow who might have been 18 for army purposes but actually barely looked 16. We looked aghast at this boy when we thought he might be made a non-commissioned officer. We were staggered a few days later when we found he had been made a lance corporal and, still worse, put in charge of the section we were in, but we agreed that we had had an equal chance and it was therefore up to us to play the game.

How well did he show us how to play the game? In a month we liked him, in six months we said he was as good as any other NCO in the battalion, in 12 months we were glad to help him carry out any difficult command he had to obey and by 18 months we would have cleaned his boots. This little fellow had a great hold on us. He seemed to have made up his mind at an early date that he would do his job, whatever was given him to do and he always got it done by first showing the way himself. We took our hats off to this lad in the end – Lance Corporal Sidney Page. Such were the fellows I found around me when I fell in on the afternoon of 12 October 1914.

Training now began to take shape. We were instructed how to handle a rifle, how to skirmish, how to take cover from observation and so forth.

Some month or six weeks passed before we began to get into uniform. Owing to the abnormal amount of khaki required, those battalions training as complete units of raw men were togged out in blue, called 'Kitchener's blue' and I duly appeared in mine at Christmas. To do this I gave the quartermaster of the company a tip to rig me out, complete with shoulder badges and cap badge. These were at a premium at the time and were only obtainable by putting the hand in the pocket. We were issued with two suits; one for working in and one for walking out. The latter were very swagger; red striped trousers and peaked caps with red band. We certainly looked a fine lot on parade, what we could do in the firing line was yet to be shown.

Milestone: Two days after Harry joined the 2nd Birmingham Battalion he and his comrades were issued with their first item of uniform – a blue forage cap – an event so momentous for these citizen soldiers that it called for a group photograph. The tidal wave of volunteers joining Kitchener's Army in August 1914 caused shortages of khaki uniforms, so men like Harry (standing, second row fourth left with pipe) were issued with uniforms of dark blue material. (David Griffiths)

Working dress: Harry was issued with a second uniform which he wore for heavy manual labour. Here (fourth from left), he nonchalantly shoulders a pick as he and his fellow Birmingham Pals take a breather from trench digging practice in Sutton Park. (David Griffiths)

Sutton Park

Day in and day out we carried on with the training; breakfast 8am, parade again 9am–12 noon and again 2pm–4pm. Some six or eight months passed before we left our billets and got into the huts which had been built close to the parade ground. The first battalion took the lead; ourselves – the second battalion – followed a week later, the third battalion continuing to occupy the nearby [Spring Hill Wesleyan] college in Moseley. The hours we kept increased, now we had reveille at 6am and were on parade at 7am for physical drill before breakfast at 8am.

To say that we enjoyed the training would be far from the truth, it resolved itself to one drab round of drill, drill, drill, intermixed with trench digging, route marching, kit inspections and guards.

After some eight months of training we began to shape into something like soldiers. The NCOs who had been created in the early days were turning out, in the main, to be first-class fellows and according to the old soldiers we were months ahead of the training book. With our advent into the huts we were more under the control of army authorities. Roll-call was called every night at 10pm and the fellow who was not there to answer was for it.

One fellow was very amusing for his ready wit. One night, creeping down a nearby street after 10pm, he was called upon to halt. He immediately took to his heels followed by the sergeant of the patrol; they both collapsed on the pavement some 100 yards distant. 'Why didn't you halt when you were called upon?' said the sergeant. 'Halt?' said the fellow. 'Did you say halt? I thought you said bolt.'

By this time it was quite evident to the country that the war was going to be a much longer thing than anyone had ever dreamt of. Trenches had been dug by both sides and from actual open warfare it had worked itself into a state of stagnation. New forces, in the shape of aeroplanes and old ideas, like trench mortars, were becoming a factor, new arms in warfare were being created in which chemists and engineers were necessary. Under these circumstances it was only natural that most of us got restless under the continual drill. With many more fellows I applied for a commission but we were uniformly refused. A few fellows with someone at the back of them got through with it, but they were the exception rather than the rule.

Within a couple of months we learnt by degrees that the various fellows who were commissioned from the battalion about this time, and who had invariably been sent out to France at once, were for the most part dead.

Saturday, 26 June – Wednesday, 28 July 1915, Wensleydale, Yorkshire

At last we made a move from Birmingham and things were beginning to take shape. Our next training area was in Yorkshire where, with larger, open spaces, larger bodies of men could be directed in manoeuvres. We were by this time taken over by the War Office and became the 14th, 15th and 16th Battalions, The Royal Warwickshire Regiment and, with the 12th Battalion, The Gloucesters, became the 95th Infantry Brigade.

Our stay at Wensleydale was very short for which we were very thankful; beautiful country but miles from civilisation.

Thursday, 5 August – Sunday, 21 November 1915, Codford, Salisbury Plain

From Wensleydale we moved down to Codford on Salisbury Plain (after firing our musketry course at Hornsea on the Yorkshire coast), the last stage of our training before going overseas. Here we fired a second musketry course. New clothing and equipment was issued and rumours were current regarding our departure and speculation was rife regarding our destination. Orders were published regarding conditions abroad and we were finally made aware that we were likely to move on Sunday, 21 November. We wondered where.

THE SOMME

November 1915 – February 1916

'First-class animals'

Towards the end of November 1915, the War Office deemed that Harry's conversion from citizen to soldier was complete. The process had taken just over a year. Now at last he and his fellow Birmingham Pals of the 15th Royal Warwicks were to be given the opportunity to do exactly what they had joined up for – to fight for king and country.

Harry's papers show that he sailed for France aboard the SS *Invicta* on 21 November 1915, bound for Boulogne. From there he and the 841 men and 29 officers who made up his battalion would be transported by train to a railhead south-east of Abbeville in the valley of the River Somme. From there his only method of transportation would be 'Shanks's Pony' – his own two feet.

The British Army had come to the Somme in the early August of 1915, a little less than four months earlier. Before its arrival the gently rolling chalk ridges, spurs and two main river valleys of this part of Picardy had been battlefields bloodily contested by the French and the Germans. The French had held the greater part of the Western Front, from the Swiss border to the city of Arras and sectors beyond, for the best part of a year while the British frantically tried to get more troops into the field. Gradually, as more and more British battalions were shipped to France and Flanders, and with the French constantly urging Britain to shoulder more of the labour-intensive, 'line holding' burden, the British Army had agreed to side-slip further south to take over more of the front line as far south as the village of Maricourt and beyond to the very banks of the Somme. This would be the extreme right flank of the entire British line on the Western Front. The looping meanders of the Somme would be the boundary between two armies, for on the opposite bank, holding the village of Frise, stood the French.

October 1915: Resplendent at last in full uniform, complete
with rifle, greatcoat and hastily procured 1914 pattern leather
equipment, Harry stands proudly to attention towards the end
of his period of military training. In a few weeks he will be
on his way to the Western Front. (David Griffiths)

By the time the Germans holding the line first noticed strange, khaki flat caps in the trenches opposite and read the English lettering on fragments of shell they picked up in the summer of 1915, the Somme had become a relatively 'quiet' sector in comparison to the killing fields of Ypres, Neuve Chapelle and Aubers Ridge. In fact there appeared to have been an unofficial acceptance of a 'live and let live' philosophy adopted by troops on either side. Given the reduced tempo and intensity of the fighting other British sectors, and compared to the dreary winter spent manning the low-lying, waterlogged breastworks of the line in the Ypres Salient or French Flanders, the deep, relatively dry and well-drained trenches dug into the chalk of the Somme came as a revelation and proved a real tonic for the British troops. It would be several months yet before the name 'Somme' would become forever burned into the British national consciousness as shorthand for slaughter on an industrial scale.

By late November 1915, however, the weather had taken its toll and any last vestiges of comfort, particularly in the Maricourt sector, just over a mile from the Somme itself, had vanished from the trenches which were becoming a morass of glutinous mud.

Moving ever eastward, mile by mile, from village to village, Harry Drinkwater trudged towards the sound of the guns and his final destination: the front-line trenches skirting the village of Maricourt. Harry was going to war.

Sunday, 21 November 1915

Daylight had not broken through when bugles throughout the camp sounded the reveille. We dressed, had a hasty breakfast and packed our valise with a 'sangfroid' as if we were going for a route march instead of a journey from which, for some, there would be no return. We were not elated. I think we were all conscious of the possibilities. My own thoughts were these; if I could find a job in England and with a clear conscience have taken it, I would have done so. We were not depressed, the monotony of our training prevented this, but at the sound of the bugle line after line of men fell in on the roadside in full marching order for a short service and so, as day was breaking, the padre read us a short lesson from a small rising and gave us his benediction. We were conscious that this was all in order and in a way it was impressive for we were starting on a game that very few of us had played before.

The service over, we marched to the station, reached Folkstone at 2pm and 15 minutes later were in the Channel bound for France.

On arrival at Boulogne we made for the rest camp [in the suburb of Ostrohove]. I was very much impressed by the absence of men and the number of women wearing black. I thought at the time that they were mourning personal loss, but afterwards gathered that in France the whole of the population go into mourning on the outbreak of war.

Our arrival caused no commotion. By this time some thousands of British troops had gone before on the same route that we were to travel. We slept the night in tents; or rather we were in tents. Sleep was out of the question, with the thermometer some degrees below freezing point, so I spent most of the night walking about in my clothes with a blanket wrapped around me.

Monday, 22 November 1915

We did not stay long in Boulogne. At 9pm the following night we entrained for an unknown destination and at 2.30am reached Longpré[-les-Corps-Saints]. There then followed one of the most exhausting marches that we had up to that moment experienced. Loaded with ammunition, rifle, blanket, ground-sheet and kit, we set out for Bellancourt, a distance of ten miles. The first five miles went down fairly well. A recruit dropped out here and there and then the weight began to tell on us all. That great little man Lance Corporal Sidney Page trudged along in front of his section, himself nearly bent double with the weight, occasionally coming along and offering to give any of us a hand if we required help.

With no sleep and indifferently fed the previous day, we trudged along leaving here and there a fellow who dropped out in the march. There was no discredit to be attached to these, they walked until they fell. Page, game to the last, collapsed on reaching our destination. We reached Bellancourt at 5am and were marched off to billets. Mine was a barn and with 20 other fellows, I lay down on the straw and slept till late in the afternoon.

This was our first experience of a rough billet. With the exception of one night, some 14 months were to pass before I slept in a bed again.

Tuesday, 23 November 1915

No parade, so look round the village. No village in England can compare to it for filth and dirt, filthy streets with refuse lying in all directions.

Harry later added to this entry, 'Months afterwards, after marching from one village to another, the reason was more apparent. With all the menfolk at the war and womenfolk doing war work, no one was left to do anything.'

Friday, 26 November 1915

Today, we left Bellancourt for l'Étoile, about eight miles distant and heard for the first time the heavy guns firing in the distance. The march was over flat country and very monotonous, reaching l'Étoile at tea-time. We were told off to billets; mine was a sheep-pen and before I had inhabited it very long I had to stuff up a hole here and there to keep out a wandering rat.

Saturday, 27 November 1915, Vignacourt

Frozen as usual during the night I was glad to be up again next morning at 5am bound for Vignacourt, ten miles distant. It is now evident to us that we are making for the trenches, a prospect I view with mixed feelings. Trains of transport pass and re-pass us during the day and during an occasional halt we gather from these some of the conditions existing up at the front which we were shortly soon to taste.

We arrived in Vignacourt on the evening of Sunday – a week since we started from England. My billet for the night was an old ballroom, and with a little more room to move I had my first bath. Johnson and myself pinched an old biscuit tin, heated some water and retired to a loft and had a good swill down.

Wednesday, 1 December 1915

Today we marched to Coisy. Here we found the conditions very much as we found them in the villages we had passed through. Poor dwellings, decrepit inhabitants, only the very oldest appear to remain and they are very hostile towards us. Straw, for which they are paid, we have to pinch. Their water supply, usually a well, they watch from the time of our arrival to departure.

Rations vary according to the conditions under which we find ourselves. Under normal conditions each man has about a quarter of a loaf of bread, sufficient jam and sometimes butter or margarine, cheese and bully beef. The latter is sometimes made up by the cooks in the form of a stew. Sometimes we eat it from the tin. These constitute one day's rations, served out each morning. Every man carries his day's food with him. Plates, forks, knives

Final march: 'A' Company of the 15th Battalion, the Royal Warwickshire Regiment, led by Company Commander Captain Percival Edwards, swing along a muddy Wiltshire lane on their last route march before their departure for France in the late autumn of 1915. Harry can be seen almost in the middle of the shot, marked with an arrow. (David Griffiths)

and spoons are now unknown, a jack-knife and fingers take their place. It is sometimes amusing to watch fellows who in private life are men of independent means, trudging along with bread in one hand and cheese in another and caked with mud.

Thursday, 2 December 1915, Lahoussoye

From Coisy we marched on to Lahoussoye, eight miles further towards the line. The frost and snow that we had been experiencing the last few days had given way to rain and the roads that were previously hard had given way to thick mud. Marching was hard. Our equipment hung like a ton weight and the leather straps cut into the shoulders. At Lahoussoye I got into conversation with one or two Army Service Corps men. From these I gathered that we were in for a fairly thin time, the land in the Somme was all low-lying and trenches full of mud.

In the evening [James] Ward and myself had a look round the village and found a cottage. Ward spotted the place marching into the village and received a welcome which was unusually cordial. After a café au lait we were given vivid descriptions of the entry of the Germans into the village during the Mons retreat. We had a thorough good warm, another drink and left better impressed with the French peasantry.

We are still very matter of fact regarding our prospective entry into the trenches. We have the worst of weather before us and have been informed that gas and gas shells are extensively used. But nothing has so far damped our spirits and I look upon it as a great relief to do something from the perpetual tramp, tramp, day after day, carrying our heavy equipment – I am footsore and fagged out.

Friday, 3 December 1915

Left Lahoussoye this morning feeling none too fit for the road. Went off at a swing but soon dropped into a slow pace. Rain began to fall, the roads were ankle deep in mud and we presented a pitiable sight as, soaked with mud from the last three days, we tramped along. I do not think any men could have done better especially when one remembers that 18 months before none of us had probably ever done a route march or handled a rifle. Only one dropped out during the journey.

From Lahoussoye we were under the possibility of enemy artillery fire and signs were soon evident of possible trouble. Army Service Corps stables covered with tree branches, and tents painted, to help afford cover from aeroplanes.

Saturday, 4 December 1915, Sailly-Laurette

We reached Sailly-Laurette in the afternoon and it would require the hand of a master to describe our feelings as we dropped on the straw of our billets, soaked with rain, splashed up to the neck with mud. I slept solidly till this morning. This evening I have been out into the village and far away in the distance could see star-shells fired from the trenches.

Sunday, 5 December 1915

We saw a bit of real warfare this morning. Six of our aeroplanes were taking observation over the enemy line and it was interesting to see shells bursting all around them. Each shell leaves a black cloud to show where it burst. This afternoon we had football. This evening I am filling in time with the help of a candle writing up my diary and writing home, afterwards to sink down to sleep, the same with us all.

Monday, 6 December 1915

Today we have been for a short route march and see for the first time the British trenches like a white streak on the skyline. We joke about our entry into them but I am conscious that we shall have a rude awakening when we get there. We appear to be here for some time and have an opportunity to look around.

Tuesday, 7 December 1915

What a great contrast all this is to England. Dirty cottages – half barns and half dwelling houses – the roads have no sort of walking path and the buildings appear to be in the last stages of decay. The principal refuse place is a pond in the centre of the village into which everything is thrown. With no idea of sanitation the few people I have seen are in keeping with their surroundings. Amongst this evil smelling lot we live and have our being.

We are billeted in barns and last night I awoke to hear something gnawing at my haversack and spent the remainder of the time patting the straw to keep off what seemed an army of rats. In the morning I found a large hole eaten in my haversack; they were after biscuits. It would be the best thing that could happen if the Germans blew the whole place up.

Wednesday, 8 December 1915

We are degenerating into first-class animals. Reveille – 7am; breakfast – a rasher of bacon. This we eat on a slice of bread with fingers and jack-knife and a mug of tea. 1pm – bully beef stew; precious little fresh meat about, 4.30pm – tea. This consists of a mug of tea and anything we have been able to save from our day's rations. In each instance we retire to the straw of our billet and feed. Our enamel mug serves the double purpose of mug for tea and plate for bully stew and is often used for washing in. A clasp knife and fingers take the place of all cutlery.

Thursday, 9 December 1915

The 14th Battalion (1st Birmingham Pals) who are billeted in an adjacent village, returned today from four days in the line: their first experience. They tell awful tales of the mud; their clothes do not belie their story. Looking out of my billet this morning I saw a squad of men pass by. They were unique, plastered from head to feet with mud; it would have been difficult to find on them a clean part the size of a man's hand. Another fellow came to the billet door and watched them as they passed. We looked at one another. Remarks were unnecessary.

Friday, 10 December 1915

Today we have done very little. Excessive movement is not allowed owing to possibilities of enemy aircraft.

Saturday, 11 December 1915

Great excitement today – burnt our billet down. First noticed the outbreak at about nine o'clock this morning and soon got to work with buckets of water. The fire alarm was given – the battalion turned out *en bloc*. Also the village fire brigade, three very old men and a pump. The fire had a good hold on the barn but we were eventually able to confine the blaze to the old building. It took all morning to put it out. We had great sport, killing rats which ran in all directions. Also cattle, a horse, pigs and sheep were killed. Damages claimed – £120.

Sunday, 12 December 1915
B and D [Companies] leave to take up their position in the line. Our battalion appears to be relieving the West Kents who returned here early this morning. They look very tired and fed up and plastered in mud. They do not appear very jovial over the prospects of winter. The weather very sharp this morning. Snow and later in the day poured down with rain.

We leave here on Thursday for Suzanne, our depot for the trenches, and then leave for what festivities the trenches have for us on Friday. We wonder.

Before any newly arrived New Army battalion was allowed to assume responsibility for a sector of the front line it first had to undergo instruction in trench warfare under the guidance of a more experienced unit. In this way it was hoped that routines, tips and hard-earned lessons could be handed down to the inexperienced so that the trenches could continue to be manned efficiently and any unnecessary casualties avoided. In the case of Harry's battalion the instructors were to be the professional soldiers of what had been existing pre-war battalions: the 1st Battalion the Devonshire Regiment and the 2nd Battalion the Manchester Regiment of the 5th Infantry Division; which had been in this sector since the previous August.

Tuesday, 14 December 1915
A beautifully clear frosty morning. Short route march and football in the afternoon. Watched an air raid in the distance over enemy lines. The aeroplanes were a fine sight, 14 in all going over in file and as each one came within the enemy shelling area it was treated to a round of shells. As I viewed all this I was glad I was on the ground, fairly safe for the time being.

As a result of the fire, smoking is prohibited in barns. Personally I am not taking any notice of it. I imagine the brigadier snug in his room at headquarters in front of a good fire whilst we in these wretched places cannot keep warm. Have nothing to do at nights except write letters and slowly sink into the straw and sleep. Lights out 8.30pm.

Wednesday, 15 December 1915

Received parcel from home for Xmas, contents very useful for the trenches. We hear now that we leave for Suzanne *en route* for the trenches tomorrow. Rumours came to the village that D Company, who left here on the 12th, have had their first casualty.

Thursday, 16 December 1915, Suzanne

Arrived here today – a very hard march. Left Sailly-Laurette punctually at 10.30am and got here at 4.30pm. Find rumours regarding the D Company casualty only too true. Lieutenant Crisp, a very decent fellow, was hit by a bullet or fragment of shell on one of those expeditions which had no special object but to keep the enemy from thinking we were asleep. The price is too great.

We are billeted in tents, 12 men in each, in the grounds of what would in England be a mansion.

We are now encamped between the enemy and our own heavy guns and the heavy artillery fire we have heard so long is now quite close. As I write I can hear the shells tearing through the air, 15 seconds to travel about four miles. We listen and hear them explode in the distance; occasionally we hear bursts of machine-gun fire. We are very close to things. Last night as I lay in the tent I could feel the ground vibrate as each shell was fired.

The grounds of this place are very fine, very extensive; here and there a lake and what were once large flower beds, now everything is a quagmire. Constant traffic of guns and wagons passing has made it boot deep in mud and what might have once been a very fine lawn is now standing room for horses with a covering overhead to keep from observation.

At night-time the camp looks very peculiar, the tents plastered with paint to make them obscure from air observation. One sees little slits of light all down the lines; those shining on the puddles of water outside give the impression of a fairy land, but not much fairy land in reality. Our boots are perpetually wet and feet cold.

Harry later added here, 'Afterwards I saw the owner of this place, a Count-de-Somme, a suspected spy in German payment. He was only allowed out accompanied by an escort. His mansion was practically the only building left intact in the village.

He was eventually found giving information to the Germans and shot. Less than 12 hours after his death the village was shelled and laid flat, including his mansion. We left that village and that part of the country half an hour after the bombardment started – we were lucky.'

Tonight we have had our first rum issue, it did go down good. Each spot seemed to warm a blood vessel and circulate the blood around the body. 8.30pm we roll into our blankets, occasionally we hear the 'splash, splash' as some fellow moves from one tent to another, or the plod of the sentry picking his way over the puddles as he moves up and down the tents. These sounds seem in time to cease and only the continual shriek of shells disturbs the night.

Tomorrow we go into the trenches and start what for 15 months we have been training for. I wonder what sort of a show we shall make.

Page, our lance corporal, has been rushing around all day trying to find any fellows who have already been in the line, getting tips from them about general conditions and the best way of getting over them. Already he is a fine little soldier. I think he will rise to great heights in times of difficulty.

Lieutenant Crisp was buried today.

For a Pals battalion made up almost entirely of Kitchener volunteers, the first casualty suffered on active service came as a great blow and a memorable event. In addition to losing Second Lieutenant Crisp – the first officer to die – the battalion lost two NCOs during D Company's first instructional tour of duty in the trenches: Corporal Daniel Greasley, 25, and 31-year-old Corporal Percy Broomfield.

Daniel Greasley of Alum Rock in Birmingham had enlisted in the Birmingham Pals on 26 September 1914. At the time of his death he had been married for nine months. Percy Broomfield lived in the Marston Green area of Birmingham before joining up. Both men now lie in Cerisy-Gailly Military Cemetery, seven miles south-west of the town of Albert on the Somme.

Ernest Geoffrey Crisp, 24, was the battalion bombing, or grenade, officer. He had worked for Lloyds Bank and enlisted as a private in the 7th Battalion of the Northamptonshire Regiment on the outbreak of war before being commissioned as an officer. Joining Harry's battalion on 8 February 1915, he was hit first by a bullet and then by shell fragments as he made his way back to the British trenches after an instructional bombing expedition on the afternoon of 15 December 1915.

He died of his wounds the following day. He lies today in Suzanne Communal Cemetery Extension.

Sunday, 19 December 1915

We are now in the trenches and paper fails to describe the situation – it is not the Germans we are fighting here, but the weather.

We left Suzanne at 4pm yesterday for here – a distance of about two miles – and had a very cheery send-off. We halted halfway along the road at a house and put on jackboots and leather jerkins and after a short halt started off again and in about an hour's time were up to our knees in mud and water. We were now indulging in a new experience, jackboots. These are actually fishermen's waders reaching up to the thigh. In these we tramped along the road the remainder of the distance before entering into the trenches. We were told to walk quietly but that was impossible, these waders were in all cases miles too large and added to our other kit we now had our boots slung round us.

We had gone perhaps a mile and reached a farm building and the word was passed back in a whisper to go steady. As far as I could see by the very indistinct light, the men in front of me appeared to be walking through a wall and then to disappear. The fellow in front of me followed and I followed him into what was the kitchen of a house, down into the cellar and out into the communication trench through a hole that had been knocked in the wall.

At first the mud was ankle deep and gradually got deeper and deeper as we advanced along the communication trench. We had not gone far before we had to duck; the enemy were sending over their evening salute of shells which were dropping around us. Very lights, a new experience for us, seemed to be sent up by the Germans in every direction; their effect was very weird in the night. By this time getting along the trench was an awful strain. To do so I had to use both elbows, one each side of the trench and with an added leverage pull one leg out, step forward and repeat again, further encumbranced by rifle, kit, rations, and boots, which I had slung about me; it was the same with us all.

After about one and a half hours of the worst plodding in mud I have ever experienced, or ever want to experience again, we reached the firing line.

My luck was out – no sooner had we arrived than I was told off with others as a ration party to fetch up the grub. Back we had to wade through the whole length of trenches to our field kitchen situated at an adjacent village called Maricourt, arriving there midnight.

These first journeys up and down the trenches I shall not forget easily. The first journey we had our kit to carry; this time it was a dixie of stew. This we carried on a pole slung between two men and when we arrived back we discovered half of it missing, partly spilt over our clothes; the weight had taken us further in the mud and every step was a tug. After dishing out the stew to what fellows I could find, I groped my way to the dugout where I was told I should find the other fellows. What a sight; the dugout was a foot deep in mud and everyone was too tired to try and do anything. It was now 1.30am so I joined in with the rest and stood against the wall and waited for the morning.

It is perhaps impossible to visualise this scene without some knowledge of the trenches. To do so one must imagine a room dug underneath the ground, dug probably more than a year ago and now in a state of decay, the sides of which were slimy with moisture that had percolated through. Here and there a prop, perhaps the trunk of a tree, supported the roof which, like the sides, was foul with moisture, which as it gathered in weight dropped down. In places it amounted to a steady 'drip, drip' and did not seem to cease, with the result that on our advent the floor was some foot or more deep in mud.

There were no bunks into which we could climb to get away from it. The size and height did not allow it; our heads nearly touched the roof. There was no possibility of having a brazier there – there was no firm ground to hold it or to stand it upon. There was no exit and the air was proportionally stale. Into this place I groped my way, now brilliantly lit by candles stuck in the wall. Some of our fellows, about a dozen, already a mass of mud from the efforts of getting along the communication trench, were ranged around the sides and one or two were leaning against the roof supports.

It was our first introduction to the trenches and a dugout. I joined them and stood against the wall. The cold was intense and nearly all the dugouts here were in the same condition. The smell which arose from the stale mud was rancid; we stirred it every time we moved our feet.

Monday, 20 December 1915
The trouble I expected with my feet did not develop. Was fortunate to get a large pair of jackboots and greased my feet and put on three pairs of socks

Maricourt mud: Several of Harry's company officers pose in a flooded trench near the village of Maricourt on the Somme towards the end of 1915. Left to right: Lieutenant Davis, 'A' Company Commander Captain Percival Edwards, Second Lieutenant Pratt and Harry's platoon commander Lieutenant Ivor Rubery. Harry experienced exactly the same conditions.

when changing into the jackboots. The trenches are in a terrible condition, anything from four inches to four feet deep in mud and water. We are in an awful condition ourselves, plastered in mud right up to our faces. Our food of cold bacon, bread and jam is all together in a sack hung up from the roof of the dugout from which water is continually dropping – we eat and drink mud.

At the time of writing the communication trench is being heavily shelled. In this district at this time the military situation is very peculiar. The British firing line is in the shape of a horseshoe, we occupying the most advanced point. It is useless for us to try and advance till the flanks are straightened out so that we have only to keep the Germans occupied. The front trenches of the Germans and ourselves are situated between two villages; we occupying one, they the other. Both could be razed to the ground by opposing artillery inside an hour, but there appears to be a mutual understanding that they shall be more or less left alone.

Tuesday, 21 December 1915

Some attempt was made today to continue the diary but my hands, perpetually caked in mud and stone cold, refused to perform the somewhat delicate operation of writing. Added to this I had nowhere to sit down. I gave up trying.

Saturday, 25 December 1915

Writing now on Christmas night and looking back over the last six days, five of which we have been in the trenches, we are thankful that we are still able to walk and not have to be carried back to billets.

The Germans have been little or no account compared with the conditions under which we found ourselves. We have had to fight against the weather, short rations, a lack of fuel and wet dugouts; a combination of things likely to knock out the strongest. Sleep we have only been able to have at periods when we could be spared and then always standing in mud. Rats that we had heard so much about we experienced and often during the night, when from sheer exhaustion I dozed off, I would be awakened by one of these fat squeaking things on my shoulder or feel it running over my head. I had approximately an hour's sleep a day.

Rations which look very nice and inviting on paper we never had, partly owing to the fact that it had been raining hard, filling up the communication trenches to such an extent that it was impossible to get along and partly because they were constantly being shelled night and day by the Germans so that provisions had to be carried over the top at night. Tea, intended to be hot, we received at midnight – stone cold. Coke to burn in the dugouts had to be left at the rear to allow for more provisions to be carried.

The dugouts that have been shelled and shaken for nearly 12 months let in water like a sieve, so that we are unable to keep even our bodies dry and it is impossible to repair them owing to exposure [to the Germans] so we have had to lump it. In moving along the trenches we had to use our elbows for added leverage, consequently the mud worked through our clothes to the body, setting up irritation. Our hands were always caked in mud which, when we ate our bread and bacon, went down the same way, setting up in many cases acute dysentery amongst the fellows.

On arriving at the firing line we took over from the 1st Devons, they remaining one night with us to show us how to go on. A sentry post consisted of three men, one on actual duty looking over the top, one by his side in the trench and the third man sleeps. This rotates every hour; if the post is in a dangerous part then two men take the place of one. In common with others I did my regular turns. It is a very creepy business looking over the top imagining every noise is a German; a rat skirmishing amongst empty tins in no-man's-land is quite sufficient to attract all our attention. Sentry duties start one hour before dusk when every man in the line stands ready for anything to happen. In the morning the same thing happens again; one hour before daybreak every man stands in the trench until daylight.

This is the survival of the old custom in war of making an attack just before dawn or sunset. This manning of the front line is an act of preparation in case an attack takes place and is called 'Stand To' and it occurs every day one hour before daybreak and one hour before sunset and lasts about one hour. It is a general custom amongst all armies.

Tuesday morning [21 December] we had a heavy bombardment from the Germans about 11am. I was in a trench at the time and moved into a dugout. Heard a fearful crash and found the next dugout to ours blown to blazes and Sergeant Horton with it. Sergeant Horton had been our physical drill instructor since the beginning of things. He was a fellow I liked.

As soon as I heard the crash I made my way out and, with the help of Sergeant [Frederick] Wassell, dug him out; he was very near a 'gonner'. Wassell and I carried him to the rear. Before we could get him anywhere near a dressing station he had departed this life – he was our first casualty and our first experience of death.

We were all very sick about it and thankful to leave the trenches that night for a night's rest back in camp. On arrival I lay down and went to sleep in my clothes, tired out, and with the death of Horton, sick of everything.

Up again early next morning making preparations for returning to the line, only to find my kit had been lost, so I was unable to shave. I had not shaved for some days now. We arrived back in those fearful places at dusk and relieved the 1st East Surreys, and started the eternal routine work all over again. When not on sentry duty we employ the night trying to pump water from the trenches and in the daytime stand in the dugouts concealed from observation.

Last night we had another lively time on sentry when the German artillery opened up on us again. I had a narrow squeak, a shell burst on the parapet. I was well wedged in the mud and heard it coming. Unable to move I crouched to the side of the trench and got covered in dirt. Was glad enough when morning came and we were able to shake ourselves out.

Yesterday evening we left the trenches and arrived back here at ten o'clock. The feeling of walking on firm, or comparatively firm, road again is indescribable. To have to plod one's way along the trenches tugging to pull one's leg out of the mud only to put it forward and tug at the other is distracting to a degree. Add to this the conditions under which we were living, knowing that when you are in the mud you are helpless to move quickly, is a strain that must eventually have its effect. To be able to walk quickly on firm ground instead of always feeling the ground give way under your feet had its effect; some fellows were singing on arrival. We were shown to our billets, mine, with others, was a barn. Blankets had been brought up for us and into these we rolled, thankful to go to sleep.

This morning, Christmas Day, we were awakened at 8am and I had my first wash and shave for a week, my kit being recovered by the Company Quartermaster Sergeant. I took my shirt off, it was thick with dried mud, and put a clean one on; the first change since leaving England, and felt a new man afterwards.

The dirty ones had already gone to wash and I fell in on parade for that purpose at 10am. We had one tub and no soap between about 50 fellows and heaven only knows how they were going to dry.

Our Christmas dinner consisted of greasy mutton and plum pudding sent by the Mayor of Birmingham. This afternoon I have been on fatigue work drawing rations till 5pm, afterwards tea. From then onwards I have been writing hard in my diary for I have an idea that I should like to keep it up – a record of my wanderings and experiences.

Albert Horton was 29. He is buried in Cerisy-Gailly Military Cemetery. Harry had been wearing the same shirt for 34 days.

Sunday, 26 December 1915, Maricourt

We were not allowed to enjoy our comfort for long. We marched here this evening for another tour of duty. We are told that this time we shall have more variety – I wonder what that means. We are here for six days. Two days in the trenches, two days in support and two days in the Maricourt defences. The latter is the last line of resistance, supposing the Germans were to break through the front line.

Monday, 27 December 1915

As one half of the battalion is relieving the other, C and D are up in the line tonight and tomorrow night. A and B are in the Maricourt defences. Very easy going here, we are not allowed outside our billet in the daytime so we sleep all day to emerge at night, sandbagging and trench digging in the vicinity.

Tuesday and Wednesday, 28 and 29 December 1915

We moved up into support this evening and things are not so comfortable. Though we have no sentry duty to do, we have to work all the night through up to our knees in mud and water, pumping out the latter. At intervals along the communication trenches, sumps had been cut into the side, to each of which a pump was connected. We have to man the pumps when not actually in the firing line. It seems a hopeless task, the trench appearing to fill up again however hard we work but we had to stick at it from dusk to dawn.

Thursday and Friday, 30 and 31 December 1915
We saw the old year out and the New Year in in fine style. We moved up last night for our last two days of this tour, relieved the men there and took over the firing line. The conditions are still the same, up against the weather and not the Germans, nearly up to our waists in mud. We have found a new diversion – in the between light at dusk, we put a small piece of cheese on the end of the bayonet [on the rifle], wait for some fat rat to come and have a nibble and then pull the trigger.

This evening, or strictly speaking I should say last evening, (I am writing this at 3am in the corner of a dugout) a party of wire cutters left our trench at 11.45pm to repair our barbed wire. They were spotted by the enemy who opened rapid fire on them which was taken up by machine guns and artillery, to which we all replied.

Saturday, 1 January 1916
At midnight I was crouched up against the side of the trench seeking protection from shells bursting overhead and very close to the parapet. The shells appeared to be going in all directions and whilst they were sending them over we came to the conclusion that it had nothing to do with our men out in front but was a New Year's salute. We wished each other a 'Happy New Year' along the trench; nevertheless I was very thankful when it was over. Our fellows came in from the wiring – no one hit. I have one more hour's sentry duty to do before daybreak. Tomorrow we go back to Suzanne to rest for two days.

Sunday, 2 January 1916, Suzanne
Left the trenches last night for a day's rest back here. It's only a day's rest mentally, as physically there is something to be done all day long. Rifle inspection, ammunition inspection, boots inspection. The quartermaster comes along and makes up all our deficiencies. Take this opportunity to change our shirts and socks and wash the dirty ones. It is a glorious feeling after a week in one's clothes to have a wash and shave and a clean change of clothing.

Friday, 7 January 1916, back in billets

We relieved the Devons on the night of the 3rd. Relieving one another is a creepy business. It is usual for those being relieved to send a man to some point decided on beforehand and he pilots us to those we are going to relieve by the best way, nearly always over the top when possible, but sometimes along the trenches. 'Splash, splash' we go along, wondering why the Germans do not hear us. Tonight they did; one fellow stumbled over a tin of some sort and kicked up a dickens of a clatter. Up went Very lights from the German lines and over came a shower of bullets, but we had ducked by this time and they did not spot us. But it is a nervy business and, like most of the other things, we are glad when it is over.

Roughly our position for the next three days was to occupy the 'knob', listening for any movement on the part of the Germans. Wedged in mud ourselves we were helpless, except to keep watch and fire our rifles – the Germans were probably as helpless.

Being in the line for three days is a long time under these conditions. Food can only be brought to us at night, which is our meal for the following day.

Tonight – 9.00pm – the ration party has just been along bringing our 'hot' drink for the night. They have had to carry it a mile and a half and by their language I believe they have had a pretty rough journey. The tea is stone cold.

When we go out on rest and return to the line again, we do not necessarily occupy the same front-line trench as the previous time, but an adjoining one in a part of the line which also comes under the control of the battalion. In this particular case the line was isolated. There were no dugouts or shelters and it was too close to the German lines so we stood in the trench. We were on duty all night and when day came we waded off to a dugout to sleep, leaving one man on sentry who was relieved by us every hour.

The duty here is light, but very nervy owing to the possibility of bombing attacks by the Germans. We are not allowed to leave the trench from dusk to dawn and so through the night I took my turn with the other fellows; an hour on sentry duty gazing over the top into nothing. Bitterly cold, I feel numbed to the bone. We are up to our knees in mud.

Breakfast at 7.30am after an hour's 'stand to'. Breakfast consists of a slice of bread and bacon and a drink from our water bottles. Bitterly cold night last night: raining hard with a keen wind blowing and with no means of keeping warm. I longed for the daylight when I could creep into some dugout. This came at last and, with the remaining fellows not on duty, crept off to the nearest shelter and huddled ourselves together to get what warmth we could.

During the day we each did a turn of fire-step duty, the fellow coming off taking the place in the dugout of the one who had gone on.

Occasionally a fellow would get up and have a munch at something, but for the most part, except when we went on duty, we stayed all day where we had lay down in the morning. 'Stand to' at 4.30pm and I watch the murky day turn to darkness. In this part of the line we have no contact with the outside world and so wait for the ration party to arrive as the one event during the 24 hours. With the ration party come the letters for us. Very pathetic it is sometimes to watch the fellows read these. Every few moments they will bring them out and re-read again or crawl off to some temporary shelter and, with the aid of a torch held low, read and re-read again. It is our only touch with civilisation which we feel we are losing contact with.

The night passed quietly. 'Stand to' at 6.30am. It is usually a creepy business watching the daybreak and straining to see signs of the enemy.

Night again. The ration party has just been along bringing rumours. We hear that we are to be brigaded with the Devons and, after this tour of six days, will return with them to the rear and offer up small prayers that it may be so.

The tea they have just brought up is funny stuff. Made by the cooks somewhere in the rear over a wood fire, the water, which is smoked in consequence, was brought to them in petrol tins recently in use and when made put into dishes used for stew. So we get a mixture of stew, smoke, petrol and tea; stone cold, always stone cold. I could not drink mine, had a try and it came up again, but nothing matters if I am getting out of this.

This afternoon the Germans gave us some hate in the shape of artillery fire. Shrapnel was flying about the trenches in all directions for a time. Lieutenant Hemus was hit in the leg and has lay in a dugout all day waiting for stretcher-bearers to come up and take him away. They arrived at dusk. I do not envy stretcher-bearers under these conditions – good fellows. They swore till they were blue in the face, getting Hemus along the trench, themselves nearly up to their waists in mud.

Last night I occupied a listening post close up to the German lines and could occasionally hear them singing. The smell is awful: rats all over the place.

At last relief came. Word was passed along at dusk that we were to be relieved that night at about 8pm. Forms loomed up in the mist at the back of us and we heard strange whispers and many curses. They were the Manchester Pals Battalion coming to take over. It takes a very few moments for the relieved man to hand over all the information he has regarding the enemy. I was on sentry duty at the time of their arrival and quickly handed over to the man taking my place and, with the rest of the platoon, made my way to the rear and to billets. It's a wretched business relieving and being relieved, the darkness adding to the confusion. We plodded our way along the trench for some distance and when not in direct line of enemy rifle fire, scrambled out of the trench on to firmer ground and made our way to the rear. Occasionally I looked back. German Very lights were going up here and there along the line, making the night seem very weird. We arrived at billets 10pm very tired and lay down in our togs and slept.

I have slept most of the day today, too tired to move. This evening I have had a wash and clean up – the best part of a wretched business.

Saturday, 8 January 1916

My rest of last night was very short-lived. About 9pm I was warned for parade at 11pm for instruction under [the Royal Engineers] in mining and sapping. Returned at 8am.

At 3.30pm we paraded for the line again. Before leaving, the commanding officer (CO) came along and said that, according to information, the Germans were becoming active in bombing raids and that they had successfully bombed one of our trenches up the line the previous night and collared some British troops.

We took over the line after dark. A wet and gusty night: ideal conditions for a raid with the wind whistling through the trenches. I could imagine anything.

Went on sentry duty at 2am; the relieved sentry reporting all clear. I had been on duty only a few minutes when word was passed down that the sentry on the left of No. 26 trench, situated on my right, had heard an unusual noise in front, like tins rattling, and to keep a keen lookout. We sent Very lights up but all was clear. I was sentry on this post again at 3am and at about 3.30 heard noises I was unable to account for – sounds like wire scraping together. The reason why I was still on sentry duty at 3.30, having already done an hour's duty from 2–3am, can be explained by the fact that our suspicions were thoroughly aroused; every man in this part of the line was on sentry.

I sent up another flare, reported the incident to the officer and awaited events, all the men in the trench standing to.

About 4am the sentry on the right spotted two men rising from the ground about 30 yards in front of our trench. The alarm was passed along and we all opened rapid fire; the suppressed excitement of the last half-hour having free rein. It was our first contact with the Germans. Amidst the din of fire we heard groans out in front and knew we had hit something. At daybreak we saw the result, a German lay about 20 yards in front, dead. Under cover of a listening post we crept out and brought him in. Scattered around were about a dozen hand grenades showing the attack was organised and the retreat rapid.

The victim was a finely built fellow – a Bavarian. On medical examination he was found to have a festering wound on the back, which makes his exploit the greater as he had travelled about 250 yards from his own line and had got partly through our own barbed wire. This is probably what I had heard. Given another five minutes they would have blown the trench to bits. The rest of his party escaped. We thus bagged the first German the battalion has been able to produce.

Amongst those immediately concerned we raffled his bayonet scabbard. I was the winner and sent it home as a souvenir.

Sunday, 9 January 1916

Trench routine all the morning, sleep in the afternoon. Guard sentries doubled in case of a repetition of last night.

We have had a rotten day; our supply of coke has given out. We are cold and plastered with mud as usual. Someone has just ventured to compare our present position to a Sunday afternoon at home, so we have all cuddled together and some are trying to go to sleep. We are to be relieved tomorrow.

Raffle prize: The scabbard of the German soldier found dead in no-man's-land by Harry and his fellow soldiers after the failed raid on the night of 8/9 January 1916. Harry referred to the man as 'Bavarian' but British sources mention only that his body was sent down to be buried in Maricourt cemetery and that the commanding officer was furious that men's lives had been put at risk in recovering it. German records reveal that there was no Bavarian unit in the line at the time. (David Griffiths)

A City Battalion Souvenir.

An interesting episode which befel the 2nd Birmingham City Battalion at the front is communicated by Mr. D. Drinkwater. A platoon of the battalion was surprised at 3 o'clock on the morning of 9 January by an enemy bombing party.

The Birmingham men were soon on the alert, however, and the enemy were driven back, but not before one of them was brought down. This was not known until morning dawned, when the body of the German, who was of a fine Bavarian type, was noticed just outside the British lines.

The City Battalion men were anxious to obtain possession of the scabbard of the first enemy to fall to the platoon, and when it was secured it was raffled for by the officers and men. The winner of the souvenir was Private H. V. Drinkwater, of Stratford-on-Avon, whither it was despatched by post and arrived safely last week.

War news: Harry sent the scabbard – its tassel still caked with Somme mud – back to his father in Stratford-upon-Avon and told him about the incident. David Drinkwater informed the *Birmingham Post* which printed the story soon afterwards. (David Griffiths)

Monday, 10 January 1916, Suzanne

Were relieved at dusk, 6.30pm, by the [16th Battalion] Manchester Pals. Very thankful to get away. We are expert by now at changing. The relieving troops come along and take up their place automatically, the relieved making every haste to get to the rear. Once on the road and clear from rifle fire and free from observation, we get our pipes on and can generally muster up a song between us. Especially so tonight, we were leaving the trenches for some little time in order to be reorganised with regular troops. Arrived Suzanne 9pm and got down to kip.

Tuesday, 11 January 1916, Morlancourt

We were not allowed to leave Suzanne without a final parting shot from the Germans. We paraded at 3pm ready to move off when a shell landed right in the centre of the village followed by others at intervals of about half a minute. The CO got the wind up and by companies we quickly moved out of the village, transport and houses going up in all directions as we passed through. We were very lucky to escape heavy casualties. I saw several fellows belonging to different units being taken to the dressing station badly knocked about. Several dead and wounded horses were lying in the road.

We arrived at Morlancourt, eight miles distance, at 7am, very tired but very cheery at the prospects of rest.

This, then is the end of our first prolonged experience in the trenches. The Germans have almost been a secondary consideration, we principally fighting the weather and the conditions. All of us suffering more or less from dysentery. It says a lot that after all this we are able to walk at all; no doubt our training in England made us very fit.

Ward and I have just been down to the village church, where the Church Army have a canteen. We sat in a pew and had a tin of pears between us, biscuits we handled with clean hands. We heard music, someone was playing the organ; it was a paradise regained.

Looking back on his diary in the 1920s, Harry added these reflections to the margin: 'Long after the war had ceased and able to review the course of events as a whole, I still look upon this period as one of the worst – a month was a long time to withstand such conditions. Today it would be a matter for conversation if by chance we got wet to the skin, in those days it was our normal existence. Add to this a lack of proper food and only eating hot food when we were out of the trenches for a day. Forever standing in mud, on occasion so deep in places that it got in over the top of our waders which came up to the thigh. Standing in it by night on duty, invariably standing in it by day trying to sleep, always with the knowledge that a well-directed shell would leave us helpless for we were unable to move except by the use of the elbows on the sides of the trench. Its effect on the mind was stunning. Already the normal life we had all been used to began to seem like a fairy story, a thought which was to be intensified before the war came to an end. Its effect upon the mind was very much like that of a bad nightmare from which one might awaken; only in this instance we were aware of its reality. This month [at Maricourt] we lived every minute in a state of fever and, in an isolated case or two, delirium.'

Wednesday, 12 January 1916

Scraping my clothes and cleaning myself.

Thursday, 13 January 1916

Equipment cleaning all day. This evening, like last night, Ward and I retired down to the canteen, which was in the local church and in great comfort sat in a pew and over some grub related our experiences during the period in the line.

Post has just come up. Shortly there will be a general scramble for letters and parcels. Tomorrow we move on to Sailly-Laurette.

Harry's battalion had left England as part of a 5,000-strong brigade of Kitchener's New Army volunteers. Now the authorities decided that whole units of inexperienced New Army troops should be stiffened with the addition of regular army battalions, even though the heavy fighting of the first 18 months had reduced the ranks of the pre-war professional soldiers. Harry's battalion and the 14th Royal Warwicks took their leave of the all-volunteer 32nd Infantry Division and were placed in a mixed brigade in the 5th Division, one of the original units of the BEF which had been in France since mid-August 1914 and part of what the German Kaiser had dismissed as Britain's 'contemptible little army'. Now Harry's Pals battalion was to serve alongside two others with illustrious histories – the 2nd King's Own Scottish Borderers (2 KOSB) and 1st Royal West Kents – both of which had seen action in the first British battle of the war, at Mons on 23 August 1914.

Friday, 14 January 1916, Sailly-Laurette

Paraded at 1.30pm today and marched here, arriving 4pm. A grand sunny day. We were escorted out of the village by the band of the King's Royal Rifle Corps.

The expected reshuffling, of which we had heard, was now to take place. Kitchener's Army was, by this time, coming out as fast as transport could bring them, filling up the gaps caused by the casualties in the early days of the war amongst the regulars.

We have been placed with the 5th Division after it had been through [the battles of] Hill 60 and Ypres and are in the 13th Brigade which now consists of the KOSBs and West Kents as regulars and the 14th Battalion Royal Warwickshire Regiment and ourselves – the 15th Battalion – as Kitchener's men.

From now to 30 January we are to spend our time in drill, bomb throwing, bayonet fighting, trench digging and so forth.

Saturday, 29 January 1916

We have had a very uneventful time, thoroughly fed up to the teeth with the monotony of things. Reveille 7am and run till 7.45. Breakfast 8am, parade 9am for the eternal bayonet fighting and finish at 12.30. For the remaining part of the day we lay in our billets and write or sleep.

My diary is now getting a duty and I keep it up regularly or, if that has not been possible, as soon as I come out of the line.

Tomorrow we move for an unknown destination. I do not think the conditions of any part of the line can be worse than that we have just left, but the Germans may be more aggressive – so may we.

Sunday, 30 January 1916, Lahoussoye

Reveille 6am, blankets rolled and loaded by 7.30. Blankets are transported in wagons, one of which is attached to each company. The blankets we roll in bundles of about a dozen and label according to the platoon of men.

Breakfast 8am, paraded 8.45 and moved off for Lahoussoye. Roads very bad and marching difficult but it is a change; arriving 1.30pm.

Renewed acquaintance this evening with the very hospitable woman and Ward, Wood and myself have an excellent supper of eggs and chips.

Monday, 31 January 1916, Talmas

Reveille as yesterday and left promptly at 9am for Talmas, about 12 miles, arriving 2.30pm. This appears to be very much as other French villages; rambling and dilapidated.

Tuesday, 1 February 1916

General inspection this afternoon. Extraordinary how quickly we have recovered from our experiences in the trenches. To see us on parade, clothes brushed and clean, no one would imagine that only a short time ago we were perpetually covered in mud. Wonderful what fresh air and grub will do.

Wednesday, 2 February 1916

The old routine – we wonder how long we are here for and where we are going.

A note here on the organisation by which we get our daily bread. A regimental quartermaster knows exactly the number of men he has to feed. This number he sends to brigade headquarters, where similar numbers are collected from other battalions under that brigade command. These numbers are for three days ahead and can be only approximate owing to casualties, sickness or recruits joining the battalion. Each brigade in turn sends the numbers collected to divisional headquarters, which in their turn have collected similar numbers from each of the units under its command. Division then hand these numbers over to the Army Service Corps (ASC) who, with their motor transport, go to ration dumps and draw the required goods. These return to divisional headquarters where the goods are split up again according to brigade returns and sent on the brigade. From brigade HQ they are fetched by battalion transport and again split up amongst the four companies forming the battalion. Cookable goods go to the company cooks to be served up as a hot meal, whilst bread, jam, and sometimes butter, is served out to us individually. A loaf between four or 14 men according to the conditions we are under and a tin of jam between four and a supply of tinned beef. This goes on daily and is how we get our rasher of bacon every morning and no more. Our tin of jam and sometimes butter and sometimes one candle for a whole billet, but the latter is rare and has to last. Tobacco we get a good ration. Generally speaking the food is enough but very rough. The postal service is served in a similar way and comes up with the rations. We are supplied with blankets – two per man – for use in the billets.

This war is beginning to have many side issues. Till now it looks as if the actual firing line is of little consequence compared with the immense organisation at the rear to keep it going. It is roughly estimated that it takes about 14 men to keep one man in the firing line.

After a long period in the line and under such conditions as we have been through, rest and recreation are required to recuperate. To lie in billets would be fatal; we should go mad with introspection, so football is becoming organised for the afternoons, one battalion playing against the other throughout the division. In the evenings a concert party has been formed by fellows in the division. They have nothing to do but to go round to villages occupied by the division and give shows, sometimes in a barn if a better place is not available.

It seems a funny war, sometimes up to our neck in mud and the following evening listening to a concert party that would do credit to a London music hall.

Thursday, 3 February 1916
Parades as usual this morning, concert party this evening.

Friday, 4 February 1916
Parades – a very uninteresting time.

Sunday, 6 February 1916
Church service 10am. QVRs [Queen Victoria's Rifles], ASC and ourselves in an orchard during this performance. I sat under a tree and ate apples left under the tree from last year, there are a lot about.

Monday, 7 February 1916
Parade as usual this morning. Hear we move off again tomorrow, but can get no information where we are going.

Tuesday, 8 February 1916, Coisy
We paraded this morning in full marching order and left the village at 10am. A brute of a march: roads in shocking condition. Reached Coisy 3pm. Have got a rotten billet with holes in the wall, no straw – have just been round to the transport lines and pinched some. I am getting a first class scrounger. Snowing hard outside and bitterly cold.

Wednesday, 9 February 1916
Paraded nearly all morning in gas helmets doing an attack. We wonder what this continual practising of the attack means, are we for it soon!

Friday, 11 February 1916
Practising the attack.

Saturday, 12 February 1916
Drill. We move again tomorrow, thankful to get away from this rotten billet.

Sunday, 13 February 1916, Fourdrinoy
We left Coisy at 1am and, preceded by the KOSB, arrived here this afternoon, our billet for the time being. Fourdrinoy is two miles from Picquigny, a railhead about ten miles from Amiens. Am hoping to get into Amiens one evening. The village is similar to all others we have been in, straggling and dirty.

As we get further from the line, things are more civilised. There are shops and *estaminets* which compare to our public houses, only that they sell cheap red and white wine at about 20 times its value. Candles we are able to buy so that now we have brilliantly lighted billets, each fellow having a couple. This is a new experience and makes life worth living at night.

Tuesday, 15 February 1916
Practising the eternal attack again. We are getting heartily sick of it and wish they would let us attack something. Trench digging.

Saturday, 19 February 1916
Barbed wire entanglements. This evening I have been to hear the concert party, a very fine show. They call themselves the Whizz-Bangs after the name of a species of shell that makes a lot of noise.

The Whizz-Bangs – their advertising assured 'no duds' – was the official Concert Party of the 5th Division and it included many Birmingham Pals in its entourage. One of these, a man who made his debut in a pantomime at Bray-sur-Somme at Christmas 1915, was Will (Billy) Kings who went on to make a career as a well-known Birmingham entertainer in the inter-war years and kept troops amused during the Second World War. He later played several characters in the original 1950s cast of The Archers.

Sunday, 20 February 1916
Have just returned from Amiens. Started off early this morning and walked to Picquigny. Caught a train and got into Amiens at dinner time. It has been a real treat to see streets of shops again and to walk on a pavement. It seems like a touch of the world I knew something about and have forgotten.

Monday, 21 February 1916
Barbed wire entanglements. I should like to wind it round some of those fat staff officers and roll them in it. It is getting as bad as doing the attack.

Tuesday, 22 February 1916
Brigade route march. Started in a snow storm and finished up plastered in mud – did 13 miles.

Wednesday, 23 February 1916
Another new phase of war came along in the last few days. Had heard of the possibility of men going home on leave; this morning it was a fact. On arriving back from the route march yesterday we heard that the leave list was at orderly rooms and in the evening the men were warned to be ready to leave this morning – we saw them off, they were very cheery at the prospect. I wonder when my turn will come along? I suppose it will if I live long enough.

It has been a wretched cold day, snowing, and I have a wretched billet. The roof lets water in like a sieve. Last night I woke up and found my blankets and straw saturated with rain; got a twinge of rheumatics in consequence.

A good old dame lives in the cottage connected with the buildings and she allows us free use of her kitchen stove around which McMillan, Patch and myself are now sitting, it's the warmest place.

We are continually speculating where we are going and what for – no one seems to know.

Thursday, 24 February 1916, Saint-Vaast-en-Chaussée

Things developed during the night. HQ were called up and parades cancelled for the day. Reveille 6am with orders to parade at noon ready to move off and reached St Vaast about 4pm. We are billeted here for the night. My billet is over a stable, very smelly, but plenty of straw.

Friday, 25 February, 1916, Doullens

Reveille 6.30am, blanket wagons packed by 7 and moved out of the village 8.30am destination unknown. Rumours were rife that we were marching to Doullens, 23 miles distance, but information very scarce and unreliable. Weather very cold, a sharp wind blowing as we set off. We had not been on the march more than half an hour before snow began to fall. Roads were good at this period, frozen hard.

We had little idea of the march that lay before us as we set out. Reached Doullens at 6pm and have been marching all day, having ten minutes' rest every hour. During the whole time of the march snow fell heavily, froze on us and froze on the roads. Our boots would not grip; we were sliding and falling all over the place. Had no food issued and water bottles froze hard. We arrived at the billet hungry and each man a mass of snow.

Our billet – a bank manager's house and we have the attic – is very cold. We rather staggered the good lady. It is her first experience of having foreign troops billeted on her. She wondered what was going to happen when we presented ourselves, 14 of us all covered in snow. Hutt, who speaks French like a native, quickly put her at ease. He told her that really we were quite harmless, but jolly cold and would like a hot drink. She gave us hot coffee all round and we thawed over the kitchen fire and then retired to the attic. No blankets, I laid down in my overcoat, too cold to sleep. I have just been out and got some grub, troops are coming into the town from all directions, French and English. Streets are full of horse and motor transport, 60,000 troops are being rushed up to Arras. We wonder what the trouble is? Hear rumours of the Germans breaking through.

For this march we were mentioned in dispatches. It was a very good performance. We had marched for ten hours in a blizzard across open country with only the regulation break of ten minutes per hour. The snow clung to our face, hands and equipment and froze hard on us as we marched along. We

Writing home: Harry was billeted in the attic of a bank manager's house at 59, Rue St Ladre in Doullens during his trying march north from the Somme to Arras. The Germans had occupied the town in September 1914 and Harry sent home this postcard of German cavalry. Today the Rue St Ladre is called the Rue du Commandement Unique. (David Griffiths)

were unable to have any food or drink on the journey. The transport got stuck and snowed up. We were carrying complete equipment, the tin hats were a godsend strapped on the back; they broke many a fellow's fall as he slipped on the road.

The band, like the remainder, was snowed up but they rose to the occasion on their bugles as we marched into the town.

Saturday, 26 February 1916
Field kitchens and transport arrived today; kitchens 4.30am and transport 3pm. No grub this morning so we went out and got bread and eggs for breakfast. Paraded at five o'clock this evening with brooms and shovels for road sweeping.

Sunday, 27 February 1916
Service at 10am the usual way – prayer book in one hand and rifle in the other, this is an old custom. Somewhere back in the distant ages, some British troops were attacked whilst at service. They had no rifles to defend themselves, so ever since rifles have been carried. There are many more old customs and red tape that will have to be scrapped if we are going to win this war.

French artillery have been streaming through all afternoon on the way to Arras, there is trouble brewing somewhere.

Ward has been very busy and fixed up a dinner at a hotel for four of us. We have had a good tuck-in, finished eight courses with ease.

We have to keep early hours here. 8pm – I am finishing my diary for the day. Candles out nine o'clock.

Monday, 28 February 1916
Writing from the billet window I can see a constant stream of French troops and transport and British Royal Field Artillery passing to and fro. Hear rumours that we go into the trenches on Friday.

This evening I have been to a concert in the YMCA.

ARRAS

February 1916 – July 1916

'I did not think we should get out of it alive'

Harry was well aware that vast numbers of Allied troops were on the move but he – and most of the infantry's lowly footsloggers – did not know why. A week earlier the Germans had unleashed a massive onslaught on the double ring of 28 fortresses which shielded the city of Verdun on the French-held sector of the Western Front.

Believing the French to be economically and militarily exhausted, the Germans intended to drain the very lifeblood out of the French armies by sucking every last poilu into the vortex of Verdun, leaving the British isolated and unable to continue the fight.

Committed to defending Verdun to the last, and with a steady stream of fresh British troops crossing the Channel, the French once again urged Britain to increase their share of the 'line holding' burden and relieve some units to allow more French soldiers to be diverted to the defence of Verdun. The British agreed and shuffled some of their divisions towards the region of Artois to assume responsibility for Arras and the trenches guarding the city out to the east.

Arras, the capital of Artois, was an ancient town, prosperous in the Middle Ages from the trade in wool and fine tapestries. Occupied by the Germans in September 1914, the French had quickly cleared them from the city but had not driven them too far. By the time the lines of trenches had solidified over the winter of 1914–1915, Arras found itself in a salient jutting out to the south-east. Surrounded by the Germans, who were never more than a mile or two beyond the ancient centre, Arras was also overlooked from the German positions on Vimy Ridge to the north. And so began the long agony of Arras at the hands of the German gunners.

By February 1916 the damage to many of the city's architectural gems, including its cathedral and the two beautiful main squares, was all too evident.

German shells regularly sought out the unwary at important road junctions, and the railway station and sidings. To move large numbers of men around on the surface in daylight was hazardous in the extreme, but below ground a medieval warren of subterranean quarries – Les Boves – had been dug out of the chalk along with connecting passageways, shelters and storage silos. There was enough space in these and in the vaults beneath the cathedral precinct and the Bishop's Palace to shelter entire divisions, and that is exactly how the British used them when they took over the defence of the city from the French.

As the 15th Royal Warwicks continued to march north, so Harry prepared to play his own small part in easing the pressure on his French allies of the 83rd and 209th Regiments of the French 34th Division. It was a march which would eventually take him 25 miles from the mud of the Somme and into the communication trenches which spread, tendril-like, from the northern suburb of Saint-Nicolas towards the front line beyond the village of Roclincourt, a couple of miles north of Arras.

Tuesday, 29 February 1916, Humbercourt

We were sorry to leave Doullens, we have had a good time and billet. We got on well with the billet folk. Before I left, Madame gave me a ring her son had made in the trenches as a souvenir of my stay. Reached Humbercourt in the evening, stayed the night and marched here to Dainville – 14 miles distance – at 6pm.

Wednesday, 1 March 1916, Dainville

Two German aeroplanes watched our arrival.

Thursday, 2 March 1916

We take over a part of the line from the French. Paraded at 6.30pm for the trenches and marched off preceded by the KOSB, West Kents and Cheshires. The night cold, dark and stormy; the roads leading to the line congested with [our] transport going up and French troops and transport returning. Several times we had to halt and fall out on the road side to allow all this to pass. Everything seemed all mixed up and horses began to get restless with the continual confusion. To make things worse it began to rain hard.

Eventually we arrived in Arras at midnight, wet through. Passing through Arras the town looked very weird; buildings down in all directions. It looked as if there had been a great fire burning out street after street, leaving only the outside walls. Sometimes these were down, blocking up the road.

This was my first glimpse of a spectacular side of the war. It seemed very strange to go marching along, seeing nothing but street after street of what were once houses of which, for the most part, only the outside walls now remained. The debris was everywhere. Occasionally we passed an odd soldier or two which added to the impression that this was a deserted city and in decay, the troops adding to the impression by the stealth in which they passed us. Later on we knew that in reality they were hurrying from one cellar to another, falling masonry being a factor here.

We reached our dugout at 1.30am, taken there by a guide, without casualties. The West Kents and KOSB were not so fortunate, they were caught in the communication trenches by shellfire and about a dozen got knocked out. Several shells came uncomfortably close to us, but we were lucky. We are in the support line, in support to the West Kents, who are occupying the front line. These dugouts are a revelation to us – 30ft below ground, reinforced with concrete and have wire bunks, one over the other.

Friday, 3 March 1916

A dixie of tea came up at 4am. We were in a fairly miserable plight after our march of last night and getting into the trenches, but the tea was very acceptable. A better edition than the stuff we used to have at Maricourt.

Breakfast at 7am. We turned out at 9am to clean up the trench and repair parts blown in by shellfire. Repairing the line in this part appears to be a very sordid business. The French have buried their dead in parts of the parapet, which is the front part of the trench above ground. We came across several of these. It was the habit of the French in the early days of the war to bury their dead in the immediate vicinity of the trenches and apparently they used this method of making the parapet. As time went on, shells and the rain washed away the earth, exposing the bodies.

Slept this afternoon.

On gas alarm sentry 8pm to 9pm. Wet and cold. Many star-shells going up from the German lines – this strikes me as being a hot part of the line.

Have just come off sentry and have nothing to do for the remaining night. These dugouts are great, am wrapped up in my bunk, it's a little palace.

Saturday, 4 March 1916

Breakfast this morning at seven o'clock. All remained quiet last night and I had a jolly good sleep. After breakfast, fatigue work as yesterday, a wretched business, kept on coming across dead Frenchmen.

The country viewed from the trenches is very dreary, nothing but trench after trench and in places the ground blown into heaps of dirt. The best general impression one can give, I think, of this area of ground or any area of ground where artillery has been firing to any degree, is that of land that has been greatly subject to a measure of volcanic eruption. The trees as far as the eye can see have been blown to pieces; black stumps only remaining in the ground. All is desolation, there is usually not a semblance of anything growing, not even grass. All is mud, shell-holes and barren. Sometimes it stretches as far as the eye can see – utter desolation; amongst this we live.

We left the trenches this evening and came into Arras and are billeted in the subterranean passages belonging to a huge convent. Here, as in the support line, we have wire beds, ie, wire netting stretched over a wooden frame. Many thousands of British troops arriving; they appear to be going straight up into the line and relieving the French.

Even when out of the firing line, infantrymen like Harry rarely got any real 'rest'. In a war which relied mainly on 'manpower', Harry was called upon time and again to provide back-breaking labour as a minute cog in the titanic and ceaseless machine that was static trench warfare on the Western Front. He was even called upon to take the fight below ground for, mirroring the fighting on the surface, the armies of all sides had formed units which had taken to digging down into deep shafts in their own trenches and then burrowing and branching out like moles beneath to lay explosive charges beneath the enemy trenches in the hope of blowing them to Kingdom Come. Far away from the light and fresh air, this subterranean war was dark, dangerous and claustrophobic work – and it was no place for the faint hearted.

Sunday, 5 March 1916

Breakfast 6.30am. Have had a brute of a day. Mining fatigue for the [Royal] Engineers. This consists of going down the mines under no-man's-land and as the miners pick the ground, we have to put it into sandbags and pass it from one to the other perhaps half or three parts of a mile, mostly bent half double

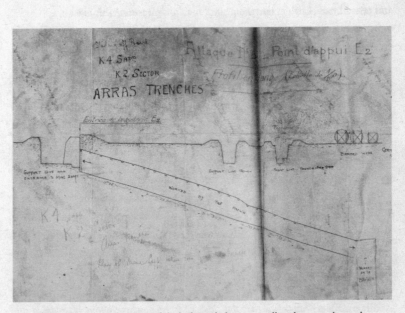

Mine map: Harry spent a good deal of time helping tunnellers dig mines beneath no-man's-land whilst serving on the Arras front. Many of the mines had been started by the French before the British arrived. Harry found this mud-stained sketch down one of the galleries he helped to work and kept it. (David Griffiths)

as we were unable to stand upright. Got back to billets at 5pm, had had no grub all day till then and was dog tired. Paraded again at 8.30pm and back again we had to go to the firing line carrying rations and have just returned this time to bed we hope, 12.30am – snowing hard.

Writing after the war about the use of mines, Harry explained, 'Mines in the locality of Arras were numerous. The war had come to a standstill, which probably no general of any side had anticipated, and it is highly probable that the high command had no real knowledge at that moment of how to deal with the situation.

'The trenches stretched from the Belgian coast right through France, separated from each other by sometimes not more than 50 yards.

'While both sides were working out how this stagnation could be overcome, the mines came into being. Unable to get at each other over the top of the ground, they started to get at each other under the ground.

'The mines in themselves were useless things. Their primary objectives were probably only two: the first was to burrow under to the other side and then blow up the opposing line of trench. By that means the stagnation could be overcome, but it created the second objective: it created a high state of nervous tension. Both sides mined the ground, burrowing deeper as they pushed further towards the other side. Then science took a hand and again check-mated the operations. Instruments were brought in which told whether there was anyone mining in the locality.

'Sometimes these mine shafts were in close proximity and both sides dug deeper and deeper with the hope of being the bottom dog as it were, so that they could, with surety, blow up the other.

'It invariably happened that the clash came somewhere about halfway in no-man's-land and then it is all finished – check-mated underground as above ground.'

Monday, 6 March 1916

Parade 7.30am and came up to the trenches on fatigue work – and it is fatigue work! Start off with a walk of about five miles and wherever we go we have to carry our rifle and equipment; the latter we have to work in. We have been digging new trenches all day long, arriving back to billet, another five miles back again. We had to go on parade at once and back up into the line again to relieve the West Kents in the firing line. Here I am at midnight and now we have to work all through the night to daybreak.

Tuesday, 7 March 1916

We worked all through last night to 6am. I felt that I had had quite enough by then, but have had to do an hour's sentry duty every third hour through the day which has only given us two hours to sleep at a time. I am feeling like most of the other fellows – half dead. Can hardly keep my eyes open.

'Stand to' at 6pm; I am in a sentry group on a machine-gun emplacement. One hour's sentry duty looking over the top into no-man's-land, one hour by the side of the sentry during which I am able to sit in the trench, and the third hour I can sleep in the dugout – this keeps on repeating through the night till daybreak.

Wednesday, 8 March 1916

It snowed all last night and was bitterly cold. It is probable that in those five words, 'it snowed all last night', one is not able to convey any idea of the actual conditions of the line at that moment. Sentry duty consisted of a man standing on the fire-step looking out into no-man's-land for one hour. The second hour he went off to a dugout to sleep if possible. Usually, when the opportunity came he was too cold to do so. The third hour he returned to his sentry post and sat by the side of the sentry. For the sentry no movement was possible – he stood looking out towards the German lines and the relief man who would follow him sat at his feet in the trench. He also was limited in his movement and so passed the night, in this instance, snowing. Sometimes rain took the place of snow; if neither of these occurred then a raid was probable.

Had a hard job to keep awake whilst on sentry duty. Passed the time by letting my rifle off across no-man's-land every now and again to keep from falling asleep. One or two fellows, of whom I was one, were found to be fast asleep at the end of their sentry when relieved by the next man. We had gone to sleep standing up and it is to be supposed that the waiting sentry was also asleep. Under military law this is a crime of the first water and so, as a preventative, the sentry fired his rifle at intervals as an indication to the next sentry that he was awake. It was an arrangement between ourselves.

We are all tired out.

'Stand to' at six this evening. Have had a little more sleep today, but not much. We are working at feverish pace almost all day and night, strengthening the trenches. I imagine something is going to happen but at the moment am too tired to trouble.

Just come in off sentry – had an exciting experience. Went on sentry at 7pm after 'stand down'. It was dusk so I put my head over the top to have a look around into no-man's-land and stopped a bullet on the side of my tin hat. I soon got my head down, the vibration made it ache for a time. This incident soon got along to Captain Edwards who presumably came to see what effect it had upon me. He had to get on the fire-step and touch me before I was aware of his presence. No doubt I was in a comatose state. After examining my steel hat, he asked me if I had been asleep when he came, and looked somewhat suspicious, or rather sounded somewhat suspicious. It was dark at the time and he was unable to see my blushes.

This place seems infested with snipers; they come out at dusk and lay in shell-holes.

Harry's honest admission that he fell asleep on occasions could have had serious, and even fatal, consequences. 'Sleeping at post' on active service – even if the man or woman on duty is completely exhausted – is still regarded as one of the most serious of military offences as it not only endangers the safety of entire units but, more importantly, risks the lives of comrades. During the First World War it was punishable by death. Field General Courts Martial handed down 449 death sentences for this offence, of which two were carried out. Two men of the 6th Battalion of the South Lancashire Regiment – both Kitchener volunteers of 1914 like Harry – were paired on sentry duty in Mesopotamia on 6 February 1917 and both were charged with falling asleep and found guilty. They were executed by firing squad on 19 February 1917.

Thursday, 9 March 1916

In an advance listening post 75yds from German front line. Notes written whilst waiting for relief to come up – 10.30pm.

The last seven days has probably been the hardest seven days for hard graft and no sleep and little grub that we have experienced since being out in France. We started well last Thursday night when we arrived in Arras soaked through to the skin and rain still coming down. Our food transport had gone astray and we had had little or no grub. Fortunately, just before starting out I received a parcel from home, which relieved anxiety for some little time.

We eventually found our dugout at 1.30am and there then followed one continual round of hard graft. The mine fatigue was no joke – a march of five miles then eight hours down the mine, backs bent handing bags of dirt and chalk from one fellow to another. Back again to our billets, another five miles walk to parade again and relieve the front line and do sentry duty all night and in the daytime repairing the trenches.

Owing to food transport going astray, food has to be hastily summoned from somewhere and was inadequate. One loaf between five of us and a few biscuits and half a tin of marmalade each per day. Added to that the weather has been bitterly cold and for the most part snowing.

The line has been quiet. Casualties: two killed and four wounded. We are very tired and cold and anxiously waiting for the relief to come along.

Have just heard that we have a ten-mile march before we can be billeted. We are not going back to Arras. We think it jolly hard lines.

Friday, 10 March 1916, Hauteville

We set out last night at 11.15. It will be a march memorable to us all. A cold wind was blowing and it was snowing as we set out along the road and through Arras. We tramped along for about four miles and were met by the field kitchens which dished us out a mug of tea.

After this, marching developed into a trail. One after another we fell in the road and were dragged on to the roadside to recover. I saw two fellows – fast asleep as they walked along – walk out of the ranks and fall into the ditch at the side of the road. We halted for ten minutes rest and I dropped down into a puddle of water and went off to sleep. Was unable to get up without help and finished the march hanging on to the arm of Lieutenant Davis one side and a stretcher-bearer the other.

As I trudged along the road held up by Lieutenant Davis and the stretcher-bearer and conscious, in a vague way, that I was articulating strangely, my mind went back to my schooldays. I recalled the rugger days and the plaudits sometimes gained on the field and contrasted it with my present exhibition. 'This can't be me,' I thought – 'how those fellows would laugh if they saw me now.' I tried to pull myself together and went headlong on the road. They got me to my feet again but I was helpless. I have a vague idea that I was taken through a farmyard and laid on some straw and then I went into oblivion.

We arrived here at 5am and I have slept solidly till 5pm. Have just had what should have been my breakfast at 5.30pm, still in my wet clothes as I was dumped down.

Am going to make my bed more comfortable and get down to it again.

Saturday, 11 March 1916
Slept solidly till 6am. Breakfast seven o'clock. Parade 10am for bath and clean clothing, afternoon scraping our clothing.

Sunday, 12 March 1916
Church parade at 10am. Whilst holding the service German planes came over and dropped six bombs on the village – no great damage done. The weather has turned out beautiful and at the moment of writing I am revelling in a beautifully sunny day; have dry, warm feet and dry boots, the first time for many a long day.

There are many things, petty in their way, which make the periods out of the line and away from the trenches one of unmitigated bliss; dry boots, socks and feet being one of them. There are many others; here we can 'lose' our tin hats, respirator and equipment for a while. Above all we can relax.

Monday, 13 March 1916
Short route march 10–11am. We leave again for the line tomorrow.

Tuesday, 14 March 1916
Reveille 6am, breakfast 7.30. We left the village at 11am en route for the line which we reached tonight.

Wednesday, 15 March 1916
Relieved the Devons in the support line and are in support to the West Kents. Have had a very uneventful march up; the congestion that we experienced last time was absent. We struck our dugout about midnight and find it infested with rats, are having to burn candles to keep them off us. This is not one of the super dugouts like we were in last time up, but a shelter in the last stage of decay. Smells like the dead.

Thursday, 16 March 1916

Occupying trenches in the village of Roclincourt on the left of our previous position. I believe all the stories I have heard about the rats, they swarm here. They are as tame and as large as young kittens and covered with mange. Some of them have scarcely any fur on their body; they look vile.

The trenches here are as good as those at Maricourt were bad. Here the engineers have been hard at work laying down duckboards – wooden platforms built up above the mud – so that one can walk with a fair amount of comfort and, best of all, keep one's feet dry.

Parade at 4pm for engineers' fatigue down the mines till midnight, boring through no-man's-land right under the German lines. Returned to Arras to billet at midnight. Arrive 2.30am to find the billet in a dirty condition – a house that has had a shell through it. Clean the dirt off the floor and sleep till morning.

Friday, 17 March 1916, down mine halfway across no-man's-land

This morning I had a look round Arras. It's an awful show; imagine a town like Bath or Leamington burnt out and you have Arras. Going along one thoroughfare I saw a huge hole in the ground – was told it was here a 'Jack Johnson' had dropped. A 'Jack Johnson' is a huge shell fired by the heaviest of the German long-range guns. It was named Jack Johnson after the black boxer of that name who had been very much to the fore in the boxing world in the days immediately before the war, and because of the havoc caused on its explosion. On this occasion it had gone right through the ground and exploded in a subterranean passage. It had made an awful mess; there were several of these.

There are still one or two shops open (probably run by spies). They keep their goods down the cellars where they stay themselves and we bartered through the grating and paid through the nose. A fellow in 'Intelligence' told me one day that they were somewhat bewildered by the frequency with which the Germans were conversant with things going on in Arras, almost from day to day. That it was the work of spies was obvious but how they got information over to the Germans was puzzling till one day, having thought of practically everything they decided to 'net' a stream which flowed through Arras and on to the German lines and then the riddle was solved. Caught in

Official pass: Although Harry sometimes contrived to slip away from the line to take a look around Arras he was also allowed into the city on official business. This pass, hastily scribbled by his platoon commander Lieutenant Ivor Rubery, allowing him to visit Arras with close friend Philip Jinks, has survived. (David Griffiths) the net were short lengths of stick or tree and hollowed out through the core a message was inserted and the ends stopped up again. They were then thrown in the stream to be taken by the current.

We paraded at 10pm and after the usual four-mile march from Arras reached the front line. Got down the saps [mines] and here I am at 2am under the ground in no-man's-land having a breather, whilst some expert engineer with instruments is listening to hear for any signs of the Germans mining in our direction. It's a very nervy business when we are working close to one another.

We knock off at eight o'clock in the morning and get back to Arras.

Saturday, 18 March 1916

A repetition of last night. Got back to billets at 10am and slept till tea-time; a wash, shave and back up again here in the mines, midnight till eight o'clock tomorrow morning.

By now I am a regular old soldier and have just collared a couple of the engineers' candles. These are supposed to last eight hours, the length of their shift, and are much sought after and are very useful.

Sunday, 19 March 1916, the 'Soldiers Rest' in vaults under Arras Cathedral

Have a night off tonight for which I am thankful. This place is a canteen rigged up by army chaplains from which we can buy coffee and biscuits.

General impressions: from an old campaigner's point of view this must be a funny war. In our training we have practised the attack; generals moving large bodies of men about from one locality to another, down valleys, over hills and in their imagination no doubt taking one village after another, whereas in actual fact here we are, slinking down mines, tunnelling under the ground, stealing out at night to put up barbed wire and crawling away again at the first suggestion of anything like daybreak to hide in our dugouts until night comes and then crawl out again. It's work that the most hardened navvy could not stand for a prolonged period. It calls for no soldierly qualities but brawn and plenty of it. Perhaps the open warfare will come and we may wish we were back in the trenches again.

There are indications of trouble brewing for someone – about a dozen different regiments came into Arras tonight.

Monday, 20 March 1916

Preparing for the line – we go back up tomorrow.

Tuesday, 21 March 1916

Paraded at 12.30am and relieved the West Kents at 2.30am. A dirty night; cold, dark and stormy.

Wednesday, 22 March 1916

In a very hot part of the line. German trenches only 50 yards away and listening posts 30 yards. We have got to keep our eyes skinned here, sentry posts doubled.

Thursday, 23 March 1916

I am one of six occupying a listening post. A brute of a night: a cold wind blowing and raining and snowing hard. The Germans are active tonight, machine-gunning our front line and sending over trench mortars and rifle grenades most of the time. The two latter are horrible things; high explosives which drop into the trench. They blow everything to blazes.

Could hear Germans out on working parties, much too close to be pleasant; am glad morning has come.

Friday, 24 March 1916

Heavy artillery drill till 3pm. I fancy the Germans are getting nervy as to the intentions of our part of the line. No sooner it is dusk they put up Very lights all along the line and keep it up till daybreak. No sooner had the artillery stopped than they started on the front line, sending over all the rubbish they had: trench mortars, aerial torpedoes and rifle grenades. They come over like lightning. We all got down into the deep dugouts which no doubt saved us casualties. We have got to work through the night when not on sentry duty, clearing up as the line gets blown to pieces in places.

Saturday, 25 March 1916

Spent all last night as I anticipated; one hour on sentry, two hours sandbagging from dusk to dawn. Tonight we have moved to the support line for a night's sleep, the first night's sleep since the 14th. We are all very tired and fagged.

Sunday, 26 March 1916

Took over the front line again today. Position rotten, the German trenches are only 30 yards away and 15 yards between listening posts. Here we do nothing but stand and listen; no one is allowed to work or sleep, just stand all night and listen.

Monday, 27 March 1916

We had a dose of it last night – the Germans sending over trench mortars and rifle grenades. One can see them coming over. They leave a trail of sparks in their flight. One feels very much like a rat in a trap, to see the trail of sparks in the air and not sure where the thing is going to drop. Very nerve-racking.

We had a few casualties and the line blown in. Like the other fellows I dodged from one traverse to another, hoping for the best, and was jolly thankful when it stopped. [Front-line trenches were dug in a zig-zag pattern when viewed from above, to confine the blast of explosions to short sections of the trench.]

'Stood to' at 8.30am whilst the engineers exploded a mine on our right. Felt the ground shake and heard a loud cheer from our fellows when the mine went up. Heard later in the day that a number of German miners went up with the mine.

Quiet today, we are being relieved tonight and back to blankets.

Tuesday, 28 March 1916

Out of the trenches and back to billets and blankets five miles from the firing line. We should have been relieved at 9pm by the 1st Bedfords. They arrived punctually on time at the rear of the communication trenches then the idiots of guides lost the way. They did not reach us till 2.30am and were then swearing like the dickens. So were we waiting for them to come.

We got away at 3.30am leaving a few remarks behind for the benefit of the guides and started for Agnez-lès-Duisans. After 12 days in the line travelling was slow. We arrived about 7am weary, worn and jolly tired. Tea served out on arrival, then to sleep. Breakfast 2pm, dinner at five o'clock and then to bed again. My bed is a rat-infested, flea-infested bundle of straw but it is soft and comfortable and there is the blessed thought that the Germans cannot drop a minnie [*minenwerfer* – literally a mine thrower, a trench mortar bomb] or a rifle grenade on the top of us.

Wednesday, 29 March 1916
Spend the day cleaning and scraping the mud off myself.

Thursday, 30 March 1916
I leave the battalion *pro-tem* and am attached to the brigade HQ for [Vickers] machine-gun instruction.

Friday, 31 March 1916
Machine-gun instruction 9am to 12.30pm. Rations good, four and a half loaves between ten men with cheese and jam per day.

Saturday, 1 April 1916
Machine-gun instruction 9.30am–12.30pm and finished for the remainder of the day.

We are now experiencing the other side of this peculiar war and are having a thoroughly good time – it is a good war. Except for an occasional enemy aeroplane which comes over to have a look at us, we might be in some quiet village in England. In this village are billeted KOSB, Royal West Kents, Gloucesters, 14th Royal Warwickshire, 15th Royal Warkwickshire, Engineers, Flying Corps and brigade machine-gunners. We have a football ground and in the afternoons can always see a good game, properly organised and, best of all, in jerseys. This gives it all a real touch of home.

The divisional band turn up and give a tune and in the evenings we have the divisional concert party, a round of mild pleasure we have not experienced before, since being out in France. Added to this the division has now started a canteen where we buy all things we require at reasonable prices – candles, matches, tobacco, soap, shirts – and are now independent of the French villagers who remain and charge us outrageous prices.

Sunday, 2 April 1916
Football and church parade. One of the relics of the past has gone to the wall; we now go on church parade without rifles.

Monday, 3 April 1916
Beautifully idle days. Brilliant weather, clear sky and tropical sun. After parade I have spent the day basking in the sun.

Harry later recalled of this particular day, 'It was a brilliant day of spring and the warmth of the sun seemed to percolate right to the backbone. After the football match I went for a stroll alone. Eventually coming to some sort of bank of grass, I lay down and surveyed the country around, which stretched for some distance in uninterrupted view. It may have been the sight of those football jerseys or the effects of the sun or perhaps the fact that here there were trees still growing instead of charred trunks, but I remember the sense of relief that came over me. I seemed to awaken from a nightmare.'

Tuesday, 4 April 1916

Inspection of machine guns by the brigadier this morning. This tour I go up with the brigade machine guns. Conditions with these appear to be easier; machine-gunners are not called upon to do fatigues and, consequently, consider themselves superior to infantry.

Wednesday, 5 April 1916

If tonight is a sample of the usual routine of machine-gunners, I am quite keen to get back to the battalion.

Left Agnez at 6.30pm with the limbers [two-wheeled, detachable part of a gun carriage used for transporting ammunition or other heavy equipment] carrying the guns and ammunition. Arrived Arras eight o'clock and unpacked the guns on the roadside. The corporal came along and gave me a couple of boxes of ammunition, 25lbs each, to carry one on each shoulder, and by the time I had reached here, the firing line, they had nearly burst me, swinging about and getting mixed up with my rifle and equipment or getting caught in the side of the trench. Each box contains a belt of ammunition and each belt 250 cartridges. We have 14 of these boxes to carry backwards and forwards, each time we change; a team consists of six men and a corporal. We seemed to be better placed for dugouts and have an emplacement built of solid blocks of concrete. Have just done an hour's sentry duty outside the emplacement. The night very cold.

Thursday, 6 April 1916

I find the position is some way from the enemy, some 300 yards. This is very easy, no strain, and everything exceptionally quiet.

Friday, 7 April 1916

Dark, cold and wet last night. Was glad when my sentry duty was over to crawl back into the dugout and stoke up the old brazier. Found a mug of tea waiting, one of the fellows had been busy brewing up on the brazier, goes down good after a cold watch.

Brilliant sunny weather today. Comparing this with our first period in the trenches at Maricourt, it is a gift. There we lived in mud and consumed it, here we have dry trench boards and dry feet. Wet feet day in and day out, running into weeks, is appalling. Here we have a good supply of dry tea and sugar and over the brazier have a brew of tea as we feel inclined.

Saturday, 8 April 1916

The Germans blew up a mine last night – felt the ground shake and went outside the dugout. Everything quiet. Afterwards I went down into Arras at 7pm. Took a couple of petrol cans as an excuse to get water if I was stopped. I dumped the petrol cans at the end of the communication trench and made my way into the town. Very curious to look at, at night: small slits of light showing here and there through the shuttered houses.

I made for the canteen, got some grub and returned. Picked up my petrol cans and rooted round some crumpled houses for a water tap. After rooting round for some time I found one in a back yard, filled up the petrol cans and made back for the emplacement and got hopelessly lost in the system of trenches. A couple of tins of water are no joke to carry for any length of time. I finally found the emplacement about 11pm. Here we wash and shave daily, it's great.

Wednesday, 12 April 1916

Things are exceptionally quiet, so rearrange sentry duty four hours on and six hours off, day and night. Rations are brought up to us every night and we cook our own. I am very good at cooking raw steak. 'Stand to' at 7pm and 4am.

Thursday, 13 April 1916

We were relieved tonight by another machine-gun company and have come back in support for four days. Our duty consists chiefly of firing 1,000 rounds per night into the air over the German lines.

Rumours are going round of a big move on; all officers and men on leave have been recalled from England. Our machine-gun men have come back looking very sick and fed up; some were stopped on arrival at Southampton and turned back. It's very hard lines when so close to home.

Sunday, 16 April 1916

Was on sentry duty from 3am to 5am. The sentry post is situated on a rise in the landscape and obscured from view from the German lines.

As the dawn breaks over Arras the town looks very weird, the bare walls of the cathedral standing out on the skyline. On this particular morning the atmosphere was very clear except that over Arras a mist was still hanging. It was above this mist that one viewed the now rugged walls of the cathedral, standing alone, so they appeared like some huge monument.

Monday, 17 April 1916, the old fort, Arras

We were relieved at 4pm and back we have come into reserve, bringing all our boxes of ammunition with us.

We were had out on parade at 7pm, carrying rations up to the line and afterwards go on fatigue work digging machine-gun emplacements. Knocked off at midnight and have just arrived back 1am. We have a few old beds left here by the last occupants and, with the aid of greatcoats and blankets, sleep very comfortably.

Tuesday, 18 April 1916

A repetition of last night, each man with a couple of bags of rations. We made our way to the firing line, handed over the grub, did some work till midnight and just arrived back. Very easy going and nothing much to disturb our peace of mind. In bed we get shaken during the night; 15-inch heavy artillery are firing from close by.

Wednesday, 19 April 1916

I have just had a very rough journey. I was detailed with other fellows to carry iron girders from Saint-Nicolas, a suburb of Arras, to the firing line. Arrived at Saint-Nicolas at 8pm, we found the girders weighed about 3cwt [336lbs] each and, four men to a girder, we started to carry them. A dark night and pouring with rain, we slipped all over the trench, falling into sump holes. We were in it over our boots in mud and nearly bent double with the weight, so we got out of the trenches and on the top and immediately slipped into a shell-hole. Down came the girder on the ground. We were fairly saturated.

We got back into the trench again but had the greatest difficulty in getting the things round the traverses. At midnight we had got about halfway and the language was foul; the prospect of another four hours of this was too much. We dumped the things in the trench, there was a state of rebellion in the air as we made back to our billets and have just arrived back at 1am in a filthy condition. Have taken all my togs off and hung them up to dry, the blankets are a bit rough. I expect we shall hear something about this in the morning.

Thursday, 20 April 1916

Were awakened this morning and told by the sergeant we were under open arrest for not finishing our job last night. Personally I didn't mind a button and rolled over and went to sleep again. Later in the morning we were had out on parade by the captain. He didn't say much except that we had got to finish the job tonight, so at 4pm we paraded and carried on where we left off last night.

With the help of a little daylight and no rain, things went a little better, but two miles of traverses to carry such things is too much. We got to the firing line about 10pm barely able to lift an arm and scarcely able to crawl back to our billet. We arrived here 11.30pm and lit up a fire and cooked anything we could find – bacon, cheese and meat. Have had a jolly good tuck-in and am about to kip down 1am. There is an awful smell in the place.

Friday, 21 April 1916

Arras heavily shelled today, shells falling uncomfortably close to our billet, trying to find the battery close by. I wish they would shut up. We go back to the line tonight; it looks like being a rotten job. Pouring with rain at the moment; a dull, dreary overcast day.

Saturday, 22 April 1916

Things got mixed up a bit last night. We thought we were going into the line and reached Saint-Nicolas for that purpose at 8pm. On arrival were told to help some of the other teams down from the line and then make for Agnez. In pouring rain we went up to the front line and helped them back with their boxes of ammunition. We had to make a return journey before we finally got all the stuff down. The trenches hereabouts are very bad, in places a foot of mud. Found, after final journey, that limbers had come up so we packed up and moved off for Agnez at 11.30pm, arriving 2am soaked again and plastered with mud. Tea was waiting and with a crust of bread that I had been thoughtful enough to put in my haversack from the last meal, was starting to tuck in when I was handed a parcel from home. What a godsend it was – we slipped the contents down us and at the moment of writing am very full; a good meal makes a lot of difference. Time – 3am.

Sunday, 23 April 1916

Easter Sunday. I awoke to a beautifully sunny day. After breakfast at 11am spent the remainder of the morning scraping the mud off my clothes. This afternoon I lay in the sun and listened to the divisional band. Back again to the billet for tea and this evening a stroll and, from where I am writing now, in a field beside a brook, I can easily imagine myself back in England.

We are all struck with the strangeness of things; one week in hell and the next in comparative bliss. It's the first nice day we have had for the last three weeks; that makes a difference.

Friday, 28 April 1916

Since coming out of the line the weather has been brilliant and I am feeling very fit in consequence. A pleasant change, after the purgatory of the line, to be able to walk upright in the daylight without any thoughts of being sniped, to wear soft caps and not steel helmets, to be able to strike a match in the dark – these are small things but tend to relieve the tension on the nerves which, by now, comes automatically every time I go near the line.

Things the last four days have been very uneventful. Finishing for the day at 12.30pm, in the afternoon the band plays and at night the divisional concert party fill in the gap. After our experience of the winter it is very pleasant, but it is all very wearying. We sometimes wonder if ever we shall get home again, the chances of time are so much against it. I seem to have lost all touch with decent civilisation. I do not think I have used a knife and fork since I have been out here except Wednesday night, and have not slept in a bed.

Wednesday night we celebrated Easter in the shape of a good square meal – six of us went down to the divisional canteen and with 18 eggs, three tins of sausages, three tins of fruit and two tins of asparagus, we retired to a cottage where chipped spuds were waiting. The two Ashbys [Corporals Frank and Howard], Ward, myself and two more constituted the party.

Saturday, 29 April 1916

Morning, sitting on the roadside outside Agnez on sentry, warning fellows of machine-gunners and hidden machine guns close by.

A glorious spring morning. Blazing hot sun and a good breeze blowing. Everything very quiet, the peacefulness of the day is not broken by the sound of guns or aeroplanes or the continual rumble of transport. From here I can see miles around the country, it is very picturesque. Towards the line in the distance stretches a long line of disused trenches dug hastily for the defence of Agnez when the Germans took Arras in the earlier days. On the left, a long belt of trees and dotted here and there an odd-looking building shoots into the sky, the remnant of what was once a large country house. Behind the belt of trees, Arras, the graveyard of many thousands of English and French soldiers – one grave contains the bodies of 640 French soldiers, gassed in the early days – and as we go up each time we leave some behind to swell the number of English.

To the right, the way to England, the road we never travel. It's always towards the line, back to rest and to the line again. The land between is all cultivated and crops are growing, attended by old men and women; it looks like a bit of rural England. Tonight it will all have changed – I shall be seven miles away standing on the fire-step and with bayonet fixed, peering over the top looking into the night, hour after hour waiting for a bombing attack or whatever else comes along.

This afternoon we have had great excitement. A couple of German planes came flying low over the village. I could easily distinguish the pilots from where I hid. They were probably photographing the location.

At the first indication of their approach the alarm was given and we all scurried to cover. The [anti-]aircraft guns opened fire on them and quickly got the range, dropping shells all round them. The airmen must have been getting mighty uncomfortable by this time, they appeared to open out and shoot through the air towards their own lines. First the foremost plane began to rock and then the second followed suit. By this time they had passed over the village and we were out in the roadway, waiting for something to happen; the excitement was intense. Suddenly the foremost one gave a lurch and nosedived and dropped to the ground behind the belt of trees. Guns from all directions firing like blazes, it was deafening. The second one lurched, turned a complete somersault in the air and dropped to the ground in a cloud of smoke and flame. As it dropped we all gave a mighty cheer. I was glad I was not one of the airmen.

Sunday, 30 April 1916

Arrived back in the line last night at midnight, nearly bent double carrying the ammo. I hope these circumstances are taken into account when I appear before St Peter at the gate. I carried two boxes slung over my shoulder by a strap; 'bump', 'bump' they went on the side of the trench on the one side and my rifle bumping on the other. My back, shoulders and chest stopping the rebound, I finished up a mass of perspiration.

On arrival we heard that the front line may go up any moment, the Germans had burrowed practically underneath and all the men had withdrawn and are now like ourselves in the support line.

We waited all night and today, but nothing has happened.

Monday, 1 May 1916

Nothing has happened today. I imagine children in England did a maypole dance this morning, it's a nice old maypole dance we are doing here.

Tuesday, 2 May 1916

The expected blow-up [of the mine] has not occurred and we are back in the firing line. I hope someone has not miscalculated. Writing at 7pm it is a glorious evening, everything very quiet. Occasionally a shell comes over from the German lines and bursts somewhere in the rear. Occasionally we reply and things die down again. Overhead the aeroplanes are busy and we watch them as they go over the German lines. One after another they go and are heavily shelled. Both sides have observation balloons up.

It all appears to be a game of compromise. If one side shells the firing line of the other, the other returns the fire, generally with interest and into the firing line opposite. It is the same with the support lines. If they shell our village where we have stores and troops billeted, up go our planes and we lay their villages so occupied flat. Everything seems to be at a deadlock, one side waiting for the other side to dash over the top which, with the clearing up of the weather, may be anytime now. With the opposing firing lines full of machine guns capable of firing 600 rounds a minute, and the front all strewn with barbed wire, they are lucky who get through.

Friday, 5 May 1916

From last Tuesday till today things have been very monotonous. Hardly a shell has come over to disturb us, but nasty rumours are about of an advance over the top. I have just had orders to return to the battalion and go tomorrow. When one is recalled to one's unit, there is always some object in doing so, I wonder what this is?

Saturday, 6 May 1916

I rejoined the battalion this morning and found many new faces; also some who I had known quite well had 'gone west'. I quickly touched for a fatigue and paraded with others for mining work at 4pm, working till midnight.

Tonight we are lucky, another party is down the mine passing the full bags from one to another and we receive them at the mine mouth and pass them one to another along the trench and in turn hand them over to another party working further along, who build up any part of the trench that may have been blown in. On this shift we have the advantage of fresh air.

Sometimes a break occurs in the chain of bags coming along, the miners are not able to pick fast enough and I employ the time crawling into a dugout and writing my diary. It's a break and the light of a candle is always friendly. Sometimes I share a mug of tea with a fellow who has just had a brew-up in the corner of a dugout. It is always worthwhile going into a dugout if one has a moment to spare; sometimes one is lucky. Am waiting for midnight to come, carrying sandbags is no picnic.

Sunday, 7 May 1916

We knocked off at midnight and had to stand in the trench till dawn. The miners had reported that they could hear German miners in their vicinity working as if they were laying explosives preparatory to blowing up the mine, in which case our attack on the front line affected would take place and so we had to pass the time walking up and down the trench waiting for something to happen. We were not unduly impressed, we had heard the story so often; sometimes the miners were right, so we had to be prepared.

Dawn came and at 4.30am I crawled into a dugout for sleep.

Probably the miners were right and something was intended by the Germans which went wrong at the last moment. At any rate, they have given us a warm couple of hours this afternoon which I am not anxious to experience again. During that period they blasted our support lines and front line with every diabolical thing they have. Starting on our front line with their light guns they sent over aerial torpedoes, trench mortars, rifle grenades and whizz-bangs. Whizz-bangs are fired from the lightest types of field guns which are consequently brought close up to the trenches. The velocity of the shell fired by this gun is terrific, hitting its target the moment after it is fired – whizz-bang!

I was awakened about 2.30pm by the continual bumping of the ground and found most of the fellows awake and on their feet. I soon gathered what was taking place and followed suit. We, fortunately, were in a deep dugout – some 30ft down and believed ourselves moderately safe unless they slung over some big stuff. We were joined by an odd man or so, who told us what was happening outside. Orders came along by runner to stay in the dugout, but prepare ourselves for an attack.

Meanwhile the ground was fairly vibrating with shells bursting, with the occasional moan of one passing overhead to fall in the rear. Personally I was not feeling very comfortable nor, do I think, were any of the other fellows. We had not experienced anything so heavy or continuous as this and taken in conjunction with last night's experience I thought the mine was probably going up any moment and they were coming over.

We oiled our rifles, cleaned our ammunition and waited events, feeling very much like rats in a trap, knowing that if a heavy shell landed fairly on the dugout, our hopes of getting out were small.

Another runner came along and from him we understood that we were being fairly plastered with shells and casualties were very heavy. Still the ground was vibrating with the 'thud', 'thud', and noise as shells fell and exploded, the sickly sulphurous smell penetrating down into the dugout.

At 3.30pm the bombardment ceased as quickly as it started. No alarm was given and we quickly concluded they were not coming over and awaited orders. Had not long to wait – at 4pm I was back in the mines, only this time I am down the mine and not along the trench.

After our warning of last night and experience this afternoon, it's an awful strain mentally. We are some three-parts of a mile under the ground; every unusual noise I think it is the Germans starting to explode their mines, which we know we are very close to. I am a bit nervy – we all are, I think.

The miners themselves dare barely peck at the chalk whilst every hour an engineer officer listens to try and detect anything of the enemy working. At this distance in the mines it is very stuffy, it consisting of one long passage barely wide enough for two men to pass and not high enough to stand upright. We work with backs bent all through the eight-hour shift. Air is got down by means of a large pair of blacksmith's bellows in the trench which is connected by a long pipe – a man blows these bellows.

Midnight – we have just knocked off. Another party takes over and does the same as we have been doing. No doubt they have the same thoughts as ourselves; wondering if they are going to be lucky or unlucky. When things are so close it is touch and go.

I can sleep now till the morning. At 8am I go on again.

Monday, 8 May 1916

Breakfast at 6.30am. From somewhere in the rear and under cover the cooks make us a large dixie of hot tea, which arrives before daybreak. Carried by ration carriers, they dish us out a mug full, or half a mug according to the amount they have spilt on the way up, and make a hurried exit back before the Germans get busy with their shells. At 8am back to the mines till four o'clock this afternoon, fetching up sandbags from the mine and stacking them along the trench ready for the night shift to start repairing the trench or throwing them out in front.

This particular mine that we have been in today is nearly finished; it nearly finished me. By the end of the shift my throat had swollen and my eyes were very sore and I was feeling generally very fed up. The miners tell us that occasionally they hear the Germans pecking and hope to catch them. This mine goes up in a day or two.

The results of yesterday's bombardment are very apparent; wrecked trenches everywhere and unexploded shells, some weighing three-parts of a hundredweight. I hear Bosky Redoubt and Observation Redoubt in the rear [two strong points] are blown in and many of our fellows past recovery.

We finished the shift at 4pm and have just made and finished a brew of tea. I can sleep now till midnight when I shall go on again and probably throw over the top of the parapet those bags of chalk I have been helping to bring up the mine today. The pace is too hard, the strain too great, it cannot last long – we are all feeling the effects. No one jokes, no one has hardly anything to say, but to sleep and work. We all have it in the back of our minds that those mines that the Germans are working will go up whilst we are down one of ours and it is not a pleasant reflection.

Tuesday, 9 May 1916
2am. We find ourselves in peculiar places at times and none funnier than this. We came on again at midnight and at the time of writing myself and another fellow are cramped in a small shelter 8ft by 3ft, in which is a large pair of blacksmith's bellows and we take it in turns to blow these, hour in and hour out.

The bellows are connected to a long pipe down which the air goes to clear the atmosphere in the mine. Occasionally word comes up that we are not blowing hard enough and that the end of the mine is getting very foul, but we know however hard we work the thing, the air will still be foul and know it is only a message sent to make quite sure we are not asleep. I know, I have sent the messages myself when I have been up near the end of the mine and felt half choked.

I have blocked up the entrance of the shelter with my ground-sheet so am able to light a candle. Writing keeps me awake. To be able to work at night anywhere where we can have a light always has its good points; it's company and we can see each other.

It has been raining hard all day and down the side of the shack mud and water trickle. We are getting fairly plastered leaning against it. A cold dark night; sometimes to break the stillness a German sniper puts a bullet into the sandbags outside. We hear the 'plonk' and for something to do, time the period between each shot.

Friday, 12 May 1916, Duisans

Nothing has happened since last entry. We carried on with the eternal sapping fatigue, eight hours on duty, eight hours off, day and night until we were relieved by the KOSB yesterday at 11pm. It was 12.30am before we got clear of the trenches and started for here – Duisans. We arrived at 3am at the break of day, very tired, very sick of everything.

Had had three halts on the roadside for ten minutes and each time I laid down and went to sleep. I think most of the fellows did the same – the officers came along and woke us up.

On arrival we found hot tea and blankets waiting for us. We quickly got the tea down and, in common with the remainder of the fellows, afterwards I rolled myself up in my blanket and went off to sleep.

Breakfast 11 o'clock this morning. Wash, scrape and shave ourselves and this afternoon, equipment cleaning. A combined tea and dinner at 4pm – the tea tasted more like soup. After this, an inspection at six o'clock. We had no time to ourselves till this was over. That passed, we are all back in the billet, glad to lie down. Some of the fellows are busy opening parcels from home or reading letters (the mail has just been delivered) or writing. Some are already well away, fast asleep.

Page, with some duties to do, potters here and there looking done in and half asleep. He's a stout little chap.

Our billet is a barn from which we can look out into the roadway. The village looks very pretty but the continual stream of transport and troops passing spoils any imagination.

We have a divisional cinema here so we shall have some entertainment.

Saturday, 13 May, 1916

We paraded for baths this morning. It was unique. With the immense amount of troops pouring into France, everything connected with them has to be organised, baths amongst everything else and for this purpose a house or convenient building – not too much knocked about – was commandeered. Into this has been installed a complete water heating apparatus; crude but sufficient. Pipes are laid along the ceiling to which were fixed sprays. It was to such a place we marched – a half-blown-in house in the village. On arrival we stripped in one of the rooms and handed in our dirty underclothes to an attendant (and they were dirty) and then passed on into the hot showers. It is the first hot bath I have had since being out in France [almost six months]. The sensation was great. I have not felt so clean for a long time but the surprise was not over. Going through the door at the other side of the room, we were each handed a complete change of underclothing in exchange for those handed in.

Though roughly done, it was well done. The water was boiling hot, we had clean towels and plenty of soap.

What a difference that bath made; still filled with the novelty we marched back to the billet singing for all we were worth, as if we had never heard of the trenches, nor been down the mines.

Sunday, 14 May 1916

Easy going all day. At 9am the CO had a parade and afterwards a church service at midday. For the remainder I have been writing and sleeping.

Monday, 15 May 1916

Today has been outstanding due to the fact that tonight we have celebrated. Had a supper of eggs and chipped potatoes, they went down jolly good.

Tuesday, 16 May 1916

Early morning run, another CO's parade and finished for the day. Tomorrow we go back up the line for 18 days, ie, six in the firing line, six in support at Saint-Nicolas and six in the reserve in Arras.

Thursday, 18 May 1916

We left Duisans at 8.15pm – arrived in Arras 10.30pm. Close and hot marching, the weight of our equipment tells in this atmosphere – four collapsed on the way up, fainted. Nothing else disturbed our march and we relieved the KOSB in the firing line at 12.30am.

The mine which Harry had helped to prepare was scheduled to be detonated on 19 May. Having detected that the Germans were also burrowing towards the British lines, the Royal Engineers had driven out a gallery and laid an explosive charge which, when fired, would destroy the German workings and eliminate the immediate threat. The 'blow' would also leave a large crater, its lips raised by earth thrown up by the explosion. This extra elevation was crucial for observation of the German lines and a coveted asset and so, before the dazed German garrison could recover their senses, the British troops would rush to occupy and reinforce the far lip of the smouldering crater. That, anyway, was the British plan.

Friday, 19 May 1916

Nos. 1 and 2 platoons are in reserve trenches to the firing line. They have little else to do but act in case of emergency whilst we, 3 and 4 platoons, are on the eternal sapping, doing tours of duty six hours on and six off in shifts of 14 men between four saps which are about ready to go up.

The Germans forestalled us this morning by about three hours. After three months of hard work the K14 mine, timed to go up at 8am, was blown in by the Germans at 4.30am. There was a terrific explosion, the ground for yards around was lifted skywards, leaving a huge crater in the ground and some of the support poles used for supporting the roof of the mine were lifted right through the ground and lay scattered around. We were cleared from the mines at 7am, the front line was cleared and we all retired to the support line. At 7.30am two of ours were blown up. I felt the ground tremble and rock, but no great damage appears to be done.

No-man's-land looks more hideous than ever now with these great holes in the ground, large enough to bury any ordinary villa, and all the surrounding ground covered with debris.

Captain Edwards, our company captain, crept out over my parapet to investigate the damage and was met by a fusillade of bullets from the German lines. He stopped one through the shoulder and one in the head – the latter would have been fatal had he not been wearing his steel helmet; another instance of their usefulness.

His progress was watched by those in the front line in the vicinity where he crawled over the top. The moment he was hit an engineer, who also happened to be watching, sprang on to the parapet and, crawling on

Trench scene: View over the parapet of the British front-line trench on the K2 sector held by Harry's battalion north of Arras. A ledge – the fire step – runs along the bottom of the heavily sandbagged trench wall while above the wall, and just in no-man's-land, the British barbed-wire entanglement is clearly visible. The entrance to a dugout can be seen to the right. The mound top right is the raised lip of earth thrown up by the 'blow' of a German mine beneath the British positions. The crater formed by the explosion was 50 yards in diameter and 30 feet deep. (© Imperial War Museums HU 87164)

his stomach, reached Captain Edwards and dragged him back to the line. The engineer was awarded the Distinguished Conduct Medal (DCM). It is worthwhile noting that the German sentry who shot Captain Edwards could also have shot his rescuer, as the circumstances were identical, if he wished to do so. If he refrained from doing so from humane motives, he was a sportsman; he had already winged his bird, which should have, and did in this case, seem to suffice.

[Captain Edwards] was got into the trench and is now gone down the line; another of the Old Guard gone; Lieutenant Davis taking his place as captain of the company.

I came off duty at midday and on again at 6pm and was detailed amongst others for a sap close to those exploded this morning. Had little to do till dark. At dusk a wiring party from D Company came along to occupy and wire the crater close by. They proceeded to crawl out with wire, picks and shovels. They had not gone far before they were spotted by the Germans who let loose rifle grenades, trench mortars and opened with machine guns and things got very uncomfortable.

By this time the sapping party I was with was also on top of the parapet doing work and fully exposed to their fire, which came over in our direction. The first shot made us pause, at the outbreak of the fusillade we dropped to the ground, I into a shell-hole, and waited till it ceased, then bolted into the trench. Meanwhile the party in front was having a warm time, the Germans keeping up a continuous fire on the crater they knew the men were making for. With a man hit they had to come in again, but returned an hour later and successfully occupied the crater. But the Germans were very restless and all through the night kept on dropping over mortars and rifle grenades. I was glad when midnight came and I was able to get back to the dugout.

Thirty-nine-year-old Captain Percival Charles Edwards from Knowle, near Solihull, was Harry's company commander and had been present at the battalion's first parade at Edgbaston Park in Birmingham in 1914. He had served as a trooper with the Imperial Yeomanry in the South African War of 1899–1902 where he received the DCM.

Captain Edwards survived the wounds Harry saw inflicted and returned to duty with the 15th Battalion in September 1916. Promoted to major and second-in-

command of the battalion, he later led it in an attack on a heavily defended position
called African Trench, near Cambrai, on 27 September 1918 and was killed near
his headquarters at a spot called, ironically, Dead Man's Corner. He is buried in
Lebucquiere Communal Cemetery Extension, between Cambrai and Bapaume.

Saturday, 20 May 1916

Was not able to sleep for long. Had scarcely got off when the alarm was given
and we all had to 'stand to' from 2.30–3.30am. Nothing happened and I
kipped down again till 5.30am.

Breakfast came along and at 6am we were back in our old corner of the
night before and relieved the sentries. Our job was simple – keep quiet,
scarcely move and keep a lookout through the periscope. That our corner was
fairly well watched by the Germans was early demonstrated. One fellow put
his head and shoulders over the top and was immediately sniped through the
head. He did a foolish thing.

We were relieved at midday and now I am lying in the dugout waiting
for the six o'clock shift to commence. Have slept all afternoon but I feel very
lousy and somewhat nervy.

Two Birmingham men of Harry's battalion were killed on 20 May. The man whose
momentary lapse of concentration cost him his life was either Arthur Jordan of Small
Heath or George Wood of King's Heath.

Sunday, 21 May 1916

6pm soon arrived and, with others, went on duty and relieved the sentries.
They reported everything quiet. To watch us relieve this post one might
imagine we were professional burglars. Cautiously we creep forward along the
sap running out from the front line, holding on to the side of the trench so
that we can the more easily put each foot down. Arriving at the post we
whisper to each other and the relieved slink back along the sap and back into
the front line.

We watched the evening close and then the Germans got busy again,
sending over mortars and rifle grenades along the front line. So long as they
did not drop short we were all right, but several had that tendency. This might
be intentional and, if intentional they were, getting the range preparatory to

a bombardment. It was all very nerve racking waiting for something of that nature to happen in the dark.

Midnight came and with it the next relief. Creeping as we had crept, filth in the shape of shells was coming over pretty frequently and, on the right 100 yards away, the Germans were bombing and shelling the craters for all they were worth.

Being relieved we started creeping back and made our way to the dugout. On our way back we passed Major Jones, second-in-command of the battalion, on the way to the front line. Ten minutes later they were digging him out of about three foot of earth. After passing us in the trench he had gone on to the crater and was stopped before he arrived there by rifle grenades. Death was instant.

We had barely arrived at our dugout when a runner came along and gave the gas alarm. C Company on the left was having a dose of gas. Every man was roused in the dugouts and we stood to till 1.30am. During this time casualties were occurring along the front line; too many for the stretcher-bearers to cope with and so I, with others, went to the front line to give help. They had by this time dug out the major, also an NCO killed with him and three other men injured by the same grenade. I helped to carry the NCO down to the dressing station at Saint-Nicolas and on uncovering him found him to be one of my pals; a very decent fellow – we had been together since the first days of joining. I could not recognise his features, they were blown away. I could only tell by his identity disk.

He was one of two brothers. The other, a stretcher-bearer unconscious of his identity, dug him out.

I arrived back at the dugout feeling very sick and laid down for half an hour at 5.30am to parade again at 6am for the mines. I was past breakfast and past any sort of exertion. Down the mines we went, passing bags of chalk one to another to be stacked in the trench ready for the night shift to deal with.

The job of the night shift was to remove the bags of chalk by throwing them over the top of the trench into no-man's-land. They would be received there by another party of men – probably lying on their stomachs because they were exposed to incessant machine-gun fire from the German front line – and from that position they would build up the parapet where it had been damaged by artillery fire.

At midday we knocked off and went back to the dugout, only to turn out again at 6pm, this time to clear away the bags of chalk we stacked in the trench this morning.

I have touched for the mine and here I am at 2am Monday, writing between the intervals of the sacks coming to the top. Outside everything is quiet for the time being and down below I can hear the miners pecking at the chalk.

At 11pm a party of our bombers went out to try and drive the Germans from an obstacle trench they have occupied close to the crater. They were only partly successful.

The Germans scented them coming and replied to our bombs with rifle fire and hand grenades. There was a mix up for a time. Our fellows, not sure of their ground in the dark, started slinging bombs in amongst themselves, quite a usual occurrence; the element of surprise not working, this time they returned.

It is six calendar months today since we landed in France and many changes have taken place in the battalion. We miss very much those who have 'gone west' and now we appear to have another dose of casualties to swell the break. New fellows arrive, good fellows no doubt, but they do not take the places of those who go down.

Major Richard Archibald Jones was among those who 'went west'. Aged 34, Major Jones had been principal of Birmingham University Training College for Men prior to joining the 2nd Birmingham Battalion in 1914. Known by many simply as 'the Major', less charitable members of the battalion referred to him as 'that blue-eyed bleeder'. Jones was said to have had a premonition that he would not return from the war; the CO, Colin Harding, remarking that some of his former students, fighting in neighbouring trenches, saw Jones during his last few days 'walking unconcernedly in the shell-swept zone'.

Monday, 22 May 1916

I came off sapping at 6am. Very tired and very sick. Not feeling like grub I kipped down on reaching the dugout. Made a sort of meal at 11am and, with the others, relieved the fellows in the mine for another six hours handling the bags of chalk from one to the other. Came off again at 6pm for rest and on again at midnight.

Brothers: Harry (standing, second right) and several members of his platoon – including the 'two brothers' Harry mentions in his diary entry of 21 May 1916 – relax during the construction of new accommodation huts in Sutton Park during the battalion's early days. Lance Corporal William James Hundy (standing, left), the first man to enlist in the 2nd Birmingham Pals, was killed by a German rifle grenade. Standing next to him, pipe in mouth, is his brother, Herbert Cecil Hundy, the stretcher-bearer who, unknowingly, dug the lifeless and unrecognisable body of his younger sibling out of the debris. William Hundy lies today in plot I of the Faubourg d'Amiens Cemetery, Arras. Herbert Hundy survived the war. (David Griffiths)

Tonight D Company send over a raiding party of 60 men with the object of bombing the German line and taking prisoners.

Wednesday, 24 May 1916

Promptly at 10 o'clock on Monday night our artillery opened fire all along the line. For 15 minutes they poured over a rain of almost every conceivable thing on to the enemy's lines. I was in a dugout at the time and could hear the heavy shells go screeching over and felt the ground vibrate as they exploded in the German lines. We welcomed this as giving the Germans a taste of what they had given us the last few days and as they tore through the air wished them a good billet.

The mortar batteries opened fire, also the rifle grenade sections, sending them over as fast as they could load. We thought no man could live through it. After 15 minutes of this hell all firing ceased except the artillery who lifted their fire on to the German support lines at the same time D Company, on our left, went over the top and advanced towards the German lines. They had got about halfway, ie, about 100 yards, and were met by a cross-fire of machine guns and rifle fire, but they still advanced. Some got to the German lines and were killed on the parapet; some got entangled in the barbed wire and riddled with bullets. The element of surprise had gone; what remnants of the Germans that remained in their front line sent up lights and so what remained of our fellows returned. It had been a failure.

Our casualties were heavy – 33 killed, wounded or missing.

By midnight the effects of the raid had subsided and we were sent out wiring the crater, a very nervy job. We did shifts of 15 minutes.

Of late, events had so crowded upon events, and the going had been so hard and of long duration, that by this time we were in a fairly high state of nerves. To remain in the crater for any great length of time, in itself something in the nature of a nightmare and becoming known on this immediate front as 'The Crater', was bordering on the vicinity of the last straw. So we did shifts of 15 minutes, which kept us more or less on the move and to a degree the nerve tension relaxed.

Crawling backwards and forwards from the crater to the trench and then working in the trench where Major Jones and Hundy were killed, at 2am we were all called in and went down the mines till 9.30 next morning (Tuesday) and I was on again at 3.30pm until we were relieved by the KOSB at 5.30pm, the end of the first period of six days in the trenches.

It has been disastrous to the battalion; our casualties are nearly 60 for that time. We arrived back in Duisans after the relief at 8.30pm and an hour later I was in a tea shop in Arras, washed, shaved and having a jolly good tuck-in of eggs and cake and bread and butter – the first good meal this week.

I slept well last night in our billet; like a log. We have a good supply of straw, lousy but comfortable, and awoke this morning for breakfast at nine o'clock. Meals are a very simple affair; just throw the blanket off, reach for your mug, an orderly comes round with a dixie of tea and fills it. Another comes round with the tin of bacon from which he gives you a rasher and, if there is any fat going, you may dip your slice of bread in it, the rest is easy with a jack-knife. We take turns at being orderly if there are no parades. Afterwards we go to sleep again, glad to forget it.

At 2pm I was on parade again and back to the mines. They are getting on my nerves. We did the usual shift, finishing at midnight, and here I am again back in the billet, writing like the dickens – 2am, Thursday morning.

Harry lated added this note to his diary entry of 24 May: 'I learnt afterwards that D Company had been practising for this raid at Duisans where we had billeted whilst on rest. Spies got to know all particulars and by some means got the information over to the Germans and they, anticipating a heavy artillery bombardment, occupied all the shell-holes in no-man's-land with machine guns which opened fire as our fellows went over.

'Ten days later a patrol out one night heard moaning. On investigating they found a sergeant wounded in the thigh and ankle. He was one of the raiding party. During the ensuing time, in periods of consciousness, he had lived on his emergency rations – a few biscuits. Apparently he had crawled to a disused trench or shell-hole in no-man's-land and afterwards was unable to move. He was eventually brought back to our lines; he was rat-eaten where he had bled and died afterwards.'

Left out in no-man's-land and unable to move from whatever scant shelter he had, Sergeant George Scrivens had also been reduced to eating the rank grasses along with the few wild flowers he could reach. Found during the night of 31 May/ 1 June 1916, he was evacuated to a casualty clearing station at Aubigny-en-Artois, nine and a half miles northwest of Arras where, weakened through loss of blood,

*dehydrated and probably with raging septicaemia from infected wounds, he died on
11 June 1916.*

Thursday, 25 May 1916

Once I was kipped down, Thursday morning came like a flash. Breakfast at
7am. We had to parade for the baths at 7.30. That over, the remainder of the
day till four o'clock I have had to myself. We paraded at four o'clock back
to the line for the mines. It's ten hours' solid graft, four hours in marching
backwards and forwards and six hours down the mines, and so at 2am I have
just returned. We wonder how long we have got to go on like this.

Tomorrow we go to a redoubt for duty.

Friday, 26 May 1916

Relieving D Company at 4pm, I find myself this evening in comparatively
serene surroundings. This redoubt, which is a strong point in the general lay
of the land, is self-contained in the way of food and water and ammunition,
and in case of a general attack by the Germans the occupants of this place
would be expected to hold on after the lines had crumpled. It is in the nature
of a fort built of earth, of which there are many around Arras. Imagine these
to be a survival of old ideas which were probably sound before this war. Now,
with aeroplanes and wireless, such strong points as these would be laid flat
before any general advance commenced; to me they seemed pretty useless.

We have a fine view of the surrounding country; it all looks very desolate.
As far as the eye can see the ground is all trenches and turned over, not a
green blade of grass is to be seen. Tree stumps stick up out of the ground:
nothing but a black charred mass. It is weeks now since I saw a bird of any
description; they all appear to be frightened away.

As I write, darkness is creeping over the landscape, the stillness is very
uncanny.

Our dugouts are very comfortable, we can move about in them.

Saturday, 27 May 1916

I hear the sergeant outside calling us out on parade, so I suppose I have to turn
out. This we all did last night, but it was a gift. We can move about at leisure
instead of crawling and crouching, and can smoke and talk; the time passed

very pleasantly. At 2am we knocked off and kipped down. There is a great sense of relief and contentment in knowing that the chances are all against being disturbed till morning.

Today, with the exception of an hour's sentry duty, I have laid in the trench, found a sunny corner, written home, slept and eaten.

A message has just come along that the Germans are putting over gas extensively a little further up the line and to keep a sharp lookout. It's dirty stuff, this gas. B Company appear to be having a dose at this moment, so the message says, and are all 'standing to' with respirators on in the front line.

Sunday, 28 May 1916

Things were a little more uncomfortable last night. We did two hours on and two off. About 1am I was on sentry and felt a mine go up on the left and both sides opened out with artillery. In the line I could hear buzzers going, giving the gas alarm. The gas did not penetrate as far as ourselves, but the bombardment was kept up till early this morning and we had to be prepared for any emergency that might arise, but with the coming of daylight, when all sides can see what is happening, things cooled down.

Today, with the exception of one hour's sentry, I have spent the time in sleep. Tonight we are on water carrying.

Monday, 29 May 1916

This was an easy job, sometimes stray shells come over and pieces of shrapnel go through the galvanised water tanks, which are half buried in the ground. These had to be dug up and taken down to Arras for repairs and new ones brought up to replace it. This we did last night, the water cart following behind as far as the communications trench.

We brought up the tank and then we carried the water from the water cart to the redoubt, a distance of about 500 yards, and at the moment are awaiting the relief party to come along. We in turn go and relieve the front line, sorry to leave.

Tuesday, 30 May 1916

We had a nightmare of a time last night. We left the redoubt about 11.30pm for the firing line, about half a mile distance as the crow flies. The night was dark; rain had been falling for some time, making the trenches muddy and slippy. Halfway along we were held up by a company KOSB for an hour who were being relieved. By this time we were soaked through, rain pouring down all the time.

Imagine it. We going one way, the Jocks going another, both parties anxious to get to their respective destination; along a trench along which there is barely room for one man to go in comfort, each man laden like a Christmas tree with things which kept getting locked with one another. It was indescribable; the language blue.

Arriving in the front line the foremost man had to wait until the remainder arrived, everyone fed up to the teeth and soaked through. It was 1.30am before the last man came along and we made our way to the old crater sector and relieved the Jocks waiting for us at 2am. We were in a fair mess, a boiling perspiration from the effects of getting up and soaking wet clothes, which in my case had come through to my legs. Added to this we were back in the crater sector which had already cost us so much and upon which the Germans seemed to concentrate a lot of attention. We 'stood to' till 3am. Nothing happened. The Germans had evidently not heard us. Relieved at 3am, we crawled into the crater and carried on with the wiring the Jocks had been doing.

The crater is the largest in the district, about 150 yards across. It is like a huge bear-baiting pit and scattered about with relics of our former scraps in the shape of unexploded bombs, someone's hat and so forth. We worked in the crater for two hours with one eye on our work and the other in the German direction, our wet condition forgotten during this period of some strain.

We left the crater at 5am and retired into the front line. Breakfast came up at 7am; a small piece of bacon. The bread we carried with us was soaked with rain.

Today I have lain in the dugout all day and over a brazier tried to dry my tunic and shirt; my trousers will have to dry on me. We are laid in a row along the dugout. Hanging around the brazier – which is in the doorway – to catch the draught are hung a number of tunics and shirts. We still have to wear our equipment and wear it over our vests. The crater alone has cost us 20 casualties so far since it was blown up. Tonight I am there on sentry on the far side.

According to latest aeroplane photographs we are 15 yards from the German listening post. Presumably when the mine went up they started digging, like ourselves, to occupy it, but we had the advantage of starting from a sap head and now hold it, but the cost of holding it is heavy.

Wednesday, 31 May 1916

Had somewhat of a thriller last night. I was on fatigue from 8.30pm to 11pm, ration carrying, fetching up our rations for today from a ration party which had brought them as far as the communication trench. That finished, we relieved the sentries in the crater: three posts and two men to a post, so that there were six pairs of eyes gazing into the darkness trying to locate the German listening post that we knew to be so close and from which we understood Germans were still digging, hoping presumably that we did not occupy the crater. We were not mistaken.

We had not been there long before we could hear sounds that were unfamiliar to us and after a whispered conversation amongst ourselves, concluded that it was coming from the German listening post and it was the Germans who were making it.

It was an uncanny night; raw, cold and a thick mist. We lay on the inside lip of the crater and hardly moved except to consult one another in whispers. Occasionally a rifle grenade came over from the German lines and dropped into the bottom of the crater, but these did not affect us. We were more disturbed by rifle bullets which came over at intervals apparently from all directions.

At the very first twinge of dawn one of the fellows peeped over the top and came along and told us that he had seen four Germans within 12 yards of where we were lying, digging like blazes. This sentry had evidently been spotted. I moved round the edge of the crater and had a look over in time to see a German putting his rifle over the top of the trench he was standing in. I ducked and warned the other fellows by signs to keep down. One fellow, very curious, put his head up and had his steel helmet knocked in by a bullet.

To the onlooker this incident might have seemed to be fraught with all kinds of danger, but in reality it was not so, taking ordinary precautions. We were in a very strong, if uncanny, position under the lip of the crater, with the Germans digging like fury only a few yards away. The logical conclusion of this was that if they kept on digging hard enough whilst darkness lasted, they would soon be into the crater and into our arms as it were. I think the same thought struck us all as we crawled stealthily, very much as a cat crawls when stalking a bird, from one to the other. Suppressed excitement was rife and we opened out, each man taking up a position and ready for anything to happen. The excitement was that of the chase rather than that of fear. It was a novel experience for us to be so close without the Germans being aware and I think mirth was mixed with the excitement.

For some reason we were told before going in that under no circumstances were we to fire; it was a great opportunity for slinging a bomb over. We sent a message to headquarters of what we had seen and were withdrawn to the near side of the crater until the mist had cleared.

At 4.30am we started wiring the bottom of the crater. It was never very clear to me why we should risk so much life and spend so much time putting barbed wire entanglements in the bottom of the crater. It seemed to me that if barbed wire was required at all it should have been placed on the far side to prevent the Germans from getting in, or if they did get in and pass through it, it would still have been an obstacle for them to have got back.

Carried on till 7am then along the sap and back into the front trench. After the mist it turned out to be a brilliant morning, sun very hot, so we spent the time working in the trench and finished, by this means drying our clothes.

We have been strafed [bombed and shelled] at intervals all day long. The Germans are very restless over this crater. They cannot quite make out what we are doing with it and what we want it for. They are taking no risks and are always bumping it, ie shelling it, as well as our front line. We return such fire, generally with interest.

Thursday, 1 June 1916, the crater

The [mine] crater has by now been completely transformed. Lying out on the far lip has been abolished and instead we have built a little shack on the near side and protecting the shack, a sandbag barrier. Behind this barrier I am now writing.

This has been accomplished by working parties working in relays every moment of darkness and in the bottom of the crater sometimes in the daylight. Looking down now the ground is one network of barbed wire.

No sleep whilst occupying this post last night. We passed the time sandbagging whilst not on sentry. It's all very nice and clean but I am of opinion that it is not very safe; it is exposed to all shellfire coming over from the German line.

At 2am it was misty and cold. At 3am we went down into the bottom of the crater and carried on wiring, always with one eye in the German direction. Breakfast at 7am.

I came on sentry duty again at 3pm and am occupying the time writing up my diary, taking it in turns with my fellow sentry to keep watch. We leave at 5pm. Everything is very quiet, occasionally a plane comes buzzing over and occasionally, a shell.

Friday, 2 June 1916

Today has been a repetition of yesterday, working all night in the crater or doing sentry duty. Dawn broke soon after 2am, cold and misty. We welcomed the daylight. The nerves get to a great tension on this job in the dark. It is quite possible for the Germans to creep along the lip of the crater and get at the back of us; daylight stops this possibility.

Today has passed very much as yesterday and I find myself in the same place as yesterday at this time, ie 'the shack', looking across to the far side of the crater from behind the sandbag barrier waiting for five o'clock to come and then a period of a few hours' sleep.

Saturday, 3 June 1916

We have changed over with the other half of our platoon. Tonight they are occupying the crater and we the front-line trench. All seems abnormally quiet. It was like that quietness before the storm.

Sunday, 4 June 1916

7am. The peace did not last long and all through the night at intervals we have had to dodge the shells and rifle grenades. Nos. 102 and 103 trenches have been laid flat and several fellows wounded. The acid smells from the burst shells has made me feel very sick and am in a somewhat nervy condition. Breakfast at the moment would turn me up. We are relieved tonight and begin to count the hours.

Tuesday, 6 June 1916

We counted the hours till Sunday, 4 June at 4pm and were congratulating ourselves that we had successfully placed the crater in a state of defence without further loss and that we should soon be away on rest. A few shells came over at midday, uncomfortably close to our front line, and during the early afternoon we got our equipment together and the trench in a state ready for handing over without delay, immediately the relief arrived.

Precisely at four o'clock the Germans opened fire with their artillery on the front line, supports and communication trenches. On the right, the 1st Norfolks were getting it and on the left I could see B Company's trenches going up in the air.

I was on sentry at the time and stuck it for a few minutes. A shell landed in front and another behind, blowing in the parados [rear of the trench] and smothering me with dirt. This appeared to be no ordinary bombardment, so I made for a shelter, hopeless if a shell hit it but useful to stop shrapnel, and found some of the other fellows gathered there. Casualties were occurring rapidly and the rain of shells kept coming over. Fellows who had been hit were calling for stretcher-bearers. At 4.30pm it was evident that we were in for something. The shellfire was furious – the trenches, both in the firing line and supports, were going up in all directions and the passages becoming blocked and telephone wires snapped. We tried to get in communication with company headquarters but could get no reply. It is a thrilling sensation to be in a bombardment but when one knows the shells are being concentrated on a comparatively small area of ground, dozens at a time, he would be a very bold man who says he doesn't get the wind up.

Even these conditions can apparently create humour. After a particular shell had burst, I heard a most awful moan going up to heaven and looking along the trench saw a fellow wriggling about on the ground. I went along to him and thinking perhaps he was hit in the stomach, rolled him on his back and put my hand under his tunic. At the same moment another shell burst on the parapet overhead, covering us with dirt. The next moment, wounded or not, he got up and ran like a hare yards along the trench. I laughed heartily – it was about the only time I did so from any incident arising from actual war and for that reason it stands out clearly in my memory.

Jones came into the shelter badly hit and plastered with dirt. I undressed him and bandaged him up whilst [Philip] Jinks stood at the exit of the shelter, ready in case the Germans came over.

Sidney Page, like a brick, kept on going along the trench in spite of the shells and dragging into cover anyone he could find wounded.

Had barely bandaged Jones when [Edgar] Eastwood came rushing in along the sap from the crater and gave us to understand that the shelter in the crater had been blown in and the sentry group buried. He was standing in the doorway, he said, when the shell landed on top burying the fellows and blowing him out; he then collapsed.

Eastwood was the son of a prominent Birmingham manufacturer and one of the type of fellows I referred to who had probably not done a day's work before joining up. Whilst we were training at Sutton Park about a dozen of us often met in their drawing room and over a cup of coffee learnt elementary French. We probably talked more about war than French but they were topping evenings. Our instructor was a good linguist and very useful in France afterwards.

Jinks and I gathered what picks and shovels were lying about and, crawling along on our hands and knees, made along the sap for the crater. We had crawled about 15 yards when a shell landed immediately on top of the trench partly burying us and it was some moments before we could pull ourselves together. I felt the force of the explosion force my head into my body and it was some seconds before I was able to see.

By this time it was impossible to go on. No trench remained in front, but a mound of earth thrown up by succeeding shell bursts. To go back was futile so we crawled to the nearest shelter. By this time the shellfire was augmented by rifle grenades and trench mortars. The ground vibrated with the explosions and the air was thick with acrid sulphurous fumes. The shelter consisted of a length of corrugated iron placed over the top of the trench. We were unable to go backwards or forwards, we appeared fairly in the midst of it. We made the best of the shelter by dragging down bags of earth against which we crouched in the bottom of the trench, hoping for the best. Occasionally I could feel the supports of the shelter wobble as a shell fell close by and exploded and all the time awful fumes came drifting backwards, fairly choking us. I could not recognise Jinks, his face was covered in dirt and black and so we hung on. We could do nothing else.

Six o'clock came and shells were still pouring over and I did not for a moment think we should get out of it alive.

At seven o'clock it ceased as suddenly as it started. We had had three hours of bombardment. For three solid hours we sat and waited, helpless to protect ourselves properly against a tornado of shells aimed at that particular area of ground where we were situated. There was no excitement of the chase here, nor, I think, fear of death so much as the manner of death, horrible examples of which we had already seen and were to see before the day was out. Later on in the day, passing along the trench I saw a couple of unexploded shells lying within a couple of yards of the sandbags against which we had been lying. How they had dropped into the trench which was once narrow and deep I could not understand but they were there and I had no time to reason. When I passed again on returning from the shack, I had more time to investigate. In all there were some half a dozen unexploded shells within the vicinity of a dozen yards. Why so many were 'dud' I fail now to understand, unless the answer is that it was a fair proportion to the hundreds of live ones that came over. But what impressed me the most was the sight of one, only a couple of feet away from the sandbags against the other side of which Jinks and I had been lying. The gods had been good.

We made our way back to the front line, dazed. We apparently had forgotten why we left it. We could not recognise it. It was a series of holes; no real trench remained. Some fellows were lying about dead and some wounded and some alive, one of whom enquired about the fellows in the shelter. And then I remembered why I had left the line.

Gathering up what picks we could find, a sergeant and myself crawled back over the top and into the crater. It was a wretched sight. Young Cooper was wedged in the doorway dead, the remainder buried under the shack.

We dug like fury for two hours, impelled by the fact that underneath the shack, now a mass of sandbags and props, we could hear someone faintly groaning and the fact that at any moment the Germans would be coming over. We took it in turns to dig. The other, from under hastily improvised cover, kept sentry with his eyes fixed on the opposite side of the crater awaiting the coming of the Germans who, fortunately, never came. It will be difficult to forget that sergeant's expression. Alternately digging and picking with almost superhuman strength, perspiration running from his face, he tugged and pulled at sandbags wedged together. We uncovered first Patch then Baker, both dead, and eventually came to Sergeant Ashby huddled up at the back and to all appearances a 'gonner'.

Sergeant Ashby had some signs of life in him so, leaving those whom we could not help, we carried Ashby down to the front line, or what remained of it, and handed him over to the stretcher-bearers and cleaned our rifles for anything that might happen. The day previously I and others had occupied the shack. We had just escaped this.

We were reduced to a handful of men. Page came along and I was very glad to see him alive; also another lance corporal called Bates and we sorted ourselves out, taking what cover remained. We had not long to wait. At 9.30pm they opened again all along the front line with artillery of all calibre; our guns replying with equal ferocity.

It was pitch dark and shells were tearing backwards and forwards. Shrapnel exploding overhead lit up the trench and by the flashes I saw the other fellows doing as I was, kneeling down against anything that afforded protection. This had been going on for some ten minutes when I was conscious of a sudden whirl in the air and knew the barrage had been lifted from our line on to the support lines. At the same moment it was shouted along that the Germans were coming over.

It will be always a matter of joy to remember how the fellows, all thoroughly well shaken, jumped out from the different places of cover and got to business with their rifles. This was our first experience of a bombardment practically all to ourselves and well it was stood. In spite of the fact that there was no cover that could be described as such, each man stuck to his post and blazed away into the darkness.

Previous to this incident we had been called on to withstand exposure and also continual, hard-slogging work at times under conditions of some stress and in the main we had stood up to it well. But it was not war as understood in the literal sense, before the trenches came into being. As war was understood – where, with bayonet and rifle one side goes for the other – this, then, was the moment when the message was passed along that the Germans were coming over. Each individual man could, if he had wished,

Buried alive: Sergeant Ashby (far left) – pictured here as a corporal in camp at Codford, Salisbury Plain, during training – was one of the men buried in the mine crater during the terrific German bombardment of 4 June 1916. Harry and an unnamed sergeant frantically dug him out and carried him back to waiting stretcher-bearers. He survived the war but his experience that day left a lasting legacy. When Harry met him in the late 1920s he appeared 'very nervy'. (David Griffiths)

have slunk into some shell-hole and away from danger, but he did not do so, he took his place in the line and awaited the oncoming of the Germans. There was no outward glory attached to it, it was all done in the dark and done so readily and passed unnoticed. But to me in that instant we justified ourselves as a service battalion, or our part of it, for when we were called upon we were found 'not wanting'.

Raper and Middleton went down, killed by a rifle grenade. The idea of friends being allowed to serve together was made manifest in this case. Raper and Middleton joined together in the early days, had since done all their duties together, spent their leisure days together and it was the same missile which took them both off together. In a way it was a fitting conclusion. Then Jinks was hit by another. We were lying next to each other when a shell or rifle grenade fell close to his legs. We carried him into a shelter, which was nothing more than a sheet of corrugated iron laid over the top of the trench on top of which some sandbags had been placed – no protection against anything but shrapnel – but he was going fast. His leg had been practically blown off.

Outside the air was livid as shrapnel was bursting, very much like flashes of lightning; come and gone in an instant, but coming with great rapidity with the attendant explosions and scattering of bullets. It was amongst this inferno, and with the knowledge that somewhere, not far away, the Germans were in our trenches and might be along any moment, that I had to try and render what aid was possible. Probably a hopeless case under the best conditions but there it was hopeless and I could do little else than kneel by his side. He recognised me almost to the last moment and asked me not to leave him. I stayed with him to the end and saw him go west.

It was quickly over and I went out into the trench again. The noise on the left of us was terrific whilst we on our part were keeping up a rapid fire with our rifles. The noise was intensified by the Germans springing a couple of mines in front of B Company. We were holding the right of the line and the Germans came in on the left. Of those that got into the trench only a few got out again, they were either bayonetted or bombed.

At 11pm all was quiet again; not a sound from a gun. Occasionally I saw from the German lines a lantern light guiding their men back in, at least those who had lost their bearings. Some never went back. We buried them later.

We 'stood to' till 1.30am until we were relieved by the Jocks of the KOSB. Day was breaking as we left the line and we had to make a hurried exit. I could not recognise the land at all; it had been wiped out of its former shape. We got to the rear and into Arras. It was by this time broad daylight and billets had to be hastily found. We were put in the vaults under the barracks.

This was another phase of the war for us and one which we were to experience much more of as time went on. The first month at Maricourt had been one of a prolonged fight against the elements, where continued exposure under conditions most difficult to describe faithfully had created a physical fever. This affair lasted only about five hours and produced war to us in another aspect. As we left our trenches in the early hours we left it a mass of shambles. Most of us possessed pocket torches and whilst some stood on sentry, others went along the remnants of trenches looking for wounded. Many we found were dead – they were a frightful sight for the most part. The KOSBs carried on as soon as they arrived and got away what wounded remained.

All our rations had gone on to Duisans where we should have arrived the night before. Under these circumstances there is always someone to come to the rescue and in this case it was the Australian and New Zealand miners billeted in the vicinity. Within an hour of our arrival they had dixies of hot tea for us and gave us their spare rations. We have stayed there all day and came on here to Duisans at dusk, ending a disastrous period for the battalion.

B Company had faced the worst. The captain, two junior officers and a number of men were buried beyond recovery in a dugout. The dugout, a very deep one, was hit presumably by an armour-piercing shell; a shell which has a very sharp point. First penetrating its object, it then explodes and the resulting havoc is fairly frightful. We were aware that the Germans had some naval guns opposite and it was from one of these that a shell landed right on top of the dugout.

Several, it is believed, have been captured and a large number wounded.

If there was no war news to record it is possible that such a raid as this would be published in England as follows, 'On the night of the 4th instant the enemy raided our lines and captured a few prisoners before being driven off.'

To the official eye they are items to publish if there is nothing more interesting but to those who go through them they are periods of great strain.

We are not a cheery crowd tonight. Already most of the fellows have wrapped themselves in their blankets and are fast asleep. With this finished I am following suit.

The loss of Jinks, one of Harry's closest friends, clearly affected him deeply. After the war, Harry added the following note about Jinks: 'I missed him very much: we had been great friends, doing many tours of duty together. It was an episode that I did not care to dwell upon for a considerable period of time. It seemed that I had lost my partner in the business and as a consequence and on all occasions, I should have to fend more for myself. War conditions made for companionship and Jinks and I, in common with most other fellows, found many occasions when we could help each other.'

Wednesday, 7 June 1916

We had a roll-call parade this morning. B Company mustered one officer and 35 men all told. Our total battalion casualties for Sunday are 120 killed, wounded and missing and well over 200 for the 18 days up the line. The roll-call was somewhat pathetic. We were standing in the open and as a name was called and unanswered we had to say if we saw the fellow killed or knew if he had gone down the line wounded.

This afternoon I went round to Ward's billet – found him alive. This evening Kilby asked me to join the Lewis gun section and I shall do so. Of the originals, they are the most intact. The idea under which the battalion was formed, that of friends serving together, has long since passed and these last 18 days have served to make it more pronounced.

If Harry was beginning to sound war weary and a little bitter he had good reason, for the period up to and including Sunday, 4 June 1916 was one which would never be forgotten by those Birmingham Pals who came through it – 4 June itself proving spectacularly brutal. A beautiful early summer's day bathed in bright sunshine and serenity, with the promise of a period of rest to follow, had been transformed into the darkest day yet in the battalion's short history. In seven hours of unbridled savagery that evening, more fury, death and destruction was visited on the battalion than in all its previous seven months on the Western Front put together.

The initial three-hour bombardment had completely obliterated B Company's trenches; shells even penetrating the old, 40-feet-deep French dugouts. Picking through the debris, clearing up and caring for the wounded had only really begun when another terrific barrage rained down on the Warwicks' trenches accompanied by the detonation of three large German mines. This was the signal for a full-scale raid – possibly 500–600 strong – which penetrated B Company's trenches; the German infantry bombing sentry posts and the remaining dugouts and making off with several prisoners, including Acting Company Sergeant Major Percy Kennard. It had been Kennard who had furnished Harry with his rail pass when they had left Stratford-upon-Avon together on that October morning back in 1914 to join the Birmingham Pals. Sometime after the war had finished he and Harry bumped into each other again in Stratford. He had then just been repatriated from Germany. Referring to the raid and his capture, he told Harry that he was eventually arraigned before some German colonel, who, learning that he came from Stratford-upon-Avon, had said how much he liked the town. He had been staying there on holiday a short time before war broke out, he had said. Kennard had apparently been well treated.

Official records written up at the time listed the casualties as three officers and 46 men killed and two officers and 29 men wounded. Eight men were suffering from shell shock and 27 were missing. Records held now by the Commonwealth War Graves Commission indicate 62 deaths that day. The names of 13 of those are listed on the Arras Memorial to the Missing including that of Private Claude Raper, who Harry saw killed by a rifle grenade; 49 others lie in the Faubourg d'Amiens Cemetery. Among them are Private Willoughby Greaves, who joined up aged 15 and was 16 when he was killed. Here, too, are those whom Harry and the unknown sergeant could not save: Lance Corporal Frederick Patch, 27, and Privates David Cooper, 20, and 19-year-old Oswald Baker. All three are buried within yards of each other, as is 20-year-old Philip Jinks, Harry's closest friend and the man he had comforted to the end.

Harry had taken Jinks's death badly. It was a hard and bloody lesson for this 'citizen soldier' to stomach.

Others are doubtless still entombed in collapsed dugouts beneath the fields near Roclincourt. The three mine craters blown by the Germans on 4 June were later christened Claude, Clarence and Cuthbert after a popular song performed by the Whizz-Bangs concert party. Two of them, now shrouded by trees and undergrowth, still lie brooding in the Arras landscape.

Sergeant Ashby was another of the wounded whom Harry met after the war, sometime in 1929. He told Harry that he had no recollections of anything happening except that everything suddenly went black. When he had recovered consciousness sufficiently to understand, he was already in hospital in England. He never went out to France again and when Harry last saw him he remarked that he was 'very nervy'.

Thursday, 8 June 1916

CO's inspection 8.30am; 10.30am memorial service in the cinema hall, which is really a barn, for those fallen.

After the church parade I, with others, had to 'fall in' and explain to the company captain the reason for having a different rifle to that one which was issued to us originally and which we possessed before this bombardment. The explanation was that ours either got so hot or dirty whilst firing that we exchanged it for the nearest cool one lying about. He said he understood all this but had to hold the inquiry. It gave one the impression that someone didn't understand the war and it was about time such customs were scrapped.

Now that the strain of the last few days is wearing off the subsequent relaxation is great. To lay and roll about in dry clothes, to walk about or to lie down according to the mood and to be rid for the time being of equipment is fine. Under these conditions we are all recovering rapidly.

At 2.30pm we were inspected by the GOC [General Officer Commanding] and, after presenting medals to the 1st Norfolks, he thanked us for our conduct on Sunday.

Friday, 9 June 1916

Reveille 7am. Early morning run till 7.45. We turn out in our trousers and shirt sleeves for this. 9.30am–12.30pm Lewis gun instruction.

This afternoon I have slept.

With the death of Jinks and so many original Pals, Kilby's suggestion that Harry join the Lewis gun section fell on fertile ground. Harry had already trained on the pre-war Vickers machine gun and so a move to the lighter, more portable Lewis gun, introduced as recently as the autumn of 1915, would not have been such a daunting prospect. Joining a Lewis gun team was no guarantee of collective safety in itself, but teams did operate as self-contained units and the prospect of living and

*working with men he had known since he joined up must have been appealing under
the circumstances.*

Saturday, 10 June 1916

Reveille and parade as yesterday. I am soon settling down to the Lewis gun.
Six in a team, we are rather self-contained, billeted together and on duty
always together – it should have its points.

Sunday, 11 June 1916

No parade, but making preparations for the line tonight.

Monday, 12 June 1916

We arrived at 1am at the scene of our former operations on the 4th.

We left Duisans at 8pm and were considerably delayed by the wretchedness
of the roads due to rain and the fact that we had to make a detour to avoid
the main Arras road. The Germans appear to have got information of the
nights we change and shell the road accordingly. The Jocks lost 30 killed and
wounded and their transport blown up when they relieved us on the night of
the 4th, ie, the night of the raid.

The trenches are good again. The Jocks appear to have put in a lot of
useful work rebuilding the line and clearing the trenches.

I miss the crater this journey. Every available man is sandbagging and
revetting, to be blown in again at some future date I expect. I hear rumours of
a wiring party going out.

Tuesday, 13 June 1916

I clicked for the wiring last night – a very creepy business crawling out in
front taking rolls of barbed wire and stakes. The ground was sodden with
rain and it was pitch dark. Quietly we crept out, trying to keep in touch with
one another and at the same time avoid the shell-holes. It poured with rain
the whole time but we did not mind this – it helps to deaden any accidental
noise. We had been working about a couple of hours and must have been
spotted by the Germans. We made a dickens of a noise at times. They turned
a 'whizz-bang' battery on us and we had to make a hasty retreat back into
the trenches.

Getting back I slipped about all over the place and fell into a shell-hole of water up to my knees. I was in a filthy state when I got back; plastered in mud. Our hands got fairly well torn handling the barbed wire, gloves are provided but they are useless. We shall probably have to finish the job tomorrow night.

Wednesday, 14 June 1916

And so we did – more cautiously than last night; we did not want a repetition of the 'whizz-bangs' coming over. Crawling out at 10.30pm, or rather we walked out with backs bent almost double, each man carrying a stake in each hand or a roll of barbed wire between two.

Cautiously we got out, stopping every few yards to find if there were any Germans about or to remain motionless as a Very light went up. Once, a Very light dropped right in front of us and we thought we were spotted. We dropped into the mud. As nothing happened we came to the conclusion that it was a chance shot and started wiring. By this time rain was pouring down again and our clothes, still wet through from last night, were quickly saturated. We stuck it for three hours and came in at 1.30am, plastered and soaked. For such occasions an extra issue of rum is waiting. We made a straight line for ours: we were in a condition for it.

No amateur pen can faithfully portray the condition we were in when we got back into the trench. The previous night we had got soaked through to the skin by the incessant rain and to that was added the mud in which we had literally lain every time the Germans sent up a Very light.

Conditions around Arras at this time allowed for no such luxuries as a change of underclothes. The moment we were back in the trench we were on sentry duty again so that the mud of the previous evening (that which we were unable to scrape off with a knife), remained on our clothes, and with the rain we were soaked through to the skin.

This second journey into no-man's-land was a replica of the night before, we alternately worked and laid in mud and water. When we got back into the trench it is probable that no part of our uniform was visible. The mud stuck to our puttees like a layer of slime and the same may be said of our clothes. In this condition we carried on sentry duty until the morning.

Thursday, 15 June 1916

We changed over last night – 5 and 6 sentry groups doing the wiring and we on sentry duty in the trench. The trench hereabouts is in a very poor condition – a relic of the bombardment of the 4th – and we move about over our boot tops in mud. Since this tour commenced my feet have been perpetually wet and frozen at night-time, my clothes more or less soaked. We are all in the same boat and have no means of drying ourselves.

This afternoon we lost four more of the old originals. A whizz-bang came right through the parapet and exploded in the trench killing Lieutenant [William] Farley, Corporal [Chester] Homer and two men [Privates Harry Hopkin and Vincent Reeve] – all old stagers formed up at Sutton. I was in a dugout at the time and heard the explosion. I went up into the trench and saw these fellows lying about; a sickly sight when one knows them so well.

We are quite resigned nowadays to losing old originals. It seems as if the fates have decreed that they have had a good run and it is time they went. Kilby asks, 'Whose turn next?' We all wonder.

I found some clean water this evening, collected in a tin from the rain and have just had a wash. Tonight I am line orderly, fetching the rations from the rear and am waiting for dusk to start off.

Friday, 16 June 1916

Our billet for this job is E Works – a kind of strong point in the line midway between the cooks' place and the front line. I did not get away till 4am and had to get to Roclincourt where, in a cellar of a house, the cooks boiled tea.

Ration carrying has its points. We arrived at the cooks' place at 5.30am along disused trenches and started by having a hot cup of tea ourselves; always a factor and very acceptable after being out all night. We loaded up and started back for the front line, every two men carrying a dixie of tea, about ten gallons between them. The dixie is placed on a long wooden stretcher, the stretcher fits on the shoulders, and back we went along these old disused trenches often knee deep in mud. The tea splashed all over us.

Arriving at the front line we issued each man a hot drink and a slice of cold bacon and made our way back to here (E Works). We repeated the same thing at midday, this time bringing up bully stew, travelling back up the trenches again. By the time we had reached the front line we were covered in bully stew, the perspiration pouring from us all. We issued each man a portion of stew and then made straight back for the cooks at Roclincourt and washed out the dixie.

Going along one part of the trench, which at that moment was not occupied, accounts for an incident where I had a narrow squeak. Apparently there was some part of the trench which was either shallow, or the parapet had been blown away so as to possibly expose our tin hat as we walked along. There was also a second such place some distance on. The German snipers in the front lines had rifles fixed and trained on these two gaps and would then watch them through glasses. When a man was seen to pass one gap he was fired at. When he passed the other, if his progress was not impeded in any way, he had passed the gap before the bullet had time to reach him. In this case it was so with me – passing a low part of the trench I suddenly heard a 'plonk' on the parados, ie the back part of the trench. It had come about a second too late. It was a trick practised by ourselves as well as the Germans.

The cooks are autocrats and we have to do this for them and return with tea to the firing line again at 3.30am. My shoulders felt as if they were parting from my body. We were beginning to feel very fagged – my legs would hardly move – but we had another journey to do. We issued each man tea and made back to the cooks. They are a mile away as the crow flies; it seems like six miles along these trenches. At 8.30pm we returned again to the line with the night tea and got back to here, E Works, at 11pm feeling fed up and done up. Sleep consists of what we can get between now and 4.30 tomorrow morning, when we return with the dixies and repeat the same proceedings as today.

Saturday, 17 June 1916

We turned out at 4.30am. Turning out is a very simple affair, you just get up off the floor of the dugout and go down to the cooks and have your drink of tea. How I envied the cooks in their job. Their eyes were nearly standing out of their head from the smoke of the fires, but it is a better game than ours – and back we went to the line, repeating up to tea-time.

Tonight we are being relieved and go to Saint-Nicolas. The cooks packed up after tea-time and our night tea we shall find waiting for us down there when we arrive.

Sunday, 18 June 1916

This we found, on reaching Saint-Nicolas at 11pm. Our dugouts here are cut in the side of a huge bank and boards let in to form a bed. Old mattresses collared from the surrounding houses serve to take off some of the hardness. We were not allowed to rest long, were called out on parade at 5am. Breakfast at 5.30 and left at 6.30 for the mines, a two-hour march back to the firing line. In this sector the miners are working against time. They have a suspicion that the Germans have undermined them and are likely to blow in the mine.

With the exception of a break for half an hour for bread and cheese, we worked like the dickens. A double shift of miners was on pecking [duty] and we had to keep pace with them, sandbagging the chalk and passing it along from one to another to be stacked in the front trench. We kept this up till 4pm. To say we crawled back is literally true – it was a considerable time before I could straighten my back. Arrived back here at 6pm, had tea and, almost best of all, a wash and shave, then gas helmet inspection. Now I am lying in my bunk – it is flea-infested and rat-ridden, but I can burn a candle here and that keeps the latter from coming too close. It's like a huge cave, this place, and from all the niches dug in the side, candles are burning. In some respects it looks like a little fairy palace, but the pairs of boots protruding, caked in mud, dispel the idea.

Monday, 19 June 1916

Reveille 7am. Marched into Arras for baths. There we went through the same performance again, handing in dirty underclothes in one room, a hot shower in the next, pass through and are issued with a clean change from the next room.

This afternoon I have been sunning myself, finished drying my tunic and trousers and, with a clean change underneath, felt very fresh and clean. We paraded at 5pm for trench fatigue in the front line. On arrival there we found we had to dig an entrance through one side of a mine crater to allow a party of KOSB bombers to go out. The Germans had concealed a sniping post on the far side and it was thought that they were digging an entrance into the crater and this party was going out to bomb them.

We finished our job at 11pm and awaited events. Sometimes, as spectators, one sees very stirring incidents of war, the setting often appropriate to the incident – it was so tonight.

Eleven o'clock came. The officer in charge of the bombing party was scanning the front over the parapet, waiting for two scouts to return who had gone out to find if the Germans were working anywhere near the far lip of the crater. The scouts returned and along came the company captain. 'Are you ready to go out Price?' he said. 'Yes sir' said Price, who, with his bombers, had been waiting in the trench. 'Well good luck and a safe return,' replied the captain and Price crept over the top followed by his 12 bombers, each carrying a bag of bombs. For a setting there was the straggling line of trenches taking on weird shapes in the darkness, in front the huge crater sides through which we had been digging and up above a weird, stormy sky – it was very impressive for the moment. We did not see the result of the raid, but made back to Saint-Nicolas and our dugouts, arriving midnight.

I have heard rumours today that the division leaves the district tomorrow for the rear for a rest.

Tuesday, 20 June 1916

Colour is lent to the rumour by the fact that there was a general inspection this morning and we have done nothing all day. From the entrance of our cave, which appears to be on the hillside, we can look across to Arras about three miles away. The walls of the cathedral standing up bare, also the monastery [of Mont-Saint-Éloi] – not a vestige of life or a suggestion of smoke. It looks like a burnt-out, deserted city, but we know that underground in the cellars there is one seething mass of life – men preparing to go up the line tonight or those who may have been relieved last night, hospitals, canteens and a few shops, all busy according to the needs of the moment.

Occasionally we hear a large shell go over and wait for it to burst and wonder if it has buried anyone.

Wednesday, 21 June 1916

Up at 5.30am. Breakfast 6.30am.

For our last fatigue in the mine we have had a tough day, very much as those in the past. At 4pm we knocked off and bid goodbye to the trenches. Tea on arriving back here. We are now awaiting the arrival of a company of the Rifle Brigade to come and take over. Our destination tonight is Duisans or Agnez, en route we hope for some quiet spot where there are fields and trees and no shells, no trench mortars and no aerial torpedoes.

Thursday, 22 June 1916, Agnez

The Rifle Brigade came up last night about midnight and 15 minutes later we were on the way here. We felt very much, leaving behind for good those buried around Arras. No one spoke of it but we all felt that we were not complete. Very silently we moved out of Saint-Nicolas and as silently tramped along the Arras road. Here and there a fellow struck up a tune, but it was not taken up and soon died down to the 'tramp', 'tramp' as we went along.

New officers in place of those fallen and new faces in the ranks did not inspire us. We had only one object in view – to get to our billet and to bed. Once fairly on the road and away from shellfire, a halt was called for a breather. Other regiments belonging to the division began to pass us as we sat on the roadside – the Jocks, the West Kents and Gloucesters – to fall out further up the road. After a rest we set off again at a good pace towards Agnez. Nearing the village in the distance we could hear Scottish pipers playing and as we rounded each corner of the road a pipe would step out from the side and play some air. As we passed it sounded very weird in the grey of the morning.

We reached here about 2.30am and found tea waiting for us and wire bunks in a stable. Very comfortable. It is a long time since we have slept on anything like it, we were soon into them and fast asleep.

We had breakfast this morning at ten o'clock and afterwards a parade for kit inspection. The remainder of the day I have slept. This evening the Whizz-Bangs concert party. They gave a tip-top show and now to bed.

Saturday, 24 June 1916

This morning we went for a route march. Beautiful weather, returned at midday. This afternoon the CO, recently returned from England after an operation, had us on parade and thanked us for the way in which we held the line on the 4th. He addressed us with sorrow and with pride, he said, as he looked around and saw how many of his officers and men had gone. No one has moved far from the billet today, being content to lie in our bunks and no doubt, as the dark comes on, to lapse into sleep.

Sunday, 25 June 1916

We were preparing for church parade this morning, busily cleaning our clothes when a message came along to fall in for fatigue. Three hundred of us paraded with picks and shovels and moved off for some unknown destination, which we reached about 11am.

After a lot of wandering about, this appears to be a locality between Dainville and Arras and we started digging big gun emplacements. We kept it up all day and marched back here this evening at seven o'clock. The remainder of the battalion went to church parade which was attended by the corps general who addressed the parade afterwards and referred to us, the 15th Warwicks, particularly. He said that we had upheld the traditions of the regiment well.

Monday, 26 June 1916

We have had to uphold them again today digging at the artillery pits, this time taking a more direct way through the village. We had a few long-range shells over and had to run for it. Apparently we are watched by German observation balloons. On the way back we passed a French battery in action on the roadside replying to the guns that have been dropping shells around us.

Further down the road we fell out again and I saw Scriven coming through a gate. Scriven and I were at school together. I did not see much of him afterwards until the outbreak of war when, by chance, we met again in Birmingham. He was just going to his depot, he had joined up so I saw him off and here we meet again. Only had time to find out what he was doing. By this time he held commissioned rank and at the moment was in charge of a party of Royal Engineers laying cables. After making arrangements to meet again, we moved off and came back here this evening to hear the Whizz-Bangs and then to sleep.

Tuesday, 27 June 1916

Wild rumours are flying about regarding what is going to happen in the next few days. It seems as if our period out of the trenches is not going to be a rest after all, but preparations for something 'over the top'. Parties of West Kents and Jocks left the village this morning in battle equipment. We have heard heavy bombardment around here all the week. Our troops, we are told, gained a mile and a half of trenches around Albert [on the Somme] last week. The air seems thick with something and no one knows what. We hear that we go back up the line this week. What our fellows think about that is not worth recording.

Tonight we are doing something all night – in the shape of digging.

Wednesday, 28 June 1916

We did the night shift, parading at 7pm. We reached Dainville at 9pm. Very curious, I found Scriven in charge of the job we had to do. He had brought over a party of engineers he had to supervise in laying artillery telephone cables. He got everything going and we then retired to the rear. Anticipating events, he had brought his haversack full of grub and we sat down and had a good tuck-in and compared our wanderings since last we parted in Birmingham. We knocked off at midnight and retired back to billets, arriving 2am.

Today we have lounged. It is very pleasant to lounge after feeling dog-tired, to let the muscles and nerves relax and gradually drift off to sleep. I have done that today.

Rumours are persistent and we cannot seem to get to the bottom of them. We all appear to be waiting for something to happen and we don't know what.

Thursday, 29 June 1916

At any rate it does not seem to prevent them from sending us on these fatigues. We did another tour this morning, parading at 7am and after a fairly sweating time, returned here at 2.30pm.

The rumours appear to be taking shape. Whilst we have been on fatigue, D Company left for the line on the right of Arras and reports say we go up shortly. I wonder what the game is? Our rest seems to be as far off as ever and as far as I can see we are on the brink of some big do.

C Company are on parade at the moment of writing. Orders have just come in for them to return up the line. The prospects do not leave us in the best of spirits. We had thought of sleep and green fields and we appear to be going back to trenches and anything that may happen.

Page comes along as cheery as ever and says, with a certain amount of truth, that if we do a tour up the line now, we shall not be doing it later on. A great optimist, Page. Someone suggests that that can be taken two ways and asks him what he means.

Friday, 30 June 1916

Still no definite news has come through but a constant stream of artillery, battery after battery, is passing our billet. From them we are not able to get news, they appear to know that something is doing somewhere, but where it is and what it is they haven't the foggiest and have no idea where they are going.

We are now confined to the village and not allowed far from the billet. Common report says that each battalion is going up for two days to get the lay of the land and some time within a fortnight we all go over the top.

Orders have just come along to keep water bottles filled, emergency rations complete and ready to move off in 30 minutes.

Batteries of artillery are still pouring past the billet. One incessant rumble and cloud of dust this last couple of days and nights.

Saturday, 1 July 1916

The emergency did not prevent us from having another dig at the artillery pits. We worked like blazes in a boiling hot sun; men from every direction were drafted on the job. For some reason there seems to be every indication that the gun pits are wanted for immediate use. We returned at 5.30pm and are awaiting events.

I was just preparing to settle down, 10pm, when in the distance we were all startled by terrific artillery fire, its intensity is so great that several of us have been into the roadway. Right in the distance the sky is livid with artillery fire and as far as we can see the sky is lit up. It all looks very weird. Both sides are using heavy guns; a long-range shell has just dropped uncomfortably close here (Agnez). Each night these bombardments have been going on but nothing like this – no doubt there is something happening.

RETURN TO THE SOMME

July 1916 – October 1916

'This is not war, it's slaughter'

By the time Harry returned to his billet on the evening of 1 July after sweating and straining digging gun pits near Agnez-les-Duisans in the broiling early July heat, events for the British had already taken a turn for the worse 12–18 miles to the south astride the River Somme. Early that morning tens of thousands of British soldiers had gone 'over the top' along a straggling 18-mile line, roughly resembling a capital letter 'L', in a joint Anglo-French offensive with catastrophic results.

While Harry and his comrades waited with bated breath to find out what their futures held, thousands of Kitchener volunteers serving in Pals battalions from towns and cities like Barnsley and Bradford, Leeds and Liverpool, Salford, Sheffield, Glasgow and Grimsby had suffered a mind-numbing 57,470 casualties; most of them before breakfast had been finished in Britain. Of that number 19,240 lay dead or dying, heaped up like so many thousand bundles of khaki rags tossed into the unkempt grass of no-man's-land or dangling from the German barbed-wire entanglements.

Preceded by a week-long artillery bombardment, the magnitude of which had never been witnessed before, what was meant to be a great Allied breakthrough, with the British bearing the brunt of the offensive north of the Somme, had, with the exception of a glimmer of success in the area of Harry's old stamping ground along the horizontal bar of the 'L' parallel to the river, been an unmitigated disaster. 1 July 1916 – the first day of the Battle of the Somme – remains the darkest day in British military history.

That evening, however, the true picture and scale of the disaster had yet to emerge. Communications at the time were poor; intelligence scarce. Harry had heard wild and unfounded rumours of British successes but the situation was still far from clear. As a lowly private he would have had no idea of the larger picture.

Tiny scraps of information would be seized on and recycled amongst the rank and file, becoming ever more distorted with each telling. Even at the highest level, the British commanders were struggling to make sense of the many fragmentary and often contradictory reports. However, poring over uncertain situation maps, they may have been unaware of the sheer magnitude of the defeat, but they were no fools. They knew that their casualties had been heavy; they knew that the German line to the north of the battlefield had hardly yielded an inch; they knew too that, despite the losses, they could not call it off. They had to fight on. The continued German pressure on the French at Verdun demanded it. They would need more guns and more ammunition – they also knew that they would need more men. Harry had avoided the slaughter of the first day but the battlefields of Picardy were hungry for more. The Somme was calling.

Sunday, 2 July 1916

What it is we are unable to gather, but we have a vague idea that we are starting an offensive movement – if that is so, everything explains itself, the artillery pits, streams of artillery passing and all this indecision.

This morning we were marching to church parade and were stopped on the way and ordered to return to billet. We paraded on the company ground and were told to pack our haversack for going over the top; all surplus stuff to be put in our valise [pack] and dumped and ready for any orders at 1pm.

One o'clock has just come and gone. We are sat round the billet yard wondering what is going to be the next move.

Monday, 3 July 1916, Sars-le-Bois

The next move came at 4pm. We had been lying about all afternoon and at 6pm we moved out of the village, but away from the firing line and trenches. We all breathed a sigh of relief. Whilst we knew the relief was only temporary, even a short relief was acceptable. We have not yet recovered from our previous shaking of 4 June.

A glorious evening, marching was hot to start, but cooled down as the night advanced. At the back of us the guns were hard at it and I thought of my experience of 4 June. We passed through several small towns and villages and arrived here at 1am, marching [13½ miles] the whole time since six o'clock with the exception of ten minutes' interval every hour.

The West Kents and KOSB preceded us and we were followed by the remainder of the battalion who had gone up the line in motor lorries.

Rumour follows us; the latest is that we entrain for Belgium – no one seems to know definitely.

Tuesday, 4 July 1916

At 7pm orders came along that we were to await further instructions, so limbers were unpacked and we kipped down for the night. Up at 6am awaiting the next move. All day nothing has developed. Have just returned from a foraging expedition – found a little cottage where they had milk, butter and eggs so I have had some; as much as I could consume. It's good stuff.

Wednesday, 5 July 1916

Still waiting events. Short route march and physical drill till dinner time.

This afternoon I have been sunning myself and watching staff officers dashing about. They seem to know little more than we do of what is happening in the trenches.

Thursday, 6 July 1916, Moncheaux

We arrived here this afternoon from Sars-le-Bois, a short march of about two hours; this seems to be a pretty village.

Friday, 7 July 1916

Reveille 6am. Breakfast 6.30. Bayonet fighting 9am–12.30pm. This afternoon I have been round the village; it's quite the prettiest we have been in. Here we have the green fields and trees and a village not in its last stages of decay. Quite good little cafés where in the evening we can get café au lait and the familiar light wines; it seems too good to last.

Saturday, 8 July 1916

Today has passed very much as yesterday. We are digging bombing pits to practise bombing, so we think we may be staying. Personally, it's the place I have been longing for for some months; away from the noise of guns and continual rumble of transport and the trenches.

Sunday, 9 July 1916

Today church parade only. We have no news of the offensive which started on 1 July. Rumour says – it's always rumour and nothing official – that it has been successful and that we are gaining ground around Albert. We know that locality – it was there we went into the trenches last November for the first time.

Today I have been lying in the sun. Occasionally one of our aeroplanes goes by overhead, the only warlike thing we hear. It is all very peaceful.

Monday, 10 July 1916

Early morning run 6.30am. After breakfast, practising the attack.

Funny affairs these 'practising the attacks' are; if we ever do any fighting in the same way as we practise them, the Germans will have some good targets and our quartermasters left with no one to provide rations for.

Tuesday, 11 July 1916

Baths this morning: these are days of tranquillity.

Wednesday, 12 July 1916

Things appear to be going well on the Somme. I hear rumours that we have advanced some distance and taken prisoners. I feel very fresh and clean after baths yesterday. It's wonderful what clean clothes will do.

This morning we added to our appearance by cleaning our equipment. Put it in water first to soak the mud out of it and laid it in the sun to dry. We were like a lot of washer-women scrubbing away.

Sunday, 16 July 1916

We were not allowed long in Moncheaux. The surroundings and conditions were too good to last. Every morning at reveille we wondered if that was to be our last day there and that we would get orders to move on. We had them on Thursday the 13th.

At noon we were told to stand to and await orders and these arrived at 7.30pm. We moved out of the village at eight o'clock prompt in full marching order.

A glorious evening. Warm marching at first but as the sun went down a breeze sprang up and, with a full moon, the country looked very picturesque. We had no idea where we were going, but assumed we were making in the Albert direction and we heard that we were to be a division in reserve to an Army Corps which was operating in this direction. The march was similar to all others with full pack; very gruelling.

We arrived at Le Meillard 4am. We have been marching eight hours [15 miles] with a rest in between of an hour for half a mug of tea. At Le Meillard we kipped down on arrival; myself in a stable. There was a good supply of straw.

Breakfast on Friday morning at 11 o'clock. At noon orders came for the battalion to stand to, ready to march off. We did not relish the idea but skipped round and loaded the blanket wagons, filled our water bottles and by one o'clock were ready to move off. We left the village at 4pm feeling somewhat stiff.

We had not been long on the march before it was evident that the brigade was moving. Met the 1st West Kents making in the same direction on a road parallel to the one we were on and the 14th Battalion [1st Birmingham Pals] were coming on behind.

Things were pretty uneventful. We passed through one or two villages and the usual dirty inhabitants came to the door of their cottage to see us go through. We still had no idea where we were going or what distance. The brigadier passed us on the march and told the colonel that our cavalry had broken through on the Somme, but to what extent he did not know. A halt was made at 8pm for a rest and tea. It's an extraordinary thing that these days I get into a mass of perspiration, as on this march, then lie down on the roadside and undo my tunic. The wind blows on my chest from all angles and I feel, in turn, hot and clammy then cold, but no vestige of a cold in consequence. Before the war I had a cold with every change of the wind.

At nine o'clock we fell in again and moved off. Here and there a man fell out, either from blistered feet or collapsed with the weight of the pack. The pack was put on a wagon and they had to follow on in the rear of the battalion. Towards 10pm we were met by motor lorries to pick up those unable to continue and from then onwards it was one long procession of lorries going backwards and forwards, picking up those done in. I noticed little Sidney Page, bent double with his own pack, helping another fellow along, himself hardly able to crawl.

By this time we were a complete brigade on the march, 1st West Kents, 2nd KOSB, 14th and 15th Royal Warwicks, all with transport, some three miles long from end to end. We reached Herrisart at 4am. We had been marching another eight hours [17 miles].

With the whole brigade assembled in one village, billeting room was scarce. We, in our platoon, had something that might have been a sheep pen, but were in no mood to find out anything about it.

We dropped our equipment and, with a pack for a pillow, I am conscious that after lying down for some short time, Page came in with an armful of straw which he had scrounged from somewhere and gave it to one of the fellows who was ill; the fellow I had seen him helping along the march. I am conscious that I slept on some stone floor.

At 8am we were awakened by the orderly sergeant to get up, pack up, have some breakfast and be ready to fall in again at 11.30am. We were all stiff and sore and little hopes had they of getting the brigade farther without proper rest.

We moved out of the village at midday. My feet were bad; I dared hardly put them on the ground. I appeared to have blisters like walnuts. First, ourselves (the 15th), then followed the KOSB, the 14th Royal Warwicks and West Kents in order. Fairly on the road the colonel passed it down that we were only going five miles; it was one of the longest five miles I have known and reached here, Franvillers, [actually eight miles] at tea-time. At the entrance to the village the divisional general [Major General Reginald Byng Stephens] and the brigadier [Brigadier General Lewis Jones] were standing, our band struck up a tune and we marched by like a brigade of Guards to collapse in our billets, soaked in perspiration and fagged out.

This evening I have spent washing my socks and am writing this with my feet in a bucket of water. Still the eternal order: water bottles to be filled and ready to move off at once. The night passed very quietly. This morning we had a church parade and orders have just been issued that we move off again in the early hours tomorrow.

Monday, 17 July 1916, Dernancourt

We left Franvillers at nine o'clock this morning, the whole brigade moving in line. Distance short, the pace easy, we reached here at 1pm.

Things here are very lively, one continual roar and rumble of transport and lorries taking rations and fodder, picks, shovels and scaling ladders to the firing line. Troops of all descriptions are in the village. I have just seen pass a squadron of Indian cavalry – weird-looking fellows – and crowds of Chinese belonging to the Labour Corps.

I have seen German prisoners for the first time today, about 250, in a compound. They were taken last night. I think they are not particularly good specimens; very dirty and very ragged, probably the last few days have told against them.

At this point we are about three miles from the firing line, or as it was last night. Every night, so we are told, 50,000 cavalry go close up to the firing line in case an opening is made ready to dash over and hold any position taken.

Tonight we have handed in our greatcoats which means only one thing; we are going over the top, probably the most exciting experience of the whole.

Huge amounts of wounded are passing by, British and German. Conditions appear to be very hot in the firing line. We hear our continuous bombardment day and night. We appear to be having indifferent success, taking each night a few hundred yards of ground and a few hundred prisoners and the cost we see passing all day long from the line; a constant stream of wounded and to the line a constant stream of lorries carrying ammunition. A very dull and stormy day.

Wednesday, 19 July 1916, in old German trenches that faced those trenches we occupied at Maricourt in November 1915

After reaching Dernancourt we were kept in constant suspense, sleeping at night with boots and puttees on and equipment by our side, ready to march off at a moment's notice. It came at 12pm today whilst the orderlies had gone for dinner. We moved off at 12.15pm towards the firing line. On the way we passed thousands of cavalry and the roads all along were congested with artillery and troops moving up to take up positions. We eventually arrived here at 5pm, in the German trenches, facing those trenches we occupied when we came out last November.

The country we can see for some distance is like one mass of ploughed ground. German equipment, helmets and broken rifles scattered all around; it looks as if they had a taste of the time we had on that 4 June afternoon and night. The trenches have entirely dried and in the side of the trench we have cubbyholes into one of which I have crept.

It is very extraordinary to occupy trenches at which we gazed for so long, wondering what was on this side. Now we have found out.

We go further forward tonight. At the moment our artillery fire is terrific – heavy shells pouring over from the rear into the German trenches three miles ahead.

Although 1 July 1916 had been a day of catastrophe for the British and Kitchener's New Army volunteers, there had been success to the south of the battlefield. There, the multiple tiers of the German front-line trench system had been breached and the pulverised village fortresses of Montauban and Mametz captured at a high price – more than 6,000 in casualties.

If the initiative had been seized at this point and the battle joined immediately in this sector, then some of the German trenches of their second-line system, several fortified villages and, more importantly, one or two expansive wooded areas may well have fallen cheaply instead of resisting capture for week after bloody week as the battle ground on towards the autumn.

But prevarication and piecemeal operations on the part of the British allowed the Germans to recover their equilibrium, bolster their defences and organise their reserves.

By the time Harry arrived for his second stint of service on the Somme, the British had inched their line forward at a heavy cost and had launched their second, and this time more successful, major set-piece attack on the German second-line system protecting the next tactically significant ridge in front of Bazentin-le-Grand and Longueval, at dawn on Bastille Day, 14 July.

The contrast with 1 July could not have been more stark. The 3.25am dawn attack, with closer infantry and artillery cooperation, was a stunning success. The German line broke and with the hinterland largely undefended and at the British Army's mercy, troops pushed on and the 7th Dragoon Guards and the Deccan Horse of the Indian Cavalry were ordered through the gap. That afternoon the cavalry charged headlong as far as Longueval and reached the crest of the ridge, just east of a large wood standing four-square at its highest point. Lacking support, however, they could get no further. Withdrawing a short distance and dismounting, they dug in for the night along the main Longueval–Martinpuich road – later named 'Black Watch Trench'.

Somme fighting: British troops resting and reorganising in captured German trenches near Bazentin-le-Petit after the heavy fighting for the Longueval Ridge on 14 July 1916. These trenches are a short distance from those held by Harry when he witnessed the attack on Wood Lane trench near High Wood and Longueval a week later and portray exactly the conditions Harry would have known. (© Imperial War Museums Q 4014)

During the hours of darkness German soldiers moved up and manhandled their machine guns into the dark recesses of both the wood to the cavalry's north and another much larger one behind Longueval to their right and in a vicious counter-attack drove the British infantry back into the open. The following day the cavalry left the battlefield and handed over their trenches in front of the woods to the infantry. It was the middle of July.

Harry arrived in the captured German trenches behind the village of Montauban four days later and his battalion was soon called upon to take its turn in having a crack at the German trenches on the ridge, including one called 'Wood Lane' which, like an umbilical cord, connected the two brooding woods behind.

The woods themselves would defy everything the British could throw at them for two more months and would not fall until 15 September 1916. By then they would resemble nothing so much as heaps of mutilated trunks and splintered matchwood and their names – High Wood and Delville or, as the men knew it Devil's Wood – would already be synonymous with the graveyards they had become.

Monday, 24 July 1916, against the third and last line of the old German defence

We left the German trenches facing Maricourt on Thursday evening about nine o'clock, later than was anticipated owing to the number of German planes up. I saw one very fine scrap between about 30 planes of both sides, flying around one another and machine-gunning the whole time, it was very exciting. One plane dropped.

The night was bright and clear. We had no instructions what we were going to do or where we were going, the whole brigade appeared to be making in the same direction by companies. It was difficult to see exactly over what country we were travelling; old trenches appeared to be all around. Here we crossed a main road, along which artillery were cantering, falling shells make their noise; we appeared to be going up a hillside across-country.

In the valley there were dead horses – must have been dead for some time, I have known better smells. There was a road running along the bottom and used by the transport. As days went on the number of dead horses grew in size and the smell was proportionally greater.

After about an hour's marching, [German] shells began to fall uncomfortably close, trying to find our artillery which, from the immediate vicinity, was pouring shells into the German lines. It's an uncanny experience to hear shells coming over, wondering where they are going to drop and in this instance, by the time they had dropped we had laid flat on the ground.

At 10.30pm A and C Companies reached some shallow trenches on the hillside. We were carrying picks and shovels and were told to make ourselves comfortable and kip down. Sleep was impossible with the awful clatter of artillery which was made worse by the close proximity of three batteries a few hundred yards away down the side of the hill, so we lit our pipes and watched the bombardment.

At 1.30am I was sent down to battalion HQ to act as runner to the company. On the way down I passed great numbers of troops who appeared to be concentrating on a point somewhere; everyone was moving at the double. I did not waste time getting down to the side of the hill, but went at the double across the main road in the valley and up the far side, arriving at battalion HQ sweating like a bull.

The HQ was a main German trench lately captured. I was not required so kipped down till morning. All day Friday [21 July] we did very little but were given to understand that the brigade was going to try and break through on Saturday night. The 1st West Kents to lead, followed by the 14th Royal Warwicks, the Jocks to follow and hold the position taken and we to follow up in support. For that purpose they all moved up early on Saturday morning [22 July] and ourselves at 8pm, B and D Companies, which had been in the line on our right, moving with us. Going was difficult, having to duck or spread out as shells dropped close by, then to get up and collect ourselves and move on until the next lot came over.

Eventually arriving at 9pm at a shallow trench about half a mile from the firing line, the artillery was in full swing, pouring over into the German lines an awful barrage of shells. The sky was livid with shell explosions and on our right a wood [Delville Wood] appeared to be on fire. No doubt it was probably a small village, we could hear machine guns and rapid fire and I imagined it was something of an inferno.

At 10pm we were in position on a roadside down which wounded came at short intervals and which eventually developed into one long procession. Those able to walk came down without help; others had to be carried on stretchers. It is at times like this that the stretcher-bearer earns his place.

Helpless to dodge or duck, he has to keep on with his load and hope for the best. From these we gathered that things were going on all right, the majority of our three battalions had gone over the top. We had not been long in our position when a message came from the front line that help was required; the Germans were preparing for a counter-attack. We moved towards the front line to reinforce. The night was a perfect inferno, shrapnel crackling overhead. The man in front of me staggered and dropped with a piece through his head. This was one of those affairs when I was within inches of a known death. I stopped and turned him over, found him beyond our help and went on.

It was no time for formalities, shrapnel was raining down and in the indistinct light we could see dead and wounded lying about in all directions. They were fellows of our brigade who had preceded us by a couple of hours. Arriving at what was an old German trench and appeared to be our firing line, we joined the rest of the brigade. West Kents, KOSB and 14th Royal Warwicks were all mixed up together, what was left of them. We filled our rifle magazines, fixed bayonets. No one seemed to know what we had to do so we peered over the top and waited for something to happen. We were unable to see what was going on, we appeared to be bordering a cornfield; the wild growth obscuring what little one could see in the darkness. Our trench, dug by the Deccan Horse and Dragoon Guards about five days previously during the first days [of the present battle], ran along a roadside just over the brow of the hill and on the other side of the field, about 250 yards, were the Germans.

Occasionally a wounded man came in and from these we gathered that the attack was not a success and that practically all the men that had gone over had been wiped out. News that we would not believe at first, but which became painfully evident as one after another came back and all told the same story, our artillery had failed to touch the front line with shellfire. Our men had been met by a mass of machine guns against which no man can advance and had all been mown down.

My thoughts at this time were extraordinary. It may have been the freedom of movement during an action, or the mood of the moment, or excitement, or the fact that we were moving over ground lately occupied by the Germans. At any rate, I had a feeling of being very elated. I felt restless looking at growing corn in the dark, so got out of the trench and walked along the road to where a fellow had just crawled in. He was a 14th Warwick, badly hit. I could get nothing from him so returned to our fellows, got in the trench and lit my pipe.

About 1am we, A Company, were ordered back to support. By this time the artillery fire had died down considerably and we succeeded in getting to the place without casualties. This support trench was in the side of a small hill. It was an effective screen for the Germans, whilst below stretched all our back areas. After waiting for some little time we kipped down at 3am.

I afterwards learned that our brigade casualties for this night's work was 1,800 killed and wounded out of about 3,500 men. It gives some idea of the intensity of the fire.

There are many side issues to casualties of war which perhaps those unaffected by the loss of relatives do not always understand or at least, pause to consider. In this instance, which was almost a common experience of all brigades who were fighting on this area of ground, our casualties for this night's work were high.

What of the after-effects of this night's work, where nothing tangible was gained? It meant the loss to many homes of one of a family, with all its attendant sorrow. Sometimes the loss was that of a support in the shape of a breadwinner and it may be that the sorrow was added to by financial stress and this may well go on all through the life of those concerned.

Of the wounded, they become a financial charge upon the nation. Their wounds are of varying degrees; some are of no consequence and are soon healed, whilst others are crippled beyond repair and often their outlook on life is changed and the change is usually not a good one. This also may go on all through the life of those concerned and their reflection can not be a pleasant one. In this instance, as in all others where casualties occur, the foregoing applies. It is the cost of gaining perhaps four or five hundred yards of ground which had no intrinsic value to either side.

War has many glories, it is the testing time for the individual as well as the nation, but the aftermath is tragedy and the tragedy lasts longer than the war. War is an accumulative effort, but the loss of life often has to be borne by the individual and, it seems, that there comes the tragedy. In war there is no such thing as equality of sacrifice.

Breakfast arrived at 10am [on the 23rd] fetched from the kitchens three miles away.

I saw a very unusual sight. The 95th Brigade, holding our right flank and a wood, were heavily attacked at dawn by the Germans who used gas. The brigade had to retire and from our position we could see them streaming across the fields, bullets kicking up the dust and dirt all around them. Eventually they took up a place on our right and rear. In this retirement the 1st Duke of Cornwall's Light Infantry lost a large number of men.

The day passed very quietly and making the most of the opportunity I had a sleep. Afterwards, with other fellows, I took barbed wire and stakes up to the rear of our front line. The smell was horrible, dead Germans were still lying about unburied. We had all our time occupied with our own affairs to attend to this.

We were relieved at 10pm by the 95th Brigade and made our way back to headquarters. Our way lay through a very narrow neck of land which the Germans continually shelled. Reaching the entrance we waited for a break in the shelling and then ran for all we were worth, arriving at the other side, about 100 yards distance, fairly panting. Arriving at headquarters we had a short rest then fell in and helped the Royal Army Medical Corps to bring in the wounded till dawn and then made our way to the rear fagged out and sick of it all. Kipped down in a trench with the remainder of the brigade and slept till dinner time.

Tonight everything is rush again. News has just come in that the Germans are concentrating in their back areas probably for a counter-attack tonight and we have to be ready to go back into the firing line.

Tuesday, 25 July 1916

The supposed counter-attack did not develop last night. From about 8pm till five o'clock this morning our artillery were pouring shells into their positions and we hear, by information gathered by aeroplane, that the German lines are a lot of a shambles and the dead are lying about in enormous quantities. They retaliated by shelling us this afternoon, where we are staying in the open. Killed a fellow and wounded several. We are right in the thick of the Somme fight here, of that there is no doubt, where, as we are experiencing, anything may happen at any moment.

We are sleeping in the open, any shell-hole that is dry. At night there is the continual rumble of transport and guns moving about and overhead shells are screeching backwards and forwards. Sometimes a shell drops close to us; one did so last night and I heard the shout for stretcher-bearers so I knew someone was hit, but I took little notice. I knew that there were crowds of fellows nearer than me to the wounded who would do all that was required, so went to sleep again. Such things are an almost hourly occurrence, even out here in the open. We give help when required and forget it. Amongst it all, the fellows who have a drop of water to spare, wash and shave. As I write now in the evening, several fellows are doing this. One is putting on a clean shirt as if he were going home – he may be, but everything points to it not being his earthly one.

Whilst resting here I saw a fellow brought out of the line nothing more than a human automaton – a broken reed. Without being wounded he had apparently stopped the full force of a shell explosion. His hair had turned perfectly white and his face had the expression of one who might have been tortured. Nearly helpless, he was holding on to the arms of a couple of fellows. An awful sight; a derelict, one imagines, for the rest of his days.

Wednesday, 26 July 1916

At 5am we went down into the valley, trench digging. The valley is appropriately named 'The Valley of Death'. I saw there a boot with a leg in it and no visible signs of an owner. It was not a usual sight – even here – and in itself looked uncanny.

It is nothing but a death trap. The Germans pour one continuous stream of shells into it day and night without ceasing. Going through the other day with a message, running from shelter to shelter, I saw a shell drop in amongst some men and knock out about a dozen and as I lay in one shell-hole, a convoy of ammunition was coming down the road and got within range of the falling shells. The drivers lashed their horses, four or six to a wagon, and raced along the road. Wagon after wagon passed me, the men lashing the horses and the horses going for all they were worth. I forgot the war, I was lost in admiration for the way the men sat on their horses and wagons as they swayed along this shell-swept road, the drivers, I could see, with their faces set and the horses frightened to death. They disappeared in the distance and I believe got safely through.

On another occasion in this locality I saw another uncanny sight. Passing over some land we came to a small ravine in which lay a large number of men, for all the world as if a battalion of men had fallen out for a rest. They lay there, some hundreds of them, British and German, all dead, stretching right round the ravine.

Into this place we went to dig trenches and shared in the common experience. We had to have some casualties before we were allowed to knock off. A shell dropped in amongst us killing one fellow and wounding several. After this we returned to our camping ground.

This evening we are awaiting events again. Some fellows have found cubbyholes in an old German trench close by; they creep in head first. This gives cover to the head and half the body, the legs hanging outside. If the cubbyholes are large enough, they have a candle burning – the little gleams of light in the trench look very cheery.

What Harry called Death Valley had originally been known as Happy Valley; British troops renamed its northernmost stretch after the area had been captured on 14 July 1916. Concealed from direct observation from the German lines, it became the only viable artery supplying the fighting line at High Wood. Thousands of men, horses and supply wagons, and hundreds of guns, constantly passed back and forth and the Germans, who had made use of it themselves, knew this. Their artillery swept it mercilessly and the gruesome results of this shelling were all too clear to Harry.

Another concealed supply route which branched off and ran east from Happy Valley/Death Valley, about halfway along its length and fed the firing line at Longueval and Delville Wood, was known as Caterpillar Valley.

Thursday, 27 July 1916

We slept till seven o'clock this morning and 'stood to' till nine, ready to go and help the 15th Brigade which had made an attack on Delville Wood, a diabolical place. I saw our Pioneer battalion, the Argyll and Sutherland Highlanders, after they had had a go at it a few days ago. They commenced the attack a complete battalion and when I saw them a few hours afterwards, only a few men remained. They had made five separate attacks and were literally blown away by machine-gun fire in the wood. Some of the fellows got to grips with the German machine-gunners and fought with their fists till they were overpowered.

News came along that the 15th Brigade had taken the wood and we breathed a sigh of relief. From our position here we can get a good view of the surrounding country. The village of Mametz lays in our rear in ruins. To our right is Montauban, laid flat, and in front, partly occupied by the Germans and partly by ourselves, is Longueval, in flames. Between us lies the Valley of Death.

Sunday, 30 July 1916

We did not do anything on Friday but were kept in a state of preparedness to move at any moment. Batches of prisoners passed us all day long and they showed signs of how hard the fighting had been. They looked a scratch lot, very old and very young mixed, and all very exhausted. Towards dusk a sergeant came along and pointing to the far ridge over the valley told us that we had to take rations there that night. We looked at the ridge; it was a halo of smoke. Somewhere on the other side of the ridge the East Surreys were situated and we had got to get to them with rations and water. No one spoke, but we knew that that barrage meant Delville Wood – the name made one creep.

We fell in at midnight, each man with two sandbags of rations slung over the shoulder and if he was unlucky he was also carrying a petrol can of water besides rifle and equipment. We started off down the hillside and into the Valley of Death. Difficulties started early. Besides the usual shells, the Germans were sending over tear-gas shells. We halted and put on gas masks, a complete head covering of flannel saturated in chemicals which passes over the head and tucks in under the tunic. Fitted with glass eyepieces and a tube through which to breathe, they are stifling.

Half-blinded by these, we made our way across the valley, shells coming over as usual. Occasionally one came very close, but there was no halting. We had got to get the rations up and be back by daylight. Sixty of us altogether, streaming over the land, one following the other. Sandbags full of bully and biscuits are no small things to carry, as we soon found out. Swaying from one side to another, we made our way over the valley the best way we could and, when some little distance up the other side, halted for a short time to allow the line to close up and to take off our gas masks. Terrible things, gas masks; one is almost choked in them without movement. To exert oneself is purgatory; I was nearly choking.

We kept on till 4am using the cover of old trenches wherever possible, the bags of rations swinging on the side of the trench and stopping our progress and adding to the delay. By this time we were getting close to our destination and on the fringe of the barrage we had viewed the previous evening, shells were falling fast. To halt was impossible, it was either forward or backward; the leading man was dead in the trench with his head blown off and the next man raving mad in the bottom of the trench.

The smell of everything was sickening, German dead were lying in all directions.

It is impossible to point to any one thing as the worst horror of war; there is probably no 'worst'. They are all so horrible in the fighting areas as to beggar description and comparison. Whilst on the Somme one lives perhaps, but only to go through it another day.

A stretcher-bearing party came through the smoke and our officer gleaned from him of the conditions in front. The road we had to travel along was literally going up from shells that the Germans were putting over. Under these circumstances he gave the order to dump the rations in the trench we were in and to about-turn. Two sergeants fell out as guards, one at each end of the line of bags of food about 150 yards long. Five hours later when another party went up to pick up the rations and carry on, they found the sergeants still where we had left them, in cubbyholes in the side of the trench, but the rations practically all blown away by shellfire. The sergeants were each awarded the Military Medal.

We returned with what speed we could muster, back to our camping place, another party being got ready to go back up as soon as the shelling abated. We rested all day but were given to understand that the division was making a push in the next 24 hours with the idea of clearing the surroundings of Delville Wood and Longueval. At 11.30pm we fell in, in battle order, each man carrying 48 hours' rations and two extra bandoliers of ammunition. We reached our position at about 2.30 this morning. Again we have done the trip down the hillside across Death Valley and up the other side again. We awaited orders all night and so far all today. We are awaiting events, employing the time cutting cubbyholes into the side of the trench we are resting in this afternoon.

Thursday, 3 August 1916

The remaining part of Sunday afternoon we spent in a restless state of mind. We had been given to understand that the Jocks [KOSB] and 14th Royal Warwicks were going over the top, the West Kents in support and we in reserve. From our position we were able to see the whole battle front; our front-line trenches on the crest of a hill or slope of ground, from where the attack was to commence. Halfway down were the support lines where we knew the West Kents were and ourselves on the opposite slope – 'Dead Horse' valley in between.

At 5pm our big guns began to bombard the German position over the ridge. We heard the shells go over and where they dropped was a line of smoke. We saw the West Kents leave their trench and make for the top of the ridge closer to the front line.

At 7pm the bombardment was at its highest. From our position, with a view across the valley and up the opposite slope, we could see our big shells dropping over the crest. The skyline was one mass of smoke. We watched for any signs of the attack.

Promptly, to the minute, we saw the Jocks and 14th Royal Warwicks leave their trench slowly, double over the crest of the hill into the smoke and then were lost to view; their place being taken by the West Kents who followed behind.

It is a thrilling sight to see lines of men rise from the ground and go forward to what, after all, is the apex of war and then be lost in the smoke of battle. To be followed by another line and another, in these instances one can think of the glories of war, and there was some glory in this instance, for the men went steadily. The staging was appropriate; it was a landscape of undulating ground. (The horrors of war I saw next day. These lines of men whom I saw go so steadily, were nearly all dead, scattered over the ground.)

The bombardment was intense, big shells from the rear were whizzing overhead. We could see the effects of the burst over the ridge. High Wood, on the left of our position, was on fire, the Germans still holding one corner. On the right of our position Longueval village had been set on fire by the

Germans and between the two extremes the front was lit up by the explosion of shells and German Very lights. In the dusk of the evening it all looked very strange and shells in return from German guns exploding close by made me feel very sick from the fumes.

It was dusk before we had any news – a message came down to say that B Company had gone up and to be ready to move ourselves. It was 2.30am before the next message came. We moved off, our pockets bulging with bombs, down the slope across the valley and up the other side, shrapnel was falling heavily.

At 4am we were in the front-line trench and relieved what remained of the 14th Battalion. It was rather a pathetic sight, a few straggling men black with heat and perspiration and hardly able to drag along – as a battalion they had practically ceased to exist. The attack had not been a success. The Jocks were relieved by the West Kents; they had suffered as heavily as the 14th. They had advanced to within a few yards of the German trench and were caught in a cross-fire from the corner of High Wood by German machine guns which the artillery had failed to blot out. The remnants had to retire back to the position from which they were relieved by ourselves and the West Kents.

On arrival we set about strengthening our position, deepening the trench and making shelter from observation. At such times as these many incidents of a diverse nature take place: from the stretcher-bearer who crawls out on all fours into no-man's-land – binding up the wounded and, pulling and tugging, brings them in – to those who volunteer to carry messages or fetch rations. In this case it was the latter; rations had to be fetched from the rear some three miles away and the journey lay through a storm-swept area of falling shells.

Four fellows set out: we watched them as they went down the side of the slope taking cover as they ran every now and again as shells came whizzing over. They reached the sunken road, paused and then, one after the other, dashed up the sunken road and out of sight. We all watched them go and then waited for their return. Some three hours passed and if they had got safely through, they should soon be returning. We did not have to wait much longer – at the edge of the sunken road they appeared – two of them carrying a dixie of tea with sandbags of food over their shoulders, the other two had petrol cans of water similarly strapped. They paused for a moment and then came into the open. Heavily laden as they were, they had no chance of taking cover in the open. We forgot the war and watched them, we were breathless.

Slowly, but as rapidly as they could move, they made their way towards us, struggling with their load. They were unlucky in a way; as they reached the open a salvo of shells came over. We saw them duck, but hanging on to the grub they did not hesitate and 20 minutes later were safe in the trench. It was one of those unrehearsed episodes which occur every day, pass and go unrecorded, but they must make an impression on those who witness them.

To a painter of pictures, whether in words or scenery, this episode affords a good subject for contemplation. Imagine for a moment yourself sat on the crest of a hill, the ground stretching away from you for some three-parts of a mile a gradual slope downwards, to culminate into a narrow neck of land, through which runs a road. Your eyes are focused on this road and presently there emerge those whom you have been looking for – the ration party now heavily laden. The ground they have to travel over before they reach you is land searched by shells; enemy artillery are probably firing at random knowing that this area of ground is probably seething with activity because of its close proximity to a road, so shells of all calibres are almost, in the literal sense of the word, poured over.

It was through this that the men started to walk. They had not got far when over came the shells and for a moment they were obliterated by the dirt as the shells reached the ground and burst. They could, if they wished to do so, have dumped the rations and made off somewhere for cover, but they continued to come on. We could see the bags of rations swinging from their shoulders and in their hands petrol cans of water. The journey was uphill and with their luggage the pace was slow. Twenty minutes is a long time to face such an ordeal of one's own free will – it was cold courage, and well done. Gradually they got nearer and nearer and then had passed through the shell zone – we gave them a cheer and then got at the food and water.

We had our grub and sandwiches. Between the digging I had periods of sleep. At dusk we moved along the trench to a trench on the right, which ran at right angles to the one we were in and which had to be continued up to Delville Wood, occupied by the 15th Brigade.

Every available man was marshalled and, armed with pick and shovel, moved along and then out on top and started to dig like blazes. A sergeant major came along half-drunk with rum; 'dig narrow and deep boys, dig narrow and deep' he kept whispering, he with the rest of us taking a hand with the pick or shovel. A shell came over and finished the career of some of us. The call went along for stretcher-bearers and we dug the harder; picks and shovels going for all we were worth.

I had not been digging long before I was sent for to rejoin the Lewis gun team and from our position some few yards away, listened to the picks and shovels going hard.

The Germans were some 250 yards away and appeared very restless, sending up Very lights two or three at a time, every few seconds. Shells began to fall very close and the call for stretcher-bearers began to be heard with uncanny regularity.

Before dawn we got down deep enough to afford cover and the Lewis gun teams crept along and occupied the trench – it had cost a dozen men to dig it during the night, most of whom were dead. We were occupying the ground over which the 14th Royal Warwicks and the West Kents had made the charge: evidence was ample.

Having made our position secure, and getting a good field of fire for the machine gun, at daybreak we lay in the bottom of the trench and awaited events. As the day advanced the heat and smell was terrible.

Here again is a subject for contemplation. With the aid of periscopes we kept watch on the land in front. Suddenly a sentry, some three or four yards away from myself, saw what he thought was some movement in a gorse bush some 30 yards out in no-man's-land. Could I see it? Together we looked hard at the spot; that something was moving in the bushes was obvious, but what it was was difficult to see clearly. Then as if by inspiration, the sentry suggested that it was one of our fellows and wounded.

The call went along the trench for a stretcher-bearer and when he came along, the sentry pointed out to him the bushes, waited for the movement to occur again and then told him of his suspicions as to the cause of it. The stretcher-bearer paused for a moment, surveyed the land and the German trenches and then without hesitation climbed over the top of the trench, lay on his stomach and started to drag himself and stretcher towards the gorse bushes, fully exposed to the German lines. We watched his progress wondering whether the Germans had spotted him and if he would get there. Still crawling on his stomach we saw him arrive at and push his way into the bushes.

Some half an hour passed whilst we all kept watch on the spot. Suddenly the bushes parted and the stretcher-bearer emerged, still on his stomach and dragging with him a man whom we could see he had bandaged up. The progress was slow; it was nothing more than a tug and a rest on his part. Soon he was exposed again to the German lines; would they spot him and fire, we wondered? Now in the open, still he tugged and pulled his man towards our lines – nearer and nearer he got to us and still no shot came from the Germans till at last he got to the trench and we dragged them both into safety. It was another of those incidents unrehearsed and unrecorded.

This was the second occasion which had come directly to my notice in which one of our fellows was exposed to the German lines in broad daylight and, watched in all probability by them, was allowed to return safely.

Towards afternoon rumour came along that the division was being relieved, perhaps that night, and as the dusk drew on we anxiously looked for any signs of relief. The strain of the last fortnight had been very hard and the last three days we had been living on bully and biscuits. Night came, but no relief; everything was fairly quiet so we took it in turns to have a sleep in the bottom of the trench.

About tea-time on Tuesday [1 August] we had orders to be ready to move at dusk, the 17th Division was relieving us. At 12.30am the Northumberland Fusiliers came up, cussing for all they were worth; they had been lost about a dozen times and were fairly fed up. Fifteen minutes later we were starting to assemble in the rear, Harry Fawke and myself bringing up the rear of the machine-gun team, then marched into the resting place for the night.

Marched back is not a good description, we doubled for three-parts of a mile over the ground that we had watched the ration carriers traverse. When under cover from possible shells we lay down and panted for breath and then made down the slope across 'Dead Horse Valley' over the opposite ridge and back to a redoubt. We moved at a snail's pace, finding our way sometimes along trenches now unoccupied, over the fields, already more than exhausted by previous days in the line and impelled by the thought, perhaps, that in front of us and away from the line meant rest and sleep.

We passed the 'glories' of war on the route: dead. Both Germans and our fellows by the score, all wrecked, sometimes beyond recognition by shellfire and they stayed behind to swell the numbers and the smell. Above these circumstances, mental and physical, we had to rise if we hoped to win.

Stayed the night on the slope of the Valley of Death, which, as the Germans were driven back, began to be gradually immune from shellfire and a resting place for the troops. We kipped down and slept till nine o'clock next morning [2 August].

Had breakfast, a wash and shave and fell in again for a camp outside Dernancourt and we arrived here about seven o'clock last night. Greatcoats were issued, tea came up, and with tea, the post.

I shall not quickly forget that night. The camp was situated on the two sides of a valley and all along the valley at dusk fires were lit, mostly from packing and coverings of parcels from England. There was a great rush for the post – we had had no parcels for a fortnight. With mine from home I lay on the ground. The relaxation was great; no shells, nothing to worry about and with a bath tomorrow. I slowly consumed my parcel, watched the fires twinkling along the sides of the slope and the stars overhead. I finished my parcel, drew my greatcoat over me and went to sleep.

It was great – I slept like a log till seven o'clock this morning and was awakened by a general movement amongst the fellows. Getting up was a simple movement. Throwing off my greatcoat I joined up with the rest for breakfast. How good it went down, uninterrupted by any fear of anything coming over in the shape of shells. We lay where we had dropped down the night before in this field. Breakfast over at 7.30am we fell in for a bath and a clean shirt, the first I had had for some weeks. This afternoon rifle inspection and we are now resting awaiting the next order to move.

Everything is bustle and hurry. Along the sides of the valley each battalion has its transport arrived. Field kitchens are getting tea ready. Very cheery to see these long lines of smoking chimneys; tea will be along in a moment. Everything that is cheery is very acceptable at the moment. The division has been in the firing line for the last 14 days. We have taken Delville Wood and Longueval village and High Wood at a cost of over 9,000 men, but we have failed to break through the German third and last line of defence. It is no reflection upon us, no body of men can advance against machine guns, especially when they are well handled and by brave men as the German machine-gunners undoubtedly are, generally speaking. Equally brave men advanced against them, but no man can go far, however brave, when he is riddled with bullets.

Like Harry, Walter Harry Fawke had joined the battalion as a private and became an officer in the Royal Warwickshire Regiment. Harry Fawke would also survive the war.

Friday, 4 August 1916
General rest day. Rumour says that this time we are really going on rest and staying for some time. We are all packed up and ready to march off.

Saturday, 5 August 1916, Airaines
Back into rest. No orders were issued, so at dusk we got down to it again. Some scrounged round for wood and soon the fires began to blaze again. Reaction was setting in. From the gatherings around the fire I could hear the latest pantomime song, accompanied by the beating of an old petrol can or biscuit tin. When I awoke at daybreak, some of the fellows were still sitting round the fire.

The transport had had orders during the night and had moved off, leaving our breakfast of bacon behind. We cooked this on the fires which were still burning. Receiving further orders, we paraded and reached the railhead and moved away about midday [in cattle trucks – usually 30–40 men per truck] passing through Amiens and Longpré of early memory.

We stopped at Airaines and detrained, moving to a field some two miles out of the village. Here we are situated amongst green fields; cows and sheep are grazing as if there had not been anything like a war on. We are not staying long here, we understand, but move on again tomorrow.

Sunday, 6 August 1916, Avesnes-Chaussoy
We arrived at this place 4pm, a miserable-looking place. We hope we are not here for long. At the moment of writing we have not yet been able to find a water supply nor a shop of any description. It's just the sort of place we may be dumped in, the billets are poor – precious little straw about.

Thursday, 10 August 1916, Villers-Campsart

We left our last village yesterday, and very glad to. It was to be our permanent place, but owing to the water supply, which did not exist, we moved on here yesterday. We are now far away from any scenes of the war. Troops here are practically unknown; a beautiful thought. This is made evident by the disposition of the French folk towards us, who, at present, look upon us somewhat as a novelty and so far have not yet started to charge us outrageous prices for goods.

We are billeted in the farm buildings of a very good class of farmhouse. Eggs and milk are plentiful and the country, just in the midst of harvest, looks very fine. It is the place I have been looking for for a long time. I hope we stay here a long time. This morning we were out on parade at 6.30 for physical drill and spent the remainder of the morning cleaning our equipment and scraping our clothes. We shall soon look like smart young soldiers again if we stay here long.

Tonight we are going on night operations from 9.30pm to 2.30am. The object of our stay here, we are told, is training in open-order and wood fighting in preparation for anything that might happen on the Somme.

Friday, 11 August 1916

Returned to the village at 2am after night operations, which consisted of racing madly over the country, digging trenches and firing Very lights and being a general nuisance to the neighbours.

This afternoon I have spent firing off a Lewis gun course.

Tonight we have celebrated our entry into these sublime parts. [James] Ward was the moving spirit – he being the French scholar. On our entry into the village we had seen what looked like very fat ducks swimming on a pond and Ward soon got busy finding a cottage that would chip us potatoes. Ward went and bargained for a fat duck and we sat down tonight, six of us, to chipped spuds and omelettes and then awaited the arrival of the roast duck. It came in on a large dish and about the size of a pigeon. We roared and told Ward he was no good at bargaining. He had, he said, seen it swimming on the pond and knew it was a duck. We ordered more chips and omelettes and finished the night in song – it's a good war tonight.

Monday, 14 August 1916

On Friday we were given 48 hours leave and Harry Fawke and myself made a bee-line for Le Tréport, a seaport on the French coast. At 8am Saturday, after a walk of about five miles – we had to carry all our equipment with us – we reached Senarpont, a railhead. Got on a train and reached Le Tréport at 1pm. We all looked a scummy lot emerging from Le Tréport station, carrying pack equipment and rifle.

Fawke and I made for an hotel. We saw visitors having a jolly good meal at one place and went in; the manager immediately sending us out. No doubt we had struck the wrong place for such as us, so we made for a back thoroughfare and eventually got a bed at the Hotel du Lion d'Or on the Rue de Paris – a fourth-rate show. It, however, provided us with a bed for the night which was all we really required. Other fellows joined us and that night about six slept in the bedroom, but I had a bed. This was the first time I had slept in a bed since leaving England. I had rather looked forward to the sensation of undressing and getting between sheets, but I was not struck with the actual experience. Dressing and undressing struck me as being a waste of time and I felt somewhat suffocated in a bedroom.

Sunday afternoon Fawke and I had a bathe. Whilst we were in the water someone entered our [bathing] machine and collared our money – it was rough luck. We had to borrow from some of the fellows occupying our bedroom.

Le Tréport is supposed to be a fashionable resort in peace time – it's a pretty place.

We returned this afternoon, it has been another peep into civilisation again. It would be very difficult to chronicle one's actual feelings. Mine were too involved. It was the second time I had been in a street of any pretentions since leaving Boulogne in November. I think it was the same with us all – here there were waiters in a restaurant taking orders from diners; for a moment it appeared rather funny and, for some reason, artificial.

Tuesday, 15 August 1916

Field operations today. Went out at 6am and finished at 11pm. It sounds a long day but we have done nothing really except lie down. I suppose it gives the brigadier an opportunity to handle his men.

Thursday, 17 August 1916

More equipment cleaning this morning; this afternoon company inspection and this evening the CO had his inspection.

Friday, 18 August 1916

Divisional route march, en route the divisional commander watched us pass by. We wonder what this means?

Saturday, 19 August 1916

Pouring with rain all day so we have remained in billets and officers have been round and given us short lectures on the compass, map reading and first aid but they appeared to only have an elementary knowledge themselves.

Sunday, 20 August 1916

Brigade church parade this morning. We are getting very fit again under this treatment; plenty of fresh air and good grub but I expect we shall get another rude awakening shortly, following the divisional commander's inspection. Rumours have started again.

Monday, 21 August 1916

Field operations in woods between Villers-Campsart and Selincourt. Orders came to headquarters late last night that after operations today, we should move to another village tonight.

At 1.30pm we moved out of Villers-Campsart and said goodbye to the eggs and milk and to prospective duck suppers and took up our position in this wood at 3pm. We make an imaginary attack at 3am tomorrow. Rumours are very strong that we return to the firing line on Wednesday and over the top.

Tuesday, 22 August 1916

Operations finished at 6am and we had breakfast in the wood. We were very much surprised when orders came to return to Villers-Campsart. We quickly sprang to it and returned to Villers at 10.30am and kipped down. I did not awake until three o'clock this afternoon, washed and shaved and afterwards I walked over to Liomer, an adjacent village. A pretty walk.

Villers-Campsart is situated on the other side of the wood and as we returned from Liomer we stopped to listen to the nightingales which were beginning to chirrup as night drew on. It seemed to be the first decent thing we had heard for a long time. We might be in England.

Wednesday, 23 August 1916

We leave here early tomorrow morning for an unknown destination. The betting is on Armentières. We are due at Airaines 7.30am. This is the extent of our knowledge.

Friday, 25 August 1916

Awoke at 1am Thursday [24th] for a drink of tea and moved out of Villers-Campsart promptly at 2.30am. The night was cool. Marching was not the terror it had been in the daytime.

We reached Airaines at 7am. Different battalions of the division were coming in from all directions. The Surreys, Jocks, West Kents, Gloucesters and the 14th Royal Warwickshire Regiment followed us in quick succession, with bands and pipes playing.

We awoke the townspeople as we passed through to the station where we found long troop trains drawn up and at 8.15am left the station, still speculating where we were going to. We might be bound for anywhere. We passed Longprè, the junction, and then we knew there was only one place for us, somewhere near Delville Wood.

We passed Amiens at top speed and eventually drew up at Dernancourt at six o'clock in the evening, back to the scene of our former exploits. We detrained and occupied the side of the valley we had occupied three weeks previously after leaving 'Deville's' Wood.

Breakfast this morning [25th] at 8am. We moved away this afternoon for this, our present camping ground known as 'Happy Valley'. Here we have tents. Tomorrow we go up the line on the right of our previous position and directly on the left of the French who we are told are going to make an attack, hoping to take the town of Combles.

The Happy Valley in which Harry found himself on this occasion should not be confused with the Happy Valley/Death Valley two miles behind the front line at

High Wood where he spent time in late July 1916. This particular Happy Valley was just over a mile north-west of Bray-sur-Somme, in the loop of a railway supply line which branched off from the main line at Dernancourt. Some six miles from the front line and relatively safe from German shelling by the time Harry arrived, the tents were used to house troops in transit moving up to, or away from, the fighting.

Harry now prepared to play his part in the Battle of the Somme once more. On the sector between the villages of Guillemont and Maurepas, three miles south-east of High Wood – which was still resisting capture – the Germans had been pushed back in heavy fighting as recently as two nights previously. Harry's company was ordered to relieve the 20th Battalion of the Lancashire Fusiliers in what had now become the front line, just in front of a position called Angle Wood.

With only French troops to their immediate right, Harry and his comrades now found themselves on the extreme right of the entire British line on the Western Front and were part of the planning for a major attack alongside the French. But Falfemont Farm – a position 270 yards away across no-man's-land which the 5th Division historian called 'one of the strongest redoubts ever made by the engineering skill of the Germans' – barred the way.

Sitting in a commanding position on high ground which dropped away towards the newly won British positions some 130 feet below, nothing now remained of the farm except a few solitary bricks; the rest pulverised into a red brick dust in the earth which showed where the buildings had been. Yet the site was protected by trenches and barbed wire covered by machine guns in well-protected, splinter-proof emplacements. Directly behind it was Leuze Wood – Lousy Wood to the troops – where German reinforcements could assemble to be rushed forward. The Germans had turned Falfemont Farm into a veritable fortress and now it had to be excised in a preliminary operation at 9am so that the main combined British/French attack could go in unimpeded four hours later. Harry's battalion had been chosen to take part.

Monday, 28 August 1916, in trenches opposite Guillemont

We left our previous camping ground, Happy Valley, on Saturday at 3pm in battle order; that is only carrying the bare necessities, rifle, ammunition, food and water, prepared for what was to be an advance on a 20-mile front in conjunction with the French.

The brigade moved up in battalions of an hour interval. After a brute of a march we reached the reserve line at 6pm and rested. At dark, we moved up to the firing line, a distance of about two miles. To say we 'moved up' describes in a couple of words a period of time which must rival hell, for during that time back came all the old nerve-racking sensations, that of being encircled in danger from shells, from gas and shrapnel bullets. Back came the old acrid smells of bursting shells, dead horses and gas. Amongst this inferno, we plodded our way. Occasionally the call went for stretcher-bearers but that did not affect us; we had to keep on.

We were given to understand before starting that our front line consisted of shell-holes only and that we had to dig from one to the other and construct a front line. We were agreeably surprised when we arrived at 1am to find respectable trenches, newly dug. Rain had been pouring down and by this time we were fairly soaked. After a previous experience of the rain, this did not greatly disconcert us but it is unpleasant to feel wet clothes next to the skin.

I spent the remainder of the night, after relief, trying to rig up some sort of shelter and dig a cubbyhole in the side of the trenches. Dawn came and with it a bombardment from the Germans causing us some few casualties. A couple of officers were hit; one called Fox from Stratford-upon-Avon.

Rain continued to pour down all morning and we were soon covered from head to foot in mud. With daylight we were able to see something of our surroundings. The trench I was in appeared to be on a rise on the ground and pushed well forward towards the German lines. To put my head over the top and gaze round would have been fatal so I did not attempt it.

During this day we lived in a continual bombardment of shells, directed on no particular trench. They covered the whole area of land stretching back towards our reserve lines. At times they fell amongst us so thickly and there appeared to be no escape from them that one fellow burst out crying. It was the only occasion during the war that I saw this occur, and in this instance it was not out of place.

Afternoon came. Still the Germans continued to bombard us. One well-directed shot fell in the midst of No. 2 Lewis gun team, placing them *hors de combat* – two killed and four wounded – and I was sent from No. 1 team to take over the position. Getting together some men who had an elementary knowledge of the Lewis gun, we dug the gun out, cleaned it and carried on.

Night came and with it the rations, bully, biscuits, and cheese and water, the ration carriers taking back with them the wounded who had all day been laying in the bottom of the trench. We had no means of keeping them dry and, like us, they were covered in mud and lying in water. Lying in water is literally correct. Imagine a narrow trench some 6ft deep and hardly wide enough for two men to pass back to back. With no outlet or communication trench to the back areas there was no means of getting them away and they lay in the bottom of the trench in mud and water.

C and D Companies came up at dark and dug trenches, connecting us up with the West Kents who had taken over on our left. On our immediate right, the French line starts. A few yards on my right, a Frenchman stands. His blue clothes look very curious in the trench. No doubt we appear the same to him.

I find I can occupy my thoughts writing this diary. It keeps me interested and is something to do.

Wednesday, 30 August 1916

Yesterday (Tuesday) was awful. The morning clear and sunny turned to rain again and at midday was pouring down in torrents quickly filling the bottom of the trench, which also meant that the mud and water reached up somewhere in the vicinity of the thigh and gradually soaked through our clothes.

The bombardment continued at a fearful pace and we were forced to kneel down in the bottom of the trench for more cover. This had been going on for some couple of hours when a shell landed right in the midst of the machine-gun team I had left the previous night, wounding and burying the lot of them, gun and all. I went along and helped to do a bit of digging and, after the men, rescued the gun. At nightfall, they all went to the rear. In this case, all the men were not killed, some only suffering from concussion and joined us again when we went out on rest. Those not wounded were considerably shaken and suffering from concussion. I was now left, the only one of the two teams that came into the line.

We collected what parts of the gun we could find and dumped them with our scratch team. This left this part of the line with one team not existing and one team manned by fellows whose knowledge of the Lewis gun is limited to pulling the trigger.

I also saw here what, on the face of it, was the tragic consequence of the incompetence of an officer; one who for a moment failed to recognise his responsibility. He had spent some considerable time looking through periscopes whilst on sentry, trying to locate the actual front line of the Germans. That they were able to fire directly on to our trench we were aware by the regularity in which they were clipping the parapet with bullets but from which direction they came it was difficult to find out, owing to the lie of the land and a thick hedge which was, in all probability, the danger point.

We reported this to the officer, one who had but recently joined us and was a second lieutenant and, it is to be assumed, was new to this rank. He came along the trench and after surveying the front through the periscope, turned to a corporal and said 'Corporal, I want you to go out and scout the front'. We all knew it was madness and so did the corporal. Replying 'Yes sir', he turned round, went a few yards down the trench, climbed over the top and a few minutes later was dead. We fetched him in at night. He had not gone more than a dozen yards. It did seem that here discipline went astray.

We continued in this state till 2am when the Jocks came up and took over.

We left parts of our equipment behind, buried by various shells. We began to make our way to the rear for two days' rest. Coming back the guide lost the way, we appeared to be wandering over a plain, picking our way around shell-holes.

It was 5am before we reached our billet; an old, disused German trench with about six inches of mud in the bottom. With picks and shovels and corrugated iron, we made shelter for ourselves.

The cook had dixies of tea waiting for us; the first hot commodity we had had for the last three days, after which we kipped down, soaked to the skin.

At 11am a dinner of stew, which looks like shaving water and goes down like a savoury, and are now awaiting tea before kipping down for the night. Rain still pouring down. We are fairly in a mess.

Tuesday, 5 September 1916

Since making the last entry we have been through the mill and emerged at the other end a very broken and battered battalion.

The wet weather of last Wednesday continued on Thursday. In consequence, a report came up that further operations were suspended and we were being relieved shortly but on Friday conditions improved and it turned out a scorching hot day. It dried our clothes and with every prospect of continuing, things took another turn. All Friday we were hard at work collecting bombs, rockets, ammo, sandbags, picks and shovels. At dusk in parties of about 30 men, we took them close up to the firing line, about two miles in front. It was evident to us that we were going to do something. Parties like ourselves from every unit in the district were moving towards the position we last occupied.

No amount of writing can in any degree convey what a reversal of things such an order brings. Imagine a strip of land perhaps ten miles in length and stretching for perhaps two miles from the front line to the rear. In daylight hardly a soul would be visible but immediately darkness came, that same stretch of land was seething with activity; small parties of men like ourselves, making for the front line, either carrying up necessities or for fatigue work.

Ammunition wagons came rumbling along, also guns, whilst in the back areas, no doubt, some thousands of men were making preparations to march up to act as support to men in the line or to take their place. All this takes place on land saturated with rain. Darkness adds to the confusion.

Things were not too comfortable. The Germans were using tear shell gas, making our eyes very watery and a well-placed shell knocked out ten of us as we waited at brigade headquarters for orders. Returning at 1am we kipped down till the Saturday morning.

The day broke clear and bright and at eight o'clock that night we moved up to the line; every man carrying two extra bandoliers of ammunition besides equipment and rifle, a bomb, two sandbags and two days rations of bully and biscuits. Every third man had a pick or shovel, Very lights and pistols. As a Lewis gunner I carried spare parts belonging to the gun. We were well loaded and we were going over the top.

The journey up appeared to be over the same plain; trenches and shell-holes in every direction, with no landmarks. It was 1am before we arrived in position and relieved the Jocks who went into the firing line leaving us in support and relieving the 16th Warwicks, who retired to the rear. We settled down without loss and the scheme was explained to us.

The Jocks were going over the top tomorrow [3rd] at 9am. Their objective was ground of which a farmhouse was the centre [Falfemont Farm]. Assuming they took the position, we went over the top at 1pm, passed over their position and took a line 500 yards in advance and dug ourselves in. At midday the French troops on our right were making an attack, also our own troops on our left.

It struck me at the time the scheme was being explained to me, how foolish someone was and what a lack of understanding they showed to think for a moment that we could advance on open ground 500 yards and to do that after we had passed the Jocks. They appeared not to have reckoned with machine guns firing at the rate of about 600 rounds a minute. How right my thoughts were eventually proved.

Our artillery steadily bombarded their position all day, growing in intensity as the night advanced. At 8.30 the following morning we were in position in the support trench and ready to dash up and take over the front line left by the Jocks when they went over.

We counted the minutes as they went by and a few seconds after 9am heard the rattle of German machine guns which told us the Jocks had gone over and had been spotted. The excitement was intense. The order was passed along to get ready and a few minutes later, we went over the top, over the rise in the ground and racing for the trench the Jocks had just left and arrived without casualties, breathless.

Once in the trench, we were safe from the bullets which appeared to be flying in all directions from the German line. All the time our artillery was still pounding away. We could hear the bark of the 18-pounders [field gun] and the heavy shells buzzing through the air. We waited for some time then wounded Jocks began to return; mostly cushy wounds from machine-gun bullets. One great fellow came along the trench roaring like a bull begging for water. He had one bullet through the stomach and the fingers of one hand hanging by the skin. I shall probably never forget this. He was a fellow six feet at least and well-built in comparison. By some chance as he came pushing his way along the trench he stopped at myself and appealed for a drink of water. With my knowledge of wounds, which was very vague, the treatment of stomach wounds particularly, I was under the impression that to drink to excess was dangerous so I refused. The look of contempt he gave me I remember as clearly now as then. The next moment I was emptying my bottle down his throat caring as little about regulations as he did.

We were unable to gather any reliable information but later in the morning understood that they were held up by German machine guns cross-firing, one on the right and one on the left.

Things continued like this till midday, punctual to the minute. We saw from over the rise of ground on our right, line after line of Frenchmen sweep down. Over the rise they came and swept down on to a wood. In their case the fight was short and sharp, about 30 minutes. Afterwards, we saw a long line of Germans coming back, some 500, so they had successfully accomplished their job.

Meanwhile a message had come in from the Jocks to say they were unable to advance and required reinforcing.

At 12.30pm assurance came from our headquarters to say that A, B and C Companies would go over the top at 12.55pm and support the Jocks, and D Company, from support, would come into the firing line and take our place.

The air was electric; machine-gun bullets kept on clipping the top of the parapet showing us how accurate the German fire was.

We counted the minutes and they seemed like years and I employed the time getting a good foothold in the side of the trench, ready to spring up and over on the word and the minutes passed. [Lieutenant] Hemus passed down the word from the left – 'seven minutes to go, get ready' and, to the second, we jumped on the parapet and raced forward.

Going over the top brings with it varying sensations according to the circumstances; in this instance as we ran forward we could hear the bullets whizzing about us as they clipped through the air and I remember thinking, as I ran, how long it would be before one stopped my canter. The same rotten cross-fire met us and as I ran, I saw several fellows fall, one fellow coughing up blood and all the time, bullets were hacking about me. I ran for about 70 yards, carrying with me all the Lewis gun things I had brought up and dropped breathless into a shell-hole headlong on to a German who had been dead for months and was fairly high.

When I had recovered my breath, I began to look about me for signs of movement from our fellows and a bullet whizzed by for my trouble. I was joined by two other fellows from whom I gathered that the same fate had overtaken us which had overtaken the Jocks. We were fairly caught by those machine guns which the artillery had failed to wipe out.

We lay in the shell-hole for some half an hour when we were suddenly mortified to see our men retiring, losing heavily as they retired. It was a sickening sight. D Company, which should have followed us over, lost all their officers in getting from the support to front line and had no one left to lead them, so did not come over.

Things were at a standstill.

The shell-hole we were in did not afford sufficient shelter for the three of us. One fellow had sunk right through the German. The smell was a bit thick. In a lull our fellows made a bolt for it back to the line. I watched the remains of A, B and C Companies struggling back, dodging from shell-hole to shell-hole. Some were fortunate and reached the trench. Some were unfortunate and never got there. One fellow in particular seemed not much more than a boy. I wanted to shout to him to drop to the ground, although he was probably some 200 yards away and had no chance of hearing me.

In my anxiety to do something I unthinkingly put my hand on the German's chest with the idea of using his body for leverage and the other hand to funnel my mouth to shout. My hand went clean into the German. I tried to rise up on my elbow but only in time to see the fellow drop to the ground and not rise again.

My position was secure as long as I lay in the bottom of the shell-hole but I was exposed to fire on my right. To attempt to go forward under the circumstances would have been absurd. I was carrying part of the Lewis gun and had no idea where the team was. To make for our line was very risky; I had been watching some of our fellows try to do so and they were lying about over the ground, shot through the back, so I lay down beside the German. I found myself covered in maggots, so as best as I was able I covered him with dirt but I could not keep the smell down. So I lit my pipe and blew the smoke into my haversack.

It was a few minutes past 1pm when I landed into the shell-hole and it was not till seven o'clock in the evening that, taking advantage of a barrage we were putting over, I ran from shell-hole to shell-hole and dropped into our trench, almost on top of our company captain who had got wounded somewhere in the stomach. I stayed with him for some time: he looked in a bad way. I spent six hours stretched out in that shell-hole. I have known better companions.

By this time the front line had been taken over by the Cheshires and at dusk I joined my battalion, or what was left of it. At 2am I found them in a trench in the rear area and not very happy with the way things had gone.

The Cheshires made an attack at dusk and met the same fate as ourselves and got badly mauled but managed to reinforce some of the Jocks who were still holding on. By this time the machine guns had been spotted, the Cheshires were followed by the Bedfords who sent a bombing party round each flank and blew the guns and men up with bombs.

This was a very good example of the havoc that can be caused by well-placed machine guns manned by men who know how to and are prepared to use them. In this case they mangled four of our battalions before we were able to proceed and there were only two of them; that is, two gun teams.

The Norfolks followed the Bedfords and eventually dug themselves in about a mile from the trench from where we started, taking a fair number of prisoners.

After resting for a short time we collected ourselves together and were taken to reserve trenches – Casement Trench, named after Sir Roger Casement, a renegade who was much in evidence about this time in connection with Irish affairs – where we are now waiting to be relieved. We left the trenches with two officers and 180 men; all that was left from those who went up.

We had some slight compensation for the tanking we have had in seeing large numbers of prisoners come in, in all sorts and conditions but with one tale. Their existence has been like hell owing to our artillery fire and they look half-starved. They say they could get no food up.

After roll-call, total casualty figures amounted to one officer and 30 men killed, seven officers – including Harry's platoon commander Lieutenant Hemus – and 144 men wounded and 49 men missing; a total of 223. When some of the missing straggled back to the British lines and told their stories, the figures were revised, pushing the totals to 63 dead, 165 wounded. The bodies of 49 of the dead were never found, or their graves were destroyed and lost during later fighting. Their names are commemorated on the Thiepval Memorial to the Missing.

The failed attacks and the grinding attrition on the Somme added to the battalion's losses incurred near Arras in early June 1916. Large gaps had by now appeared in the ranks of the proud Birmingham Pals of August and September 1914. These gaps were gradually being filled by drafts of fresh men from Britain but for the surviving 'originals' like Harry, the essential character of their battalion was changing.

After the war, Harry added the following reflection: 'As time went on and event succeeded event, I came eventually to believe that I was ordained to come through the war alive. Time and again I missed death, so it seemed, by a fraction, but I always missed it. Many other occasions had yet to arise where one might say there was no reasonable or perhaps possible escape, yet somehow I got through.'

Saturday, 9 September 1916

We remained in Casement Trench [two miles back from Falfemont Farm] all day Tuesday [the 5th] watching hoards of prisoners come by. No one moved, for we were fairly secure but occasionally a shell came over looking for batteries firing but no great damage done so we slept, thankful to forget it.

This is not war, it's slaughter. No man, however brave, can advance against a sheet of bullets from the front and a shower of bullets and shells from overhead. It appears to me to be that the side will win who can supply the last man, supposing the economic conditions hold out.

Wednesday morning, the 6th, we awoke to find the batches of prisoners still coming in and gathered, from the intelligence department, that in the advance on the 20-mile front of which we had been a part, our affair was the only one that had not been immediately successful but that we were now pushing forward and things were going well.

We left Casement Trench at 2.30pm and reached this camp about 5.30pm, a short distance in the rear and up to today, the 9th, have done nothing but straighten ourselves out, reorganise ourselves and replace lost equipment.

We have had hopes that we had finished with the district for some little time but signs are that we have got to have another packet before we go.

Huge drafts arrived today, making the battalion up to strength again. It's a very worrying business, this getting to know a fellow, going up the line and afterwards finding out no one knows what has happened to him. His place is filled by the next draft up and so it continues; officers and men alike. The infantry are beginning to be known as 'gun fodder'. I think it is an apt description.

Monday, 11 September 1916

We moved back up towards the line yesterday morning, the 10th, and lay in Casement Trench till the evening. All day long a battery of French 75s

[75mm quick-firing field gun] has been firing close by. In the afternoon I went along and had a look at them firing.

They are fine-looking guns and well-handled. I did not stay long. With the aid of long-range shells, the Germans are trying to find these guns so I just had a look at them and returned.

We fell in again at 7.30pm and moved off at 7.45, no one knowing the nature of the business we were in for. We reached brigade headquarters at 8.15pm and stayed till dark.

Our artillery was very busy, the continual noise a bit nerve-racking. At dusk, guides arrived and we moved off to the left of our previous position. The night was fine and moonlit. We moved along the side of a valley and over a far crest of a hill.

We had been moving about an hour and were well in the open before things began to get warm, the Germans, sending over chance shells, got very close at times. Arriving at the crest we had to run down the slope across the valley and up the other side, shells falling thickly. We arrived at the top in some disorder, everyone having done 500 yards in record time. Troops seemed to be assembling from all directions, a shell falling here and there, putting some out for all time.

We lay down and guides went forward to try and find the positions we had to occupy, meanwhile troops were coming into position and some appeared to be leaving. From the questions I could hear asked, things seemed to be in a perfect mix-up and things were extremely uncomfortable. Amongst the confusion we could hear the call continuously going up for stretcher-bearers as shell after shell came over. Someone stopped part of it.

We lay in the open for about an hour when an order came for us to about-turn, and back we went. We were taken another route and after about two hours along trenches and over rough ground we arrived at the scene of our former exploit last Sunday, ie, Falfemont Farm.

Time 3am. We were fairly safe from eventual observation here so selecting a trench – the trenches here were nothing more than banks of earth thrown up hastily for cover as we pushed forward each night – the company officer got us down into it and told us what had happened during the night. We were supposed to relieve a regiment in the line. The guides, after crawling about from trench to trench, found that the Middlesex had relieved the part we were supposed to occupy so we had 'about-turned' and here we were. Someone had bungled somewhat.

The part we had been in was Leuze Wood and the ground was sufficient indication that there had been hard fighting. The dead were everywhere, British and German, and the smell was strong.

After a short rest we made our way back here to brigade headquarters and arrived at 5am. Except for the period of time we lay waiting to relieve, we had been marching about since 8pm the previous night, over trenches, over shell-swept areas and in full pack. We were thoroughly done in and on arrival back we found cubbyholes, kipped down and here we had stayed all day, wondering what was going to happen next.

Tuesday, 12 September 1916

Had a sleep last night and awoke this morning to find nothing had happened to necessitate the prospects of us going up the line and so have remained in reserve all day, our friends the French 75s barking at intervals.

Whilst out on reserve, I saw a very unusual occurrence. Besides the French battery of guns there was also one of ours. These were in gun pits with a layer of netting and canvas overhead to keep them from aerial observation so that only the muzzle of the gun was visible, just protruding above the level of the ground.

A fellow whom I knew well, careless of where he was walking, passed in front of one of the guns whilst it was in the act of firing. The shell did not actually hit him but went right in front of his stomach. The concussion forced that part of his anatomy into the chest and he dropped down dead; a horrible sight.

Occasionally a heavy shell comes over but we can hear them droning in the distance and have time to scurry to cover before it falls and explodes.

A gorgeous evening. Aeroplanes are thick overhead, buzzing backwards and forwards. From these we can gather the extent of our advance. They appear to go some miles forward before they get shelled. It is very satisfactory but the cost, we see it every day, long streams of wounded passing back in ambulances. The positions we have lately taken we seem to be holding. The Guards and the Middlesex went over last night and found the German trenches empty.

Wednesday, 13 September 1916, in trenches outside Combles

We have had to have another packet at the Germans before we leave the line and go out on rest. We were sat round the old brazier in an improvised shack last night watching it burn down before turning in for the night – ie, sleeping on the ground – congratulating ourselves that we should not have to go up again before relief came, when we were suddenly startled by an orderly rushing in and telling us to parade in ten minutes for the line. The French had taken part of a village and we had to take over their old line for the night.

There was nothing for it. We soon got into harness and a few minutes later were making our way towards the line, following a guide. A glorious moonlit night, almost as light as day. We made our way over the line we had jumped from the other Sunday and across what was then no-man's-land. I looked out for my friendly shell-hole and its German occupant but I could not find it. There were still several dead lying out. No doubt they will be brought in and buried at the first opportunity; they do not look nice in the moonlight. Arriving at the – or what was the – German trench, we found it a very spacious affair with cubbyholes and shelters and moved further forward and reached our position at 2am.

We found a few Frenchmen waiting for us. These we relieved and got our gun in position for emergency. On our right, Combles was on fire. It's a unique sight to see a whole village on fire. A few stray shells came close by and morning came with nothing more exciting happening.

On our left, Leuze Wood was being shelled without interval but this died down as the morning passed. Judging from this no doubt we have a firm hold on the place, making the Germans withdraw their guns. One heavy shell falling between here and Leuze Wood presented me with a part of itself. I heard it whizzing through the air and next thing I knew there was a terrific knock on the arm. Most of the fellows close by heard the smack and came along to see the damage, so I took my tunic off and rolling up my sleeve, there was a tiny spot of blood trickling down. I kept the piece of shell as a souvenir.

The day has passed very quietly otherwise and we are awaiting a relief to come up. We believe we start leave to England again when we get out.

Thursday, 14 September 1916

The QVRs came up last evening at 9.30pm. No shells were about at the time but it was cloudy and wet. We handed over the position and made our way to brigade headquarters and after resting marched on to the rear and lay down in the open at 3am.

Breakfast at 8am. We moved off shortly afterwards with no idea where we were going, passing through Morlancourt. We reached Méricourt [-l'Abbé] after five hours hard marching. We passed large numbers of cavalry on the road all making for the line.

Here we are billeted in the cinema hall which has, in turn, been used as a cattle market, hospital and concert hall. We are very crowded so I have got a truck to sleep in tonight, there is another fellow sleeping between the wheels underneath.

I shaved this evening, the first for the last few days. I grew a respectable beard in that time and look quite different. After the operation, it's very refreshing to get it off. We are speculating what the next move is to be.

Saturday, 16 September 1916

We can get no information as to what is going to happen. Leave is the chief topic of conversation. Rumours are strong that we are making for the rear and that leave in large batches is going to start. Personally, long ago I reached that stage where home seemed to be a thing I once remembered. It seems to be a thing I once knew in some age long ago and have been, since then, living in a different sphere. It has seemed, in a way, to make that former time always conscious in my mind but helpless myself to reach it.

If leave does start no doubt mine will come in turn. I am looking forward to the experience.

We have done practically nothing this afternoon and as dusk comes on and as we feel inclined one after another to get down to it, ie, sleep, a few fellows besides myself are writing with a bit of candle stuck in bottles, or in the wall.

I slept well on the truck last night. Hoping for another good night tonight.

Wednesday, 20 September 1916

Our quiet repose in Méricourt, where the division was on reserve work and from where we hoped we should entrain for the rear and for rest and leave, was rudely broken. Early on Monday morning [18th] at 6am, orders came round to make preparations for the line again.

Imagine our frame of mind. We had all been reckoning on rest and, best of all, leave. We had understood we were going to entrain for some back area and all that that means; real rest and sleep, good grub, a regular post bringing parcels and letters from England, somewhere where we could lay in the sun and read the newspapers out from England, where we could have dry clothes and a regular supply of clean ones and where we could wash and shave every morning. Instead we were going to have another dose of the mire. To say that any fellow expressed any sort of pleasure at the prospects would be absurd but on the other hand every fellow kept his disappointment, written on each face, to himself and made preparations for the line.

It was a fine exhibition of discipline and much can be ascribed to that, but tradition also plays its part under circumstances of this description I think.

It was on 20 July that we first entered the Somme battle and, with the exception of a short break, have been fighting on that front without rest. Our casualties in the battalion have been enormous; draft after draft had, as time went on, been sent to make up losses and consequently, there was not that coordination amongst us which comes with close contact of one man with another, for we had no time to know one another before some position required attacking and then followed the attendant losses and another draft arrived to replace all this. New officers whom no man knew: we had to rely on the fact that they were officers.

Those who had been fortunate enough to come through the fray could be well described as 'war-worn troops' and those who had been through it only in part were not much more fortunate. A period of rest was within our grasp; a period that was long overdue, badly needed and leave was our one topic of conversation.

Suddenly, at 6am our thoughts were flung to the other extreme – back to the line and its certain casualties. Outside it was raining hard.

At 9am we moved out of the village – the 14th Warwicks, ourselves (the 15th Warwicks), the West Kents and KOSB. A vile morning: rain still coming down in torrents with every prospect of a soaker. We had no idea of our destination or what position we were going to take up.

Small carts were used for the transport of Lewis guns. We pulled them along by hand.

As we marched along the road, we of the Lewis gun teams had to pull the extra weight of our light carts along a road which, with the constant heavy traffic that had passed over it, was not much better than a broad track thick with mud and what with the rain coming down without ceasing we were soon wet through.

I felt that I was glad I was one of these fellows, if one could be glad with a lottery as great in its personal element as any man has perhaps to face. Here were ranks of them; ranks of 'men in the street' as it were, plodding along towards that lottery, knowing full well that for some there would be no return, marching towards it when they knew that they should be marching the other way towards rest and safety.

The onlooker may ask how it was that the men did not grumble, in view of the traditional prerogative of the men in the ranks to grumble if they saw fit to do so. The reply seems to me to lay in the fact that that traditional prerogative applied to the petty things of army life: too many fatigues, not enough variety in the food and so on. As long as they carried out that which it had been given them to perform they reserved to themselves the right to grumble but this, and many other instances, it was different.

Here the men had already performed that which they had been called upon to do and in consequence were exhausted and were being called upon again. It was the ability to visualise what might have been and, with good reason, could easily have been, that made this occasion appear so fine. Here there was cause to rebel and it was a very just cause, but because it was assumed the need was great, they rose to it to a man and marched back to the line without a grumble. Perhaps we were too done in to do so.

Passed through Morlancourt and rested for dinner outside what was once the village of Montauban at 4pm. Of the village, hardly a brick remained. There was not a wall two feet high. The whole place in the early days of the Somme offensive had been moved skyward and lay in all directions; a mass of bricks and shell-holes.

Rain was still coming down and had been doing so all day without exception. We were soaked to the skin. We had been marching all day through it with only a few minutes interval every hour for rest. In spite of the hard travelling we were bitterly cold from a keen wind blowing.

In the absence of orders or anyone knowing what we were going to do or where we were going, we made temporary shelters with our ground-sheets and in pairs or threes, made what little protection we could from the elements. Orders came at 5.30pm and we moved closer up the line. Travelling was bad. The road was inches deep in mud and congested with traffic of every description; ambulances coming down from the line and ammunition columns and transport going up.

With our Lewis gun carts we were unable to keep the pace with the battalion. We had ropes on to the carts, pulling for all we were worth but the mud beat us in the end and we got stuck and the battalion went on, leaving us to follow. With more leisure we got more ropes on the wagons and got going again, enquiring as we went the direction the battalion had taken.

Our way lay through Trones Wood and on the way we passed a party of Guards busy at a burial. We were told it was Asquith's son.

We passed through Trones Wood pulling and tugging at the carts and finally got stuck on the far side at 1am up to the axles in mud and thoroughly well done in.

With nowhere to sit down, sodden with rain and boots full of mud, we tried to light a fire but it gave more smoke than heat. We stood round it till dawn [on the 19th].

What a sight it all was. The wood had been attacked and counter-attacked some 20 odd times before we eventually took it and the dead were literally swarming all over the ground; British and German mixed up together, and showed how hard the fighting had been. It all looked ghastly at the breaking of day. There was not a tree standing; some had been entirely uprooted by shells and had fallen in all directions and those that remained standing were blown off at the trunk leaving a black, charred mass.

I went into some of the trenches and the same sight presented itself, British and Germans all mixed up together. I did not go far.

With daylight we took stock of our bearing and gathered the Germans were well ahead, some three miles over the crest and our battalion about a mile further on. We were making preparations to join them when up came our kitchens. They, like us, had been stuck in the rear and held up by traffic. From these we were able to get a drink of tea. There could have been no better drink at that moment.

In the afternoon we caught up the battalion, pulling our gun carts the remaining distance across country. On arrival we found them still awaiting orders and lying in the open, so we followed suit.

I found a shell-hole and dropped into it dead beat and slept till this morning and we are still waiting now at midday, equipped and ready to move anywhere.

Raymond Asquith, the eldest son of the then serving British Prime Minister Herbert Asquith, served as a lieutenant in the 3rd Battalion the Grenadier Guards. Regarded by many of his generation as a brilliant intellect, Asquith had served as a barrister before the war and, given his father's position, had felt duty bound to join up in early 1915, despite his age. Initially joining the London Regiment, he transferred to the Grenadier Guards in order to serve overseas, a move which caused a serious rift with his father, which was partially healed when Herbert Asquith met him on 7 September 1916 during the Prime Minister's visit to the front.

Eight days later, on 15 September 1916 – the opening day of the Battle of Flers-Courcellete – Raymond was shot through the chest as soon as he rose to lead his men in an attack on the German trenches north-east of the village of Ginchy. He died of his wounds an hour later in a shell-hole being used as an improvised dressing station. He was 37.

Today Raymond Asquith lies buried in Guillemont Road Cemetery – some 280 yards or so from the eastern fringes of Trones Wood, through which Harry was dragging his Lewis gun cart.

Friday, 22 September 1916

We waited at our place in support all day on Wednesday [20th]. We were, we understood, reserve to an attack on our right. We were, however, not required and were relieved at 8pm by the Grenadier Guards and made back to another position called Chimpanzee Trench – the old brigade headquarters [280 yards from the southern edge of Trones Wood]. About two miles across country, with the Lewis gun trucks we had to take a route via the road and, after wading along for five hours sometimes held up by mud and the traffic, we finally got stuck again at 1am along the Maricourt road. Traffic in all directions was in difficulties, the mud in places some two feet deep, or almost burying the wheels of our wagons to the hubs.

Some idea of the depth of mud on what was, in normal times, something akin to a main road can be gathered by the fact that as we pulled the cart along, we suddenly struck an obstacle in the mud. On investigation, we found a dead German, spread-eagled and completely submerged.

We built a fire and sat round till daybreak. At dawn we made for Chimpanzee Trench reaching it in time for breakfast, plastered in mud and very tired. We found the battalion lying in the open, finding what cover they could get in some trenches and shell-holes.

Fawke and I did the same, finding a shell-hole for two. We rigged our ground-sheet overhead and crawled in with our breakfast, which was a slice of bread and bacon and a mug of tea. Consumed this and went to sleep. I slept till four o'clock this afternoon and afterwards had a wash and shave in the usual manner when close to the line, in half a mug of water, but it was very welcome.

Afterwards we cleaned the guns and kipped down again in our shell-hole and slept till this morning (Friday). Today we are given to understand that we are the brigade in reserve to our division who attack Morval within the next few days.

The day is bright and warm. It has given us an opportunity to dry our clothes and wash our socks.

Sunday, 24 September 1916, reserve trenches in front of Morval

We left Chimpanzee Trench on Friday evening and took up our position in the reserve line the same night. Ordinarily the distance is about an hour's march across country. After wandering about for three hours and eventually finding ourselves close to the firing line, shells dropping uncomfortably close, the guide admitted that he had lost his way and had very little idea where he was. Orders were given to about turn and we took shelter in a disused trench whilst the guide went back to brigade headquarters for another guide, both returning in about an hour's time.

With a fresh guide we retraced our steps some distance and eventually relieved the DCLI at 1am in the reserve line facing Morval. The reserve line appears to be an old German main trench recently taken over by the London Territorials Division and the 56th Division and well honeycombed with shelters and funk holes. We kipped down till daybreak.

In reserve we have had very little to do all day but watch the passing of time and, in this instance, observe our artillery getting the range of Morval and the surrounding strong points held by the Germans in preparation for the attack on Morval which, rumour says, is tomorrow.

From this line of trenches the village is straight in front, about 1½ miles in a dead line with a valley in between. The Germans hold a line of trenches on the outskirts of the village from which they retire at dawn and occupy only at night.

From the point that I am now sitting in the trench on the crest of a hill, I can see the surrounding district. Down the side of this hill our men are entrenched. The valley is no-man's-land. Up the far side are the German lines, with Morval and Lesbœufs, the two villages we are going to attack, about three-parts of the way up. The valley curves right round on our right, where the French are going to have a packet at Combles and try and finally clear the district. I believe if all goes well, the French and ourselves should enclose the village and join forces on the other side.

An artillery officer has just arrived. He says the show comes off tomorrow and as I write, a shell from his battery comes over and falls in the vicinity of Morval and he telephones back instructions. They are registering their battery.

Like Trones Wood, this ground was not taken without a hard fight; broken equipment and dead are lying about.

Monday, 25 September 1916

The attack on Morval and Lesbœufs starts at 12.30pm today. It is now 8am. We moved back from the reserve line last night, the 14th and 15th Brigades occupy the firing line and support line and the KOSB took over the reserve line from us and we moved backwards and formed an extra reserve. Reaching our position I was in a party detailed for digging so back we went to the firing line. We had to dig some sort of cover for bombers who were going to rush a German strong point.

Silently we crept out. To work was difficult. In the distance we could see an earthwork about 50 yards away. We had hardly put a pick in the ground and over came a shower of bullets. We lay flat on the ground and built a sort of barrier with anything we could find. Behind this we scraped some sort of a trench and by the time we had got cover for the body, we had to return to the rear. Day would be breaking shortly.

On the way back, troops were still pouring into the trenches ready for the attack and we made our preparations on reaching the battalion, which we have just finished. We wonder how the day will go. The morning is brilliant.

Reports kept on coming from the front lines saying progress was steady and casualties small in number whilst the Germans were surrendering in masses. The latter was confirmed by the steady stream which passed our position.

When it became evident that we might not be required, I could view the proceedings with a more detached mind.

Tuesday, 26 September 1916

We made a breakfast yesterday morning of anything we could get hold of and tea. The cooks came up from the rear and made this for us. Then we made more preparations. Two days' rations of bully and biscuits were issued, bombs, flares, picks, shovels and sandbags. Towards dinner time we were in a fair state of preparedness.

We were told that the chances were against us being called up but we had to be prepared. The morning continued brilliant and so we waited events.

Punctually at 12.30pm our artillery opened the bombardment on the villages and surrounding German positions and we all stood to, ready to act. The noise was deafening from the rear of us and from the front and from both flanks, guns of all calibres poured one continuous stream of shells over on to the German positions. The ground shook and vibrated with the firing. We looked at one another. We had been in such bombardments ourselves but on the other end, and we knew the effects.

In less than half an hour, the first batch of German prisoners passed us and we knew that our fellows were getting busy in the German lines but could get no information. We were still pouring over shells. At 1.30pm orders were passed along to be ready to move at any moment. Shortly afterwards in columns of platoons, the battalion moved forward.

The first two or three hundred yards was easy going until we began to get amongst our own light batteries and had to encounter the reply from the German guns. It was one of the few instances when I preferred to remain in the infantry. The [German] replies came in the shape of 'heavies' which came crumping over. They served to spur us on. We reached the crest of the hill at the double, over the top and dropped in the old main German trench, fairly blown to the wind.

The whole panorama was exposed to our view. When I had recovered my breath, I got up to look. Across and up the opposite slope, I saw the 14th and 15th Brigades advancing line after line. They appeared to rise out of the valley and, as one line, went up the hillside to be followed by another some 200 yards behind and then another and another. It was an exhilarating sight. We could see each man distinctly and they appeared not to have many casualties but kept on advancing, to divide as they reached Morval and, surrounding the village, they disappeared over the crest of the hill.

Morval itself was obscured in smoke; our artillery the whole time pounding it to dust. That their fire was accurate, we could tell by the reddish haze that hung over the place; there would not be many bricks left standing when they had finished with it.

In the meantime, large batches of prisoners were coming in which gave us the idea that the attack was going well. By this time our artillery had abated, the haze cleared and we could see what was left of Morval. It looked, and was, a heap of ruins.

As our men moved forward so we advanced down the slope of the hill occupying any trench or shelter that presented itself, to eventually find ourselves in a trench very near to the bottom of the valley. There we stayed and awaited orders.

The German fire, which up to now had been fairly hot on us, began to slacken. This was a good sign; we knew they were taking their guns further back. Still the prisoners were coming in in batches, the unwounded carrying the wounded on stretchers. They were not a bad-looking lot of fellows on the whole.

With the ceasing of the German artillery we began to breathe more fully. Some of our men coming back wounded told us that all the positions aimed at had been taken and that our men were digging in some 200 yards over the ridge and that our casualties were comparatively small.

We were still to have a warm few minutes. A tank coming up in the rear got stuck in the mud and was unable to move. This is the first mention of a tank although it was not the first time I had seen them. Sometime before the offensive started, I had seen them when on rest and had marvelled at their very intricate machinery. We were told then that they were 'hush-hush' affairs. I nevertheless fully explored its interior. It was beautifully made and fitted with Daimler engines, I believe.

In this instance, we cussed it for a long time as it was drawing heavy fire from the German guns. The ground was so sodden with rain, the rollers in consequence would not grip and it was sending out smoke from the exhaust in clouds which were easily spotted by a German observation balloon – the last to remain up in this sector – which directed the fire from a German heavy gun battery. This battery made us feel very uncomfortable for a time, dropping heavy shells in close proximity but it did not last long. They also had to withdraw.

We lay in the trench all night; everything satisfactory further forward.

Early this morning [26th], one of our fellows passed by wounded and drunk. He had been having a rummage round a dugout: said he had found bottles of beer and, by his description, enough to keep the army going. When he said he had had the lot before coming back we understood. He sold me a trench dagger and a pair of excellent field glasses for 11 francs.

He seemed very satisfied and so was I; he had about half a dozen pairs slung round him.

Assured that we were not moving for some little time, I went and had a scrounge round but more particularly to see the trench we had dug the night before the attack and from which, I afterwards heard, the Surreys sprang and captured about 50 Germans. From there I went on to the strong point. It was in an awful mess, blown to pieces and many Germans with it. I fail to understand why they did not wipe us out the night we dug the trench. We were right on the top of them, they must have heard us. Probably they had had the wind up too badly.

From there I went on to some machine-gun dugouts, magnificently constructed in the side of a bank. In the entrance I found one fellow wounded. He looked fairly scared when he saw me. He was a typical German with hair standing up like barbed wire. He motioned the [sign of the] cross and I gathered he was wounded but I could not find out where. I felt him all over and coming to the conclusion he was more shell shocked than anything, I gave him a drink of water, propped him up outside the dugout and left him for our ambulances to deal with as they scoured the district and made my way inside the dugout.

It was lined on each side with wire bunks and nearly each bunk was occupied by a German, dead. How they came to be there I could not find out. It still remains one of the things I am unable to explain. The dugout was constructed in the side of a rise in the ground so that it had an entrance and an exit in the open bank. The dugout itself was like a huge tunnel lined on each side with wire bunks four deep and practically each bunk had a dead occupant. It was not that which, for the moment, appeared so gruesome as the fact that each one was wearing a gas mask, the chemical container of which gave them the appearance of having a snout, like some animal.

The unoccupied dugouts I found had bedding of sorts and sorting this over, I discovered an automatic revolver which I collared. Passing on along the dugout I made a couple of turns and found myself outside again, having seen enough to make any ordinary man sick. I made my way back to our fellows.

I found them having a breakfast of biscuits and bully and joined in. The wounded are still being brought in and a few Germans rounded up from dugouts in the village. Occasionally the Germans send a few shells over and a few have dropped close, making us get down to the bottom of the trench, but they appear to be fired at random.

It's a gorgeous hot day. We are being relieved tonight and leave the Somme district for good and jolly glad to get away.

In this very successful attack, the 5th Division took 1,500 prisoners including a general and his staff at very few casualties to ourselves.

On our right, in conjunction with the French, we encircled Combles, the French occupying it.

The first day of what later became known as the Battle of Morval – 25–28 September 1916 – was a stunning success when judged against the many other costly failures of the five-month-long Somme campaign. Planned with very specific objectives which were limited to the German front line as it then existed and the villages of Morval, Lesbœufs and Gueudecourt behind, the British guns deluged the German trenches, dugouts and many of their gun batteries on the day before the battle, and were able to provide close and effective support for the infantry when they went over the top at 12.35pm on 25 September with the help of tanks.

The first day of the battle had had a profound effect on Harry; the 5th Division, of which his battalion was a part, had taken all its objectives by mid-afternoon. One member of the division, Alfred Thomas 'Todger' Jones of the 1st Battalion of the Cheshire Regiment, had single-handedly captured scores of prisoners, 102 of which he marched back across no-man's-land to the British lines under shellfire, following up with a lone 'hunting expedition' in no-man's-land tracking down German snipers. He was later awarded the Victoria Cross for his actions that day.

The Battle of the Somme would grind its way on through the drenching rain, the biting cold and the sucking Somme mud into late autumn for another eight weeks, claiming thousands more British, French and German lives. But, unlike many of his comrades, the Somme could not claim Harry.

Friday, 29 September 1916

We lay in the trenches last Tuesday and towards tea-time information came along that the relief had arrived behind us at last and, towards dusk, would come and take over. The weather, which for the last few days had been warm and dry, turned chilly and cold.

At 7pm the Shropshire Light Infantry came along and we handed over and started to make our way to the rear and were very glad to go, hoping the Germans would keep their guns quiet during the proceedings. Troops by this time were arriving in masses and there was some congestion.

We had gone about 100 yards when heavy shrapnel began to come over. We stuck it for some few yards and then made a dive for cover. The ground was congested with troops; those coming in to relieve and those returning from the forward areas. Shells were falling fairly thickly around us and our guns immediately opened fire in reply and for a time it looked as if we were going to get caught in a gun barrage.

With the other fellows, I dropped into the bottom of a trench and took what cover was available. After about three parts of an hour of this, and it seemed like a week with our departure so near, the shelling ceased and we hurried to the rear where we reassembled and marched on and away from the Somme.

We passed through Montauban, left Maricourt on our left and eventually reached our transport lines close to Carnoy at 1am. I breathed many small prayers of thanksgiving that I had come through the Somme offensive alive and without injury. We kipped down in the open: weary, worn and dirty.

Breakfast at 8am. We washed and shaved, for many the first for a week.

Now that it was over we had time to reflect on our losses since our advent into the Somme, of the many good fellows that we had known who had gone west, Sidney Page was amongst them.

Much has been omitted regarding Page. At no time was he in appearance more than a boy and a very thin, anaemic-looking one at that, but perhaps no fellow amongst us played the man better than he did. In his capacity as lance corporal, he had controlled his section by example and his example was of the best tradition. From the time when he was given a stripe until his death, I never knew him flinch from what he conceived to be his duty. No circumstance ever seemed to break his pluck, whatever his thoughts may have been, he rose to them as they came along and no duty he tackled was left undone. We had come to understand him as being of that stuff of which, perhaps, the best type of men are made, or one of the best type, who have sound principles in life and knowing them to be sound cling to them and follow them through thick and thin. No varying of the weather or environment seemed to affect him. He kept an even tenor through it all. His tenacity to his principles in life made him brave and his honesty of purpose was beyond all question.

I saw him killed carrying a message from one trench to another at Falfemont Farm and knew it was because he would not ask another fellow to face the danger. He got back to the support [trenches] with it and in returning to his men was shot through the heart, doing his job as he had always done it, without hesitation whatever the conditions. He died as we had known him to live, always facing the problem in hand. We missed many such as he; officers, NCOs and men.

In the afternoon, we moved further to the rear to an encampment – 'The Citadel' – [between the villages of Fricourt and Bray-sur-Somme] arriving towards evening. The accommodation was insufficient for the whole battalion so we made fires and prepared to sit round them till morning. By night the camp, which is situated on two sides of a valley, looked very picturesque with these fires burning all along the slope.

We were getting fairly comfortable, revelling in the thought of comparative freedom, when suddenly we heard the drone of aeroplanes and orders shouted to put out the fires. We chucked our overcoats on ours and stamped on it. Almost immediately we heard the loud explosions of bombs dropping. Within two minutes, the whole valley was in darkness, the bombs appeared to be uncomfortably close.

It was all over in a couple of minutes but we did not light any more fires. I scrounged round and found a truck and in this I spent the remainder of the night till Thursday morning. I afterwards heard that the bombs fell in the Bedfords' camp next to ours, killing five fellows and wounding about 17 others. Jolly hard lines after going through the Somme.

At 11.30 on Thursday morning [28th], we fell in and marched to Dernancourt and entrained for an unknown destination. After a slow journey but in gorgeous weather, we reached Longpré. Going along we hung outside the cattle trucks and breathed the air and watched the fields as we passed by. It was a great change again. Some of the fellows were singing for all they were worth.

Longpré. We stayed the night in billets. Kipped down at 2am and woke up this Friday morning to find the gutters running with water. It had evidently started to rain after we kipped down and with every prospect of more to come.

We left Longpré at 1.30pm. Raining hard and from then till seven o'clock tonight we have been continually on the march, with very short intervals for rest, raining more or less the whole time.

We arrived here [Villers-sur-Mareuil – a little way south of Abbeville] soaked with rain and perspiration. It was intended that we should go further on but under the conditions we had had enough; the next village was some miles away and it was still raining. So here I am, billeted for the night in an open barn with plenty of straw and a binder for a backrest, finishing my diary and then to sleep.

Corporal Sidney Page of Balsall Heath, Birmingham, had first come to Harry's attention when the 2nd Birmingham Pals were forming in 1914, and he went on to make a huge impression on Harry during the battalion's service on the Western Front. They were separated on the battalion's roll by just 15 numbers – Harry's was 161, Page's 176 – so they had joined up at roughly the same time.

Sidney Page was one of the 63 men killed on 3 September 1916 at Falfemont Farm and his body was one of the 49 which could not be found at the end of the war. His name is inscribed on the Thiepval Memorial to the Missing on panels recording all those British and South African soldiers who were killed on the Somme between the summer of 1915 and 20 March 1918 and have no known grave. More than 90 per cent of those commemorated on here died between 1 July and 18 November 1916.

This imposing structure – a massive, stepped pyramid of red-brick and stone with intersecting arches flanking a high central arch and the whole supported by 16 piers – was conceived by Sir Edwin Lutyens who also designed the Cenotaph in Whitehall. It was unveiled on 1 August 1932 by Edward, HRH the Prince of Wales.

Saturday, 30 September 1916

I slept lustily in spite of the open barn. Got well buried in the straw and this morning awoke to breakfast at 8am. No orders had arrived and after waiting for some time, I arose and I had a stroll round the village in search of something in the grub line. We cast our eyes upon a duck which appeared to want a home but there was nothing doing. We tried several cottages for eggs and milk or butter. They were all blank, so we returned to the barn and had stew and slept the afternoon.

This evening we went out and collared some apples we saw lying about this morning and are lying now consuming them. It's a glorious evening. The sun has just gone down, leaving all the landscape for a moment wrapped in shades of purple. For a moment it was possible to lose oneself and forget there was a war on. Civilisation seemed real and home just over the road but it was only momentary. More rumours have just come round that we move on again tomorrow.

Monday, 2 October 1916

Rumours current on Saturday were confirmed early yesterday morning by orderlies coming round and waking us up for breakfast and parade. We left the village at 12.30pm and, reaching Abbeville, entrained at 3pm. No destination was given but popular opinion was that we were going to a quiet part of the line to relieve another division with the GOC's promise of a rest still fresh in our memory. We were not in the best frame of mind as we left Abbeville about 5pm, the whole battalion transport entraining.

After a tiring journey in cattle trucks, we arrived at Lillers at 11pm. Hot tea was waiting on the station. We detrained and had a mugful each and moved away at 1pm.

Till now we had no idea where we were bound for. As we moved out of the station, the word was passed along – Béthune – which we reached and passed through at 4am and reached our present billet an hour later as day was breaking. The night had been fine and the conditions had been good for marching. After the first hour, motor buses met us along the road and picked up the halt and lame.

We kipped down on arrival. My billet is a loft over a cow house, plenty of smell but this did not prevent me from going straight off to sleep and sleeping soundly till 11 o'clock this morning. It was raining hard and has continued to do so all day. We leave here tomorrow for nearer the line.

We wonder what new experience we shall encounter here. We hear that there are no trenches but that huge breastworks form the front line. At any rate they will not be worse than the Somme, although villages with nasty-sounding names are situated in this part, Festubert, Givenchy, Neuve Chapelle, la Bassée, all scenes of former hard fighting.

Over a decade later, having put time and distance between him and his experiences on the Somme, Harry felt able to reflect on the battle in broader terms. His diary entries at the time – 'the side who will win is the one who can supply the last man' – recognise the attritional nature of the fighting. Interestingly, he also seems to conclude that despite the horrors he and his comrades faced on the battlefield, the twin pillars of duty and honour which had driven so many to join up in 1914 had brought out the best in some of them, raising them above the slaughter, the squalor, the death and destruction to find a higher purpose they would not have known in civilian life: 'The Somme battles as a whole from our nation's point of view were a failure, although not an inglorious one. Bravery is not a commodity of any one nation, although it may be apparent in some nations more than in others, but it cannot be said that the Germans were lacking in that respect when it is remembered that, invariably when men and guns are pitted against each other, the guns win.

'Even so, we had failed largely in our object.

'It was not entirely due to the resistance of the Germans, although we never underrated their qualities. It seemed during this period of the Somme as if the heavens themselves were against us and on nearly all the occasions when we made any attempt to go forward the sky would open and pour on us a deluge of rain to

damp our ardour, so that when a battle opened, we generally went forward literally soaked to the skin. We invariably reached the firing line exhausted.

'This was not all that the wet summer caused in the way of delay. The wet, gloomy days did not allow for observation so that our aeroplanes could get the information that was so relied upon. Under cover of the haze, the Germans were able to dig trench after trench so that they had always something to fall back on and we could never get to their last line of defence to break through.

'These, generally speaking, were the conditions we were up against and the men that were up against them were what we would probably describe in general terms as the ordinary workman or his like. Not soldiers by profession, it sometimes did seem that at last they had come into their own and, being given a job to do, they knew no failure individually whilst they had strength to carry on. Like us all in varying degrees, they were the children of circumstance and for some, in their civilian lives, their circumstances were not good. Some were cradled in idleness, and that probably seemed the natural life to live but here it all changed.

'Many are the stories one can tell of who was fighting on this front; of the often heroic efforts of some of these men. They became a daily occurrence as the fighting grew hotter but they came and went unrecorded, except in the minds of those who saw them.

'It may be that in the scheme of things many a man, who, ready when the call came, found that after being adrift for so long in life they had reached the shore at last, for they often offered and sometimes gave their life for another.'

FRENCH FLANDERS

October 1916 – January 1917

*'We wonder sometimes why we are left
whilst others come and are gone in no time'*

After two stints on the battlefields of the chalk uplands of the Somme and one at Arras in Artois, Harry was about to serve on his third stretch of the Western Front in the damp and smoky region known as French Flanders, lying between Armentières and the valley of the River Lys to the north and the slag-heaps of the French coalfield around Béthune and la Bassée to the south. Characterised by grimy villages amid low-lying, marshy meadows criss-crossed by thousands of dykes and drainage ditches and unrelieved by any large woods or high ground worth the name, it was, after two years of trench warfare, battered beyond belief. Truly, it was a desolate place in which to wage war.

Although a novel sector for Harry, it was, by late 1916, all too familiar a sector to the British Army. So familiar, in fact, that even Harry could reel off the names of towns and villages which, for the men who had fought in these Flanders fields of 1915, would always have an ominous ring.

In March 1915, the then still relatively small and inexperienced British Army had gone on the offensive for the first time in its own right when it launched an attack against the German line around the village of Neuve Chapelle in an attempt to secure the vital ground of the Aubers Ridge beyond and, in so doing, deny the Germans the advantages of observation whilst at the same time menacing Lille. Preceded by a bombardment the ferocity of which had never before been witnessed at any point on the Western Front, the German line was overrun and, in another two days of heavy fighting, it was driven back 1,000 yards and beyond the village. But Aubers Ridge remained in German hands.

Even whilst fighting for their very existence during the Second Battle of Ypres – 22 April–25 May 1915 – the British were urged on by the French to push again at another point on their front, to coincide with a French effort further south in Artois. Once again, the British objective was the capture of Aubers Ridge. The attack was launched on 9 May 1915. The Battle of Aubers Ridge lasted for just one day. No ground was taken and 11,185 British soldiers became casualties. A week later, the British tried once more. This time the battle lasted for ten days and would become known to history as Festubert, but the results were depressingly similar; heavy losses for no appreciable gain. A smaller-scale attack, in mid-June 1915 at Givenchy, was also a dismal failure.

When all the reckoning had been done, the final 'butcher's bill' of British Empire and Dominions forces for the fighting at Neuve Chapelle, Second Ypres, Aubers Ridge, Festubert and Givenchy amounted to over 100,000 men of which some 21,000–22,000 were killed.

At Festubert, what had been the old British front line came to be known as the OBL and when Harry arrived it was being used as a support position to the firing line. This, then, was the battlefield – a battlefield few visit today – steeped in blood and misery, towards which Harry was marching.

Wednesday, 4 October 1916

We moved up yesterday evening and occupied billets at Festubert and later on we, the Lewis gunners, came on into the line, a guide directing the way.

It was a glorious evening as we marched out of the village. It seemed weird to us to relieve the line in daylight. Before, we had always done it almost on our hands and knees and after dark, hardly daring to whisper and glad when the rotten job was over and here we were, marching along the road and whistling. We soon struck a main trench called Barnton Road and into this we dropped. The floor was in good order; duckboards all along. Underneath, we are told, is anything up to three feet of mud and water.

After we had been walking up the trench some three-parts of a mile, we were somewhat surprised to see cooks boiling water for tea and a little farther on, men walking about apparently in the open and further on still a huge breastwork was erected which apparently went as far as we could see to right and left.

We were greeted by a strong north-country dialect. They told us they were the Yorks and Lancashires, 31st Division and there was no doubt about it by their brogue.

Taking over a machine-gun post here and there along the line, our first enquiries were as to the general conditions. We gathered from their conversation that there was very little shelling but that the Germans were always likely to sling over rifle grenades, trench mortars and *minenwerfers*. We pressed them as to the last time a bombardment with these things took place and found out that about a week ago, they sent over one *minenwerfer*. We were able to smile in a superior kind of way.

We got to business, got our gun in position, found shelters and settled down. Dark had by then come on and we had no further opportunity of seeing our surroundings. During the night a few Very lights went up but otherwise all was quiet.

With the break of day this morning, we were able to take stock of our position. The country around here is very flat and marshy, making ordinary trenches impossible. Instead of trenches we have enormous breastworks erected with bags of dirt, several feet thick at the bottom and about ten feet high. Instead of dugouts we have shelters built of corrugated iron and mostly against the breastworks. These have the great charm of being clean inside and very comfortable.

On our right is Givenchy, in ruins, which we hold and on the left Neuve Chapelle, the Germans holding la Bassée and Lille. The line appears to be very quiet. We did not get a shot over last night nor has anything disturbed the peace today.

It is very novel whilst in the line to get up and walk about and walk for 100 yards with the country we occupy open to view instead of gazing along a trench and seeing nothing but dirt and dirty fellows.

The cooks apparently come up with the battalion and in a line further back, only about 100 yards, cook our meals. It strikes me that the Germans have only to look and must see coils of smoke going into the air and I expect we can see the same in the German lines. What a game circumstances sometimes make of the war.

The division comes in tonight and takes over from the 31st Division.

Blazing the trail by moving up into the line ahead of the rest of his battalion, Harry had bumped into some Yorkshiremen. Although his battalion would actually relieve the 11th Battalion of the East Lancashire Regiment – the famous Accrington Pals – three battalions of the York and Lancaster Regiment were in the same brigade. Raised exclusively in South Yorkshire, the 12th (Sheffield City), 13th (1st Barnsley Pals) and the 14th (2nd Barnsley Pals) had initially been made up entirely of Kitchener volunteers, just like Harry. The assaulting battalions of the 31st Division had literally been smashed to pieces on the opening day of the Somme offensive on 1 July 1916, suffering some 3,600 casualties of which 1,349 had been killed. By nightfall on that first day some units – with almost every officer and most of the men who had gone into the attack becoming casualties – had practically ceased to exist.

Of little further use on the Somme, the Pals of the 31st Division had been sent north almost immediately to what was, by July 1916, a relatively quiet sector in order to recover and refit. Harry and his battalion were now going to go through the same rebuilding process on a new and unknown front.

The neglect of the intricate drainage system as the farmers had fled the fighting, coupled with almost two years of shelling, had rendered the ground in the Festubert/ Givenchy sector a foul-smelling, ill-drained marshland. Towards Givenchy particularly, localised flooding dictated that there could be no continuous front line, merely a series of unconnected posts – 60–70 yards apart – built up of short stretches of sandbagged breastworks with a few dugouts which the British called 'islands'. With considerable gaps between them and all approaches to them having to be made across the open during the night, these posts were aptly named.

Once ensconced in an 'island', the handful of men which constituted its garrison was effectively trapped for their six-day tour of duty. Apart from taking turns on sentry duty or, in Harry's case, attending to his Lewis gun, there was little else for the men to do except to shelter from the worst of the weather and lie down quietly, sleep, eat, read and write. Given such a humdrum routine, boredom had the potential to become a greater enemy than the German troops opposite.

Thursday, 5 October 1916

The battalion came in last night at 7.30pm, D Company and a platoon of A Company occupying the firing line, the remainder staying in the support line with the cooks. Rain came down during the early part of the night; a wild and unsettled night.

After the Germans and ourselves had paid our tribute to our respective causes in the shape of machine-gun and rifle fire, we made ourselves as comfortable as possible taking turns at sentry an hour at a time.

With our return to stationary warfare organised, sentry duty starts again, watching the night pass gazing over the top into the darkness. Here there is not much fear of attack; if either side wished to move they would first have to cross a swamp. This sureness of security only tends to make the night seem longer.

At dawn we retire to the second line and return again at dusk. This part of the line is under observation from the right. From some high ground occupied by the Germans they can see right into our back areas. Today we have laid in our shelter all day smoking, reading, and sleeping and eating.

This part of the line is very peculiar. Actually it is waterlogged and we hold it by a series of posts called islands. These islands are held mainly by Lewis guns and a few men and we are kept in contact with one another by a patrol whose duty it is to walk up and down and keep in contact with each post all through the night.

Except in parts, the ground is mostly under water where the ground has been dug up to make the breastworks. Over this water trench boards have been placed. It has the advantage that we shall not be short of water for a wash and shave.

Friday, 6 October 1916

Went into the front line again last night at 6pm. Everything very quiet. The front line is occupied on our battalion front with eight Lewis gun posts. We have orders to fire 500 rounds per gun, per night. This we did. The gun on our left would start with a burst of fire, a short interval and the next gun would start and so along the front. It served to pass the night but we had no idea what we were firing at.

The Germans replied, occasionally sending a bullet across. As night wore on, everything quietened down. Only the splash of the patrol could be heard passing to and fro. Daybreak came and with it we retired to the support line and had breakfast. We have our meals in style and every morning get a rasher of freshly cooked bacon and a mug of hot tea.

Today has been very dull, cold and overcast. I have viewed life through very smoked glasses. The tension of the Somme is beginning to wear off and we are experiencing the aftermath. Added to that we all appear full of colds and chills and generally fagged out.

Saturday, 7 October 1916

Everything was very quiet in the line last night after firing our 500 rounds. Everything settling down to an almost uncanny stillness. Frogs croaking in the marshes and rats, of which there is a good supply, squeaking and running about, are the only noises to break the stillness except the patrols as they pass along. The night was very cloudy but dry and as usual I passed every third hour looking over the top and gazing into darkness.

With daybreak I received orders to pack up and return to the transport lines, ready to proceed on a Lewis gun course. Here was a bit of joy. I was not long in packing up and reaching the transport. I reported to the transport officer, found a billet for the time being and then had dinner.

This afternoon I have been down to the baths, there to have a hot bath. I soaked in it and [received] a clean change of underclothing.

Tea-time arrived and with it a disposition to move. A very likely cottage was pointed out to me by one of the transport fellows and to there I adjourned. An hour or so later I emerged feeling very full and comfortable – or uncomfortable. When I paid up I found I had consumed ten eggs and a large dish of chipped spuds but it is an occasion to celebrate.

After this I returned to the transport lines. Here all was bustle, getting rations ready to go up the line. The wagons take them as far up the road as is possible and there are met by parties from the line who carry on unloading the limbers and taking the rations up into the support line where the bacon is handed over to the cooks and the bread and jam to each man.

Tomorrow I leave for Étaples for the Lewis gun course.

Sunday, 8 October 1916

I left the transport lines this morning in time to reach Béthune at 11 o'clock. Here I met other fellows from the division and together we entrained and left the station at 11.30am. Reaching St Pol we detrained and went to a rest camp awaiting a connection. We found units from other divisions had arrived and continued to arrive and we left the camp some 500 strong, the representatives of about 150 different units.

Reaching Étaples at 10pm after a wretched journey – and railway journeys under these war conditions can be wretched – we marched to Paris-Plage [near Le Touquet], a distance of about two miles and one mile from the coast and are now settled down in tents.

I am looking forward to this course. It has the reputation for being really interesting and under good conditions.

Monday, 9 October 1916

We all went on parade this morning and were broken up into small squads, each squad under an instructor. Our fellow seems to know his job in many ways. He started off by trying to put the wind up us. After reciting the virtues of the Lewis gun – which he knew off by heart from constant repetition – he informed us that he had an 'awkward squad' which, by the way we all appeared to be gazing at him, we should soon be in, but by this time we are old soldiers and fully understand the ways of instructors, especially sergeants. So we gazed the more and smiled.

At 2.15pm we were on parade again and got down to the work. This afternoon has certainly been interesting. The instructor is a good fellow; he knows the gun upside down but we are not quite sure whether he has been any further than here to fire it. Parades finish for the day at 4.15pm. Afterwards, tea.

This evening I have been across to the canteen, of which we seem to have a good supply, and after writing home and now my diary, I am turning in for a night's sleep. No sentry duty every third hour, no squeaking rats to keep me company but here I take my tunic, trousers and boots off, roll myself in a blanket and then sleep till morn.

Tuesday, 10 October 1916

Parade at 7.45am. Breakfast eight to nine o'clock. Parade again 9am till 1pm and again 2.15pm–4.15pm, which makes a fairly full day. This evening I have been into Paris-Plage which, in pre-war days, was a very fashionable resort by the sea. I had a good supper and returned to camp 9pm and to bed.

Wednesday, 11 October 1916

Parades today as usual. This evening I have been round the camp. We are situated on sand dunes between Paris-Plage and Le Touquet and the camp has accommodation for some 3,000 fellows. We are complete with canteens, EFC [Expeditionary Force Canteens], YMCA and Church Army. Into these we retire in the evening and get coffee, cakes and short meals of sorts.

It is ideally situated, practically encircled by woods. We have the classes in the open at a trestle table on which the gun is placed and we sit round, the instructor expounding at one end.

Thursday, 12 October 1916

Went into Paris-Plage this evening and walked through the wood – a topping evening for October. In the town I sampled the steak and chips department of a restaurant. Had a bath afterwards at the hotel – it was great to get into a bath again – and then returned to camp.

It is two years ago today that we went into training at Sutton Park in Birmingham. It seems like a lifetime, in another sphere.

Friday, 13 October 1916

Been for a stroll through the woods. They are very pretty. Found a cottage and, round the oven fire, chips, steak and coffee departed.

Our course finishes tomorrow and back we go to the line again, our places to be taken by another contingent of individuals who are making preparations some miles away along the British front, anticipating, as we have realised, a week of repose.

Saturday, 14 October 1916

We were on parade till noon today. The major portion of the morning was spent in the different methods of carrying the gun and operating it in open order under fire.

At 5pm we of the 5th Division moved off for Étaples, a base camp, to await trains. We arrived at 7pm and found the place to be a huge affair of many departments like a town built of huts and tents.

After a lot of searching we found someone who knew something about us and we were put in tents, 20 to a tent. We can keep warm all right; we are like sardines, all feet to the pole. We are not the cheery crowd we were coming down. I think going back has something to do with it. We leave early in the morning, so to sleep.

Sunday, 15 October 1916

We were awakened at 3am and told if we got a move on, we could get tea before starting off. We got a move on. I was one of the first out to get a mug of tea. We left the camp at 4am – a dark, raw, cold morning. The coldness seemed to go through me. One of those periods in the 24 hours of a day when the prospects of travelling in cattle trucks and then towards the line makes life not worth living. I think we all felt very much like that but no one groused. It was part of the life we had come to accept as warfare – one day in heaven and, perhaps, the next day under conditions that would rival hell.

Before entraining, a YMCA motor buffet drew up, providing us with hot coffee, tea and biscuits at a nominal cost. The day broke clear and sunny and it was not till after we had waited about six hours that we moved out of the station and reached Béthune at two o'clock this afternoon. Here we detrained and all splitting up, we went in our various directions. I made my way here, to the transport lines. Passed through Béthune. There were very few people visible, except our military police. On through Essars and reached here 5.30pm.

Have just had tea. They make good tea down here at the transport lines and I stay here the night. Tomorrow I go forward and join the battalion in the line.

Monday, 16 October 1916

Which I did this morning, leaving the transport lines at 9.30am. I reached Givenchy at midday and reported to battalion headquarters, afterwards joining the rest of the machine-gunners.

I had struck unlucky whilst I had been at Paris-Plage, the battalion had been out on rest and I found them making preparations for returning. I joined in the preparations and at 3pm we left the village and relieved the KOSB in the line.

The relief was a gift. In this part of the line, the country being so very flat and swampy, there are no points of any worth for observation. Each side does not know what the other side is doing and due to the general lay of the line, has no interest in finding out.

In daylight we can see what we are doing and everything passes off smoothly.

Tuesday, 17 October 1916

We find ourselves situated on the right of our previous post and somewhat isolated owing to the ground. A distance of 500 yards is held by ourselves and a team of brigade machine-gunners, being kept in contact with one another by the patrol passing to and fro.

We stay here day and night and have no contact with the outer world. We fetch our rations up at night and cook here in the daytime. The way to and fro is under German observation from the edge of a crater on our right [what the British called 'Northern Craters', 500 yards north of Givenchy], only some few yards but quite sufficient for us to stop one (ie, a bullet).

Our cooking utensils are not elaborate. Three-parts of a petrol can is the kettle, the remaining quarter – cut off – is the frying pan. A petrol can with the top off and holes in the side makes a brazier. We found them all that was necessary. This morning, after coming off sentry at 6am I got busy with the brazier. Had the wind up for a short time until the smoke cleared and then put it in the open. To boil the water and cook the rashers of bacon was easy. By 7am I had breakfast ready, called the fellows and we had breakfast and sat round the dying brazier. Dinner of bread and bully and at tea-time another brew of tea.

The day has passed not unpleasantly. We have ample time to read, write and sleep.

Kilby of our team is a humorous chap. Swears that during the night he was awakened by fleas crawling over him as large as beetles. Stuck it till they started to bite. Something is always happening to Kilby. I felt the fleas all right but I couldn't spot mine. They seemed to be all over me. This place swarms with them.

Wednesday, 18 October 1916

On sentry last night 8–10pm, 2–4am. The night cold and stormy. Occasionally a Very light went up from the German lines and we sent one back to let them see we were awake but it soon died down. I fancy the Germans must see, as we do, the absurdity of this stagnation and, having paid tribute to their cause and the night by firing a Very light, box up till breakfast time.

The day has passed very quietly. It has been cold and overcast so we have had the brazier inside the shelter. Kilby is giving way to a quiet song; Fawke is well away in sleep. I fancy he has slept most of the day.

We are living a great life here. Wash and shave every morning and a wash again at night before starting duty for the night.

Thursday, 19 October 1916

Had a wretched time last night. Poured with rain practically the whole time I was on sentry 6pm–8pm and again midnight–2am. When I came off at 2am, the old brazier was going in the shelter. The smell nearly stifled us but it was warm and cheery.

One of the fellows, Arnold, had been brewing and I found a mug of tea waiting, besides a couple of candles were burning. It's like going into the Palace after an hour on the fire-step. It's a side of warfare we have not experienced before and as far as possible we are making the most of it. Nightly, we get a good supply of coke, dry tea, grub and water. We can do what else is required ourselves.

Friday, 20 October 1916

The weather cleared last night. Bright and fine overhead so a patrol was sent out into no-man's-land. I was on sentry at the time and watched them go out. They dropped over the breastwork and went splashing out, they could not help it. They had got about 100 yards and up went a couple of lights from the German lines, followed by bombs and rifle fire. Things were lively for a short time and our fellows returned, leaving one behind. We searched the front for him this morning through glasses but cannot see him lying out anywhere. He has either been captured or is lying in a shell-hole.

Today has been clear and sunny and some strafing with trench mortars has been going on on our right. I suppose we are going to wake up this part of the line with raids and trench mortars.

Although the front around Festubert and Givenchy was seen as a 'quiet' sector, that is not to say that Harry's battalion was indolent. Nightly reconnaissance or fighting patrols – sometimes two per night – consisting of a junior officer and a handful of men, went out into no-man's-land to gather information on the nature of the ground and the condition of the German wire obstacles and trenches.

At exactly the same time that Harry began his first stint of sentry duty in the dark of the evening of 19 October, a fighting patrol of eight men and a Lewis gun team under Second Lieutenant Charles Herbert went out to either capture a German or, as the battalion diary puts it, 'wipe out' one of their patrols. Herbert had only been with the battalion a few weeks and, as he led his men on a crawl through the mire of no-man's-land, they bumped up against a larger German party which challenged them in broken English.

There ensued a short, sharp firefight before the Warwicks scurried back to the safety of their lines. When the roll was called, one man could not be accounted for and he failed to turn up the following day. An NCO volunteered to go out in broad daylight to search for the missing man without success. He did, however, return with a bizarre tale. He had discovered that the Germans had adopted an unusual early warning system, the battalion diary noting his report that 'geese are penned in near the enemy wire to give warning of anyone approaching'.

The missing man from the original patrol turned up six days later, and Harry recorded his tale: 'Said he had lost his bearings and did not know which were our lines. He had wandered about all night and lay in shell-holes in the daytime.

'This was the second occasion on which one of our men had got lost in no-man's-land. The first was at Arras where a sergeant lay out in the open for ten nights. This was explained by the fact that he was wounded and for some time unconscious.

'In this instance that was not the case but is probably explained by the fact that we were new to the line and the man had not yet got his bearings or had not picked out any particular landmark that would differentiate our lines from the German. His opportunity for escape would now be small and he would have to make it at dusk or dawn and then probably both lines would appear to be very much alike. In the daytime he had to lay in a shell-hole for cover and was saturated with mud in consequence. He had lived on his emergency rations which every man carries and at last, driven by hunger, he chanced his luck and was fortunate. He was sent to the transport lines, in the rear areas, and soon recovered.'

Saturday, 21 October 1916

The West Kents had a bombing stint last night. Entering the German lines from the crater end they found it empty but soon found a party of Germans whom they bombed and then came in again.

Bitterly cold all last night: a sharp frost. For me the night passes uneventfully enough whilst on sentry. The only noises I could hear were the frogs and rats, the former croaking and the latter squeaking and running about in all directions but it is not going to be uneventful long if we are going to start raiding and trench mortaring.

Today is bright and clear. We have all spent the day adding our bit of work to the shelter in the shape of replacing broken sandbags, adding extra supports and leaving the place clean. Some of our predecessors have gone to some trouble to print a notice and put it up in the shelter to the effect that if each lot of occupants does a bit, no one will be called upon to do a lot. The scheme is good so we have been doing our share today.

Whilst digging, we came across some of our rifles, broken and rusty. Also a skull buried about a foot down probably belonging to Canadians who fought hard here in the early days of the war in 1915.

Tomorrow we are relieved and go to Gorre for a few days' rest.

Sunday, 22 October 1916

The relief came up this afternoon in the shape of the Jocks and we got safely to the rear. C Company's gunners were not so lucky. Got spotted passing over an exposed few yards and lost a man.

Once on to the main roadway, we were secure from observation and awaited the limbers. They were late in coming but on their arrival we packed up and made for here – Gorre – an hour's march and arrived at 8pm.

We are billeted in the stables, coach houses and outhouses belonging to a huge château. All these places are fitted up with wire beds like ships' bunks and open out on to a courtyard laid with stone. No doubt this place belongs to some French aristocrat. It looks a fine show.

There appears very little to do here. As I write, most of the fellows are getting down to sleep. We found a winter issue of blankets awaiting us. Arnold and Harry Fawke are wrapped up in theirs and are well away. I am following suit.

Only one man of the battalion was recorded as being killed on the day the battalion was relieved. Harry had recorded the death of Private Ernest Rowland Smith, probably shot by a sniper due to a momentary lapse of concentration. Ernest Smith is buried in Brown's Road Military Cemetery, Festubert.

Monday, 23 October 1916

Breakfast 7.30am. We spent the morning cleaning the gun and making up deficiencies.

Tonight we have all been to see the Whizz-Bangs, the divisional concert party, who have set up in the village. It is the first time we have heard them since prior to the Somme. They are an extraordinary good show. Billy Kings, the leading humorist, is a scream in himself. They have employed the time rigging themselves up with new scenery and costumes. A motor lorry is detailed to carry this about from place to place.

Tuesday, 24 October 1916

After parade, the afternoon turned wet and cold so I slept. In the evening the Whizz-Bangs, and then on to a cottage for an egg and chip supper. The cottagers appear to be more wide-awake to the possibilities of making money. The village is very prettily situated and almost encircled by trees; separated from Beuvry by the la Bassée Canal and three miles from Béthune.

Thursday, 26 October 1916

Arnold and myself have been into Béthune. Left here, Gorre, at 3pm and 30 minutes' sharp walk along the la Bassée Canal brought us into the town. It is forbidden to walk about in daylight so we made for a teashop and then stayed till dusk. We had some excellent French pastries and tea.

At dusk we made our way out and had a look round the town. It's a fine show and assumed almost natural conditions except no lights were showing. Most requirements could be bought. We went into a local cinema that was still showing. Afterwards to a café for eggs and chips and back here to Gorre.

All troops had to be clear by nine o'clock and civilians indoors.

Friday, 27 October 1916

To Béthune again this afternoon. Had a look around the cathedral.

Saturday, 28 October 1916

Relieving the KOSB this afternoon at 3pm at the same position we occupied last time and back to the same old shelter. Found things very quiet. At dusk the Germans traversed our breastworks with machine-gun fire and, getting tired of it, soon stopped the game.

I am writing sitting in the shelter waiting for the time to go on sentry, a candle for a light and bags of rats for company, squealing and running all round the place. We appear to be doing tours of duty of six days at a time. Six days in the firing line and then retire to Festubert for six days in support which consists chiefly of doing fatigues all day long with the assurance of a sleep at night. Return again for six days to the firing line and afterwards back to Gorre for six days rest, or what is called rest.

Sunday, 29 October 1916

On sentry last night 10pm–midnight, 4–6am. Nothing occurred to break the stillness. Whilst on sentry I passed the time potting at, with my rifle, anything that presented itself in the shape of a Very light going up or trying to bayonet a rat as it ran by.

The night passed and with it daybreak. My turn to be cook. At 6am I started to stoke up the old brazier, boil the water and cook the bacon. An hour later we were all sat round with a mug of tea and a slice of bread and bacon. That finished, a wash and shave followed. The remainder of the day I have slept and read till tea-time. Got going on the old brazier and soon had a petrol can of tea ready. This is my last duty for the day in the meal line. We have tea through the night but whoever feels inspired makes this. There is always some going for those coming off sentry duty in the night.

Monday, 30 October 1916

One day follows another and scarcely anything happens to break the even trend and monotony of things. Following last night today has been cold and for the most part raining hard. We get our dugout in an awful mess coming in with boots plastered in mud. We would like to take them off but often it is the unlikely thing that happens and it is not worth the risk. So the time has passed as other days, in sleep and reading and waiting for the night.

Tuesday, 31 October 1916

The night came and with it, sentry duty: 8 –10pm, 2– 4am. Round about 3am is a wretched time to be on sentry. It was made more so last night by rain and a cold wind blowing in my face. I wrapped my ground-sheet around me and cuddled up to the side of the traverse for a bit of shelter. No Germans would come across on a night like that. They would have required waders or boats.

I sent over a few bursts of machine-gun fire to let them see we were awake. They must have thought what an idiot I was and hard up for a job.

Arnold relieved me at 4.00am. He came stepping along the trench from the shelter, cussing the Germans and everything else that made him turn out on such a night. I didn't stop to hear all he had to say but got back to the shelter and made the most of the two hours before breakfast.

Today cold and raw. We have spent it in the shelter, the six of us. The brazier has been well stoked. Outside we are over our boot tops in mud and water.

Wednesday, 1 November 1916

All quiet in the line last night and today is the reverse of yesterday. We have had a brilliant sun all day. It makes it a good war.

Most of the morning I was employed on washing and shaving. For the wash I took my shirt off. We all did the same and commenced an offensive of our own on fleas with which we appeared to be swarming. My stomach was raw in parts where I had been scratching. I found my shirt covered with them. So enwrapped have we been all afternoon in this murder that the day seems to have gone in no time. For the moment I certainly seem more comfortable. Tonight we hear that the battalion is sending out a raiding party. It strikes me as being a pretty hopeless job. They will either get bagged and, if they are not jolly careful, drowned – apart from the ever-present possibility of getting shot.

Orders have just been sent along to say that at dusk, a party is going out and we have to cover them with the Lewis guns. Our business in this case was to watch from our sentry posts for any firing from the German lines and reply to it with our machine guns with the object of preventing them from firing, whether they spotted our fellows or not, and to cover the party when they returned.

Thursday, 2 November 1916

The night came on cloudy and showery. We could hear parties of Germans on our right at work. Faintly through the night we could hear a pick as it struck some hard substance. From that we gathered they were working on the mine craters on the right. A very interesting problem of how to get hold of a German prisoner was developed. A prisoner was badly required for identification and information.

During the afternoon we sent over some shells into their barbed wire, breaking it up, making it less of an obstacle and something for the Germans to repair.

At 6.30pm a party went out consisting of about a dozen men, two officers and two Lewis guns and took up a position opposite the gap in the wire made by the artillery and waited. The scheme was that when the Germans came out to repair the damaged wire, the two guns would open fire on them, the dozen men and officers would rush forward and collar a man and bring him in. Their return would be covered by the two guns and we in turn would cover the return of the two Lewis guns in case the Germans attempted a rescue or counter-attack.

On paper the scheme was perfect. In actual operation, it left a lot to be desired. Going out, the machine guns, delicate under the best of conditions, got plastered in mud and would not fire. The machine-gunners, crawling along, dragged the guns behind them, wrapped in ground-sheets. Men and guns were soon plastered in mud and soaked with water.

The Germans came out all right but brought a covering party about twice the size of our own which lay out in front of their men, apparently unconscious that our fellows were within 20 yards of them.

After lying out for three hours on the boggy ground and nearly frozen, our fellows crept silently and stealthily back.

Today bright and sunny, I have been carrying on with the flea hunt, known as 'chatting'. These creatures appear to live in the ground and in wood when they are not living on us. They bite like the dickens. Daylight is going and with it starts our night sentry. Kilby and Fawke have just gone on [duty]. Arnold and I follow them.

Friday, 3 November 1916

The night was clear and warm. Our aeroplanes very busy overhead signalling with coloured lights to someone. It may be part of a scheme to make the Germans think we are going to try and make a move on this front and so keep them from sending reinforcements to the Somme. The lights may mean nothing but the scheme is invariably effective keeping the other side in a state of indecision.

We are hopelessly outdoing the Germans in the aeroplane department. Whilst our front ceaselessly swarms with them patrolling up and down and keeping in touch with our troops all along the line, we seldom see a German plane nowadays. If one does move in sight it keeps at a safe distance behind its own lines and turns and goes further back if ours make a suggestion of going for it.

We were relieved at midday and moved back here, on the east side of Festubert and in reserve. Here my job is road control on the main road which passes through our lines and through the German lines – my special mission: to stop everyone and examine their papers.

There appear to be a few civilians still knocking about living in partly blown down houses; probably spies but we can never catch them.

Saturday, 4 November 1916

Strolled up and down the road last night from 6–8pm and midnight–2am. Not a soul moved in sight the whole time. I kipped down at 2am.

Breakfast this morning. I strolled through Festubert. It is the same as all villages where any fighting has taken place. The roadway is blocked in parts by houses fallen in, blown down by shellfire. Here and there a living room was exposed to view and in some cases a little broken furniture remained. I went in one room and looked in a cupboard. There were books placed probably as they were left when the occupants fled. On the mantelpiece an old clock, broken, and a few broken ornaments and the floor littered with debris from the ceiling. Many of our fellows had been there before me. The whole place looked like what it was, a deserted village fast falling into decay.

I made my way back to my post. Fawke on the roadway was sunning himself and I found Kilby singing. He had just received a parcel. We finished Kilby's parcel this tea-time. It consisted mostly of cake and we all like cake. The day has been bright and warm.

Sunday, 5 November 1916

On patrol last night 10pm–midnight and 4–6am. The night cold and stormy. I got my pipe out. In the distance, like a huge semi-circle, the Very lights were going up from the front lines. They are not entirely satisfactory these night patrols. There is no danger and very small prospects of anything happening and one has plenty of time for reflection.

On the Somme one had no time for reflection. There, one had to act and always be ready to act on the instant. Here, things were reversed. No immediate action has been called for and so one reflects.

Monday, 6 November 1916

Patrol last night 8–10pm, 2–4am. Beastly night: raining the whole time, the roadway filthy.

Today I have been instructing a class in Lewis gunnery; some dozen fellows from the company. In case of casualties any time, they would have an elementary knowledge of the guns and help to form a gun team.

The type of fellow who comes along nowadays does not compare with our original battalion. Some of these fellows are young farm lads; had never seen a rifle before joining up. A machine gun is beyond their comprehension for the moment – it's like talking to wood, but they are willing to learn.

Tuesday, 7 November 1916

Road patrol last night 5–7pm, midnight–2am. Poured again all night. At 2am, when I got to the billet, I found that it had come through the roof on to where I was lying. I am pretty well hardened to anything by now so I laid in it. Rain was dropping on to the other fellows asleep so I had no choice.

Awoke this morning feeling very clammy and damp but as I have felt the same so many times before, once more would make no difference.

Wednesday, 8 November 1916

A repetition of former nights on road patrol. Lewis gun class today. Rain still coming down.

Tomorrow we go back up the line and, as conditions are, we shall probably be more comfortable, at least have a dry shelter. Here we are wet and jolly cold. A bit of bad luck really. Had the weather been good, we could have enjoyed ourselves out here with its comparative freedom and freedom from observation and shellfire.

Thursday, 9 November 1916

Orders were issued late last night to parade at 7am ready to move up the line.

The evening was clear and passed quietly and at 5am we knocked off patrol and relieved the KOSB at 9am in the line and on the right of our previous position. We found a shelter six square feet for six men. No use to us, so we set about building another with sandbags and shovels. We have been sweating all day and have now a respectable addition for half of us.

The position here is on a slight rise on the ground. From it we can see some miles around the district. Some 800 yards in front is the German line and behind that a few battered houses and behind these a village, probably where they go for rest. Behind us lies Festubert, le Plantin and Givenchy in one straggling line and equally battered.

The intermediate country has all run wild, a mangle-wurzle growing here and there the only signs that it was once cultivated.

Trenches have been dug through this rise and we are up to our knees in mud and water, the result of continual hard rain these last few days. Wading along through it reminds me of our Maricourt days.

Kilby has just come in from the fire-step. It appears that whilst taking the gun from the shelter to the gun position, he dropped it in the mud and has had to take it all to pieces and clean it again. He is cussing like the dickens.

Friday, 10 November 1916

Our life here grows very monotonous. Tours of six days' duty, each following on with nothing exciting happening, either in the line or out. Last night passed as all the other nights had passed; I taking it in turn to do our sentry then back to the shelter to sleep, to wake again in the morning and wait for the night for it to start again. It is all very wearying but it shines when we compare it with the Somme.

The mud here has silenced Kilby. Even he has not much to say but is sat in the corner of the shack scraping his clothes. He appears lost in thought.

Saturday, 11 November 1916

Night passed again. I was awakened early this morning by the rats. Already they are swarming in our new shack like rabbits; quite tame. We shoo them off and we can hear them go pattering away only to return again and, if we are asleep, run all over us.

To counteract the mud we have a good supply of coke to keep us dry and warm. It is a point of honour for anyone awake, day or night, to stoke up and keep it going.

Sunday, 12 November 1916

The Germans were busy last night on our right on the brickfields sector, sending over trench mortars. I watched them go through the air, leaving a trail of sparks behind them as they went. They are easy to follow and easy to dodge providing they do not come over too thickly. Our part of the line seems immune from such things.

Monday, 13 November 1916

Close and muggy today. I am fairly fed up with this. At one time I used to think if only I could sleep for a night uninterruptedly, I could stick everything else. Here we have nothing to do but sleep all day long. I can't sleep today, don't want to. We all seem to be suffering from mental inertia and cold and wet feet.

Wednesday, 15 November 1916, Gorre

The KOSB came up at 10am and we returned back here to Gorre in time for dinner via le Plantin and the la Bassée Canal. Glad to get away for a few days.

Glorious weather today; sunny and dry. We have got our old billets in the château stables. Most of the fellows are in their bunks and, wrapped in their blankets, are asleep.

It is a great sensation after wearing clothes for a period of days – especially boots that are soaked in mud – to take them off and lie down and to feel the warm blood circulating around.

Thursday, 16 November 1916

Breakfast 8am. I have spent the day in common with all the other fellows, scraping and cleaning my clothes. The mud is soaked in and caked on our clothes and our method of cleaning is the only way. Scrape them first with a knife, beat them afterwards with a stick and then brush them. By the time we go back to the line, they are fairly presentable, only to get caked up again and the performance repeated.

Friday, 17 November 1916

Went into Béthune this afternoon and back this evening at 8.30pm. Very cold and a keen wind blowing.

Most of the fellows are asleep, well tucked-up in a couple of excellent blankets and any surplus togs going. Outside our heavy guns are firing.

Saturday, 18 November 1916

Woke up this morning to find snow on the ground – a cold business, washing and shaving.

This afternoon I was innoculated against fever. For this we get 48 hours' rest which means no parades and this evening Arnold, Fawke and myself have walked down to a cottage in the village, the home of refugees from la Bassée, who make excellent café and chipped potatoes. We are constant patrons here whilst out on rest and at the moment of writing we are sat round the fire waiting for a supply.

The frost and snow of this morning has turned to rain. It is coming down heaven's hard at the moment. It's a beastly night.

Sunday, 19 November 1916

Twelve months ago to the day we landed in France and, with the exception of the transport men and headquarters staff, only a handful of the old original men remain. Most of the absentees lie buried around Arras, Maricourt, Longueval and Delville Wood and Morval. Some have returned to England wounded.

The battalion as a Pals battalion was badly shaken on 4 June at Arras and practically ceased to exist after our first time up at Delville Wood. Since then drafts of men have come up from time to time but not men of the same stamp. Some of these, before they have hardly known the war, have been killed or wounded and their places being taken by other drafts and so it goes on.

We wonder sometimes why we are left whilst others come and are gone in no time – perhaps in a day or week or month – whilst we few appear like the brook, going on to the end.

Writing after the war, Harry reflected with some weariness on how his experiences were being understood back in Britain: 'Popular conception, or at least that which was published for public consumption at home, of the thoughts of the men in the trenches regarding the danger amongst which they dwelt, was usually erroneous. To read some accounts one might imagine that the men regarded the trenches as a sort of happy hunting ground for adventure. But to those who had experience of the trenches and caught sometimes the wistful and often pensive look of contemplation on a fellow's face and knew from intuition what channel such thoughts were taking, knew also that no great spirit of adventure was here – there was no real opportunity for adventures but a wondering, unexpressed in words, how long it would be before his turn came, as come it must.'

Monday, 20 November 1916

Ward is leaving to take up a commission in the RE tonight and we have a duck supper.

James Walter Ward had become one of Harry's closest companions. Originally a corporal in the 15th Battalion, he was commissioned as a second lieutenant in the Royal Engineers and would eventually be promoted to lieutenant. There is little doubt that Harry would have missed his friendship keenly.

Wednesday, 22 November 1916

We relieved the 14th Royal Warwicks in the line last night on the left of our previous position and in the position we first occupied. We found the shelters insufficient. We appear to have more men. I spent the night, when not on sentry, walking about and trying to keep warm. At daybreak we started building another. It seems as if, at this sort of work, we are rather good. At any rate, we work hard to be comfortable and besides doing other duties during the day we have now a very presentable shack, clean sandbags and with a corrugated iron roof. I am sitting in it now.

Things seem to be livening up along the front. Last night there was a raid from our lines on our left, whilst the Germans were dropping over trench mortars on our right. Division says we have got to keep them on the jump, expecting something to happen. That is all right but divisional headquarters do not have to stop the dirt in the shape of trench mortars that come back.

Day closes very early making night longer and more sentry hours to do.

Thursday, 23 November 1916

Quiet in the line last night and bitterly cold. I came off sentry at 6am hardly able to move, nearly frozen stiff.

At daybreak we had our usual issue of rum. The size of the issue made us jovial for the rest of the morning. It was like manna from heaven falling on a desert. I felt every drop circulating through my body, turning my inside from a frozen mass into a glow of warmth. In this state I lay down in the shelter and slept like a log.

We do not take much notice of dinner time. It consists of bread and bully and can be consumed anytime without preparation so I slept till about three o'clock this afternoon, stretched myself and had a wash and shave and bread and bully.

The Germans appear to be very busy in their lines at nights. Patrols going out report noises like mortar being shovelled. Probably they are constructing a machine-gun emplacement which will have the attention of our artillery when it is completed.

We are all very much concerned about a number of geese they keep over there. Last night when I was on sentry I could hear them quacking. Today we have all heard them but cannot spot where they are. They are probably kept as sentries on some isolated part which they are unable to occupy.

This was a new idea to us although very old in warfare. The ground occupied both by us and the Germans was very little better than swamp land and apparently the Germans had a portion that was probably worse than ours and untenable under any circumstances so they had penned in the locality a group of geese which started to make a clatter when approached. It was a simple but effective method of holding this particular part of the line.

The rum issue which so cheered Harry was a source of comfort for thousands of British soldiers battling the weather as well as the Germans on the Western Front. Dispensed only at the discretion of commanding officers – some units whose COs disapproved of the demon drink went 'dry' – each man was allowed one-eighth of a pint per day. Served undiluted at 80 per cent alcohol by volume, it was potent stuff and, as Harry's observation proved, could work wonders on a soldier frozen stiff and depressed after a night on sentry duty in late November.

It came up to the trenches in earthenware jars stamped 'SRD', and the various theories as to what the letters stand for has become the stuff of First World War myth and legend. Most people believe it was an acronym for 'Service Rum Distilled', although it is actually short for the very dull 'Supply Reserve Depot', which was responsible for issuing, collecting and refilling rum jars and much else besides. Though factually incorrect, the best interpretation came from the soldiers themselves – 'Seldom Reaches Destination'.

Friday, 24 November 1916

The weather is very trying: one day a sharp frost and the next day muggy. It was very muggy last night and the same today and I feel more or less in a feverish state, accelerated by broken sleep. Six days in the line at a stretch is quite long enough.

Everything very quiet in the line: a few star-shells the only signs of visibility at night.

Today we have been working, sandbagging close up to the breastworks. Every few nights we have to put a fresh layer on top owing to the swampy ground. It is continually sinking in.

Saturday, 25 November 1916

We seem to have the 'wind up' lately for some reason. All machine guns along our line have orders to fire 1,000 rounds of ammunition per gun, per night. We interested ourselves doing this last night, some 16 guns firing at intervals. The ammunition costs the country about 16/- [16 shillings] per 100 rounds so it costs approximately £128 per night in cartridges for our little entertainment of making sparks fly from the German barbed wire.

We have to do this every night.

It gives some vague idea, however vague, of the enormous amount of money that must be spent on munitions. Here we are occupying a front of perhaps some 300 yards in length and on what is a very quiet front of the line and firing our guns, which are nothing more than portable machine guns, blowing into the air £128 from this one small arm of warfare alone every night. It takes about 15 minutes to do it.

This morning broke raw and cold, turning later into rain and has continued all day.

At dinnertime the Germans blew up a mine on our right. I felt the ground tremble. I put my head out of the shelter in time to see a huge column of smoke and earth up in the air but I soon poked it back again as huge pieces of dirt came falling around. We cannot understand the Germans mining here; the ground is too sodden to mine. Probably they have got a little dry patch and are teaching their young miners. At any rate, it has served to awaken Kilby from his state of inertia and for the moment he is quite lively and somewhere outside, busy surveying the landscape for a convenient place to put the gun to fire into the crater tonight.

Sunday, 26 November 1916

Kilby carried this out very satisfactorily to himself. Apparently the Germans did not mind. He had no reply from them.

I was on sentry 2–4am and in a brute of a night; bitterly cold, raining and blowing – how those two hours hung. I fired off my quota of the 1,000 rounds, watched the sparks fly from the German wire as the bullets struck it and then covered up the gun and got close to the side of the trench for shelter.

The patrol came along. One of their number had fallen into a shell-hole of water on the way and things were blue. I could hear him cussing as they returned, his wail being eventually obliterated by the wind and rain.

Bitterly cold again today. Our shacks are not proof against this wind. It seems to come from every angle.

Monday, 27 November 1916

This evening we have retired to a line of support trenches called 'Old British Line'. Here I believe we do fatigue work, helping the engineers do something. From my experience with fatigue parties with the engineers we shall at least keep warm.

In reply to our 1,000 rounds per gun, per night, the Germans are getting busy with trench mortars and rifle grenades. They have just sent over a dose. They are wicked things; blowing all the surroundings into the air where they explode and leaving a huge hole. We shall have to repair all this damage.

Tuesday, 28 November 1916

We slept all night and today have been bringing up engineers' materials from the rear to build shacks with.

Tonight the Lewis gunners in general have received a note of congratulations from the division on the accuracy of the machine-gun fire. We are led to believe that information was to hand, via the intelligence department, that a raid on our trenches by the Germans was intended during one of these last nights but was stopped owing to the activity of our machine-gun fire.

Such a thing is quite possible of course. They (the Germans) have recently stopped one of our raids by sending out a large covering party, larger by far than our attacking force, to cover their men whilst they worked, unknown to themselves and it is quite possible the reverse applies, that we stopped a raid by our continued machine-gun fire but as we view no-man's-land – waterlogged – we wonder whether division are leg pulling.

Wednesday, 29 November – Saturday, 2 December 1916

These days spent in the Old British Line can only be treated in a general sense; the work so monotonous, that of hauling from the rear loads of props and corrugated iron and then erecting them for shelters. We have sweated day in and day out, fully realising what we anticipated, that we should keep warm from daybreak to dark, then to retire to our shacks and to sleep. Rain or fine we have had to stick at it so that now on Saturday night, Kilby is reduced to a state of complete prostration and from a corner of our shack has just stated that he does not mind if it snows ink or the Germans come over in hoards he is not moving for anyone. He looks incapable of moving. We are plastered in mud from head to foot and personally, I just feel whacked.

Sunday, 3 December 1916

This morning, we had another sweat with the engineers. Knocking off at midday, we prepared for the front line wondering which is the greater evil; the front line or what we have been doing? We took over from the 14th Royal Warwicks at 4.30pm and had barely settled in when over came a trench mortar and up went a part of our trench. This was followed for the next 15 minutes by a perfect hail of trench mortars and rifle grenades. As many as half a dozen at a time were in the air and directed on the spot we are occupying.

A considerable portion of the line was receiving the same treatment. We have no cover of any sort against these things so we had to dodge from traverse to traverse, dodging backwards and forwards as they fell. It was a brute of a quarter of an hour running from traverse to traverse with our heads in the air, watching them come over and wondering where they were going to drop.

Kilby, of course, is not satisfied. He wants to go back now to the engineers' fatigue and is at the moment somewhere outside helping to build up the breastwork blown in. He and Arnold have just relieved Fawke and myself from sentry and for the next two hours, they do a bit of sentry sandbagging. I hope I am not awake at 2am when he comes off. He will be so irritable.

Monday, 4 December 1916

Bitterly cold, I have slept all day in an honest endeavour to forget it. Before tea, we awoke to the fact that we had no coke and so scrounged around for wood. We found some, soaked in rain and mud and, waiting for dark, induced it to burn with the help of bits of candle. We eventually got it going. It smoked like the dickens and Fawke started to boil the water for tea. For a time things went well until he upset the whole lot over the fire pulling up a cloud of smoke and out went the brazier and our prospective tea gone west. It has put the tin hat on everything.

We are all very cold. Poor old Kilby is past speech. In this part we have a hot drink brought up at 8pm called tea, from the cookhouse, made with petrol water. I have tasted worse stew.

I hear we had casualties last night from the strafing but do not know the fellows.

Tuesday, 5 December 1916

Fairly quiet last night. The tea came along at 8pm and, with it, the issue of rum for this morning. We all in turn looked at the rum and with a single thought to get at it. It is the only thing which gets us off to sleep in the mornings, so we hung it in its accustomed place.

Whilst I was on duty at midnight we set up a strafing of trench mortars on our right to which the Germans replied with the same and rifle grenades added. It seems very senseless and a silly game, taunting one another with no apparent object of gaining anything. I suppose the idea is to keep one another guessing.

Thursday, 7 December 1916

Last night we had a patrol out close to the German lines. After lying there some time they were astonished to hear the Germans cheering and making a dickens of a noise, beating, apparently, tins of some description. I heard the latter whilst on sentry, lights going up all along their line. Our fellows took the first opportunity to return. I helped them in over the breastworks. They had got a dickens of a wind up. They thought for a moment they had been spotted.

This morning at daybreak the reason for all the noise is made clear. We found a notice board stuck in the ground facing our lines informing us that Bucharest has fallen to the Germans, so we trained our Lewis guns on the notice boards and blew them down.

The arrangements for changes of clothes for patrols after they have been out are excellent in this part. After they have been crawling about in front in mud and water for a couple of hours, sometimes up to their knees in water and always lying in 'bogland' they retire to the rear, to le Plantin, where hot baths are waiting and a complete change of clothing throughout and with enough rum inside them to sink a ship, they sleep for the remainder of the night.

Sunday, 10 December 1916, in the cottage at Gorre

Friday night, the 8th, we had another game of hide and seek along the trenches. At 6.30pm we opened with trench mortars on the German lines. Our batteries had orders to fire 600 over before 12.30am so we made ourselves as scarce as possible and waited for the German reply which was not long in coming in the shape of torpedoes, rifle grenades and *minenwerfers*, the latter horrible things and make a hole in the ground large enough to bury a horse and cart easily.

Rifle grenades and trench mortars dropped around us; blew in our parapet and *minenwerfers* blew in Cover Trench.

We repeated our previous operation. With heads turned skywards, watching them as they came over, we dodged from traverse to traverse. This reads as humorous on paper but in actual fact it is something of a strain, caged in as we were along the breastwork which was being aimed at and blown up by these things. To get back was impossible. Not only were they falling at the rear as well but the ground is a mass of shell-holes and full of water so we had to go sideways. All the time they were coming over; sometimes falling at a safe distance and sometimes covering us with dirt after contact with the ground.

We finished dodging after half an hour. We cussed our batteries that started it and hoped the Germans were in a worse mess than ourselves.

Thoroughly exhausted, we helped to get our wounded away, of which there were a few, and started at once to rebuild the breastwork which in places was so blown down as to expose us to view in daylight. Always with one eye in the air, we worked throughout the night till daybreak, sandbagging and clearing away the debris.

The morning broke raw and cold with a thick Scotch mist. I felt chilled to the bone but warmed up after the rum issue. Breakfast came along at 7am. By that time, we had the breastworks in a fair state of repair again. Breakfast finished, I turned in to kip in our shelter and had what sleep was obtainable which is very little. As a rule, the fleas and rats are responsible for an agitated mind.

The mist of the early morning turned into rain with every prospect of being a soaker. The ground is waterlogged and with a grey, dismal sky and after 18 days in the trenches things are not at their best.

I awoke towards three o'clock in the afternoon feeling cold and stiff and awoke Kilby, Fawke and Arnold. We had dinner of bully and bread, cleaned the [Lewis] gun, and made preparations for the night.

At 5pm we were about to 'stand to' when the 14th Royal Warwicks came up and took over the line. Rain was still pouring down as we packed up and made for the rear to 'Estaminet dump'. The limbers were waiting for us. We packed our guns and ammo and waited for the other teams who were not long in arriving. Limbers packed, we marched back to Gorre and arrived about 7pm, soaked in rain.

Billets, blankets and hot tea were waiting for us. The latter we soon despatched. In the billet, a brazier was burning, giving out a warm glow. It was very welcome.

I stripped, hung my clothes up to dry and wrapping myself in blankets, rolled into kip.

A vile night outside; raw and cold and raining hard. I was thankful for the prospects of six days in front of us during which I should not hear that never failing command 'stand to' which every evening signifies a night of weary sentry. With these thoughts in my mind, I went to sleep thankful to do so and forget everything.

This morning breakfast at 8am. I found my clothes in a fair state of dryness and after breakfast dressed. The major part of the morning we have spent in cleaning the gun. That finished, I have made my way round to the cottage where, with a good fire and the prospects of a good dinner of eggs and chips, I am beginning to smile again.

Friday, 15 December 1916

The last six days at Gorre have been very uneventful. The time has been occupied chiefly by parades till dinnertime. During the time, we have had baths – always looked forward to – bringing with it a change of underclothing.

Whilst out on rest, Fawke and I went and saw Rutter, the company captain, about a commission. He promised to put forward our names with a recommendation for that purpose.

At 2.30 this afternoon, we left Gorre and relieved the 14th Royal Warwicks in the line at 4pm. We found them in a bit of a mess. They have been having a warm time during our absence, the parapet and shelters knocked in from whizz-bangs and trench mortars and things generally in a muddle. The rain of the last few days has not improved matters. Mud is everywhere. The remaining shelters, which have any hope of keeping us dry when it rains, are inches thick in mud on the floor and the sides are plastered in the same stuff. The 14th Battalion, which we have just relieved, look as if they have been rolling in it.

Outside it is a villainous night; pitch dark, damp and cold. To get along the trench is a work of art. If one slips off the trench board track, the chances are that one goes into a shell-hole of water or slips up and measures one's length in foul, sticky mud.

9pm. I am sitting on a box in a shelter contemplating the outlook. At 10pm I go on sentry for two hours and again from 4–6am.

Although Harry had been content to serve in the ranks earlier in the war, perhaps the departure of their close companion Ward had spurred both him and his friend Harry Fawke to go in search of officers' pips. Captain Donald Alfred Rutter, who had been with Harry's battalion since the end of the Somme campaign, would doubtless have been sympathetic to Harry's request to be put forward for a commission as an officer, as he had trodden the same path a year earlier.

Originally a corporal in the 7th Battalion of the Norfolk Regiment, he had been in France since the end of May 1915 and had been commissioned as a second lieutenant in the Royal Warwickshire Regiment three months later. When Harry went to see him he was in command of D Company. Rutter survived the war and retired in 1925.

Saturday, 16 December 1916

We spent all available time last night putting up shelters again, trying to keep out the elements. We appear to be fast developing our Maricourt days again, when we principally had to fight the weather. All night long it was bitterly cold with a rawness that literally went right through one. Handling wet sandbags my fingers were dead and numbed by this morning and my feet had very quickly reached this stage early in the night.

With daybreak came rum and with it followed the thaw but our shelters are not in a state of habitation and today we have been scraping the ground inside, trying to get to a dry surface. Kilby is sitting on a box in the corner. He looks very disconsolate about it all.

Kilby could cut a better dash down Regent Street than where he is situated at the moment but he is a great fellow and will rise to it after he has recovered a bit.

Sunday, 17 December 1916

The conditions are beginning to get hold of me a bit. In the line the Germans were quiet last night. Whilst on sentry duty I could hear our fellows just behind me working hard on the shelters and slipping about in the mud, I too take my turn with them when relieved from sentry.

It is impossible to be cheery under these conditions and today I am the reverse. I have a fit of acute depression. I see, or think I see, the uselessness of it all; of these useless bombardments which we give them and they give us in return, with their attendant casualties, causing some fellows awful wounds and suffering and in some cases causing families the loss of their support in peace time. All this with no other object than to keep each side guessing what the other side intends to do.

To those in higher spheres in the army, these passing casualties appear nothing. They know that in the rear, there are drafts ready to take the place of those knocked out and these drafts come with unfailing regularity so that a general has invariably a full or nearly full quota of men to draw upon.

What of us who remain to go through it all? Fortunately, or unfortunately, under the conditions here, we are developing a high state of fever. Arnold, not physically strong, sticks it all like a brick but from his expression and occasional flushed face, one knows what he is feeling like. He is not an exception, he is becoming the rule.

So the day has passed. Tonight we hope to get the shelters something like inhabitable and with a brazier, no doubt we shall perk up.

Monday, 18 December 1916

Last night was cold and foggy. I was on sentry duty 5–7.30pm and midnight–2am, nearly frozen. I could occasionally hear the Germans working in their lines, apparently pumping water from their trenches.

We are still supposed to fire our 1,000 rounds per gun, per night. It's a fearful waste and we seldom carry it out. Most of the time, my fingers are too stiff with cold to pull the trigger.

By daybreak, we had our shelters in a fair state of repair again, but no coke.

Breakfast came along at 7am. We had this and our rum and after the thaw, Kilby, Arnold, Fawke and myself laid down in a row, getting as close together as possible to keep warm. We all must have slept pretty solidly.

I was the first to awake at 3pm. Leaving the others still at it, I got up and washed and shaved, an awful job with cold water in December but it is refreshing and now I am awaiting dusk to go on sentry.

Tea came along at 4.30pm for which the others woke up.

Tuesday, 19 December 1916

The night was bitterly cold. I came off duty at 6.30am. The day broke steely grey and gave a finishing touch to my frozen condition. I was numbed to the core when rum and breakfast came along. We afterwards followed yesterday's experiment of lying together in the shelter but it was not a success today.

Snow began to fall at dinnertime and has continued till early this morning.

With rations tonight has come a bag of coke. This has put new life in us. Fawke is busy at the moment trying to start it going with the help of some candles on the wet wood. There is a dickens of a smoke and smell but there is also the prospect of a fire and for the moment nothing else matters.

Wednesday, 20 December 1916

The night passes as former nights. Taking my turn on sentry, looking out into the night, Very lights were going up along the German line but nothing happened.

This afternoon we have had another strafing. The first one came over – a minnie at 3pm – and there then followed for the next half an hour, a perfect inferno of *minenwerfers*, trench mortars and rifle grenades. As in previous cases we rushed from one place to another and back again. The Germans over the other side must have worked like fury to have fired them so quickly. The air seemed thick with them.

After about half an hour of this it ceased and, as before, as soon as it had finished we set about getting the wounded back to the rear. There were three only in our immediate vicinity. Then we surveyed the line. All our work of the few last nights lay flat in the mud. We had not a shack standing. Corrugated iron that we had been to some trouble to scrounge and brought up here to form a dry roof lay buried bent and battered.

We dragged our equipment and belongings from amongst the debris and it lies stacked in a corner of the fire trench.

Our thoughts are very mixed as we survey the mess. We have worked hard building these shelters, working all through the night and now that we had them finished, they are laid flat again.

Thursday, 21 December 1916

We all 'stood to' last night till 8pm and then started to rebuild the shelters and breastwork. We had nowhere to sit down so find something to work at – it was about the best thing that we could do. We worked all through the night till 6.30 this morning, doing our tour of sentry duty in between.

Working on the shelters was bad enough, handling half-frozen sandbags in the dark, standing on slippery boards or standing in mud, but it was far preferable to sentry duty where one has nothing else to do but stand and look out into the night. Here the conditions allow the thoughts to wander and our thoughts nowadays are not good to contemplate. We see only the wretched mess of it all. That is not to be wondered at. There is nothing in our lives to counteract it.

Today we have a makeshift shack of sorts in which we are all sat. Kilby is asleep, which is as well.

4.30pm. Tea has just been along, not bad stuff and plenty of it. Kilby wakes up for this when he hears it's hot and plenty going. If we are lucky, we shall get another dixie up tonight at 8pm. In the meantime we lie and await the dusk and start sentry again.

The thought of sentry makes me shudder. I am in no frame of mind for it.

Friday, 22 December 1916

Daybreak was cold and grey. It was a fitting surrounding for my thoughts. They were equally as cold and grey.

With the issue of the rum and breakfast, things seemed better and we all kipped down.

At dinnertime, I had orders to come into Givenchy and take over billets for the machine-gunners. Promising our fellows to find them a dry billet, I lost no time in getting away but I had barely moved when over came a minnie. Fancying this might be a forerunner of others, I made my way to the rear along Ware Road [a trench 250 yards or so north of Givenchy] with some speed. I was not mistaken. At 3pm, as on Wednesday, the Germans opened a continuous barrage on our breastworks of minnies, grenades and trench mortars and heavy shells into Cover Trench and the OBL.

I watched the bombardment from the village, jolly thankful that I was not in it and rather sorry for those who were. The line was some three-parts of a mile from where I was standing. Hanging over it all was a haze of smoke, whilst we who watched could hear the repeated thud and crack as the things fell.

I took over the billets from the Yorks and Lancasters and went to meet the teams from the line. They had been unable to leave till dark, owing to yards of the breastworks being blown away.

I met them about 7pm at Barnton Road Trench. Church of our team had been killed and all the men were more or less in a state of collapse. I found Kilby, Arnold and Fawke intact but very much shaken. From them I gathered that the bombardment had been fearfully heavy and the line was fairly flat. Coming down from the firing line in the dark they had been falling into shell-holes and into the mud. They were plastered in mud and soaked from head to foot.

We made our way here. Tea was waiting and we were preparing to take our things off when orders and bombs were issued. We were to sleep in our clothes and equipment and be ready to reinforce the firing line. So here, at 9pm, we are standing or sitting about in the billet and I suppose we shall have to await daybreak before we can start to get ourselves dry.

Twenty-seven-year-old Arthur Percival Church was not one of the original Birmingham Pals but the Royal Warwicks had been his only regiment, although he had no apparent connections with Warwickshire.

Arthur Church is buried in Brown's Road Military Cemetery.

Saturday, 23 December 1916

Daybreak came. Most of us got off to sleep during the night wrapped in blankets. Breakfast at 8am: baths at 10am. This afternoon – cleaning the gun.

All today our artillery has been tanking their lines and posts, repaying with interest what they gave us yesterday. As I write, shells are going over and in the distance we can hear them fall. I suppose we shall get this back in time.

Our billets are stables. They are dry but cold.

Sunday, 24 December 1916

Wild and stormy all day, we have done very little in the shape of work for the most part, lying in the billet asleep.

A big draft has just arrived for the battalion. We are making some preparations for tomorrow. Every billet is having a fire for which we have been scrounging wood and at dark we are lighting up. We have covered up all holes likely to show the light and are risking the rest.

Monday, 25 December 1916

Christmas Day. A very festive day. Breakfast at 8am and after breakfast the mail came up from the transport lines, bringing over parcels. We all seemed to have them, mine from home, and we appear to have been eating all day.

It's a great time when parcels come up. We waited for the limbers to roll up so it was this morning. Nearly the whole battalion was on the roadside and we watched the transport men throw off bag after bag to be sorted out into companies and from companies into platoons. We followed this process this morning till eventually four fellows came staggering into the billet, each dropping a bag of parcels after them and from then onwards as each succeeding fellow got his parcel, there were sounds of tearing cloth and paper to resolve itself in munching as fellows produced cake, fruit and chocolates.

Dinnertime, 12 of us had a bust. Two shoulders of lamb had been produced from somewhere and taken to the only inhabitant in the village; some old dame who was a good cook and had got a room left in her cottage. To there we repaired armed with jack-knives and plates. Givenchy was one of four villages scattered along the main road. Each village could best be described as a pile of ruins. There was not a cottage intact amongst the whole lot. Since 1914 they had been subject to bombardment and in many places the ruins were becoming overgrown with moss and grass. How this old woman preferred to remain under such circumstances of loneliness and desolation it is difficult to imagine. Her house was partly blown down and at any moment, a shell might finish it but she lived on, the only inhabitant.

We sat down on anything we could find in the cottage and finished off the lamb. We had little else but the meat. There are no vegetables in this district.

Returning to billet this afternoon, I slept till tea-time. At dusk we lit the fire and all the evening, we have sat round the old yule log and as I write now, it has nearly burnt out.

Most of the fellows have rolled themselves up in their blankets and are fast asleep. A few, like myself, are writing but we shall not be long before we follow suit.

Tuesday, 26 December 1916

Cold and wet all day. We have done nothing but lie in the billet. This evening we lit up the fire again. It fairly fills the billet with smoke but it is very cheery.

Here, we are early birds. With the night, our thoughts turn to sleep and now, 8pm, most of us are well away in sleep. There is nothing to keep awake for and one is never certain when one will get the next night's sleep.

Wednesday, 27 December 1916
Today I have been back in the line on fatigue. At 3pm a party of us went up and helped to clear up the rubbish from the bombardment. We knocked off at 8pm.

Like ourselves, the fellows in the line are having a very thin time of it. Christmas Day they spent wading about in the filth, trying to get some sort of cover up, always with one eye in the air.

We left them at 8pm and have just got back. We are not allowed to take our boots or puttees off, so getting down to sleep is very easy. We just roll our blankets around us and, with equipment for a pillow, get off.

Thursday, 28 December 1916
Awoke this morning. The day has been very cold and grey. We are not allowed a fire during the day owing to the smoke but with night, everything has been prepared and we light up the fire. A couple of candles melting on the top of the wood soon produce a blaze. We are sat round the fire now, hoping that nothing will disturb our night's rest.

Friday, 29 December 1916
We were relieved this afternoon, the 1st Devons taking over our billets.

I clicked for a fatigue. The battalion left the village by companies, whilst we on fatigue went back to the line and helped with the work of getting the place straight. At 7pm rain was coming down and with every probability of it continuing, we knocked off and made back for Essars where the remainder of the battalion had gone. It has poured all the way back and we arrived here in what is now our usual state, wet and sticky.

Saturday, 30 December 1916, Essars
Here we are able to undress and this morning, my things are passably dry.

Situated close to Béthune, the village is of the usual French type, long and straggling.

Sunday, 31 December 1916
New Year's Eve. Tonight I have been into Béthune to celebrate the New Year's Eve. Béthune looks very weird at night. The streets were filled with troops.

Everyone in the locality seems to have gone in to town for the occasion. The Scots were making the most of things, parading up and down the street and with the help of French wine, obviously happy.

Little slits of light which percolate through the shutters of doors or windows told us which were the cafés. Into one of these, Fawke and I went. It's a work of art getting into these places quickly so that a flood of light does not get into the street. Once inside we sat down to an egg, chip and steak supper. This café, in common with all the others, was crowded with our fellows from different parts of the line. One might have imagined it was a meal before some football match. All was laughter.

We made our way out at 8.55pm, staying to the last moment. Streams of fellows were going in all directions. Here and there a chap told us that he was a Queen of the May or made similar remarks but everything was very orderly. Most of us had a long walk in front of us.

Fawke and I arrived back 10pm. Here most of the fellows were in bed and asleep. A few late birds were still writing. We wish them a Happy New Year and safe return and now, following the majority, to sleep.

Saturday, 13 January 1917

Our tour for rest was originally six days and then back again but the following morning after we came out of the line, men collapsed right and left from various causes; trench fever, frost-bitten feet, colds or temperatures, all arising from the conditions that we have been experiencing, from exposure, mud and cold. For a time the sick parade almost mustered a good proportion of the battalion. Under the circumstances, I think they have decided to prolong the rest, every so often bringing up extra troops from the rear to make up the breach.

Things have been taken very quietly. Parades of sorts up to 12.30pm and then finished for the day. The parades have been mostly things essential; baths, Lewis gun classes, gas helmet drill and so forth. Then in the evenings to Béthune, there to hear the Whizz-Bangs, by now a concert party of some note, installed in the theatre which is quite new and a very fine building. We are able to get a stalls seat for a very few pence and are able to sit in comfort and hear a show equal to the best in London.

Such a place has its effect. It serves to bring us back to civilisation. To our mind the fact is that these conditions that we are experiencing now are only transitory and that if we have the good fortune to live long enough, we shall emerge from them and see our homes again; back to beds and bedrooms, meal tables with tablecloths and attendant cutlery and the small decencies in life which help to make it worth living.

On 6 January, the Germans bombarded Béthune with heavy artillery for a couple of hours. I could hear the shells go roaring past overhead. The following day I went into the town and saw the damage done. Many houses had been wrecked and many killed and wounded and some are still buried. They were still trying to dig them out as I passed.

On the 8th, I was made an acting sergeant with a view to a commission ahead. With me are Kilby and Fawke. Together we were interviewed by the brigadier [Lewis] last Thursday, the 11th, and after a few elementary questions, he signed our papers and this morning, the 13th, we have been interviewed by the divisional general [Stephens] in Béthune.

We found him quite genial. There were a number of fellows for the same purpose and he saw us each separately and afterwards collectively, telling us the duties of an officer. He spoke as it were from a great height but we did not mind. We were all struck with the idea afterwards that, as far as the duties of an officer were concerned in this war, we know far more about them than he knew or was ever likely to know, regarding trench war as affecting junior officers at least.

So now I find myself a sergeant under instruction and awaiting orders to return to England. With me are Kilby and Fawke. We have said goodbye to the Lewis guns and sentry duties on the fire-step and in fact go round with the officers on duty at night. To say we are fit again is far from the truth. In many cases one can still see the flush on the face of a fellow here and there and I know from experience that such fellows will soon be down after a few days in the line with a high fever. Other fellows can break small pieces of skin and flesh from their toes – frost bitten. On the march, these will break out into sores and they will be done.

Under present conditions, we could get fit again in time but tomorrow we go back up the line.

The winter of 1916–1917 was seen as one of the most severe of the war and, according to some, was the coldest witnessed in this region of northern France for a generation.

Sunday, 14 January 1917

We moved out of Essars at 2.30pm, leaving in companies for the trenches.

A beastly day; the roads were ankle deep in mud. As we moved along, a raw cold atmosphere made marching hard graft and we were not in a happy state of mind when we took over the line from the DCLI at about 5.30pm.

The usual blockages occurred in the communication trenches when battalions are being relieved, especially where the means of exit are limited. Here we have only Barnton Road Trench and Ware Road Trench and in Barnton Trench we got fairly jammed, delivering and relieving men meeting halfway and both wanting to get to their destination.

Kilby, Fawke and myself – acting sergeants and understudies – found a shelter in Cover Trench where we have dug ourselves in. We are complete with old brazier and fusty old sandbags but we are dry and soon we shall be warm with a bit of luck. For the three of us, this may be our last tour of duty with the battalion before leaving for England.

Monday, 15 January 1917

Last night, I was fetched up at 1am to prowl around with the officer on duty. The night was bitterly cold. The shell-holes of water and swamp land were all frozen over, upon which lay a thick covering of snow. Black patches here and there showed where some fellows had stepped unwarily and had fallen in a shell-hole. We walked warily ourselves, keeping as close into the breastwork as possible.

Backwards and forwards we walked along the distance of the beat, occasionally stopping at a sentry post, then on to the next and back again. It struck me as being very humorous, being under instruction with an officer only lately out from England whilst I had been through the Somme, Arras and had had a dose like this last year. I think he sees it too. He went out of his way to make himself decent.

We finished at 3am. When I got back to the shelter, I found Kilby had scrounged some rum from somewhere. With this inside me, I slept till this morning.

Tuesday, 16 January 1917

I was on duty last night with an officer from 1am to 3am and our beat lay along a part of the line now entirely submerged in water some three or four feet deep in places, so we decided to crawl along the top of the breastwork. I had a jar of rum strapped to my back for the outpost. We started to crawl along the breastwork. The officer, going first, rubbed the frozen snow off as he crawled along.

I had gone about a dozen yards. I missed my hold on the frozen bags and slithering down the side of the breastworks, fell into no-man's-land into a shell-hole and up to my waist in water. The fact that I was exposed to the Germans did not stop me from scrabbling out quickly and lying flat on the ground. The Germans appeared not to hear me as I lay there for a moment. Nothing happened so I quickly climbed up and on to the breastworks again and, with the jar of rum, joined the officer at the sentry post. Wet right through, I was bitterly cold.

I made my way back over the breastwork, this time making sure of my hold. I dropped down at the first opportunity and made my way back to the shack. Taking my togs off, I wrapped myself in sandbags and my greatcoat and got off to sleep.

Breakfast this morning at 7.30am. My clothes were dry by this dinnertime. I was glad to get into them. I have been feeling at a disadvantage stripped, because one has to move quickly if a shell comes over.

Wednesday, 17 January 1917

On duty last night 1am–3am; bitterly cold and snowing hard. Going along the trench our path was pretty well under water and sentries, a mass of snow. Moving along the trench, we were nearly frozen. The sentries were numbed to the bone.

At 3am we finished. Back in the shack I took my boots off, rubbed my feet with oil, changed my socks and got off to sleep, Kilby taking the next watch.

All day both sides have been quiet. I think we are too busy fighting the elements to think about fighting one another.

At 8pm, Rutter, the company captain, sent for me and read me my marching orders. I leave on the 22nd for England. I found Captain Rutter in his shack, coiled up underneath his greatcoat on some sort of a bed.

Rutter's shack was no better than our own and consisted of sandbags built against the second line of breastworks. Barely high enough to stand upright in, the bed consisted of two boxes upon which succeeding inhabitants in the shape of company commanders had added their quota of rags to help make it soft. The shack was no more than eight feet square. Inside, the sandbags were almost as slimy as they were outside from the moisture which had percolated through. The floor was mud. There was no brazier at that moment.

Outside it was bitterly cold; it was nearly as cold in the shack. The door consisted of an old army blanket hung over the entrance. The sole illumination was a candle. In common with all the shacks, it looked and smelt fusty.

Beside him he had papers scattered about and a candle burning. A couple of junior officers were sitting in a corner. They were all shivering like the dickens with the cold. Sorting his papers out, Rutter, with a smile, read out my instructions and afterwards handed them to me. They read as follows:

OC A Coy

15/161 Pte (a/Sgt) Drinkwater H V will proceed to Transport Lines on evening of 19th inst. & will report at DIV. HQ. 14, Rue Gambetta BÉTHUNE at 8.30 am on following morning for interview with Corps Commander.

Dress for interview, strip belt & side arms.

He must be prompt and must take MT393 with him; this may be had from Orderly Room. He will proceed to England via Boulogne on 22nd January 1917.

17/1/17 G A Wilmot Capt & a/Adj.

The other two officers smiled and so did I. They knew what I was going to, whilst I knew what I was leaving behind. This moment impressed me very much, as such instances are likely to do. It involved the fact that I was going to leave the trenches for a prolonged period of time. I was going to something that would be akin to Arcady compared with the hell we were living in.

The order meant that I was leaving all this and going back to England, somewhere where I could walk and talk with ease, where the order of life would not be reversed, where I should sleep at night and where illumination would not be limited to a single candle, where I should have a proper meal and above all, where there would be no minnies or shells. It was the prospect of the contrast which impressed me and made me smile.

Then, as now, the British Army set great store by its paperwork. The mysterious 'MT393' was nothing more sinister than an application form 'for appointment to a temporary commission in the regular army for the period of the war'. It was specifically designed for men, like Harry, who were then serving in the New Armies, Special Reserve or Territorials and who had not been a cadet in the Officer Training Corps or attended university. In addition to asking for references as to 'good moral character' and a 'good standard of education' MT393 asked a series of mostly mundane questions such as name, address and date of birth, but there were others which were firmly rooted in the age of Empire and Britain's dominant position on the world stage including Question Four which enquired whether the candidate was 'of pure European descent'.

Thursday, 18 January 1917

I did my usual tour last night 1am–3am. The snow is about six inches deep and bitterly cold. The snow serves one useful purpose at least, covering the whole country in a cloth of white, covering up and hiding huge craters, shell-holes and piles of trench rubbish, making a hideous shell-battered area of ground something akin to natural; but it is only passing. Soon it will melt and the locality will be worse than before.

Six days is about the limit of endurance under these conditions. The rum issue is almost doubled, tea – hot – comes up three times a day, dry socks every three days and we rub our feet every morning with whale oil but all these things are almost trivial. To combat the conditions dry socks are no good with wet boots.

Tonight is my last night. I hope the Germans will not shell us. Tomorrow I go down to the transport lines en route for Blighty on Monday 22nd.

Tuesday, 23 January 1917, in rest camp in Boulogne

Night-time. I did my last tour last Thursday night [18th]. Those fellows that I knew I wished goodbye as I moved along the line. Under different circumstances there might have been moments of regret in spite of the conditions but the fellows I knew best had gone and I had no regrets.

The following morning I said goodbye to Fawke and Kilby whom, I expect, will soon follow me and made my way to Gorre to the transport lines, finding a billet for the remaining days. I had no duty to do but scrape and clean myself. I had a bath and clean underclothes.

Monday night I left the transport lines and met Ward in Béthune. Together we adjourned to a hotel for a farewell dinner. We parted late in the evening, he to his billet and I to the station.

We were supposed to leave at midnight. At 1am the Railway Transport Officer told us that the train would not leave till the morning so we spent the remainder of the night in an adjoining YMCA hut.

We eventually left Béthune at 10am on a bitterly cold day. We left in a snow storm and arrived at Boulogne at 6pm after a wretched day in travel. Half the carriage windows were missing and the wind came in and nearly froze us. At Boulogne we found the last boat had sailed for the day and so we have moved up to a camp for the night.

Wednesday, 24 January 1917

We marched down from the camp this morning but it was not till 3pm that we had finally got on board and an hour later we left the harbour for England. And so I crossed the Channel again after being 14 months in France. During that time, I had not missed a day's duty from any cause and had only slept in a bed for one night.

We reached Folkestone about 6pm. A train was waiting and I reached here, home, late at night.

OFFICER CADET

February 1917 – July 1917

'Your men will not take you seriously'

The attrition rate amongst company officers during the first 18 months of the war, and particularly amongst the ranks of junior officers such as second lieutenants and lieutenants, had led to serious concerns in the War Office about officer shortages. With the existing reservoir of candidates who had experienced at least some level of officer training virtually dry by early 1916, the War Office had decided that officer commissions would only be considered in the cases of men who had seen some service in the ranks.

In February 1916, in a move designed explicitly to control and standardise officer training, the War Office began to form Officer Cadet Battalions (OCBs) at various locations around the British Isles and by the end of the year, there were 23 such OCBs, of which 21 were for the infantry, each having a strength of some 500 men and offering a four-month course of officer training.

By that time, with shortages in the numbers of company level officers severely exacerbated by the heavy losses during the Battle of the Somme, the commanding officers of units on the Western Front were being asked to supply suitably qualified non-commissioned officer candidates for officer training. Loath to put the names of their most experienced corporals and sergeants forward and run the risk of losing them to the detriment of their units, some commanding officers either selected able and experienced 'rankers' or jumped at individual requests made by men like Harry and his friends and raised them to 'acting' non-commissioned rank. So it was that Harry left the 15th Royal Warwicks in January 1917 and headed for the 7th OCB at Moore Park, north of Fermoy, in County Cork, the only OCB located in Ireland.

Cork itself was a major army base and headquarters town for large units of the British Army and had played a central role in recruiting for four Irish regiments – the

Royal Munster Fusiliers, the Leinster Regiment, the Connaught Rangers and the Royal Irish Regiment – all of which fought with distinction from the very opening battles of the British Army in Europe and in other theatres such as Gallipoli.

Fermoy – including Kilworth barracks a little further north – also had a long history and tradition as a garrison town and training centre for the British Army, and by the time Harry arrived and was pitched headlong into this new world of officer training at Moore Park in February 1917, complete with a hat with a white hatband, it was probably at its peak in terms of sheer numbers and was teeming with men.

It seems that Harry set aside his daily diary during his busy time at the Officer Cadet Battalion in Ireland, recording his experiences there while on his way back to France to rejoin his regiment.

7th Officer Cadet Battalion, Moore Park, Fermoy, Ireland

I was granted three weeks leave before joining up with a cadet school. My thoughts and impressions of home life after a prolonged period in France in the ranks were in common with those of most fellows so situated.

I rebelled against the necessity of undressing and dressing every night and morning. I felt confined in a bed in a bedroom and wanted the open air. I had got used to the hard ground for sleeping and did not take very kindly to a feather bed but with the mornings came breakfast on plates which had not the remnants of previous meals still adhering to them and tea without grease floating on top. I used a knife and fork again. All these things quickly served to squash my first impressions. Slowly I gained my civilised instincts and appreciated civilised things.

The holiday over, I reported to Budbrooke Barracks, Warwick [the Royal Warwickshire Regimental Depot] and found other fellows like myself awaiting orders to proceed to a cadet school.

By this time there were cadet schools all over England; Oxford, Cambridge, Winchester, Aldershot and so on and from reports, some appeared far better than others. One had no chance of selection but went where one was sent and I was sent to Ireland. I gathered that the school was a good one from a housing point of view but that the discipline was as hard as iron. Other fellows [at Budbrooke] were detailed to the same school and together we left Warwick, travelling via Holyhead and Dublin and reached our school – the 7th Officer Cadet Battalion, Moore Park, Fermoy, County Cork in Ireland. There were a stream of fellows doing the same as myself and together we reported to the orderly room and were allotted to our huts and a place in the school routine.

Our first impressions were not cheery. Arriving at our hut, we found one or two fellows still remaining from the last course. From these, we gathered particulars of the place.

From all accounts, the CO, a Welshman, was a brute of the first order. One slight deviation from the orders of the camp was sufficient to get a fellow turned down and sent back to his regiment. The fellow speaking was a victim. From his account he and another fellow were practising bayonet fighting one day two months previously whilst on field operations, they having nothing else to do. The CO caught them and, apart from taking their names, said nothing else till the last day of the course and then, reminding them of the incident, told them that as they could not take sufficient interest in their work, they could not become efficient officers and so were turned down.

On every hand we heard such stories and could not help but believe that there was something in them to contemplate. The general opinion was that about 50 per cent of the school passed at the end of the course, 25 per cent were given another month and the remaining 25 per cent were assumed to have committed some small offence or were really incapable of taking a commission and were returned to their units. It was two of the last 25 per cent who were remaining and giving in these particulars.

If we had any doubts on the matter they were quickly dispelled. The CO, Colonel Williams, lecturing to us the following morning, said in his general remarks: 'You fellows have come here from France under the impression that you are all going to be given commissions. Let me tell you at once, you are not.'

It was not a happy start for us.

Colonel Williams himself was a hard man; a hard man to himself as well as to those under him. He carried his arm in a sling – the result of a wound in France – and the arm was slowly withering away in consequence of the wound. He was also wounded in the back. He had had two sons killed in the war and his wife had died from shock and we had the result; a man afraid for one moment to relax, lest in that moment he might break down altogether, and who viewed the world as a hard place. He made us the subject of his views. In France he had had the reputation for being a brave man and considerate to those under him.

Under the guidance of this man, the whole school, some 500 cadets, soon got down to work. Three days a week we were on parade from 7.30am till 10.30pm on field operations. Two days were, generally speaking, spent in drill, map reading and topography and so forth. Saturday morning was always a brute. The colonel came round and inspected our huts. Nothing escaped him. He moved things on our shelves to see that everything was dusted, turned down the bed clothes, would move everything under the bed and would inspect minutely every particle of equipment polished and hung up for inspection. We cussed him but admired his persistent industry. On his departure from the hut, the inspection was not over. He sent back to each officer in charge of the hut his observations and, if his observations were not satisfactory, the officer concerned passed them on to us.

Apart from all this, the officer in charge had to keep a daily record of our bearing from every point of view, showing whether we were progressing satisfactorily, down to the minutest detail; well shaved, boots always clean, rifle and equipment spotless and kept so and whether we were always alert and taking an intelligent interest in our work. This was a daily affair sent in to the colonel every night and had a great bearing on our eventual destination.

It began to become a strain and the strain was not long in making itself manifest. Old soldiers in the school refused to submit to what they considered being bullied and applied to be sent back to their units. When this was refused they went out and got drunk and with such a charge against them, the colonel had no difficulty in sending them away.

Our evenings were not wasted. We were given a whole stack of books which we had to study and write reviews on various topics which were in turn inspected and passed, or corrected and returned to be done again.

After six weeks of this, we had a break of three days holiday, to return for another six weeks.

This second period was worse than the first. Even the officers immediately concerned with our training began to feel the effects of this concentrated effort exerted by Colonel Williams. My officer, Captain Patrick, sent from France suffering with shell shock and to the school for a comparative rest, was given two subjects bearing on military training to study and on which he had to lecture to us and be prepared to answer questions. His first lecture was a scream. Shaking like a leaf, he knew little of what he was talking about.

Towards the end of the course, things got very tense. We were examined individually on all the subjects we had been studying and a report sent in to the CO. Any doubtful case, the name was sent into the CO and he would come himself and take the cadet. That was usually the last straw. Sometimes he would come uninvited and, picking out a cadet here and there, would turn him inside out with questions.

He had what appeared to be a pet one and used it on more than one occasion. Coming along to a squad of cadets at drill, he would stop this performance and call some poor unfortunate fellow out and pointing to a fairly large tree, he would say, 'I command you to fell that tree, what are you going to do?'

The fellow, thinking of his drill book, replies something as follows: 'I should detail four men with ropes etc, two men with pegs etc, two men for the saw etc' but long before he had finished the recital Colonel Williams would break in, 'Stuff and nonsense. You and I could fell that tree by ourselves.' He would walk off, presumably highly satisfied but if the fellow had made that suggestion, he would probably have been told that he had not been reading his drill book and it would be remembered at the great day of reckoning.

Taking the company in drill was, generally speaking, the examination we feared most. I was fortunate. A major, the second in command of the school, took me and I passed through.

The next examination was that set for cadets by the War Office. In other schools, this was the deciding factor. Here it was not. Colonel Williams was the deciding factor.

What the result of this was I never knew but I believe I did moderately well.

All these things led up to a climax of which Colonel Williams was the central figure. Three days before the camp broke up we were to know if we were going to be commissioned, retained another month or sent back to units.

During the day, we paraded by platoons and were interviewed separately. My turn came and I went into the room. Facing me was Colonel Williams sitting in an armchair with papers, books and reports spread out in front of him. Sitting each side of him were the two officers concerned with myself.

'Well Drinkwater,' said Colonel Williams, 'your company commander recommends you, your platoon commander recommends you, therefore I shall recommend you to be commissioned but there is one thing that has been noticed.' Here he made a search amongst his reports and papers. 'That you smile whilst on parade in charge of the company. If you do this on parade, your men will not take you seriously,' and he dismissed me.

I left the room considerably more relieved than when I went in, conscious at any rate that I was fully qualified to hold a commission.

That night we celebrated and the following day broke up the camp. Crossing via Dublin and Holyhead, I reached home again for a month's holiday, afterwards reporting to our overseas depot at Parkhurst, Isle of Wight, where I am now staying, and awaiting orders to join a battalion overseas again.

PASSCHENDAELE

August 1917 – November 1917

'Hell made manifest'

By the time Harry was ready to sail once again for France, the third and most ferocious battle to bear the name of the bruised, battered and beleaguered town of Ypres had been raging for three weeks. The British had launched their huge offensive in Flanders on 31 July 1917 with the aim of driving the Germans back once and for all from their commanding positions on a half-moon of high ground and excising the lingering threat to the vital, British-held channel ports of Dunkirk, Calais and Boulogne, just two days' march away. Pegged back to a trench line which formed a rough semi-circle around Ypres to the east and threatened on three sides by the Germans, the British intended to strike out and drive east to capture the Passchendaele Ridge – their first objective – before forging ahead to seize Ostende and Zeebrugge – linked by canal to Bruges. In doing so they would deny the German U-Boat fleet access to the North Sea and thwart the submarine threat which had crippled Allied shipping.

But that was not all. Just as the Somme had become the mass burial ground of thousands of British soldiers, the German army too had bled profusely into the earth of Picardy. Given the enormous German losses, the British reasoned that another major effort at 'Wipers' would finish them off, as the Germans would have to stand and slug it out or risk losing the Channel ports and the vital rail hub of Roulers (Roeselare) 12 miles to the north-east.

So far, however, Third Ypres had not gone to plan. Three weeks into the battle, the British were not even halfway towards the Passchendaele Ridge, which should have been taken early to serve as a jumping-off point for the rest of the offensive. Far from fading away, the Germans had put up a fierce resistance from heavily defended positions studded with numerous ferro-concrete infantry shelters *and machine-gun pillboxes which resisted the attentions of all but the heaviest calibre shells. This, coupled with a period of unseasonably wet weather, which had coincided with the start of the offensive, had slowed the British advance to a snail's pace.*

Arriving back in France, Harry was now poised to enter another great battle; the maelstrom which was the Third Battle of Ypres or Passchendaele as the men came to call it. This time, however, it would be different. As a newly-commissioned officer, Harry had acquired rank and privilege and wore a different uniform from the private soldiers he would command. He had even gained a servant. But with this came responsibility. Raised above the masses of the led he was now expected to lead his men into battle. Now he held men's lives in his hands.

Wednesday, 22 August 1917, Rouen, France

My peace of mind at Parkhurst, Isle of Wight, was very rudely broken about four days ago. I was called to the orderly room and given my marching orders and after three days leave, I sailed across again this morning, landing at Le Havre. We were brought by boat up the Seine, a most glorious river journey.

Tuesday, 4 September 1917

In huts here, we have had a very easy time awaiting our further orders. Amongst all this is movement for war troops constantly coming and going, some from England en route for the front, others coming down from the line and returning to England, always a changing scene.

I had my orders this evening. I am gazetted to the 16th Battalion, the Royal Warwicks, a sister battalion to the 15th in which I have served up to now. It will probably seem very peculiar to go and relieve the old battalion in the line. We are all in the same division, the 5th. I leave here tomorrow with others; officers and men.

Gopsill, another fellow joining the 16th Battalion, and myself go together. I believe we are taking a number of men with us.

Harry's reference to being 'gazetted' was acknowledged as being the means by which all military notifications were officially recorded in the London Gazette, *Britain's official newspaper of record. Until notification appeared in the* London Gazette *no promotions or awards were deemed to be official.*

Harry's elevation to the rank of temporary second lieutenant in the Royal Warwickshire Regiment appeared on page 7439 on 21 July 1917 in a lengthy third supplement to the Gazette of Friday, 20 July 1917. Harry's name is the last in a batch of seven newly-commissioned officer cadets, which also includes the name of John Eustace Gopsill, a man who had served on the Western Front as a sergeant with the 10th Battalion of the Royal Warwicks from 18 July 1915 until being wounded in January 1916.

Friday, 7 September 1917

We paraded at the reinforcement camp in Rouen at 1pm on the 5th, officers and men of all regiments going up the line rejoining regiments. At 4.30pm we moved out of the station. We who were going to the 5th Division were under the impression that we were bound for Béthune and with that idea, five of us, the complement of a carriage, got in a stock of fruit, grub and drinks and settled down for a 24-hour train journey back to the line.

Towards dusk, fed up with reading, I settled down to a sleep and woke up next morning at 6.30am with a bump at Étaples. Here we were told that we had a couple of hours to wait so went to the Officers' Club for breakfast, where those priceless commodities, clean water and soap, are provided.

Breakfast of porridge and bacon and served by English girls of the WAAC and off again at 8.30am. At St Pol we of the 5th Division were hauled out of the train and told to await orders which came along shortly afterwards and we all split up into our various directions to join battalions belonging to the division.

Gopsill and myself set out followed by the men we were taking to the 16th Battalion. Boarding a light railway we were taken across country for some few miles and eventually dumped at a small village that appeared to be up in the air and miles from nowhere. We were given a general direction and told that if we marched on we should eventually find some troops who would again give us some general idea where the 5th Division lay and the 16th Battalion in particular.

The instructions were vague but we set out and after marching some couple of miles, we met some transport belonging to the 5th Division. From these we could get nothing definite but they believed that a battalion of the Warwicks was billeted in an adjoining village.

Leaving Gopsill and the men behind (it was raining hard and we were fairly wet), I set out for the village some two miles ahead and was considerably relieved to find I had hit on the right place and so made my way to the battalion headquarters to report myself and the men left back in the village.

I found the colonel, Lieutenant Colonel [Grahame] Deakin, extremely nice and explained I was the forerunner of other men left in the village behind and if he would give me some transport, I would go back and bring them along. He pressed me to go and have a drink and I was as equally insistent in a humble way that I should go back first with transport and bring back the other fellows, whom I knew were like myself, fairly wet.

He was so insistent that I said 'I do not drink, sir'. It was an unfortunate remark to make in a way and followed me all the time I was in the battalion. In after days, when I had a drink of French wine, I always heard the same remark – 'Drinkwater, you are degenerating: when you joined the battalion you told the colonel that you did not drink'. (The colonel afterwards told me that it was not so much the words as the half pathetic way in which I said them which struck him as being so humorous.)

At any rate our differences were quickly solved by Gopsill himself arriving with the men. In the meantime, he had got reliable information and come on to the village [Grand-Rullecourt].

The men were handed over to the RSM [Regimental Sergeant Major] and together we were introduced to the officers of the battalion, amongst whom I was surprised to meet Stanley Henson. I am impressed with the style of the officers here. As a collection they appear to be an extremely decent lot of fellows from the colonel downwards. Stanley Henson, from his experience with them, is of the same opinion. Stanley Henson and myself had been known to each other from the time that we could first remember.

Although I have been here only a few hours I am feeling very much at home. It might be the fellows or the dinner or the prospects of a night's sleep or it may be that the ordeal that every officer has to go through – that of joining a new battalion – is finished.

Stanley Rawle Henson was a year younger than Harry and, like Harry, he was a Stratford-upon-Avon man. Before the war Stanley and his twin brother Percy had helped their father James run the family farm at Lower Clopton, a hamlet north of the town. With both families being staunch Wesleyan Methodists, the Drinkwaters and Hensons were well known to each other, the Hensons always hosting the annual chapel summer fêtes on their land.

A relative newcomer to the 16th Battalion, Stanley Henson had been commissioned as a second lieutenant from an officer cadet battalion less than a month before Harry, reporting for duty as recently as 6 August 1917.

Although badly wounded, Henson survived the war and returned to Stratford.

Saturday, 8 September 1917

Today I have been able to gather particulars of what has happened since I left the division in January. After la Bassée they went out on rest for a time, there to recuperate and fill up with drafts, to return to the firing line again at 'Oppy Wood' where I believe they have had a very thin time and had only come out on rest the day before yesterday, which explains the difficulty we had in finding them.

We are out of the line for a considerable period of time. This is very fortunate for me, giving me an opportunity to get to know the folk.

I am billeted with [W] Sewell [another relative newcomer who joined on 18 July], a jovial kind of fellow. He speaks well of the battalion, as all the fellows do with whom I have come in contact so far.

My bedroom window (I sleep on the floor) looks out on to the village green, now used for the parking of our transport.

I was awakened early this morning by the clatter of horses as the transport men got busy, taking the horses for exercise or for water. It brings back all the various thoughts and feelings I had during the time I was in the ranks. I find at one moment I am half glad to be back again where things are moving and the next moment, when I hear of the awful slaughter going on up in the line and can fully picture the feelings of those who go through it, I wish I were back in England again and would willingly, if I could do so with a good conscience, be a boot black or crossing sweeper.

Sunday, 9 September 1917

Today I have been posted to C Company. The officer in command, Captain Charles Lacon, has the reputation of being a good sort of chap.

OC: As a newly commissioned officer in the 16th Battalion of the Royal Warwickshire Regiment, Harry was posted to Captain Charles Lacon's company. Harry held his new commander in high regard, remarking that he was '*a fellow whom I came to like... He had no sense of discipline or fear and was universally liked by the men. Like us all... he was a subject for the psychologist. A product of Eton and British Columbia he was educated at the former and had lived a greater part of his life in the latter; discipline to him was irksome.*' (David Griffiths)

Lacon had arrived at the battalion with what Harry called 'something of a halo' following an incident in 1915 when he had calmly taken photographs from the decks of a sinking ship after she had been torpedoed by a German submarine.

The British steamship Falaba, bound for Sierra Leone, was torpedoed in St George's Channel by the German submarine U-28 on 28 March 1915. Fifty-three crew and some 50 passengers, out of the ship's complement of 240, were killed, including one American citizen. The death of Leon C Thrasher, a mining engineer, led some in the US to call for a declaration of war but although diplomatic tensions rose between the US and Germany the situation was resolved before it came to blows.

Charles Lacon's remarkable photographs certainly made a huge impression at home and abroad. The New York Times of 31 March 1915 proclaimed 'PHOTOGRAPHS TAKEN ON SINKING FALABA, Show Havoc Done by Submarine's Torpedo – Englishman Went About, Camera in Hand'. At home the Daily Mirror, to whom Lacon sold his shots, claimed the way the photographs were taken was 'romance in itself'. After the explosion Lacon, it seemed, had calmly helped to lower lifeboats, issue lifebelts, soothe fellow passengers and 'when there was a moment to spare … went about, camera in hand, snapping pictures here and there … oblivious of the danger'.

When, at last, the Falaba had keeled over and her funnels were almost level with the water, Lacon had finally deemed it wise to stop snapping and, wrapping his camera in his mackintosh, had jumped ship. He was in the water for over an hour, clinging to a plank, before the trawler Eileen Emma fished him out. Carefully unwrapping his camera, he found the leather case was ruined but that the camera, and, more importantly, the film, was safe.

In an age when communications were still relatively primitive, the immediacy of these images from an actual 'war zone'– especially of an event as shocking and controversial as this – made them highly prized and Lacon was able to capitalise on his foresight.

Less than two months later a German U-Boat sank the liner Lusitania with the loss of more than 1,000 lives, including more than 120 US citizens.

Given Charles Lacon's track record of serenity under pressure, there was little wonder that Harry had confidence in his new company commander.

Monday, 10 September 1917

The duties are light. Parade this morning 8am–12.30pm.

Felt somewhat strange at first at the reversal of things. Going on parade, I imagined everyone was making a special point of looking at me and I wondered if all my buttons were bright and fastened but I soon recovered and shortly afterwards I was inspecting a platoon like a warrior. It is very amusing to watch the NCOs come and salute me. I remember the first day I joined up in 1914. I saluted an NCO, not knowing better then.

We finished at 12.30pm. Lunch, sleep, tea, dinner has composed the rest of the day and now to bed on the floor. The floor is hard but I sleep very warm and comfortably otherwise.

Monday, 24 September 1917

From the date of the last entry until today we have taken things very easy. New drafts have arrived to make up the casualties. We have spent the time in the mornings as we commenced, drill till 12.30pm; mainly bayonet fighting and practising the attack. I have been given a platoon to command. The platoon sergeant, Sergeant Badger, is a fellow well over six feet high and as well built. He amuses me when he comes towering up over me and salutes. I look gravely back; he has the reputation of being a very good soldier and always struts about as if he were fully aware of it. He knows his job and his place so that his bearing adds to his worth. The men I like. There are one or two old crocks but generally speaking, they should be able to put up a good show if in difficulties.

The afternoons have been spent mostly in sleep, tea and dinner; sometimes bridge afterwards and then to bed. Very pleasant when one reflects that it might be so much worse and that not far away.

This has its finish. Tomorrow we move at dawn 'back to the land'. We don't know where but now that the time for departure has come, my thoughts regarding being glad to be back again here are all gone. The others are very much in the ascendant.

As far as possible all our things are packed up and ready to move – we wonder where we are going to?

Tuesday, 25 September 1917

We left Grand-Rullecourt this morning at daybreak reaching the railhead at 10am. A blistering hot day, we arrived one mass of perspiration. Entraining finished, we moved out again at 11.30am and reached St Omer at 4pm. Here we detrained.

St Omer is one of our main headquarters for the British Army and appeared to be thick with troops, who, as we passed through, appeared to have nothing to do in particular and wanted to look very busy doing it.

We reached here, Serques, after a march of five miles. Many stops occurred on the way to allow streams of traffic to pass. We were glad of the rests. It has been a boiling hot day and every mile seemed like half a dozen with the sun beating down on us.

We reached the village at 7am. The men had plenty of straw and I can boast of a bed and clean sheets which I am about to fall into.

Wednesday, 26 September 1917

This is a very pretty village. We appear to be off the beaten track. No sounds of war in any way penetrate to the village. Looking out of my bedroom window, everything looks very peaceful. We are here awaiting further orders. I do not suppose we shall have long to wait.

Thursday, 27 September 1917

Rumours are very busy. We can get no definite information except that we are for it somewhere, sometime. We have been hanging about all day ready to move off within half an hour.

Friday, 28 September 1917

I was awakened at 6.30am by my servant who told me that the battalion was moving and I had to take on an advance party at once. I tumbled out of bed and into my clothes and went down to the orderly room. A glorious morning; the sun was shining and there was a nip in the air. I was glad to be up and about.

At the orderly room, I found some of the men already waiting. I received my instructions, got the remainder of the men together and at 7.30am we set out for our destination some 15 miles away. The party I was in charge of were the 'halt and lame' belonging to the battalion: fellows with sore feet and so forth.

We started off at a good swing to get warm and then gradually as the day got warmer, cooled down the pace. We passed through St Omer and rested for half an hour at a village just outside. I had had no breakfast so found a café for coffee, roll and butter.

We pushed on again marching; very tiring by now. We had got on to the main roads again and were constantly held up by the streams of traffic, troops, artillery and supply columns going to and fro.

At six o'clock in the evening, we were passed by the brigade. We were now only three miles from our destination so I fell out the men till the brigade had passed.

I had barely started again when in the distance I saw a crowd of staff officers on horseback approaching. As they were preceded by lancers flying Union Jacks, I assumed some 'great gun' was approaching and drew up on the roadside to let them pass.

A few moments later, up rode Sir Douglas Haig [the Commander-in-Chief of the BEF]. He dismounted. I called the men to attention and saluted him. He was very unassuming. After inspecting the men, he enquired after myself; asking who I was and what service I had done. Wishing me 'Good evening', he mounted and rode on, followed by his entourage, whilst we fell in and reached our destination at 7.30pm.

Reporting our arrival to the orderly room, I found the mess room a temporary affair but it provided a meal and I am now turning in to kip. This appears to be only a rest on the way.

We are all under canvas which has been pitched under trees to afford some sort of shelter from air observation.

It did not fall to every man who had served on the Western Front as a private and was in his first few weeks in command of a platoon to meet 'The Chief', a man whose post-war reputation was, and in some quarters still is, much maligned for his prosecution of the war but who was still in command on 11 November 1918 when the Germans signed the Armistice to end the fighting. Harry seems to have been, as he was on many occasions throughout the war, in the right place at the right time.

Saturday, 29 September 1917

There is now no doubt where we are bound. About 12 miles ahead is the Ypres front and it is there we are going. Here we get the aftermath of a night's work up in the line. Convoys of ambulances have been passing during the day, it has almost amounted to a steady stream, whilst in the distance, all last night and today, we have heard terrific gun fire.

We have just been told that we are down for a show somewhere up in the line. I have the feeling again, as I had on that November morning in England in 1915 when we first came over to France. I would do anything I reasonably could to get out of the affair. The contemplation is almost as bad as the actual experiences and they are really brave men who, having experienced bombardments to any degree, can contemplate another without turning a hair.

We are none of us very happy tonight. Some of the fellows have already gone to kip and I am following suit. It is as well to get all the sleep one can.

A large draft has arrived today from England; officers and men. With this added number, we are a fairly strong battalion.

The wet weather that had been hindering the British improved towards the end of September allowing them to embark on a series of what they termed 'bite and hold' operations – advance and bite off a chunk of German-held ground and then hold it at all costs. One such operation, the Battle of the Broodseinde Ridge, was scheduled to begin on 4 October and, judged against other phases of this bitter campaign, it would be hailed as a welcome success. But to the south of the battlefield, about half a mile north of the village of Gheluvelt and the infamous Menin Road, the ruins of the Polderhoek Château and its series of interlocking, pillbox defences, would refuse to yield. Stubborn and painful thorns in the Allied side, the château position would have to be taken if the advance was to continue and Harry and his comrades had been brought north to 'Wipers' to try.

Sunday, 30 September 1917

I was awakened twice during the night by the terrific gunfire. Lying on the floor of the tent, the ground seemed to vibrate with the firing. I was not sorry when this morning came. I scarcely slept all night and with the morning, breakfast. After breakfast we sorted the men out detailed to our company and

I organised the men detailed to my platoon. Sergeant Badger quickly got my flock together; his big form usually towering over the lot of them. All I was left to do was to consent to this or that and the job was done.

This afternoon the officers went over to corps headquarters to study the scheme for the proposed attack. It all looks very formidable. The ground was taped out, German strong points, pillboxes, woods and belts of barbed wire were shown. It was very difficult to raise any enthusiasm over such a proposition.

The staff officers spoke glibly of the affair: how our artillery would smash everything and we should walk over, but those who had had some knew better. There are many slips between the cup and the lip.

We understand that we are the brigade in reserve. It might mean much or little.

We walked back to the camping ground. A little to our right [south] towered the 'Mont de Cats', a huge rise of ground topped by a monastery belonging to the Trappists. It is interesting as marking the limit of the German advance in 1914. In the cemetery many Germans are buried, including a German Prince – Prince Max of Hesse.

We use it now as a Red Cross hospital.

It has been a glorious day, almost tropical sun from morning to night. We have nothing to do now but sit tight and await orders.

Monday, 1 October 1917

We are still awaiting orders.

Tuesday, 2 October 1917, Westoutre

They came early this morning. We fell in and moved off at 11.30am. We crossed the frontier from France into Belgium. It was indicated by a couple of sentry boxes, occupied by soldiers of their respective country.

Tonight we are billeted in the open and have to be cautious not to show lights. German aeroplanes are busy overhead. At intervals we hear explosives in the vicinity, where they are dropping their bombs. Tomorrow we move further up and the next day, right into the line.

Saturday, 13 October 1917

The battalion fell in about 2pm on Wednesday the 3rd. We were all feeling fairly fit. We had had some large drafts and made quite a good show as, with band playing and a good swinging step, we moved out of the village. As we moved towards the line, the roads presented an unusual sight for us. Hung up, like huge festoons from tree to tree, both sides of the road were long lengths of netting or canvas painted to represent part of the landscape. It was like marching in a huge channel, the camouflage stretching up some 15 or 20 feet from the ground.

The closer we got to the line, the more congested became the traffic. A constant stream of motor lorries taking supplies to the line, ammunition columns and artillery passed or re-passed according to their destination.

It was well after tea before we reached our destination – Ridge Wood. It was, as its name implies, a wood running along a ridge, situated close to the village of Dickebusch. The weather was unusually warm and we were able to sit about in comfort.

On arrival, the cooks got busy and soon, sitting along the hedgerow of a field, we were enjoying a cup of excellent tea and awaited events in the shape of orders. These were not long in following us up and dusk found us on the move again. We said goodbye to the transport as we passed them and moved away in platoons at 50 yards interval. It is necessary, when a large body of men are on the move close to the line, to march in small numbers so that a bombing attack from the air has not the same result should a bomb drop amongst them.

I wished Charles Lacon, the company captain and 'Nappy' Harwood goodnight as we moved away, they staying behind. Now that the casualties are so heavy, each company leaves behind a percentage of officers and men to form a new company if those in the firing line get wiped out. Charles Lacon and Harwood were staying behind this tour.

Two officers with the surname Harwood were serving with the battalion at the time – Second Lieutenant Arnold Harwood, who sometimes filled in as acting adjutant, and Lieutenant Maurice Harwood. Given that Arnold Harwood had performed the role of adjutant – the CO's right-hand man for all things administrative – it is highly likely he would have been the one left behind as part of the nucleus of officers.

Utter desolation: The appalling conditions on the battlefield after the fighting for the Broodseinde Ridge on 4 October 1917 during the Third Battle of Ypres – Passchendaele. The mutilated tree stumps screen a German concrete pillbox that withstood the British shelling. Harry was moving up to attack the pillboxes at Polderhoek Château on the day this photograph was taken, across duckboard tracks just like the one in the bottom right corner. (© Imperial War Museums (AUS) 1049)

Darkness came quickly [on the 3rd] so I sent a couple of men forward to keep in touch with those in front. We were constantly being held up by traffic and apart from the fact that we were going to a place called Bedford House, I had no idea of my destination.

After a march of about two miles, we were pulled up and I gathered we had arrived. Troops were thick on the ground and I was told we were on the verge of our reserve line and preparations were being made for another push.

Bedford House, we found, was the ruins of what was once a fine country house, under which some energetic engineers had tunnelled and made a fairly substantial place. This was battalion headquarters. We were billeted in what were once artillery shacks and the men had to lie in the open.

What Harry knew as 'Bedford House' was actually the ruins of the moated Château Rosendal (Kasteel Rozendaal), also known as Château Kerskenshove, which, before the war, had been a grand country mansion set in pleasant wooded parkland south of Ypres on the road to Messines. After the death of Gustaaf de Stuers, the original owner, his second wife Louise Perez had rented the château to a M Janson, a French entrepreneur from Armentières. It was Janson who changed the name from Château de Stuers to Château Rosendal.

After its partial destruction, what was left of its ruins and deep cellars had, by the time Harry arrived in October 1917, been turned into headquarters, billets and medical facilities for the British troops. It is now the site of a large Commonwealth War Graves Commission cemetery containing more than 5,000 graves in several plots, with the moat incorporated into the design. Today all that remains of the original château is a short flight of stone steps and the last vestiges of the brick-built ice house.

We had barely arrived when rain began to pour down. There was no cover for the men so they had to stick it. Most of them tied their ground-sheets together in pairs and by lying close to one another, tried to get a little added shelter and warmth.

We had no orders regarding our movements but understood that a push was being made the following morning and we were in reserve in case help was required. We hoped that such would not be the case and tried to settle down and have a sleep. Evidence of a push was made apparent later at night by our heavy guns firing, intensifying as the night wore on.

Usually when an attack was about to take place, the heavy guns of the attacking side would pour over to the enemy side an almost continuous stream of shells with the object of smashing up barbed-wire machine-gun emplacements, trenches and of course, men. Sometimes an attack would be developed without this bombardment so as to create an element of surprise but this was usually a failure and an intensive bombardment was generally the preliminary to an attack.

I was unable to sleep so got up out of the shack and went across to see how the men were going on. The rain had somewhat abated but there was still a thick drizzle falling. I found my platoon, they were quite happy under the circumstances. Some were walking about with their ground-sheets wrapped round them, whilst some were laid on the ground asleep, no doubt in a pool of water.

I returned to my shack but sleep was impossible. The ground regularly vibrated with the artillery which by now, 2am, was simply pouring out shells into the German lines.

We were anxious for news. An early breakfast came along at 6am but no news of the attack. Towards 10am the first wounded began to arrive. We were situated on the roadside and close to a dressing station and from these we gathered that as far as they knew things had gone well but they, being wounded early on, knew very little and were not anxious to stop and discuss anything. It brought back all my former experiences of the Somme to see the men plastered in mud, clothes cut away here and there according to their wounds. Some were able to walk and made straight for the dressing station, others were being carried. They all had an expression of relief, one of having done their job and now for sleep and something to eat regularly.

Shortly afterwards droves of prisoners began to arrive and then a long procession of motor ambulances bringing in the wounded.

We were able to gather nothing definite except that generally speaking, all the objectives had been taken with the exception of one or two positions which still remained in the Germans' hands. All were agreed that the conditions were terrible. The mud was knee-deep and in parts a morass had formed into which our men had gone and were not seen again. Some bore distinct marks round their waists, bearing out their story showing how far they had sunk in and showing, without exception, the utmost signs of fatigue.

This may seem somewhat strange, yet it was true. It is difficult to explain with certainty the morass but the probable explanation is that a large stream had been dammed somewhere in the German lines and had overflowed and lay in a hollow part of the land. Shells continually dropping into it, this would soon give it the appearance of mud and it was probably into such a place as this that our men had gone. During the Somme, and at night, it was not a frightfully uncommon thing to lose a man when going backwards and forwards to the line and no one having seen him hit, the general inference was drawn that he had fallen into a shell-hole and, too feeble to struggle out, had been submerged in the mud and water and lost to sight.

Under these circumstances, the men were not communicative and we did not press them for news but I had a sense of feeling that we had not been as successful as was hoped. It may have been the lack of definite information or seeing only this long procession of wounded. At any rate, my thoughts were diverted by the arrival of 'bivvy' [bivouac] sheets for our men. I saw that my flock had their share and returned to our headquarters. The colonel had, in the meantime, telephoned through to say that the push had been on a 12-mile front and that we had penetrated about a mile. It had been successful but not outstanding. One wonders how anything could be outstanding under such conditions; our men stuck in mud and shot down like rabbits by machine-gun fire.

After this news, we all felt more reassured and I went over with Walters to tell the men definite news. They had been very busy with their bivvy sheets and were settling down making themselves as comfortable as circumstances would allow.

Hoping our help would not be required, we settled down for the night. Walters, Gopsill, Hutchinson and myself were the officers concerned in charge of platoons, with Captain Byrne, second-in-command of the company, normally in charge on this occasion.

Night came and with it our artillery, still firing all day, it never ceasing day and night, intensifying its fire, shaking the ground and making it impossible to sleep. Before turning in, I went across to my platoon. They seemed happy enough, singing and joking at their condition. Wished Sergeant Badger goodnight and then stayed in the road for a time and watched the artillery fire in the distance.

A brute of a night: pitch dark and drizzling. Hardly a soul about except the sentries patrolling the road and our own sentries in the field adjoining. I did not stay long. Hoping that orders would not come along to move that night, I turned in to sleep or, rather, to lie down.

At noon next day, orders came from battalion headquarters that we had to move up at dusk towards the firing line, dig ourselves in and act as support to the troops occupying the front line. We set out at 5pm in platoons at 100 yards interval. Rain had been coming down all day and although fine at the moment, and with a moon, the ground was muddy and slippery. Our difficulties were added to by the men being heavily laden. Besides their usual equipment, each man was carrying either a pick or a shovel, two extra bandoliers of ammunition, aeroplane flares, bombs, sandbags and so on and so the pace was slow as we picked our way round crump holes full of water, blown-in buildings and old trenches. It was dusk before we had gone far and pitch dark when we reached our guns, which were firing for all they were worth.

Our guns in this part of the Ypres Salient were numerous. The 18-pounders in front were on average only 15 yards apart from axle to axle and guns of all calibres were stretched at short intervals to 800 yards to the rear. It was these rear guns that we were now coming in contact with. And then the game started. Our road lay through batteries of these heavy guns. To speak to the men was impossible. The noise was deafening and the flashes blinding and the ground vibrating with the firing. Through this lot we had to march for three parts of a mile. We had not gone far on the way before a couple of my men lost their nerve and by the flashes of the guns, I saw them dancing about, waving their rifles in the air and making the most hideous noises. It was no time to hold an inquest so I sent them back and hurried on, shells from the German guns making us very uncomfortable at times.

Their case was, so far as I could see, a genuine one of nerves quite gone. The conditions were hellish. We seemed to be situated in a circle of gun flashes, the close proximity of which were blinding for the moment. The noise was terrific and the ground shook with the combined firing of our guns and the explosion of shells as they came over from the Germans – it was hell made manifest.

We eventually cleared our guns for a time and marched straight into a German barrage that they were sending over to find our artillery. At this point, we were in Sanctuary Wood. We came up to the preceding part of the company. A halt was made and we got the men into the nearest cover, some trenches close by. Shells were dropping uncomfortably close to us.

Things were very nervy. Pitch dark night, in a wood, in a district we had not been in before with only maps to guide us to a very indefinite destination, are not things to inspire confidence. Added to this, shells appeared to be falling so close that at any moment, we might get a dose of them. Hutchinson and myself, standing in an exposed position on a corduroy track – a road made of wood piles like railway sleepers and placed closely together – decided to join the men in the trench. This particular track was a well-known landmark to the troops, running from near Hellfire Corner [an important road and rail junction just over a mile east of Ypres along the Menin Road, shelled frequently by the Germans] across the land and through Sanctuary Wood where we were at that moment. We had not left our position more than half a minute when a shell landed on the exact spot. We congratulated one another.

The men lay in the trench, whilst in an adjoining shell-hole the officers held a conference as to the best thing to do. To push forward in face of the barrage seemed madness but we had got a job to do before morning and the night was getting on. To stay seemed equal madness. In parts the wood was on fire, where falling shells had found a dry billet and the fire in turn was exploding dumps of artillery ammunition. Under these circumstances, we decided to push on.

Sergeant Badger got my men together and found that three were missing. Leaving him in charge of the platoon, the CSM and myself searched the shell-holes in the vicinity and eventually came upon them, half-buried and dead, hit by a shell. One of them was my servant, a very good fellow. Pushing a rifle in the ground and a tin hat on top to mark the place, we left them. We could do no more for them and rejoined the company.

Time was beginning to press. We had to dig ourselves in by dawn and had yet to find our position when we got to the locality, which we had not then reached. We got a move on and, tired and a mass of perspiration, we arrived after a fearful journey round craters full of water, over ground one mass of mud and ploughed up by shells, to a part where we were told we had to dig in; A, B, C and D Companies, more or less in line.

It had taken us eight and a half hours to reach the position we were making for, a distance of not more than five miles as the crow flies and probably not so far. By far the greater part of the time had been taken in getting from Sanctuary Wood.

My map showed the German trenches as they were on 30 June and it was now October. In the intermediate time, the ground, already honeycombed with trenches, had been subject to perpetual bombardment from our guns, creating in places swamp land and craters, obliterating sometimes possible landmarks. It was over this land that we made our way. After Sanctuary Wood our only guide was the map and compass.

The men, laden to an unreasonable degree and unable to get a foothold, often slipped into the shell-holes and we would pause to get them out. Sometimes we were lost and another pause would occur whilst we could find our bearings again. To do this, it was necessary to get into a trench so that we could use a torch.

Meanwhile, shells were coming over. From these there was no rest and we had casualties in consequence. To stand motionless in a locality which is being heavily shelled soon tells on one's nerves. It was so in this case, as each pause occurred and shells still continued to come over, the men got restless, scattering in the dark to any cover as shells came whistling through the air, then to be collected again and pushed on. No officer was sure that he had all his men after each successive halt nor was he sure of his direction. The only reliable guide was our compass and it was by this aid that we eventually got somewhere near our position, saturated with perspiration.

We started to dig.

We made pencil marks on our maps before we set out from Bedford House but it is highly improbable that each trench had the relationship of position of one to the other as shown, as in actual fact we never saw the trenches in daylight from above ground.

Time, 1.30am. After getting our bearings, officers, NCOs and men started to dig like blazes. There was no rank nor breathing time; the one who could dig the longest without stopping was the best man. Badger and myself took a pick and shovel and kept time with our platoon. The soil was soft and sandy and as day broke, we were well down and obscure from all observation except aeroplanes. We had done a good night's work and with the coming of day, lay down in the bottom of the trench for food and what sleep we were able to get.

The morning was fine, so after about a couple of hours' sleep, the men got busy in the bottom of the trench, digging deeper down and strengthening the sides. I had no means of communication with the other officers except by climbing out of the trench. As I had no idea of the land and how much we might be under observation if we moved about on top, I remained in the trench and awaited the dusk. By midday, the promise of the morning for a fine day passed and by evening, rain was pouring down. Our shelters, only of ground-sheets stretched over the top of the trench, fell in and the bottom of the trench began to fill with water. Things were not made more comfortable by the Germans dropping shells in our locality.

When dark, I went across to the OC Company, Captain Byrne, to see what information I could get. I gathered nothing from him; he appeared to know very little himself and so I made my way back to my platoon. I gave Hutchinson and Gopsill a call on the way. Like myself, their platoons were dug in and awaiting orders.

With the men, I stood up all that night. The bottom of the trench was mud, slowly filling with water and still the shells kept on coming over. They were probably only chance shells but too close to be comfortable. With daybreak, a new factor presented itself. Our trenches, which were so easy to dig, appeared equally as easy to fill up again. Huge cracks appeared along the sides and as the day progressed, fell away with the weight of rain and into the bottom of the trench, in places blocking up the way.

German aeroplanes came over at intervals and we wondered if we had been spotted, as shells kept on falling in our vicinity with nasty regularity. Night came again and I went across to the other officers but found that they were no better informed than myself. No rations came up. This gave us hopes that we were only here temporarily and that relief in some shape would come at any moment.

Rain continued to come down in torrents and although we kept our clothes fairly dry with our capes, we were well over our boot tops in mud and water and our feet were proportionally wet. The night came and went very much as the night before. We scraped cubbyholes in the side of the trench and sitting in these, tried to get as much sleep as possible. Before turning to a sleep myself, Sergeant Badger and I went along the trench. The men were wonderfully cheery under such conditions – our rations for some reason had been very scarce whilst here, principally biscuits, jam and water. (Afterwards I gathered that rations were sent up each night in double quantities but that the ration parties failed to get through the barrage of shells that the Germans were sending over. Their casualties were such as not to leave any doubt about the problem of getting food to the front line. Later on, several parties of small numbers of men, six or eight, were more successful.)

Some men were asleep in the cubbyholes, hanging their feet in the water. Some were awake chatting and joking to one another. No one had a grouse and everyone frightfully cold and uncomfortable and wet.

Morning came and the day passed. German aeroplanes had been constantly overhead all day and we knew that if not already spotted, we should not remain so for long.

The men's morale was good but we were all wet, wretchedly cold and with no regular supply of food, although we had been considerably helped in that direction by the inclusion in our rations of spirit stoves and tinned vegetables and meat.

The night came again; cold, wet and raining and with the night came the German shells, dropping here and there. They appeared to have no object in view in firing the shells; falling too straggling.

Towards very early morning, about 3am, I went over to the OC D Company and found my own company officer and two or three more, discussing things in general. They appeared to me to be sitting in a trench that was open to the direction from which the shells had been coming. After giving them my views on their position, I moved away to what seemed to me a safer position, some 12 yards away. I had barely got there when a shell lobbed into the middle of them. I hurried back on hearing their shouts and found them in an awful mess. My own officer – Captain Byrne – and another, the D Company captain, were both hit, also Stanley Henson. Stretcher-bearers came along and we quickly bandaged them up and got them out of the way. There were three men besides, one badly hit. We were only able to find parts of the other two; they seemed to have stopped the full force of the shell.

Morning came [on the 8th] and later in the day, orders followed that we had to relieve the firing line that night. As a battalion, we had lost heavily whilst in this position and we were glad of the prospects of getting away from it. The shellfire had by now become intense at intervals.

We left the trenches when it was dark, [Second Lieutenant W] Walters acting as company captain in the place of Captain Byrne. The ground was in a fairly bad state. The shell-holes were deep and full of water, the ground deep in mud and the men heavily laden with picks, shovels and sandbags. We moved slowly and cautiously, winding round shell-holes and trying to find firm parts of ground to walk on. I led the way for my platoon and Badger brought up the rear. Although we had only some 500 yards to travel, it took us some two hours to do it.

I and my platoon were sent slightly to the left in support of D Company who were occupying the front line and we arrived in a perfect salvo of shells. I got my men into a trench which was to be their billet for the time being. They had scarcely settled down when a shell dropped amongst them, killing four. It was a dangerous position, so I moved them closer up to D Company and then got into my headquarters which was a cellar belonging to a lodge, which in turn belonged to a château [Polderhoek Château]. In pre-war days this must have been a charming spot.

The lodge was some 200 yards from the edge of a cluster of trees not sufficiently dense to be called a wood and in the centre of the trees, some 400 yards from the lodge, was the château, situated on a ridge: the view was extensive. The extensive view was now the only thing which remained of its beauty. The château and lodge were in ruins; the intermediate ground pockmarked with shell-holes and cut up with trenches. There was not a tree standing, they had all been blown down by shells.

Harry added later: 'Some years later, I again visited this place. The site of the château is marked by a pile of bricks – all that is left – instead of the avenue of pines and all the elaborate gardens that once existed. Corn would now grow here, for it is ploughed land. The extensive view was all that remained. The rest had been wiped out of existence.'

We held the lodge, the Germans held the château. No actual buildings, except walls, of the lodge or château existed. They had been long since blown down by artillery. It was the cellars in both instances that were occupied. The cellar

I found was occupied by D Company and brigade machine-gunners as their headquarters but the most welcome sight of all was to see a candle burning. I had not had a light for nights past and its glow was very cheery. That its recent occupants were Germans was evident by the amount of German equipment strewn about and the sides of the walls were reinforced by blocks of concrete.

We had reached another stage and wondered what was going to happen next. We were only fit to be taken out of the line at the first opportunity and given a night's sleep and some food. The rations seldom reached us; small parties got through occasionally and it was on these that we relied for sustenance.

I had scarcely been in the cellar a few minutes when such a party arrived, bringing a supply of rations and rum. Under these conditions, I fondly looked for relief but instead had a message at 10pm by runner from Walters, who was acting captain, asking me to go to his headquarters.

Stuffing my pockets with grub and with a bottle of whisky from D Company rations in case he was without food or rum, I returned with the runner taking Sergeant Badger. Rain was pouring down. Our condition was pitiable. My boots were full of mud and had been so for some days and I was fairly wet through, either by rain or perspiration. We were, without exception, all the same.

We followed the runner over what seemed to be about a mile of ground although it was a very short distance. He had to stop every few yards to take his bearings. We found Walters at last. With him was Hutchinson. They were standing up to their knees in mud and water. They had no covering. Their shack – which was a ground-sheet stretched across the top of the trench – had fallen in.

They were both shaking as if they had a bad attack of ague and could scarcely speak from cold. I handed them the whisky and food down into the trench. Their expression of thanks was rather pathetic. With this tonic they recovered somewhat and Walters told me he had operation orders for an attack on the château at dawn.

It was impossible to do anything there. Rain was still coming down hard, so they both climbed out of the trench and back we all went to the cellar and there studied the scheme for the attack, or that part which applied to us. The scheme appeared sound on paper but our condition made success improbable. We wished that those staff officers concerned, somewhere, high up in rank, who had ordered the attack, had undergone the same conditions as ourselves during the past week. There would not then have been this absurd affair.

We heard afterwards that when the brigadier received the orders in the first place, before they were handed on to the battalions concerned, he tried to get it stopped and when told that it must take place, wept, knowing very well the result must be disastrous in our weak condition.

Walters and Hutchinson, having got a good idea of the scheme, returned to their platoons – they never reached them, both were hit [and wounded] by shellfire on the way – whilst Sergeant Badger and myself got our platoon NCOs a few at a time down into the cellar. There we explained the general idea. The whole battalion was attacking the château and two pillboxes, supported by the Norfolks on our left.

One can nearly always admire discipline and always the disciplined self and on this occasion, the latter was very evident. Although the platoon NCOs must have been as conscious as I was of the improbability of the attack being successful, they made no word of comment but studied the scheme, took their orders and then went up the steps and out into the night to their sections. I did admire them. They showed every sign of fatigue but would not express it in words.

Rain was coming down steadily as I moved back with my platoon some 50 yards to the jumping-off line; so were German shells and another of my men went 'west'.

I met W. O. Field, the battalion Intelligence Officer. He told me he had been unable to mark out our position; he had been unable to get any tape. So I took my general direction from the stump of a tree which he had pointed out.

These small attacks had become such highly organised affairs that it was usual, when circumstances permitted, for an officer, under cover of darkness, to creep out and lay long lengths of tape on the ground to indicate the front line of the attacking force so that they could creep straight to their position and finding the tape, know that they were correctly situated.

As each successive Very light went up in the district, so I got a few more of my men in position and quickly had them in line. Other officers were doing the same so I went along to find out who was on my right and left. There was the usual confusion. It was fine overhead now but pitch dark. The men seemed tired and done up and in places were lying down in thick mud. The officers had no clear idea of the men on their right or left or their objective and like myself were trying to find out and get some idea before the attack. I was unable to find Walters anywhere. He appeared to be lost. No one had apparently seen him after he left me at the cellar and I was afraid he had got knocked out on the way back.

I met one or two officers. They were all having casualties from falling shells and the men were very naturally getting nervous. We were going over in two waves, A, B and C Companies supported by D Company with the Norfolks on our left. Our particular objective was the two pillboxes, A Company and the Norfolks dealing with the château. My platoon was in the first wave to go over.

Punctually, at 5.20am, just as day was breaking, the barrage opened on the château and pillboxes. We advanced and in less than two minutes, we were amongst the Germans who were lying out in shell-holes around the pillboxes and château.

Keeping well in line, we received and inflicted casualties but our men were going strong and according to plan, my platoon were keeping their eye on, and making straight for the pillboxes, the Germans running before us as we advanced. I was the left-hand man of my platoon so that I could keep them from straying into the party who were attacking the château. Actually, I was the left-hand man of the attack upon the pillboxes. Although the attack on the château and the pillboxes was one scheme as a whole, the attack on the château was taken from a slightly different angle which left a space of some few hundred yards between myself and their right-hand man. Glancing [right] along the line as we closed up to the pillboxes, I saw my bombers and others crawling on their hands and knees close up, trying to find an opening to drop in bombs.

My platoon machine-gunner, who was advancing with me and slightly to the rear carrying a Lewis gun, was hit in the head and fell down. Hearing him fall, I looked round quickly and quickly back again and saw a German stretched out in a shell-hole. I let fly with my revolver. He was not more than ten yards away but I missed and he got up and bolted towards the pillboxes. I dropped into the shell-hole he had just left.

Pillbox fighting: Two of the pillboxes at Polderhoek Château which Harry's
battalion attacked on 9 October 1917. Taken three years after the war, the top
photograph is a German's-eye view towards the skyline at 'C', which approximates
the jumping-off line from which Harry's platoon advanced, his men moving in
line abreast towards the camera. The fighting that Harry vividly describes took
place around the pillbox that has been marked '1'. The bottom photograph shows
a close-up of the rear entrance of the pillbox that Harry attacked. (David Griffiths)

This was another occasion, one of many, where it seemed that with the average fortune of war, I should have had my career stopped. I was well advanced in front of the men and proclaimed myself an officer by my uniform, which I had not been able to change and one can only explain this incident by saying that, presumably, we surprised the Germans and were on them before they were aware of it and this particular German aimed past me and shot at the machine-gunner as being the most dangerous. He had no time to get in a second shot as I was not more than about a dozen yards away from him and advancing towards him. If this is the logical reasoning, it seems the most logical. It shows this particular German soldier in a high state of efficiency, who could pause to reason under such conditions.

Bullets were flying about in all directions so I stayed a moment. I glanced to the right; saw our men were still crawling up to the pillboxes whilst on the left, our other men, A Company and the Norfolks, appeared to be getting round the château. It all took only a moment and I was up again and going forward. We seemed to be making good headway when, for some unexplained reason, my platoon and the remainder of the battalion on my right began to retire. Glancing to the right again, I found to my consternation that there was not a soul between me and the pillboxes and looking backwards saw them all retiring and 50 yards to my rear. I dropped into a shell-hole and glanced to the left. Our men were still attacking the château so I waited, thinking that perhaps they had retired for good reason and would come back again.

I was within 20 yards of the pillboxes and knowing them to be occupied by Germans, I dodged from shell-hole to shell-hole and lay down beside a fallen tree – out of their line of fire if they spotted me – and waited again. I had a good view of the château being attacked; I was within 100 yards of it.

Before the attack, Lieutenant Gopsill, who joined the battalion with me, had often expressed a very keen desire, which appeared almost an obsession, to see inside the château and apparently had peered at the ruins from all angles. When the actual attack took place, he almost raced on in front of his men, taking cover as it was afforded and made straight for the château and entered it. It is to be assumed that to this, he owed his life. Probably the Germans, seeing him coming on almost alone, allowed him to do so. He was the only one to enter the château, was last seen fighting with his fists and was taken prisoner. Why he should have had this obsession and brave everything to bring it to a consummation was difficult to understand. Apparently in his desire to get there, he left his men without a leader and it was not a sound policy to pursue.

The Germans were putting up a good fight. One German from the top of the ruins was slinging bombs amongst our men. I could see him, but apparently they could not yet [see us]; still our men on the left kept crawling closer, taking cover in shell-holes and behind fallen trees.

I waited some ten minutes for our men on the right to return. They did not do so and seeing Germans emerge from the pillboxes – I was within 30 yards of them – I watched and waited for my opportunity. I bolted over a rise in the ground and, obscured from their view, waited again and then made my way to the rear to try and find my platoon.

On the way back I picked up Crisp with a bullet through the leg. We stopped in a shell-hole and I put a bandage round the wound. It was of no consequence, scarcely bleeding, and together we bound up one or two fellows we saw lying about then made our way back to where we thought our men had retired to and what was our front-line trench. We had nearly reached there when we must have come under observation from the pillboxes. At any rate, a machine gun was turned on us and Crisp joined the 'great majority' with a bullet in the brain (we were walking arm in arm). I dropped down and found Crisp beyond help and, crawling on my stomach, tumbled into the trenches myself, almost on top of Walters who was lying on the top of a couple of dead Germans, with a piece of shell through the chest.

The attack both on the château and on the pillboxes was a failure. Gopsill was the only one to reach the château and then to be taken prisoner. In both cases, we got to within a dozen yards but apparently had not sufficient stamina to push the attack home.

When he was killed on 9 October 1917, Temporary Second Lieutenant Frederick George Crisp, aged 20, and no relation to Ernest Crisp, the first officer to die in Harry's original battalion, had been serving on the Western Front for almost exactly two years. Like Harry he had also joined the army as a private and had been an officer cadet in Bristol. On receiving his commission he had been posted to Harry's battalion on the same day as Stanley Henson.

Crisp was buried where he fell on the battlefield – the spot was marked on a sketch map drawn by Harry – but his grave was destroyed during later fighting and his name is now one of almost 35,000 inscribed on the panels of the Memorial to the Missing at Tyne Cot Cemetery near the village of Passchendaele. He left a widow, Ellen.

I found the remnants of the battalion in charge of a lieutenant as the senior officer and two second lieutenants, both wounded, and the men halfway up to their knees in mud. I waded along the trench and found Sergeant Badger. He had got most of the platoon together. From him I gathered that when the men had got to the pillboxes, they heard the word 'retire' given. They should have known that it did not come from us. The Germans may have shouted it or, what is more probable, our men were too exhausted to carry on. The two officers who should have led them lay somewhere around, wounded.

Leaving them in charge of Badger, I went back along the trench. Sewell had put himself in charge. Hutchinson and Wilks were the only other two officers who had got back and Hutchinson was fairly well hit but carrying on for the time being.

We organised ourselves in case of counter-attack. Alternate men cleaned their rifles whilst the others were ready in case of attack. Slightly wounded men waded up and down the trench, collecting and cleaning ammunition and handing it out to those who were short.

Hutchinson, Wilks and myself divided the line up roughly into three parts and each took command over a part. We had a good field of fire and there was no great emergency so I went back and saw Walters. He looked a 'gonner' and said he felt as such. He had a nasty wound in the chest and was deadly pale. He was lying on a couple of dead Germans to keep him out of the mud. He told me then that he had not actually taken part in the attack. Apparently after leaving me in the cellar last night, or what was really early this morning, he had attempted to make his way back to his headquarters and although it was only a distance of about 500 yards had got lost and was wandering about until daybreak. It was then that he got hit and was found and brought in by our fellows.

The time was now about 8am. Shortly afterwards some Germans came down the opposite slope into the valley. We opened fire as they came down.

Fortunately for us, or themselves, they came no further but occupied some old trenches.

Towards dinner [lunch] time, assuring ourselves that the Germans did not intend to attempt to reach our front line, we took things more easily. The day passed miserably dull and cold, raining at intervals. The men were very exhausted but they set to trying to clear the trench of mud. It was a hopeless task. We were in it up to our knees but it served to keep them occupied.

At night came rations. A good supply of rum was got through and we dished it out to the men. We all warmed up under its influence. Later on, Field, the Intelligence Officer, and [Second Lieutenant] Devine were sent up to reinforce us. We hoped they had come as guides to take us back but apart from the fact that they had orders to join us, they knew nothing about what was likely to happen. So we waited, hoping for relief. At dusk the men got ready to move away and we anxiously watched for relief. We waited all night. Midnight came and no relief.

At 3am we saw a number of men appear from the rear and thought at last relief had arrived but from the officer in charge we gathered that they had not come to relieve us but to reinforce us and we were not being relieved that night. They were a company of the 14th Warwicks with orders to reinforce us and attack again next morning.

Several British battalions had now been broken on the Polderhoek Château position but while the Germans in the cellars and pillboxes hung on, British successes further north could not be exploited. There was nothing for it but to try again and so a further order was issued just before midnight to the effect that Polderhoek Château was to be 'assaulted and captured at all costs' at 2am on 10 October. This time, however – and incredibly, given that it had repeatedly resisted several units attacking simultaneously – the task was handed to just a single battalion of the 14th Royal Warwicks, of which only one company of perhaps 200 men under Captain Herbert Clement, had managed to haul its way forward across the morass in the pitch-black night to Harry and his comrades, now clinging desperately to the string of mud-filled shell-holes which passed for the British front line.

Quite memorable was the meeting and subsequent discussion between Sewell and the captain of the 14th Battalion in the pillbox. We, the remnants of the

16th Battalion, were fit only to be, literally, carried out of the line and given food and sleep. Some of the men could barely stand and yet here were orders brought by a captain who had himself brought a mere handful of men only, to attack the pillboxes again at dawn.

Sewell, with all the eloquence he could muster, pointed out the foolishness and impossibility of again making the attack under these conditions and the 14th Battalion captain, whilst agreeing with all Sewell said, nevertheless had orders to carry out the affair. They sat there in the pillbox; both covered in mud – clothes, hands and face – the one unwilling to let his men be slaughtered, which is what it amounted to, and the other unwilling to disobey orders. They both looked as if they had the responsibility of the war on their shoulders, the hour of early morning helping to this end. At daybreak the captain went along the trench to see the position for a possible excuse consummate with his conscience and was sniped through the head. By some means this second attack was cancelled.

Born in Battersea, south-west London, Herbert Clement had served as a private in the Warwickshire Yeomanry and had been commissioned as an officer in the Royal Warwickshire Regiment on 29 August 1914. When war broke out he was living in Olton, near Birmingham.

Not one of the original officers of the 14th Battalion of the Royal Warwicks – the 1st Birmingham Pals – Clement had nevertheless served in the 17th Reserve Battalion which had supplied reinforcements for the Birmingham battalions. He had crossed to France on 25 May 1916 and by October 1917 was in command of A Company of the 14th.

Herbert Clement was 29, a year older than Harry, when he was shot in the head in the early hours of 10 October 1917. He has no known grave and is remembered today on the Tyne Cot Memorial to the Missing near Passchendaele.

The men were almost ready to shoot themselves or anyone else who came near them as they took their packs off to stick it for another night. However, the reinforcement from the 14th Warwicks took off some of the strain, allowing our men to relax.

Before daybreak another ration party got through, bringing rum, cigarettes and food. They had had an awful time getting through. They said it was impossible to dodge the German barrage and had casualties in consequence. Hutchinson, who was hit, went down with the ration party early in the morning.

Towards dawn [on the 10th] a runner came through from battalion headquarters to say that we were being relieved that night. The men bucked up considerably at this news and we all tried to settle down for the day to await the night and relief. My food for the two preceding days had been a piece of bread on the first and a piece of bread and cheese on the second, on both occasions taken from the dead. The rum, cigarettes and food were issued to the men. The cigarettes were particularly welcome; some of them had not had a smoke for days.

The ration party was followed by a runner from battalion headquarters saying that relief was coming that night for certain. With that news we settled down for the day. The men had for the most part scooped holes in the side of the trench and in these they sat, their legs hanging in the mud.

Devine took Hutchinson's place and, with Wilks, we took alternate hours throughout the day on duty in the trench spending the remainder of the time in the pillbox. To get to the pillbox entrance was difficult. A shallow and dry trench led to it. The trench was not more than two feet deep and led off from our front line. Three of our men were sniped and lay dead in the doorway before we were able to discover that we were being fired at from the pillboxes we had attempted to take, so we had to crawl backwards and forwards on hands and knees.

The day dragged on. The Germans for their part were quiet and we had no desire to disturb them. Half the men's rifles would not fire, they were so choked up with dirt. No Lewis guns were in action, they also were choked. We had one brigade machine gun left and that was minus the tripod. The gunners fired the gun by holding it on the parapet. So we waited for the night to come. Sergeant Badger got ready what remained of my platoon so that when the relief did arrive, we could get quickly away.

Towards 8pm I was on duty. Feeling too dead to wade up and down the trench, I sat in a cubbyhole and dozed like the men not on duty, hanging my feet in the mud. I was awakened by a sentry coming along and reporting that the Germans were using signal lights in the valley so we all prepared for an attack. No attack developed and we were still waiting when the relief arrived.

They reported that the Menin Rue was being very heavily shelled and, as far as they could gather, so was the surrounding district.

I was the only officer left of my company. Getting the men together as best as I could, I told them of the conditions and warned them that if anyone fell out on the way, no help could be given, that we had to go for all we were worth, to stop and help one man might mean half a dozen being hit. So we set out, Devine leading the way and taking with him a company – or the remnants of a company – which had not an officer left.

We had not gone far when the shells came buzzing over. Devine, not sure of the way, was leading us over shell-holes and mud, the men slipping in all directions. Travelling over such ground would have been difficult for fit men. To us it was a form of torture. As we wound round the craters representing half a battalion, we must have presented a pitiable spectacle, a few dozen men and a couple of officers.

Although it was characteristic of the usual return from the firing line where there had been any hard fighting – the men being exhausted – this affair seemed to have more than its fair share of bad luck for us.

To all battalions in the British Army, the pride of regiment is a thing which is strongly cultivated and often strongly upheld by the men. It was so with us. We had what was almost a battle cry: 'Heads up, Warwicks.' We had a bugle call to which we could chant it and we sang it on the march.

To all this, this march back was the contrast, a few dozen men – probably about five or six dozen, no more – representing half a battalion of men (500) staggering back to the camp. No other word could describe it; backs bent from fatigue and covered in mud.

It was a blessing that the night was dark and we could not see one another to any degree of detail. The language was foul and the appearance equal to the language. We left the trenches, the mud of which reached to the vicinity of the knees and stuck like glue, and started to make our way towards camp. No sort of order was kept, in single file we trailed over the land. Sometimes a man would fall into a shell-hole and immediately up would go a wail from him and, being the last man, I paused to pull him out. They barely had the strength to get out themselves and I was not in a much better condition.

Sometimes it was the shells that came screeching over to fall in our vicinity that would send the men scattering or to lie down in the mud to be collected and then to push on again.

Sometimes when returning from an affair of this description, the troops could look back upon something as being well done. Here, we as a battalion had been given a job to do and it had failed and it is highly probable that it had failed for no other reason than that physically we were not in a fit condition to undertake it. There seemed the bad luck for us.

We reached Inverness Copse and then Clapham Junction. The latter was a huge underground dressing station first dug out and used by the Germans as such and now being used by us. We halted for a moment whilst Devine dived down into what appeared to be a huge shell-hole and emerged in a few moments with a guide to take us into Ypres.

Still shells were falling, huge things crumping over. The men were in a highly nervous state: one moment almost imploring those in front to push on and the next moment scattering and lying down in the mud as each succeeding shell dropped. We started on again, the guide leading the way. The fact that the faster we went, the further we got away from the shells helped us forward and each man knew that if he dropped out under the circumstances, there was no help for him as everyone was almost past doing anything except walking automatically. We reached and passed Hellfire Corner without casualties along the Menin Rue. Here our guide left us and we continued down the road.

Passing our [gun] batteries we met some lorries that had just finished unloading ammunition and were returning to Ypres. Into these we bundled the men and arrived into Ypres. The lorries were going in a different direction to ourselves so we got out at the Cloth Hall – when I passed it was still burning in parts – and in the shelter of a side street, stopped whilst I passed round my water bottle of rum which I had filled before leaving the line.

It was good stuff and warmed us up considerably. Leaving the street, we struck out for the camp, Devine leading the way. We had barely left Ypres when we were met by battalion orderlies and further on found the field kitchens waiting for us. They had been brought up as far as possible and situated on a by-road and had hot tea and bread and cheese waiting. It was the last stage. The men were relieved of all equipment and overcoats and, carrying only their rifles, made their way into camp in their own time under guidance of runners.

Devine and myself took the company horses and shortly afterwards, at 3.30am, rode into the camp at Ridge Wood. The remainder of the battalion followed us in about two hours afterwards. They reached the camp, nothing more than bedraggled automatons; weary and worn and exhausted to a point almost beyond human endurance.

Major Quarry, the second-in-command, was waiting for us and from ten days of perfect hell, I was transferred into a perfect paradise, a scene fit for a banquet.

During our absence in the line, the 'dumped personnel' under Major Quarry had been preparing for our return, realising that we were probably in for a hot time. The pioneers were brought up. These built canvas shacks in the wood. Braziers and coke were got up; beds were hastily made of wire netting stretched on a wooden frame, so that when we arrived back, the men found a good, hot meal waiting, a change of clothes, hot water to wash them and then a shack to sleep in. All this in the middle of a wood and everything had been carted there from some miles from the rear.

For the officers (there were only three of us left out of 17 who went up to the line), a miniature fairyland presented itself. I was taken into the mess, a long canvas hut, brilliantly lit by candles. Candles were everywhere and, warmed by braziers, it was a perfect paradise for the moment. A table was laid complete with tablecloth and on the table were more candles. Lowe, the mess corporal who never appears to be tired, appeared with a hot meal. Arrayed along the table was champagne and wine. The meal was great. I waited for a short time for the remainder of the battalion to arrive but too tired to stand, I was carried to bed and undressed.

Here another scene presented itself. My valise had been brought up and laid on a bed in one of the canvas shacks. The shack itself was brilliantly illuminated and, best of all, a brazier was burning throwing out a warm glow. Once inside my valise, I was soon asleep, the end of a gruelling ten days.

We had accomplished nothing and lost heavily: considerably over 300 men and 14 officers of the 17 fighting officers who went up. Sewell, Wilks and myself were the only three to return unwounded.

The attitude of mind of the troops towards the question of possible death was an interesting one when it was under discussion, which was rare.

Some fellows were born fatalists and would clinch all argument by saying that if a bullet or shell had got his name written on it, he would have to have it when it came along. It was an argument in a way that was very satisfactory because, argued the fatalist, if the fellow referred to came through a battle uninjured, 'your' shot has not been fired yet. If he got knocked out, the fatalist said, 'I told you so,' and cheered fully applying the same plane of argument to himself, and awaited the missile that was going to put him out for all time, if he thought there was one with his name so inscribed.

But there was one side of the mind complex which had little or no part in the thoughts of the average soldier and that was pessimism. There were a few, a very few, who were pessimists and it was curious to note that under circumstances where perhaps it may have been most permissible, it was conspicuous by its absence.

The general line of thought on this question was, I think, this. That if one went about looking for trouble by unduly exposing himself, he very soon got it, whether he was a believer in fate or fatalism or not, and it was a very sound line of thought to take. It, at least, showed a healthy mind. The argument was not necessarily finished from the fatalist's point of view for, he argued, what of those times when no sort of cover is available and yet some individuals will go through affair after affair and come through with a whole skin.

As I reviewed the last ten days, to that there seemed no reply that would answer the query if I applied it to myself alone, for during that period I had seemed to have more than my fair share of narrow escapes. Generally speaking, the reply lay in the fact that these narrow escapes were the common lot of all the infantry when they were in action, often facing a hail of shells and machine-gun bullets. Under such conditions, death comes very near and yet passes by.

Many lives lost can be ascribed to the fact that a fellow sometimes temporarily loses his head and does that which he would not have done under more normal circumstances and the circumstances were often diabolical in the extreme but that arose from the action of the enemy in which fatalism had no share.

It was not unusual to find men who attributed their safety to divine interference as being the most reasonable construction they could put upon the fact that they were still alive and when one reviewed the circumstances, it often did seem the most reasonable.

There were those who had a premonition that death was near, who put their affairs in order and did not return from the front line, and there were some who did return. There was never anything conclusive. There were also those, the great majority, who had no tendency towards fatalism, who doubted the possibility of a premonition being attributable to anything but a momentarily low state of health, who tried to keep their head when circumstances were difficult and with that aid, to hope for the best, so far as they were personally concerned.

It was a matter for congratulation, however transitory it may have been, to have lived to view a hole in the ground upon land on which, a moment before, Hutchinson and I had been standing. It was the first moment in this space of time where the fraction of time and distance made the difference.

The next incident occurred at 3am when the instincts, one might think, are at their lowest ebb. After warning a gathering of fellows of their risk, I moved away and shortly afterwards two of them ceased to exist and the remainder were wounded, the result of a shell.

The attack on the château and pillboxes brought with it many opportunities for departing this life and some were outstanding; the German who fired past me when, by my dress, I should have been the target; the friendly tree trunk alongside which I lay for cover, whilst on the other side and not 30 yards away the Germans came out of the pillbox and looked for stragglers to shoot; Lieutenant Crisp and myself walking shortly afterwards back to our line arm-in-arm and he being the unfortunate one to be shot in the head. These were outstanding incidences of many more in this hectic ten days when life was not worth the smallest coin of the realm. As I reflected upon the many incidences during this last period in the line, I wondered under which category I came.

The following morning I was awakened about 10am by my servant with breakfast and what clean clothes I had. He told me that the battalion was moving away shortly so I dressed and had a wash and shave; the first for the last ten days. I presented a respectable appearance outside but underneath I was caked in mud.

The men had in no way recovered. Most of them had a touch of fever and their feet were in bad condition so moving was slow. By degrees they were put on passing motor lorries and by tea-time had been conveyed some distance to the rear to a place called Curragh Camp [near Westoutre]; hutments for passing troops. We stayed here the night and till yesterday dinnertime.

The men had taken their boots off over night and were unable to get them on again so passing lorries were chartered and so, by degrees, the battalion was got away. I was with the last party and after about an hour's lorry jolt we arrived at our billet; a farmhouse outside Berthen.

It was raining and pitch dark when we arrived and found that only about half the battalion could be accommodated in the buildings. The remainder waited outside in the rain, awaiting the arrival of tents; very feeble arrangements for men who were almost exhausted to the last degree. They made the best of it. They pitched the tents on rain-sodden ground and scraped the wet earth away. We commandeered every available bit of straw and with old sacks and rags or anything that was dry, settled down fairly comfortably.

The officers were not much better. We were given a room in the house, no fireplace and a stone floor, broken and wet with moisture coming through. We were all too done up – those who had been up the line – and too fed up at our losses to do anything but lying down in our valises, we got close to one another and, by degrees, got off to sleep, thankful to be clear for a time of the 'Salient'.

I awoke this morning [13 October] feeling stiff and cold. I was awakened by the general noise of servants bringing in breakfast. They had some difficulty in getting at individual officers we were packed so close together on the floor. There was nothing doing in the way of parade and having consumed my breakfast, went to sleep again.

Towards midday I got up and started to sort myself out and by lunch time presented a respectable appearance, a tub of water helping to that end. The men for the most part have spent the day scraping their clothes and seeing the doctor. The latter is an excellent regimental doctor. During our last days up in the line, he occupied a pillbox situated on the Menin Rue for a dressing station and there, standing over his boot tops in water, he carved and cut our fellows as they arrived wounded. He carried on night and day in spite of the shells and the fact that one landed in the doorway and killed and wounded nearly all his helpers and stretcher-bearers [at 1.15pm on 7 October]. He was awarded the Military Cross. To him our men have been today with sore and swollen feet and trench fever.

This afternoon, I went across to the billet to see my flock. For the most part, they were asleep, wrapped up in blankets and this evening, they have hobbled off to the local *estaminets* to find a fire and cheap French wine.

The Commanding Officer, or a General Officer under whom the officer may be serving, may, if he wishes to do so, state here in his own handwriting the fact that an officer has shown aptitude for any particular duty or employment, or if he has special qualifications for any particular branch of the service. Any marked acts of gallantry, or any special duty well carried out may be mentioned.

Any such statement must be signed by the officer making the entry.

Rendered valuable services & displayed great courage & devotion to duty during heavy fighting round POLDERHOEK CHÂTEAU. YPRES. 6/11ᵗʰ Octʳ 1917

G H Deakin Lᵗ Col
Comdg 16/ R War

2/4/18

Official recognition: Harry's part in the fighting for the Polderhoek Château position did not go unnoticed although he had to wait almost six months – until 2 April 1918 – before his CO, Lieutenant Colonel Grahame Deakin, saw fit to note his contribution in Harry's record of service: 'Rendered valuable services and displayed great courage and devotion to duty during heavy fighting round POLDERHOEK CHÂTEAU, YPRES. 6/11th Oct 1917.' (David Griffiths)

We have had a supply of wood and coal sent up and around the fire, most of the officers are now sat. The older officers appear to miss very much those we have lost. They have little to say but sit looking into the fire. At the moment it seems to be the only cheery thing we have.

The doctor whose dedication, fortitude and professionalism had so moved Harry was 26-year-old Captain John Aylmer Tippet of the Royal Army Medical Corps. Tippet's citation for the award of the Military Cross in November 1917 read:

'When his dressing station was blown in and nearly all the occupants killed, although much shaken, he immediately organised a new station, and for eight hours dressed and tended the wounded without rest. Later, when the battalion moved forward, he went through a heavy barrage to the new dressing station and worked continuously for six hours. During five days he had practically no rest, and dealt with 300 casualties.'

As for the Polderhoek Château position, further attempts to take it towards the end of 1917 were repulsed with similar bloody results and it resisted capture until the end of September 1918.

Sunday, 14 October 1917

This morning I was on parade with the platoon, sorting them out and seeing what actually remained. We have heard today that the 14th Battalion, Royal Warwicks Regiment have had a shot at taking the château and took it with 200 prisoners after hard fighting but after withstanding two counter-attacks they fell back at the third with their rifles and machine guns choked with mud.

Harry added later: 'This was one of many instances, and they were the rule rather than the exception, which showed the intensity to which the fighting was carried. We were not the first to try and take the château and pillboxes but after our attempts we were followed by the 14th Battalion so that it was captured at last. It was the Germans now who had got to act and they did do so, not resting until they had recaptured it. In this instance they were successful at the third attempt.

'So it was throughout the war, generally speaking, so far as the Germans and ourselves were concerned. The most forceful instance of this with which I came in contact was Trones Wood which was attacked and counter-attacked some 20-odd times before we eventually took it for keeps.

'*Cambrai and Bourlon Wood was another example on a larger scale. We caught them napping and bit right into their line and they, in return, took it nearly all back again and it was not until 9 November 1918 that we retook it again. So the war went on – on the Western Front which was the crux of the fighting – swaying backwards and forwards until at last, the Germans sank in economic exhaustion.*'

Monday, 15 October 1917

We are beginning to knock ourselves into shape again with drill, bayonet fighting and short marches. The time goes very slowly and I get fearfully fed up. It seems a useless waste of time and energy to train each man, almost independently, in his particular work and then in the first stint lose the great majority and have to start again with fresh men.

It is remarkable the lure a football has. Yesterday afternoon, footballs were procured for the men. On their arrival, not more than half a dozen men hobbled out and started to kick one about, to be joined later by others as they woke up. They turned out in slippers or anything they could get on their feet and kicked the ball about till tea-time. This afternoon practically the whole battalion turned out, still hobbling. They have been playing for the remainder of the day.

Had a route march been suggested or anything half so strenuous, they would have had a lot of remarks to pass and no doubt, by some means, they would have passed on their opinions to us.

Tuesday, 16 October 1917

Went into Bailleul this afternoon; a small country town. There is an excellent officers' club and a good variety show in the local hall. It serves to bring out the extraordinary features of this war. Last week we were well in the mire but tonight I have seen quite one of the best music hall turns of London, Du Callon, with his ladders.

Wednesday, 17 October 1917

A large draft joined us this morning; for the most part fellows of good physique. Mostly cavalrymen from the base drafted into the infantry.

Chicken for dinner tonight, jolly good. A gramophone has been sent up from battalion headquarters and with this, we are sat round the fire.

The pioneers have been busy making us beds; wood frames with canvas stretched over. They are very comfortable after the floor.

Am feeling very much off-colour tonight. I suppose it's the reaction and wretched weather outside; rain pouring down.

Thursday, 18 October 1917

The rain of yesternight has continued today. Am not feeling cheery and think a dram of sleep and to forget is indicated and so turning into kip – 9.30pm.

Friday, 19 October 1917

Vile weather continues. The farm buildings, or the vicinity of them, is getting like a ploughed field. Chicken again tonight. Am beginning to feel much more cheery; perhaps it's the chicken.

Saturday, 20 October 1917

Another draft of officers and men arrived this morning making us up to fair strength and rumours are going round that we are shortly returning up the line again.

Had a footer match this afternoon. Met the colonel. He says that [Harry] Wilks and myself are down for a month's course at the X Corps School not far away. A bit of joy for Wilks and myself.

After the match, I walked into Bailleul and have just returned, midnight.

Monday, 22 October 1917

The fat has been in the fire today. This morning we had an inspection by the brigadier and he picked several flies in the men and strafed the colonel. The colonel in turn strafed the company captains who in turn rounded on the poor subs [subalterns] and we had it in the neck, so we have turned round on our respective platoons and made them parade again.

We leave here tomorrow for the line.

Tuesday, 23 October 1917, Ridge Wood

Back to our old locality – Ridge Wood – which we reached at six this evening. Nissen huts have been built and the whole place appears infested with rats and fleas.

Owing to the nightly traffic and heavy rains, the ground is over our boot tops in mud and we move about on duckboards built up from the ground. Getting about in the dark is difficult. Practically every moment someone outside is missing their footing and slips into the mud. They don't hesitate to say what they think and appear to blame everything on the Germans. The Germans know we occupy the wood and [planes] come over about every other night and drop bombs.

C Company officers are occupying one shack. It is an awful squash. On arrival we got our servants to work. They cleaned the place out, produced a brazier and bits of dry wood from heaven knows where. Later coal came up and at the moment of writing, we are sat round the brazier, smoked to the wide and dry and warm.

It's a beast of a night outside: raw and cold. The wind is howling through the trees and not far away our guns are pouring stuff over into the German positions.

I have just been outside. After winding about on the track almost scared to walk lest I fall into the mud, I found my platoon. They are billeted in a large hut and appear quite happy to stay there. Not knowing when the next night's sleep may be, most of the subs have turned down to it. I am following suit. We are situated some five miles from the firing line and have our valises with us. We have no definite orders but think we are the brigade in reserve for another push which comes off, on the 26th probably. The guns are preparing for that day.

Wednesday, 24 October 1917

We had no orders last night so I did not hurry to get up this morning (getting up in this case means rolling out of my valise and putting on my tunic). My servant got fed up with waiting about and brought my breakfast in. I sat upon the floor, quickly cleared it and lay down again, the other subs doing the same thing.

Here movement is greatly restricted and apart from gas helmet drill in the huts, we have done little but lie about awaiting the next move. I do not suppose it will be long in coming. Somewhere in the line, they will find something for us to do.

Have just heard from battalion headquarters that I go down on the course tomorrow. This is a bit of luck to get away from this rat and flea-infested place. Already I feel full of fleas. Wilks goes with me.

Outside, a beastly night; pouring with rain and a cold wind howling through the trees. The guns still pouring over shells into the German lines, they never seem to cease.

Beeteson suggests that the Lord should help the soldiers on a night like this, to which we all reply, 'Amen.'

Thursday, 25 October 1917, X Corps School

Wilks and I left Ridge Wood this morning. The mess cart came up for us and we left with our servants and valises, a fresh and sunny morning. We were glad to be going away for a time. Both Wilks and myself were still feeling on the shaky side and we congratulated each other on our prospect of a rest from it all for a short time. As our old cart jogged along the road, we were constantly held up by troops, mostly Australians and New Zealanders with transport, going up the line to take up their position for a push up the Passchendaele Ridge.

We arrived at the school about 1pm and found that it had only just been moved there and was more or less in a confused state.

The position is very fine. Situated on the spur of a range of hills [just over the French border], we can see for miles around. In the distance, Poperinghe lies in the valley, to the right Bailleul and in the rear Mount Cassel towers up above all and at the foot of the hill Boeschepe. It is all very pretty, very picturesque, the intervening space a panorama of camps, villages, roads and rivers but it is difficult to appreciate it at its real value. The continual roar of heavy guns in the distance continually reminds us that this is no tour but war, turning what might be a paradise for the eyes into a hideous nightmare.

There appear to be many amongst us who have experienced the latter to a large degree – it leaves its mark and in different forms. Some fellows are morose and sit on their bed looking into space apparently, others are just the reverse: jocular, bubbling over with apparent joy at the prospects of a month up here but in all cases the eyes and face tell the story of a thick time in the Salient. But our prospects are very good and we are here for a month and live only for the day.

The accommodation here is surprisingly good – a real eye opener to us. In Nissen huts, eight to a hut, we each have a proper bed and mattress and a good supply of blankets.

Officers from every battalion in the corps are here. The eight comprising our hut are one each from the Black Watch, Royal Scots, North Staffs, Hertfordshires, two from the Devons and Wilks and myself. One of the Devons I recognised; he was with me at the cadet school in Ireland. We ought to have been very elated at such a chance reunion but we smiled and shook hands. He for the moment is one of the morose ones and I am not too cheery.

Have just had dinner; a topping affair, sitting at table in a chair with green foliage on the table. The table itself is complete with cloth, glasses and cutlery and the mess room illuminated with a good supply of oil lamps. The food itself, mostly army rations, goes down better when well served and this meal has been no exception. To laze over a coffee and afterwards to turn into kip in one's own good time is bound to have its good results.

Coming across from the mess hut to the sleeping quarters, I stopped to view the scene. It is very wonderful – a complete arc of flashes here and there, livid patches showing that some village is burning whilst the whole line in the far distance is dotted by various types of star-shells both of our own and German, each variety having its own meaning but everything is spoilt by the infernal roar of the heavy guns. They never seem to cease day or night.

We are all turning into bed early. One or two are already there including Wilks. It's a great place, bed, when one is tired and I am that.

Saturday, 24 November 1917

From the day of our arrival [25 October] nothing very startling has happened. It was generally a round of exercises of varying description, the same in this school as others.

The policy pursued has been quite an enlightened policy. Instead of working us to death, as is often the case in these schools so that one feels far worse on departure than on arrival, things have been taken steadily and we have had a fair amount of leisure time.

Parade at 7.45 for a breather before breakfast and that meal at 8am. Parades of varying description 9am–12.30pm and again 2–4pm have usually constituted the day. The parades have often been extremely interesting, especially in the case of one of the staff lecturers who was a staff officer during the early days of the war and operated in the vicinity. He has on occasions taken us over the 'old ground' and explained the positions held by the Germans and ourselves. An awfully nice fellow, he is never tired of telling us the story of how he first came in contact with the Germans.

Early in November 1914, he was adjutant of his battalion and was sent forward by his commanding officer to reconnoitre the land, the battalion camping for the night in a field. Their information was that German scouts were believed to be some 15 miles away, up ahead. Taking a captain with him they rode some two or three miles forward and seeing a wayside cottage made direct to it and on arrival, found it to be a small *estaminet*.

Teaming up the horses, they went inside, sat in the parlour and ordered wine. They had not been there many minutes before up rode a couple of men in strange-looking uniforms. Thinking they might be Belgians, they assumed an air of careless ease but kept an eye on the door, the strangers also eyeing them and the door. The [spoken] German was unmistakable. Our fellows, unarmed, sprang through the door, slammed it after them, sprang on their horses and tore down the road and apparently got some small distance before the Germans, recovering from surprise, had time to open the door and fire at them with their revolvers. Their aim was not good and the two got away. He is never tired of telling the story. He roars over it; so do we.

We have had lectures four nights a week 5.30–6.30. They have been of an unusually high order, given by chiefs of corps on their special work in their respective corps. The social side has been developed by concerts and concert parties from the surrounding camps. Occasionally I have walked into Bailleul which, at night-time, assumes the air of a flourishing town.

We have all improved under the treatment. Personally I am feeling very fit again. If only those infernal guns would stop firing so that we could forget the war.

Rumours are current that the Italians have had a setback somewhere and some of our troops are leaving the Salient for Italy.

The school breaks up on Thursday next and after the examination on Monday, the remainder of the time will be spent in sports, assault of arms etc. The whole course has been so successful (it's wonderful, the effect a bed, good grub and fresh air has on one), that we are looking forward to this, regretting that it is the finale and not beginning.

We spent the major part of this morning making final arrangements for the sports. Had lunch and was changing to go into Bailleul for the afternoon and evening when a message came round ordering all officers of the 5th Division to remain in camp and to pack up and be ready to join their battalion.

7pm. We have waited in all afternoon and evening but nothing has yet come through. We wonder what it means, whether we are going to reinforce a push which has just taken place at Cambrai or are we going to Italy? We wonder. In any case we are going to miss the last few days here and all officers concerned are looking very fed up. The betting is equal on Cambrai and Italy. No one has any definite information but we are swayed by each successive rumour which arrives every few moments.

Since Wilks and I left Ridge Wood, the battalion had had one or two nasty knocks in the line and rumours, via our respective servants and which are generally unreliable, say they are somewhere in the rear. We are patiently awaiting lorries to arrive to take us to them, wherever they are. We hope there will be no long list of blanks and vacant places.

Sunday, 25 November 1917

We sat up till late last night. No information came through so about midnight we turned into bed and were awakened at 8.30 this morning by the mess sergeant who said we had to report to the town major in the village at nine o'clock. We jumped out of bed. Heathfield [Harry's soldier servant] came in and dashed about with the result that at a few minutes past nine, I, in company with others, went down into the village. Here we found details of everything. The 5th Division was gathering together, lorries drew up and at 10.30am we left the village. The betting is in favour of Italy.

The morning was beautifully clear with a 'nip' in the air. The buses, which had done duty in London for many years before the war, fairly shook us up.

We reached Hazebrouck about midday and after a meal (my first) left again at 1pm. Passed St Omer and arrived here [Hesdin] at six o'clock this evening, which appears to be the destination the corporal in charge of the buses was given.

We expected to find someone awaiting our arrival with further orders but found no one. A messenger was despatched to the town major who knew nothing about us, the same with the local camp commandant.

The railway transport officer was next resorted to. From him we gathered that part of the division had passed through the station and some details were encamped some two miles away but he had received no instructions and knew nothing definite.

It was evident we were there for the night. Valises were dumped at the casualty clearing station. The men went to the camp and we spread ourselves over the hotels in the town. So tonight finds me sleeping at the Hotel Chemin-de-Fer with Wilks, a Cheshires and an artillery officer wondering, in common with the rest, where we are going. The room we are sleeping in has one bed. We tossed for it. I lost and am sleeping on the floor.

Monday, 26 November 1917

Had an excellent night's sleep and was awakened by Heathfield at 8am with a cup of excellent coffee. Breakfast at 8.30. Someone had been out in the meantime and brought back information that we had to leave Hesdin by the 9.30 train. We left at 10.30 and arrived here (St Pol) about 1pm.

The railway transport officer seemed to know something about us. At any rate, he soon had the ranks lined up and marched off to the local camp and we were told to report to the town major only to find that he had no idea where our battalions were but believed they were coming into the district sometime today and would we call again in the evening, which we did at 6.30pm. Still no news, so we spread ourselves over the town and awaited events.

Wilks and I have found a jolly good billet at the Hotel-de-France. We are rather enjoying this freelance travelling, no one owning us for the moment and free from parades. It is one of those occasions when, for a moment, one can pause to enjoy the war but it will not last long.

Wilks and I have just come in from the town. Odd details of the division have just passed through, followed by the 13th Brigade. From these we gathered that there is no doubt as to our destination – Italy. Seven days' rations per man have been drawn, we are told. We wonder what it means? Will it be worse than the Salient? On the whole we think not. Nothing can be more hideous than that.

ITALIAN INTERLUDE

November 1917 – March 1918

'Tonight it has been a very good war'

Italy and Austria-Hungary had been at loggerheads for years over hotly-disputed territory on their shared borders and yet, since 1882, Italy had been bound to both Germany and Austria in an alliance which, on the surface, offered mutual support and military assistance in case of external aggression. However, this 'Triple Alliance', as it was known, was no happy union. Simmering suspicions and territorial resentments between Italy and Austria went unresolved and relations deteriorated markedly in the years immediately prior to the outbreak of war in Europe in 1914.

Given, then, the mutual enmity which already existed between the two countries, when Austria declared war on Serbia in 1914, Italy feared that she would eventually suffer the same fate as had befallen Belgium and Serbia at the hands of her larger, more rapacious and more militaristic Triple Alliance partners. After first declaring herself to be 'neutral', Italy then threw in her lot with the Allies in April 1915, finally withdrawing from the Triple Alliance altogether on 4 May 1915 and completing a remarkable volte-face by declaring war on her erstwhile partners 20 days later.

When the fighting started in earnest in 1915, the Italians initially achieved moderate success against the Austrians on the battlefield on a front straddling the River Isonzo, which ran from the mountains beyond the Venetian plain in the far north-east down to the Adriatic. Although the front line ebbed and flowed for the next two years, after the 11th Battle of the Isonzo the Italians actually made ground. Then, in the autumn of 1917, came the catastrophe they called Caporetto.

Beginning on 24 October 1917, in just 17 days a joint German/Austrian sledgehammer had crushed an entire Italian army and substantially reduced two more on the anvil of the Isonzo front, and had pushed the Italians back 70 miles to the River Piave. There, after streaming across to the west bank and blowing the bridges behind them, the Italians finally checked the Austro-German onslaught. Italian losses in men and materiel had been enormous but, more worryingly strategically speaking, the assault left the forces of the Central Powers not much more than 20 miles from the gates of Venice.

For their part, Italy's new partners had already discussed plans to rally to Italy's aid should they need it, and now the call came loud and clear. France, still weakened by its own failures in major offensives on the Western Front in the spring of 1917 and facing 'work to rule' mutinies in the ranks as a result, nevertheless readied several divisions for Italy while Britain, albeit still heavily engaged in trying to claw its way, inch by bloody inch, up on to the Passchendaele Ridge near Ypres, not to mention the rest of its 'line holding' commitments in France and Flanders, diverted 200,000 men south towards the Med to shore up the new Italian line on the Piave. Harry Drinkwater was one of them.

Tuesday, 27 November 1917

Things were in a more or less confused state this morning until a staff officer came into the town with definite orders as to where the different battalions were situated.

Wilks and I arranged our plans accordingly. He came on this morning with our servants and valises whilst I remained behind, collected all the details for our battalion [then at Heuchin], together from the rest camp – about 70 in all – and left St Pol about 10.30am.

The men were very cheery. They had heard all about the prospects of Italy and whilst not stopping to think of the possible inconveniences of trying to stop a momentarily victorious army well supplied with guns, thought only of the prospects of getting away from the Salient for a time. They were full of song in consequence as we swung along the road.

I had been given no map or route regarding Heuchin but had been told its general direction. Everything was bustle and hurry and, despairing of getting anything reliable from anyone reliable, we set out. After going a couple of miles up what I thought was the most likely road from my vague instructions, unable to find a signpost to help me, I halted the men and we sat on the roadside and waited for someone to come along with a map of the district. I had not long to wait. A despatch rider came along and from him I gathered we were some distance off our correct course.

We struck off across country and about 2pm found our direct road. The men were very sick when they found we were still only a short way out of St Pol. They were carrying every mortal thing a soldier is supposed to be supplied with. I knew their feelings quite well, so choosing a convenient place on the roadside, we fell out and, as succeeding motor lorries passed, got a few men at a time on these with instructions to await us at Anvin, a village some distance up the road.

At 4pm I arrived in Anvin myself with the last party and found those who had gone on before awaiting our arrival.

We left Anvin and reached here [Heuchin] at 6pm.

Handing the men over to the RSM, my first thoughts were for the battalion. Found no great damage had been done to them whilst I had been away. Half of the officers were away – home on leave – the remainder were in the best of health and number. There were a few new faces but no vacant places.

Dinner over, we are full of the prospects of Italy. [Captain and Adjutant Alfred] Sayer is the only one who appears to regret the change. He says that we shall be nothing but 'gun fodder' against the Austrian artillery but he is an old pessimist and we point out that conditions can scarcely be worse than the Ypres Salient, to which he reluctantly agrees.

Heuchin appears to be a very pretty little village and little frequented by troops which perhaps accounts for the accommodation. We have a room in a cottage where the officers can gather. It has a stove of some sort but gives out no heat. At the moment Sayer is trying to tickle it into a flame but he does not appear very successful.

The accommodation is not good so bed is indicated.

Wednesday, 28 November 1917

We move sometime tomorrow – today things have been easy, a rifle inspection our only effort.

Thursday, 29 November 1917

Midnight. A and B Companies, with part of the transport and part of headquarters, entrained this afternoon at Anvin. Ourselves (C Company), with D Company, the remainder of the transport and headquarters entrain at 2.30am.

At the moment of writing, close on midnight, the remaining officers are sitting around the mess fire waiting to fall in and march to Anvin.

Someone has just remarked how matter-of-fact we are regarding the prospects of the journey, taking things as if such journeys were an ordinary occurrence every month and Italy well known to us all. It is a mood one gets into if one has done any extent of fighting. The prospects of a seven-day train journey, with all its attendant changes of scenery, is a prospect many might envy but I think if any of us were told that he was not going but was to be shot instead, he would have accepted it with the same lack of demonstration that is being exhibited now. Trench warfare dulls the faculties. One is unable to appreciate things at their proper value – perhaps it is as well whilst in the line.

We leave here in a few minutes – ie, 12.30am – and entrain at Anvin.

Friday, 30 November 1917

We fell in last night (or early this morning) promptly at 12.30am. Bugle blowing woke us. It was time for parade. We said goodbye to our last French billet – we hoped it was the last – and, awakening those who had dozed off around the stove, we buckled on our equipment and joined the men outside.

A few of the residents of the village, aroused by the bugles, put their heads out of the cottage windows. They were greeted by cheers from our men as we passed through the village and out into the country. After a march of some three miles, we reached Anvin railway station.

A huge train – in length – was waiting. The men in cattle trucks, 16 to a truck, were provided with their blankets and with the ability of old campaigners were soon at home.

The officers (four to a carriage) also had blankets, an unlimited supply and with these, we were quite warm.

A glorious moonlit night. With men, horses and transport aboard, we moved out of the station punctually at 2.30am.

Using the four corners of the carriage as headrests, we found that by dovetailing in our legs, we could make quite a comfortable bed on the seat. At least I thought it was, as with the blinds down we, in our carriage, got down to it and I straight off to sleep.

I slept well till 7.30 this morning when the train pulled up with a jerk at Longueau, having passed Abbeville and Amiens during the night. The jerk must have bumped my head and I awoke with a start. A Frenchman was passing the carriage shouting something which I later gathered was that 400 gallons of boiling water was waiting.

The cooks on the train soon stopped his tour along the coaches and, on being directed to this wonderful supply of boiling water, soon had tea made and passed along the train.

Heathfield came along later with a bucket of warm water for washing. I did not anticipate this but quickly got my shaving gear into action outside the carriage and by the time we made a start again, was feeling very fresh and clean.

After an hour's rest with an opportunity to stretch our legs outside the carriages, we reached Creil.

A most glorious morning and equally glorious scenery. We appear to be going along the rear of the French lines. French troops and transport are at most of the stations.

The railway alternately runs through woods and valleys with roads and streams running and intersecting in all directions.

We no longer hear the rattle of heavy guns. This is all very peaceful and unspoilt by the war.

Louvres – 1pm. Here for an hour and for lunch; all the servants have been drafted in as orderlies. With a truck to themselves, they bring our meals along from the cooks and, being next to the cookhouse on the train, no doubt make a very good thing of it. The men seem very happy, apparently spending their time when awake sitting in the doorway of their trucks.

After leaving Louvres we stopped for an hour at St Denis. French troops and transport filling all the station surroundings.

Our train is a huge length, like a snake, twisting around the curves of the lines.

Mesgrigny-Méry – we have just pulled up here for the last meal of the day before settling down for the night.

As before, our arrival appears to be expected. Frenchmen are running along the train no doubt to find the cooks who will shortly provide us with a hot drink, a meal and then for a night's sleep.

Slept excellently last night. Before settling down, hot coffee was passed along and afterwards with the hot water that remained the cooks made tea so that we were thoroughly warm when the train moved out of Mesgrigny station.

Saturday, 1 December 1917

I dozed off to the strains of our men cheering but at what I did not trouble to find out but getting well down into my blankets, was soon fast asleep. Had an idea that Beeteson had his feet in the small of my back but it did not prevent me from getting well away.

A halt was made at 5am at Les Laumes apparently for breakfast and it was 7.30am before I awoke and, raising my head, found we were in the midst of most gorgeous scenery, wild, mountainous country. The mountains in the distance appear covered with fir, pine and gorse whilst the valleys below appear under vine cultivation. It's a wonderful scene.

The train appears to be going along at a rapid pace. Almost as I write, the mountains give place to table land, still under vine cultivation, intersected by a stream here and there.

Dijon – 9am – stayed here a short time only. The orderlies came along with breakfast, bully and eggs. On enquiry at the station, I found we had been passing through the Burgundy district. This accounts for all the vine fields.

Macon – 1pm – a two hours' halt here. All the troops have been off the train, stretching themselves. They are in excellent spirits and full of back-chat.

Lyons – 5.15pm – drew up here for an hour to allow the Lyons Express to pass.

I had an extraordinary experience here. We had no sooner drawn up in a siding (it was dark) than hawkers (old men and women) came along the train selling the most trifling things. They were usually accompanied by more or less pretty young women who, in broken English, got into conversation with the men and usually, when leaving, left their address with a request for the fellow concerned to write to her. They did not stay long and appeared to always have one eye in another direction. Have just heard that they were spies. Have no doubt that the addresses they gave are useful for their own purpose but no use for tracing them. I expect they have got what information they require.

The letters have been collected and men warned against these folk.

Sunday, 2 December 1917, Arles

7 am. Here for an hour, for a wash and breakfast. Heathfield is rising to great heights. At every prolonged stop, he comes along with a bucket of warm

water for washing and a hot drink which he has been busy making, along with the other servants, also a supply of chocolate obtained from the canteen on the train. This is a great institution. A part of a truck has been set apart where the men can go and buy things they require to help the journey along. They form up at every opportunity.

We seem to have made some sort of circular tour. It's all very pretty and after our last experience, very wonderful. The Alps on our left stand out very distinctly, the tops covered with snow.

Miramas – 10.15am. Along the side of the Mediterranean Sea. A brilliant morning and scenery beyond description. A pen fails to describe one's feelings. Only a short time ago, our life consisted of being cold and soaked with rain and mud, with no reasonable prospects of life before us, living continuously day and night in conditions not fit for a dog, eating when we could and anything we could get, keeping awake only by the conditions we were under, knowing that at any moment an ill-directed shell might blow us to pieces, from shells that were literally, at periods, being poured over; an end that we had seen come to many of our fellows during that period and would as quickly come to us. From all this we had escaped and viewed instead a panorama which, under the circumstances, I shall not forget.

The morning is warm. The men, with their tunics off and shirt sleeves turned up, watch, as we all do, the unfolding scenery as mile after mile something new and more impressive comes into sight.

We are running along the coast within 200 yards of the shore. Trees, of unique shape to us, are growing in the sands, trees of various types with various shades of foliage. These continue right around the bay we are travelling. On the far side of the bay, the land is cut in terraces from which oranges and lemons appear to be growing, whilst here and there a frescoed house. Beyond all this, the hills – it's grand.

We passed through Berre [-l'Étang] at 11am. Still the same type of scenery, trees growing almost on the edge of the sea. As we pass along, cottagers come to their doors and give us a cheer, the men cheering for all they are worth in reply. If they see a stray dog or cow they cheer. They cheer at the slightest provocation. I think they are intoxicated by the conditions, the scenery and the sun.

Marseilles at 1pm. We were told that we were six hours behind schedule time and so our stay here was short. Engines changed and we were away again and at the moment of writing, 3pm, we are passing through the Chaîne de St Cyr, a chain of hills covered by pine and fir trees. We drew into Toulon – 6pm. Have just met an English lady on the platform. Hastily getting a postcard, I wrote home telling them as best I could, without stating definitely that I was on the way to Italy. She promised to post it through the French post.

La Pauline – 8.30pm. Travelling very slowly, we passed through La Pauline and drew up here (Les Arcs) at midnight. I was fast asleep when Major Quarry came along and aroused us to supervise the dishing out of coffee.

Getting out of my blankets and on to the platform, I found huge lights burning and from a fenced-off portion of the station yard, came the smell of coffee in the making. Orderlies soon formed up and the coffee issued to the men.

Bitterly cold outside. I went along the trucks to see my platoon. They appeared very snug, half of them were asleep. Those awake sat up and had their coffee. They expressed the hope that this journey would not end. Wishing them goodnight, I came back to the carriage.

McKinnell and Beeteson are already back and tucked up. I am filling up the minutes writing, waiting for Clews to arrive so that I can get down to it. A glorious moonlit night outside but very nippy.

Several of Harry's travelling companions were interesting characters who between them had accrued considerable combat experience.

Rugby-born James Jessie McKinnell had crossed to France in September 1914 as a private with the 1st Battalion, the Honourable Artillery Company (HAC), had seen heavy fighting during the First Battle of Ypres in late 1914 and been commissioned into the Royal Warwicks in May 1915.

John Clews had also served in the ranks on the Western Front since the autumn of 1914 and by the time of their Italian sojourn was already a decorated war hero. During the Battle of Poelcapelle, at the Third Ypres, Clews had been the first of his battalion to reach the German trenches, but by then almost all his officers were down. Clews took command of his platoon and led his men to their final objective. He was awarded the Distinguished Conduct Medal for 'conspicuous gallantry and devotion to duty … setting a splendid example of courage and resource throughout the whole action'.

Both McKinnell and Clews survived the war, Clews going on to serve as a captain in the Second World War, seeing service in North Africa.

Monday, 3 December 1917, Nice

I awoke at 7am as we were on the outskirts of Nice. Getting out of the blankets, I went to the carriage window and looking along the train, found I was a comparative latecomer to watch the scenery.

On the one side, the sun was just rising over the Mediterranean, throwing a long beam of light over the sea. Under its rays, the sea appeared golden, tapering off to a deep blue. I went to the other side of the carriage and that was a wonderful sight. Towering up on to the skyline was a range of hills and on these hills, houses were built after Swiss chalets; each a different pattern and a different colour. Splashes of fir and pine dotted the landscape, the whole practically one mass of various colours from flowers growing in profusion. Upon all this the sun rose and one was speechless with its beauty.

I hardly knew which I wanted to see most, the sea or the land. I awakened the other fellows and together we gazed upon it all. To us it was wonderful. A few minutes afterwards, we drew up in Nice station.

We were greeted by someone calling 'Good morning' and were assailed by English ladies (YMCA workers) bringing along coffee and cakes.

Had just sufficient time to run up and down the station for a warm and then moved off again.

Menton Garavan – 8.30am – we went slowly through Monte Carlo and had a good opportunity of seeing the locality and the casino and drew up at Menton Garavan.

An English girl came along the platform and told us that some thousands of our fellows had passed through during the last three weeks.

This is our last stopping place before passing over the frontier into Italy.

ITALY– 9.15am – have just crossed over the frontier. Entering a tunnel, we were greeted on emerging by Italian soldiers. Cheering by our men is now a common occurrence every few minutes. The Italian soldiers were greeted with an extra burst as each succeeding truck emerged from the tunnel.

Vintimille [Ventimiglia] – 10am – the first Italian station. A frontier station, it is a huge place, all bustle. There are many Italian soldiers here. Their officer's uniform is very gorgeous, trimmed with astrakhan and much braid and complete with a very showy sword.

Have just been along to the exchange and got my money turned into lira which appears to be equivalent to our shilling.

Heathfield has just come along to straighten the carriage. It's in a fairly decent mess. Have given him some Italian money, which seems to have impressed him. He has gone off to show it to his fellow servants probably and no doubt then to blow it.

The day is turning out gloriously hot. The commanding officer has gone off somewhere for fresh instructions regarding our destination. At the moment we have not the faintest idea what part of the line we are going to but have gathered that the Austrian push has stopped on the banks of a river and that the emergency is not pressing.

Bordighera – 11.45am. We left Vintimille at 11.15, passed through Bordighera and have drawn up at San Remo (12.15pm).

On arrival, gushing Italian women came along the train with wine and fruit and flowers so that, at the moment, the men have flowers stuck in their caps and in a lot of cases are the proud possessors of a bottle of wine or fruit of some description. It's a type of war they have been looking for for a long time and are enjoying it to the full and at the moment, are very busy trying to pick up useful phrases of Italian. 'Vino' seems to come very readily, so does the wine!

Porto Maurizio – 2pm, Andora – 2.45pm, Final-Marina – 4.30pm, Savona – 6pm. This afternoon has been a perfectly triumphant journey. Passing each town or village, we have been greeted with much shouting and flag waving, whilst from all houses along the route, flags are hung from conspicuous windows. Whenever the train stopped for a few minutes near any habitation, out would come the ladies of the house, bringing bottles of wine to find many willing recipients waiting with outstretched hands to receive the gift.

We drew up here, Savona, at 6pm. Lusty cheering from a neighbouring train told us that some of our fellows who had preceded us were in the vicinity. By the constant repetition of cheers that is going on, I imagine they have imbibed well of the atmosphere and wine.

I have no idea how long we are here for but believe the commanding officer has gone into the station to get fresh orders.

The glorious day has turned to a starlit evening with a decided nip in the air. I am remaining in the carriage, tucked up in the rugs.

McKinnell has gone out for news. Beeteson is fast asleep.

Genoa – we left Savona at 7.15pm and at nine o'clock drew up in Genoa station. Here our previous welcome was eclipsed by what followed.

We had barely stopped when the whole length of the train was raided by Italian women with wine and fruit and flags of the Allied countries – it was thrilling to a degree.

We had barely recovered from the ovation when an Italian officer came along and, with the aid of an interpreter, made known the fact that a spread was awaiting the officers in the buffet.

Tumbling out of the carriages and straightening ourselves out as far as possible (travelling days on end does not improve one's appearance), we made our way to the buffet, Richmond leading the way. The sight was a feast for the gods. Spread along the length of the room was a table laid out fit for a king; fruit, wine, champagne and attended by Italian ladies, wearing some sort of Red Cross apparel.

The Italian colonel led off with a speech in Italian, our Italian knowledge was limited to the one word 'vino' and so had no idea what he was saying but words like 'Inglese' and 'France', we were able to understand, referred to us and France. He eventually sat down.

All this time we had been eating and drinking whilst each of us had been decorated by an Italian flag and had bestowed upon us chocolate and fruit for the journey.

The Italian colonel's speech over, he sat down at the head of the table and someone had to reply. No one knew Italian and after a lot of pressure, Richmond got up to reply in French. He had not been speaking more than a minute in broken French when he discovered how very limited his knowledge of the French language was. We could see that he was getting fairly tied up; occasionally giving imploring glances down the table for help. Knowing Richmond, I hardly knew how to stand and keep my face straight. We were all being reduced to a state of hysteria without the opportunity to let our feelings go.

He was on the point of collapse when an orderly arrived saying the train was ready to start. Filling our glasses and drinking, presumably to the Italian Army and anything else they liked to couple with it, we hastily emptied our glasses and with farewells, made for our carriages.

We left the station amidst wild applause from the Italians to which few of the officers, at least, were able to reply. I lay in the bottom of the carriage, McKinnell and Beeteson on the seats and we roared at Richmond's effort in speechmaking.

The men rose to the occasion, waving Italian flags with which the Italians had supplied them or bottles of wine, which was more to their taste. They cheered back, relieving us of a duty which for the moment, we were unable to undertake.

It had been a great hour and we left Genoa under the impression that, with our arrival, Italy was safe.

From Genoa, we have changed our direction, leaving the coast. We have struck off inland and appear to be going through high ground [the Appenine mountain range].

I feel much too awake for thoughts of sleep so am tucked up on the seat and writing my diary up. McKinnell is reading, the others are trying to doze. Midnight has passed. The train keeps grinding on.

Tuesday, 4 December 1917

Parma – 8.00am. Awoke to find Heathfield rattling at the carriage door with breakfast and a bucket of warm water.

A beautifully sunny morning, I have had breakfast, washed, shaved and am now awaiting events. All the troops are out on the siding, some still washing in any old tin they can find. Parma looks a magnificent place from here.

We left the station siding at 10.15am after a very useful couple of hours walking about in the vicinity of the train. We are anxious now for the journey to end. We all have a desire to explore some of the Italian towns which, from a distance, look very picturesque – in keeping with some of the inhabitants we have seen.

We appear to be passing many small towns at each of which the usual greetings are exchanged and we pass on.

Este – 5.30pm. The end of our journey. Transport was unloaded and drawn up outside in the station yard, rations unloaded and collected and an hour later we were ready to move off but apparently someone was not ready for us and it was 9.30pm before the men were marched to the local barracks and the officers to various residents in the town.

The interpreter who had preceded us was in charge of the arrangements for the officers and we all trooped after him, dropping, as we went, an officer here and there.

A glorious moonlit night, it was very uncanny prowling from one street to another (everyone was indoors and no street lights). Occasionally from an archway (the streets were a succession of archways with the pavements and shops underneath), an Italian policeman would step out and with his cloak thrown over his shoulder, looked for all the world like a bandit, or our conception of one.

Wednesday, 5 December 1917

We got into our billet at 12.30am and after an excellent night's sleep went into a local café this morning for breakfast. Had an extraordinary omelette with an apple rolled up inside but, with the coffee, it was jolly good.

Lunch midday at a local hotel. We have orders to move at an hour's notice and everything is packed up ready.

We left Este after tea. At a few minutes to five o'clock we 'fell in' in the local market place. The roll called, two men were found to be missing and at the moment of writing have not yet reported. No doubt they are at some café, drunk to the wide.

The wine is much stronger in this country than in France and the men have not yet gauged its strength.

On arrival here [Saletto] we were met by the quartermaster who had preceded us to arrange billet accommodation and received something of a shock when he told us that we must not be surprised if the tone of our welcome was not so warm as we had previously experienced. Nothing had been openly demonstrated but that there was a definite feeling against the British because they, the Italians, said had it not been for us, the war would have been over – there is no doubt about that, the rest would have collapsed!

With the men placed in local barracks, we were taken by guides and runners to various houses for the night. Field, the Intelligence Officer, took three others and myself to our house, the occupant of which was anti-British. On arrival we found a sentry on the door placed there by Field to prevent them locking up the place. The occupant refused to see us so the required bedrooms were commandeered and at the moment of writing, I am reposing in a most gorgeous bed in an equally gorgeous bedroom. The floor is all mosaic pattern, set in cement.

Leading up to the room is a wide marble stairway complete with marble pillars and huge palms, probably someone's ancestral home. I feel somewhat of an intruder under the circumstances but I also feel very comfortable.

Thursday, 6 December 1917, Cologna Veneta

We left Saletto at ten o'clock this morning and after a march of about 15 miles reached here in the early afternoon. We were met by the battalion interpreter, a Frenchman speaking almost every language under the sun who, with the billeting party, had preceded us. From him we gathered that the impression regarding ourselves is pretty general and that we should not have to look for exhibitions of the wild demonstrations we had had on the journey into the country because they would not be forthcoming. On the other hand, they looked upon us as easy prey and he warned us to keep our eye on our goods otherwise we shall have them stolen; a warning we were not surprised to hear. Several of us have already missed small things. The transport has lost a set of harness.

I have an excellent billet, very similar to my last.

Friday, 7 December 1917

Compared with English and French towns, Italian towns are unique. The main streets invariably consist of a series of arches built over the pavement, so that standing in one of the open squares, one sees nothing but a series of archways all around and one has to penetrate these to find the shops. It all looks very picturesque.

Here, the town swarms with Italian soldiers, mainly batches in chains. They are, I understand, those who ran away during the Italian retreat. Chain makers will be busy for some time.

Taken as a whole, the Italians do not appear an energetic race. They stand for the most part at street corners and with their capes thrown over their shoulders look more like conspirators.

Saturday, 8 December 1917
We can get no definite information where we are bound for. The only reliable report is that there is no immediate need for us up in the line so whilst they are deciding the next move, we are taking things easy, an inspection in the mornings of some sort, either rifle or kit, and finish for the day.

Sunday, 9 December 1917
The king of Italy [Victor Emmanuel III] motored through this afternoon, causing some slight commotion.

Monday, 10 December 1917
Had a most glorious view of the Alps this morning. We marched some distance out of the town and from a high hill, saw in the distance the Alps, snow-capped and stretching, so they appeared in a half-circle around. A clear air and with brilliant sun striking the tops, it was a wonderful sight.

Tuesday, 11 December 1917, Brendola
As we were leaving the mess room last night, a despatch rider came up with moving orders and we left at 9.45am and arrived here at five o'clock this evening. We appear to be on the side of a mountain. We saw the village at 1pm as we were marching along what was probably a plain and it has taken us the remainder of the day to get here. It has been a continual climb all afternoon.

Am excellently billeted again and, very tired after the march, am turning into kip.

Wednesday, 12 December 1917
From my bedroom window I can see the road we came along yesterday, twisting like a snake through the valley. A wonderful view, the hills for the most part are cultivated and, with vine trees and foliage of some description, stretch in all directions.

Occasionally during the day we have been enveloped in clouds as they pass from hill to hill. We must be very high up. It is very weird.

Under these influences, France and the war seem like a nightmare which I have experienced and have awakened from to find it a dream but I expect I shall awake again before long and find this to be only a passing dream and the nightmare the reality.

This evening, the battalion concert party gave a show in the local hall: quite a successful do. After our men had been seated, the natives were invited to fill the remainder of the space. Being free, they did so with haste and as far as they understood, enjoyed it apparently.

Thursday, 13 December 1917, [Sant'Andrea Di] Barbarana [south of Vicenza]

We were not allowed to stay long in Brendola. At 8.30am this morning we had orders to move and left the village at 10am.

Our destination, eight miles as the crow flies, lay through the hills we had been admiring so much. We negotiated the first hill all right and by a series of corkscrew roads got over the next hill, perspiration literally rolling out of us in the effort; the men were carrying full marching order.

When we got to the next series of hills, the trouble started with the transport. Whole companies with drag-ropes were detailed to help the mules pull the wagons. We dropped one over the ledge. It stopped, smashed to atoms on a ledge some 60 feet below and it was 8.30pm before we got into billets, whacked to the wide.

Friday, 14 December 1917, Veggiano

We left again at ten o'clock this morning and compared with yesterday, the march has been uninteresting. We are in the plains again.

At 1pm we halted on the roadside for lunch and arrived here about 4pm.

On the way, we passed through the first warlike preparations we have seen, a huge belt of barbed wire, stretching right across country.

This evening, right in the distance and very faintly, we can hear big guns firing.

Saturday, 15 December 1917

No news yet of our ultimate destination. We appear to be marching from one village to another with a general direction towards the firing line, wherever that may be. Report says that it is partly up in the mountains and thither we are bound but reports and rumours are not to be relied upon, often being spread abroad by our intelligence department for the edification of spies, which no doubt abound, then we do something entirely different.

Sunday, 16 December 1917

McKinnell and I walked into Padua this afternoon, ten miles distance. Along the road, we stopped an Italian officer in a car with whom we finished the journey.

Arriving in the city, we said goodbye and many thanks to the Italians – in French – and made our way into the town. Passing over a bridge, we watched for some minutes, the bridge being mined ready to be blown up if emergency arises. Trenches were being dug in the town and barbed-wire entanglements erected. It struck us as strange, all this in an otherwise perfectly normal town.

After wandering about for some little time, we saw a sign advertising English teas and we went into an excellent café with wonderful pastries and passable tea, for a coffee-drinking community. Padua is very fine and we have thoroughly enjoyed the day, the buildings very gorgeous from an architectural point of view.

At dusk, we made our way back to camp. Coming along the road, we heard lorries lumbering along behind us and awaited their approach. To our joy, we found it was our mail that we had been waiting for for so long (we had received no letters from home since leaving France). We climbed up on top of the bags and arrived back in time for dinner.

The advent of the mail was soon echoed through the billets and at the moment of writing (after dinner) is in the process of being sorted out, eagerly watched by groups of men.

Monday, 17 December 1917, Campo San Martino

Awoke this morning to a thick snow on the ground. Moving orders had come in during the night and at 9.30am, we left the village.

The snow turned to slush later on and made marching very unpleasant. We halted at 1pm for an hour and for dinner along the road side. Passed through Piazzola at 2.30pm and saw one of the palaces belonging to the king of Italy, gorgeous in conception. A balcony appeared to run around three sides of the place and, draped with huge curtains at intervals, the whole, built after the style of a Swiss chalet, was most wonderfully decorated externally.

Arriving here later in the day, we found jolly good billets awaiting us in a large house. The occupants got wind and bolted, leaving behind nearly all their furniture and beds. I have a bed.

Tuesday, 18 December 1917

We are very prettily situated on the banks of the river Brenta which winds for a considerable distance around our locality before being lost to view.

In front of us, the mountains, snow-capped, and in the distance, we are told, fighting is taking place.

The Italians are very active in this part, digging trenches and gun positions and apparently getting ready for another retreat.

There are many Italian soldiers in this village but they do not appear to have the energy or enthusiasm of our fellows. They appear to have no life in them and I do not think they would be of any use in a scrap.

Wednesday, 19 December 1917

This morning I took my platoon to see the various positions and strong points the Italians are making in the vicinity. We discussed their advantages and disadvantages. Some of the men gave really excellent reasons for their opinions and left me with the impression that they would make, with little training, really intelligent NCOs, which are always an asset.

News and information is scarce but we are given to understand that there is no reason why the Italians should not hold on indefinitely, although it only requires the Austrians to put a few shells over and exit the Italians. They appear to have all the stuffing knocked out of them, so we are told.

The men in company with the officers are having a royal time. Fruit and nuts are very cheap. This, together with the mail, which always brings huge consignments of parcels from England, has made them, for the moment, almost independent of army rations.

The glorious weather continues; we are all feeling fitter for the change of conditions.

We remained in this village until 22 January. During this time, we led a perfectly natural life, well-billeted and well-fed, with sufficient parades to keep us fit and no more. We came to look upon Campo San Martino as our permanent resting place.

We did not anticipate when we marched in to Campo that our stay was going to be so long. We had been rushed out of France and through Italy but as the days went on and no orders came through, the commanding officer was informed that we were likely to stay here for some little time. Accordingly our thoughts turned to Christmas preparations and action was taken accordingly.

The regimental quartermaster sergeant went out one day and returned driving 13 turkeys and a couple of geese. Ovens were built, company quartermaster sergeants got busy and with the mess cart drove into Padua and returned stacked with Christmas fare. The men decorated their billets with green foliage.

Tuesday, 25 December 1917

Christmas Day. No building was found to be large enough for the whole battalion so each company had its own dinner. We, C Company, besides the turkeys and geese, had the army issue of beef, 160lbs of plum puddings and nuts, fruit and beer was bought locally.

No parades that day, the men spent the morning scrounging for wood for the ovens which were kept going by relays bringing in the fuel.

6pm arrived, the time for the dinner. The men were seated at long tables, erected for the purpose in their billet and we took our places amongst our platoons. Lacon, as captain, took the head of the table. It was a highly successful dinner. The turkeys were great.

With the prospect of another dinner afterwards, I ate sparingly and we left the men to it. At 7.30pm they were arriving at that stage when they were best on their own. One or two were beginning to slip under the table but Christmas comes only once a year and in war, often, does not come again. I went round last thing to see if any of my platoon could do with their rum ration. Some were still game but most were asleep, full of turkey and beer.

The Royal Warwickshire Regiment

CHRISTMAS, 1917
NEW YEAR, 1918

For the Past—Remembrance.
For the Present—Best Wishes.
For the Future—Good Fortune.

WITH CHRISTMAS GREETINGS

AND ALL GOOD WISHES

FOR THE NEW YEAR

From *David S.*

Christmas cheer: Harry spent Christmas Day 1917 in a camp near Padua in Italy, in what seemed a different world from the constant dangers of the fighting on the Western Front. He enjoyed a memorable festive period and even managed to send a regimental Christmas card back to his father in Stratford. He later remarked, '*We reached such a normal state in life during these days that Christmas cards were printed and sent out from England for the battalion.*' (David Griffiths)

At 8pm the whole of the battalion officers gathered at battalion headquarters mess and sat down to dinner. Toasts, turkeys and plum pudding and afterwards song, concluded a very successful Christmas. We left shortly after midnight. On the way back to my billet, I reflected upon my previous Christmas Days since the war broke out. 1915, I was in Maricourt and spent most of the day scraping mud from my clothes; 1916 I had spent in the trenches and cooked my Christmas dinner in the trenches. The war had brought many changes. This was one of the most acceptable.

We had a little diversion on Christmas Eve. Led by the colonel, we went round to brigade headquarters and standing outside the house, sang carols to the brigadier which we had been practising.

The brigadier, a very stern style of man, who thinks only of war, invited us inside. We found him poring over maps of mountains. He was very cold and not at all festively inclined. We wished him a Happy Christmas and returned.

With Christmas Day over, festivities did not cease. The following day, C Company sergeants had a do to which we were invited. Again, Christmas fare predominated as did the Christmas spirit. We left them later in the evening, still singing – those who could.

The following day, the 27th, we were reviewed by General Plumer after a short divisional route march. It was mercifully short. No one felt like marching.

With the passing of Christmas, festivities died down. Parades in the morning were continued and I usually finished up the day by a walk into Padua or amongst the local scenery which almost equals anything Wales has to show, always with Mount Grappa in the distance, snow-covered and looking very majestic.

The last day of the Old Year, I went into Padua. During the last few nights, Padua has been the object of several bombing attacks by the Austrians and Germans. Beautiful moonlit nights, they come over, drop their cargo and scoot back. It is our only contact with actual war but for those underneath, it is very unpleasant. One dropped close to our general headquarters in Padua, knocking out some officers.

As I left the town in the evening, streams of civilians were leaving, wheeling their beds into the surrounding district to return again in the morning. They are a very windy folk, the Italians. Up in the air one moment and down in the dumps, the next.

Returning to the mess at Campo, most of the officers stayed up till midnight and, wishing each other a safe return, we turned into kip.

Tuesday, 1 January 1918

The 1st was a glorious day with bright, warm sun all day. Walking round to a local church in the afternoon, heard a lot of chanting going on. They appear to keep up some sort of festivity.

In the evening, C Company officers entertained the colonel, the second-in-command and the adjutant; a very successful evening. Enlisting the help of the company cooks and our servants, we sat down to an excellent spread.

MENU

Sardine salad

Clear soup

Boiled bream and sauce

Rissoles

Roast goose and apple sauce

Stone cream and chocolate

Scotch eggs

Cheese

Dessert

Coffee

A very complete menu; these are little affairs which help to keep one in contact with civilisation. It was a great success. We broke up about midnight.

As I walked back to my billet, I could not help contrasting this phase of war and that of my first experience in France how, in those days, often soaked in mud and water, I was glad to drop on some straw in a barn for a night's sleep, too tired to take my clothes off, whilst here I was walking back to a bed after a dinner that would have graced most hotels in London. War is very peculiar. It makes one live from day to day. This is only an interlude, we shall wonder someday if it ever existed but we live only for the day and tonight it has been a very good war.

On the 3rd, Milner and I walked into Padua and met an Italian officer, with whom we had previously become acquainted, for dinner. The mode of conversation was in the French language and very slow.

We stayed until about 10.30pm and discovered we were too late to catch any transport going our way, so walked it and arrived back in camp 2am in fine style after a glorious walk in the moonlight.

With no prospects of a move, hot baths were erected for the men and we settled down to more training. Lewis-gun pits were dug where, all morning, firing went on. With the exception of the night bombing raids, this was the only sounds of war we heard.

On the 9th we had a blizzard; snowing hard all day. We awoke to find the snow some 18 inches deep in parts. The country looks very pretty in consequence, as if someone had placed a huge sheet over the whole of the landscape with Mount Grappa in the distance as the peak. Upon all this, the sun would shine during the daytime. Its effect upon the mountain tops was unique, turning them into various hues as the sun sank down.

On the 12th, a leave party left for England, the first since we have been out here.

Sunday, 13 January 1918

A diversion from our daily round is caused by small parties of officers and NCOs being taken up the mountains to see the Italian positions there. Leaving Campo San Martino at daybreak, they are taken as far as possible in motor lorries and then climb up. A party went off this morning. All day it has been raw and foggy. Personally, I sat by the fire, glad of it.

On the 15th, I took a fatigue party to Camposampiero, a village some five miles away. I reported at the railway station and relieved a similar party of the Cheshires.

From information, apparently an air raid was expected on the town on the 18th and our job was to clear the petrol dump from the station to some isolated land.

The 12th Gloucesters relieved me the following day and I returned on receipt of orders, the following day, the 17th.

The party which went up the mountains met British troops up there who say there is no enemy within 1,000 yards of them. They appeared quite contented to stay up there.

The weather for the last few days has turned muggy and raw, obscuring Mount Grappa.

Monday, 21 January 1918

Heard this morning that the division is making a move on Wednesday towards the line, taking over a sector from the Italians.

Tuesday, 22 January 1918

Twelve months ago today, I left France for England to take my commission.

The news about our move has been confirmed and we leave tomorrow on what is reported to be a 60-mile trek to the Piave. We have had a topping good time here. After Ypres, it has been very useful.

Wednesday, 23 January 1918, [Sant'] Ambrogio

We left Campo this morning at 9am. The battalion paraded in full marching order and promptly to the minute, we moved off, the band – full of beans – leading the way and blowing lustily.

The villagers were sorry, I think, at our departure. The men had apparently made many friends who turned out to watch our exit.

The morning was dull but turned out brighter as we marched along. We stopped every 50 minutes for a ten-minute rest and at 1pm stopped on the roadside for dinner which had been stewing in the cookers as we marched along.

We fell in again at 2pm, passed through Noale. The sun by this time had become intense for marching and the men, in full marching order, began to feel the strain but our 'esprit-de-company' is good; unwilling to drop out, the men plodded along, consigning everyone who made them carry such a weight to purgatory but still they kept on plodding along, the sun scorching down making us all wet with perspiration. It came clean through our clothing and stained our leather equipment. It was at least a novel experience, in January.

We arrived here [Sant'Ambrogio] at 6pm. After a march of 20-odd miles, three men only left the ranks of our company and they kept up with the transport in the rear and joined us immediately we got to billets.

8pm. Everything is quiet in the village. The men, those that have been able, after a rest, adjourned to the local cafés for a drink. They have for the most part returned to their billet for sleep. I feel like a sleep myself and am turning in, feeling very tired.

Thursday, 24 January 1918

Resting all day. We move on again tomorrow.

Friday, 25 January 1918, Paese

We fell in again at 12.30pm and after a short march, reached here. The sun has been almost tropical in a cloudless sky. In the distance, we can still see Mount Grappa covered in snow.

On arrival, we found the artillery in possession of the village and the best billets but we are only birds of passage, moving on again shortly. By some happy dispensation, I have got a bed but it is not so with all the officers.

Saturday, 26 January 1918

We expected to move on again this morning. Limbers packed and men ready to move off when orders came through to unpack again. Subsequently I heard that we, the British, had relieved some Italians who, coming from the line, had collared all available billets and so we are unable to move forward until they get away.

The weather is perfect, a cloudless, blue sky and a gloriously hot sun. At the moment of writing, am sat on the steps of the local theatre. The 1/4th Gloucesters (48th Division) have just come in. Overhead a few of our aeroplanes are buzzing around, doing nothing in particular. In the distance, the mountains, snowcapped, appear. They are a dividing line between us and the war.

I am feeling very lazy with nothing to do but sit in the sun. I am feeling very happy with the war. I think we all are.

Evening – a gorgeous moonlit night. Aeroplanes (enemy) are very busy in the locality. In the direction of Treviso we hear them go buzzing over and wait to hear the bombs explode in the distance.

Sunday, 27 January 1918, Povegliano

We arrived here at 5pm and are within five miles of the line. We took over the billets from the Argyll [and Sutherland] Highlanders who were leaving to take over part of the front.

Air raids appear to be frequent in this locality. Last night they came over, we are told, and dropped bombs just outside the town.

My luck is out tonight, I have no bed so am using the next best thing – my valise, which Heathfield has laid out on some bags of straw. It's a good substitute. I expect someone will miss their bags of straw tonight. Heathfield is a good scrounger and it is not for me to doubt his honesty when he says that the bags of straw had no owner.

Monday, 28 January 1918
Had a peaceful night, undisturbed by any aeroplanes. Sentries are posted all over the town to warn the inhabitants (what is left of them) and ourselves of their approach.

Tuesday, 29 January 1918
B and C Company officers went up into the front line this morning to inspect the positions. It was a unique experience.

Taking all the available bicycles, we left here at nine o'clock and rode through what appears to be a valley towards the Alps, which the Austrians hold.

A beautiful morning, the mountains stood out very clearly. The smaller and lesser ridges were easily defined and through glasses, we could distinguish small woods of pine trees. It was all very different to anything we had been used to in France where, sat in a trench, we were not able to put our head over the top.

On the way, we passed through a couple of villages without a single civilian inhabitant. From some of our troops who had begun to take possession, we gathered that the villagers had long since stampeded, leaving everything behind them. The stampede seemed very unnecessary. Many a man had got an excellent bed to sleep in – making the best of good conditions as equally as they were able to make the best of bad conditions, which they had so often had to do.

We rode on till about 10am and, finding a house on the roadside, we dumped our bicycles inside the gate and walked on.

The country was spread out in front of us for miles, finishing up on the skyline with the Alps. Somewhere between the mountains and ourselves ran the River Piave, upon the far banks of which were the Austrians, on the near bank the Italians whose positions we were going to inspect and which we are to take over.

After walking some little distance, we found a communication trench and by this means, made our way into the front line.

We were met by the Italian colonel in command and with the aid of our interpreter, whom we had brought with us, were given interesting particulars of the conditions there in general and came away with the general feeling that if possible, it is a better war in the front line than in the rear.

The ground appeared to be somewhat elevated. We could see, for a couple of miles, the country behind the Austrian side of the river and then the rising ground until it gradually merges into the mountains and the mountains to the skyline.

Returning, we picked up our bicycles and arrived back here this afternoon, a very interesting day amidst most gorgeous scenery. An unorganised tour under peace conditions could not have been more picturesque.

I had not been back long when, hearing a fearful clatter of machine guns in the air, I went outside the billet just in time to see a couple of our men come down in parachutes from one of our observation balloons. Austrian airmen (or German) had suddenly appeared from nowhere and before the balloon could be hauled down, had set it on fire by machine-gunning it.

Wednesday, 30 January 1918

This morning one of our planes got mixed up with a couple of German planes and was their unfortunate victim. We watched them for some time and in the end, our plane burst into flames and fell, apparently into the Austrian lines, the occupant falling out whilst it was still some thousands of feet in the air.

This afternoon, I played rugger. Turned out for the battalion against the Norfolks and am sore and as stiff as a board in consequence.

Thursday, 31 January 1918

I have had to work the stiffness off today. I did not feel anything like a parade this morning and tonight we go wiring around one of the adjacent villages – Arcade.

Friday, 1 February 1918

We returned a few minutes to midnight last night and I had barely got into bed when those blessed aeroplanes came over and our village was their object this time. They appeared to come in droves. Several houses are down. They gave us a very uncomfortable hour.

Tomorrow we leave for the line.

As Harry scrutinised a trench map of the Trentini sector, he noted that the area of responsibility entrusted to the 16th Royal Warwicks included that section of the line which stretched from the old river crossing at the Ponte Priula as far as the village of Nervesa a few miles to the north-west. Behind lay the village of Arcade, while immediately in front of their positions the River Piave had split into several channels creating islands of various sizes, each of which appeared to have a name.

From the map Harry could make out the few piers which remained from the collapsed road and rail bridges at Ponte Priula. These had once linked the communities on either side, but there was no longer a friendly welcome on the other bank. Now the only way across was by boat or, at this time of the year, by wading across. Both methods were extremely hazardous, for a little way inland on the bank directly opposite lay the tiny hamlet of Barco – in front of which lay the Austrian Army.

By the time Harry's battalion was in place it was clear that the threat to Venice had diminished a great deal. The Germans had already suspended major offensives and had pulled several of their divisions out of Italy. But the Allies could not be complacent; there was no way of knowing if another attempt would be made to cross the Piave. For now, however, the front appeared almost serene.

For the men like Harry, who had fought and slogged their way through the Somme and the slough of despond that had been Third Ypres, they were to find that although this was war, it was not war as they had come to know it.

Saturday, 2 February 1918, on the banks of the River Piave

Midnight. After leaving billets, we picked up guides at the village of Arcade and relieved the West Kents here at 8pm. Too dark to see our actual conditions and how we are situated. After strolling along to see that all my platoon were either tucked up in a dugout (it is bitterly cold) or were on sentry duty and knew their job, have returned to my dugout which is excellent, complete with bed, chair, table and looking-glass, procured no doubt from some neighbouring house.

With the prospects of a tour of duty for a couple of hours at 4am, bed is indicated.

Sunday, 3 February 1918

With the break of day, a wonderful view unfolded itself. I forgot all about the war, enraptured with the conditions. The River Piave running down from the mountains is, at this point, some 800 yards across from bank to bank. At this time of the year, the bed is nearly dry and the only remaining water running is a stream some 20 yards across and running very rapidly, criss-crossing from side to side as it flows on, eventually to empty itself into the sea in the vicinity of Venice.

The banks of the river are unusual. Although the stream at this time of the year is narrow and comparatively shallow, leaving a large expanse of the bed dry, with the coming of the rain, the snow in the mountains melts quickly and down comes a raging torrent of water rising, I am told, with great rapidity. To counteract the terrific force of water on the banks as it swirls down, huge concrete walls have been built, about ten feet high, several feet thick at the base, tapering off to about a foot at the top. It is behind this wall on our side, we are dug in, the Austrians dug in on the other side of the bank and similarly protected and the 800 yards divides us.

These were the conditions we were told before we came into the line but speech fails to describe the scenery. Straight ahead, looking across the river and about ten miles distant, rise the Venetian Alps, rugged and snowcapped and which culminate on our left with Mount Grappa, from which vicinity the Piave has its source.

From the Austrian side of the river, until one's view is obscured by the Alps, the land rises in tiers and each tier appears to have a different type of foliage until as seen through the glasses, finishes up with pine forests and then the snow and mountain tops.

Amongst all this, dotted here and there, are houses, the outsides of which are frescoed in different colours, with clusters here and there which no doubt denote a village.

Upon the whole landscape the sun arose this morning and as it arose, it turned the view into different hues which, in their turn, were reflected in the river.

This is not all that adds to our comfort. We are not in trenches. A main road runs along the side of the wall so that we step out of our dugouts, cross the road and we are into what was before the war, a vineyard. At one corner of the field, buildings, which were probably used for grape pressing, have been turned into company headquarters where we, the company officers, have our meals. At 7am, I made my way there for breakfast and found a breakfast ready that would have graced many a home – porridge, eggs and bacon with an abundance of bread, butter and tea. All this was spread out on a table, complete with tablecloth. It was wonderful.

The day has been uneventful. For the most part the men, when not on duty, have been lying out in the sun which has been blazing hot.

Occasionally a shell has come over from somewhere up in the mountains but they are small and comparatively harmless (2-inch mountain guns).

With the dusk, we turn to duty again. I am on from 8–10pm and again 2–4am, walking along the sentry posts.

Tuesday, 5 February 1918

And with the dawn, back into dugouts, there to sleep and keep out of observation whilst day lasts. During the night, several enemy planes went over. We heard the explosions and back they came, searchlights from all directions trying to pick them up, a regular Brocks [fireworks] display.

Very interesting was the method adopted by the Austrians for guiding their aeroplanes back at night in the dark. From somewhere in their back areas and at stated intervals, there would shoot up into the sky a long column of lights, very much like fairy lights. For about half a minute, they would twinkle and then suddenly disappear.

Our airmen have retaliated this afternoon by going over in droves. They were fired at by guns somewhere in the mountains.

Wednesday, 6 February 1918

The general came along the line this afternoon and wants to know what is on the other side, so by some wonderful means someone is going to cross over the stream and investigate. Looking through my glasses this afternoon, I saw a sentry some six miles away up in the mountains walking about in front of a house; probably someone's headquarters. It's the first sign of life I have seen in the Austrian vicinity, usually all is very quiet.

Thursday, 7 February 1918

The calm was slightly broken this morning by a salvo of whizz-bangs from the Austrians. It was only of a few minutes' duration and soon died down. One hit our stone wall and took a piece of concrete out the size of one's head.

Very misty all day, we could barely see across the river. I suppose they thought that with the bad light, they could fire with impunity.

Friday, 8 February 1918

Taking advantage of the mist, Lieutenant Ward and a couple of stalwarts crossed over tonight. Dressed only in bare uniforms (and dirty sheets with holes for head and arms), each armed with a bottle of rum and a revolver and roped together, they dropped over the wall at dusk and we watched them enter the water. They were soon in difficulties and besides being roped together, were holding on to one another for support. We could see the water washing around them as it came pouring down.

The Austrian side was only just obscured from our view but dark came on very quickly and the last we saw of them they were still holding on to one another and trying to force a way through the stream, well up over the waist in water. They returned at 8.45pm after lying over in the Austrian lines [on the island of Lucca] for two hours.

They had chosen a part of high ground where no wall exists and, creeping into some bushes, started to have a drink of rum each but Ward says that their teeth, clattering on the bottle necks, made such an infernal noise that they had to stop and so lay in wait for something to happen. Frozen nearly stiff, they attempted to reconnoitre the ground and had barely moved before they came upon a patrol of Austrians. The recognition was mutual and both sides dropped to the ground, Ward and Co. withdrawing and eventually re-crossing – they were too cold to carry their investigations further.

Saturday, 9 February 1918

The night passed very quietly and all my duty consisted of was strolling up and down the road along the company front. Occasionally I went into a Lewis-gun position and to pass the time away, fired a Lewis gun. In France, we used to so pass the time by trying to hit the German barbed wire and create sparks. Here we tried to create sparks by clipping the top of the wall opposite – it serves to pass the time which, at night and under these conditions, hangs somewhat.

Still dull and misty, we can just see the wall opposite. After that it is all haze. Raw and cold, it smells like rain so have spent most of the day in my dugout which, with the aid of a brazier and some books, is extremely comfortable.

Sunday, 10 February 1918, Arcade

The battalion left the line tonight and I came on here this morning to take over the billets for the company. It's the only time I have regretted leaving the line. C and D Company officers are billeted together in a practically furnished house. The inhabitants have long since fled leaving all behind them. We have a bed each and living rooms complete with furniture, all in carved oak. Lesser things, such as cooking utensils and china, have departed. A few broken cups and jugs lying about gives one the opinion that the first comers had a jolly good scrounge around.

Going into a bedroom, I found a crucifix still by the side of a bed, much damaged, inlaid with mother of pearl. The back has slides behind which are minute stones, inlaid, which probably have much meaning to a Roman Catholic.

Monday, 11 February 1918

The military situation is rather ridiculous. From my bedroom window (which is in the front of the house and boarded up inside), I can look right across the river and to the land and mountains on the other side. Opening the shutters this morning, the whole landscape unfolded itself to view. I could see the houses on the hillside which we know are used by the Austrians for observation purposes and where I saw a sentry walking. They can see us equally distinctly and, with artillery, each side could lay the other flat but neither side has started yet but I think our generals are getting a bit restless. I should not be surprised if we do not move something somewhere shortly.

At 9am I took a party out road-making in the locality of the lines. I don't doubt that from somewhere up in the mountains some eight miles away, the Austrians were hauling up guns, both sides making use of the mist which came over the country.

Returning at 1pm for lunch, several officers have been practising revolver shooting in the adjacent yard.

With the dusk, fires are lighted; the windows blocked up to obscure the light. We sit around the fire – a game of cards and then bed.

Tuesday, 12 February 1918
Road-making, 9am–1pm.

Wednesday, 13 February 1918
Orderly officer for the day.

Thursday, 14 February 1918
Road-making, and on my return heard the first rumours of our reposeful life being broken.

Last night a patrol went over the Piave and buried some iron bars to which is attached rope which in turn they buried in the bed of the river as they returned. These, we are told, are to guide rafts over when required.

The engineers have orders to build wooden bridges for crossing. This means only one thing. We are going over.

The patrol was under the command of the irrepressible Captain Charles Lacon.

Friday, 15 February 1918
Had orders this morning to be ready to take a party up to the river to cross over tonight but the mist of the last few days has cleared and with the moon up, it has been cancelled.

I expect we shall have Fritz over to haunt our dreams.

Saturday, 16 February 1918
Road-making.

Sunday, 17 February 1918
No duty so I lay in bed. Heathfield ministered to my wants in the shape of breakfast and later on in the morning, hot water for a bath.

Revolver practice this afternoon and this evening, the fire. Tomorrow we move back to Povegliano.

Monday, 18 February 1918

The DCLI relieved us and we marched on here. A glorious moonlit night, Fritz was hovering somewhere overhead. Searchlights by the dozen were trying to pick them up.

Tuesday, 19 February 1918

This morning I heard that one of the planes had been brought down outside the village by the anti-aircraft guns, so strolled along to see the wreck. A huge thing; the engine was completely buried in the ground from the impact and the remaining part smashed to atoms, the occupants with it. Taking a few small parts as souvenirs to send home – one of which was a piece of canvas belonging to a wing which shows it rather cleverly 'doctored' in colour to blend with the darkness of night and dashboard lamps – I returned to billet.

Apparently seven [planes] were brought down in the vicinity after they had bombed Treviso and were returning. In this part of the line, we are doing tours of eight days – eight days in the line, eight days in support in Arcade and eight days rest as here. Under these conditions, there is very little difference. It is, comparatively speaking, all rest.

Wednesday, 20 February 1918

The proposed stunt [attack] is developing. All officers in our brigade gathered at a rendezvous and the scheme presently proposed was explained to us.

This raid, which is of fairly big proportions and offers a good target for the enemy, was supposed to be very secret. A whole brigade (us) cross over the Piave supported by the RE, RAMC and Royal Field Artillery, taken over by the Navy who are coming up from Venice in boats. We have to form a bridgehead on the other side and hold on for two days, then withdraw.

The object is to give the Austrians the impression we are making a definite attempt to form a crossing for future operations, necessitating them withdrawing troops from the vicinity of Venice (to which they are too close to be pleasant). Should they do this, the Italians will attack them down there and drive them back to a safer distance.

Very picturesque on paper but 5,000 men crossing the bed of a river without a shrub for cover for some 800 yards and shot at by artillery which is the last word in accuracy is a bit of a problem if it is going to be done without overwhelming casualties.

Thursday, 21 February 1918

On parade this morning. The battalion moved to the training area some three miles away, outside the village of Villorba and have spent the day passing over an imaginary river in imaginary boats. Without the actual effects, it has all been very dry and dull but with the actual effects, I imagine we are going to have all the excitement we require.

We returned at 5pm scorched from a blazing hot sun.

Friday, 22 February 1918

A repetition of yesterday. We shall have no rest until this affair is over.

I was awakened at 2am by bombs dropping in the village, the Fritz planes droning overhead. They come over at odd times, drop a load of bombs, scoot off back to their lines and return again with another load. It's very disconcerting – spoiling the night's sleep.

All night long from dark to dawn, ammunition wagons and artillery are rumbling past, taking up positions ready for the show.

We are told that the whole of the British artillery in Italy is being concentrated on our front to support us when we go over and it looks as if such is the case. We have passed huge stocks of ammunition on the roadside and guns, covered by trees and sheets from aeroplane observation, to be moved again as soon as dusk arrived.

Saturday, 23 February 1918

10pm. Today the order of things has been changed and tonight finds us on the training area again.

After a day of comparative rest, we paraded at six o'clock this evening for training under more or less the same daylight conditions under which we shall go over – whenever that is.

The ground has been laid out with tapes describing the course of the river over which we have to cross and as we practise we pass small knots of men who tell us they represent shingle, solid ground, swift-running stream, bank and so forth, the idea being to get into our minds that we shall meet such-and-such a thing, which in turn should tell us how far we are from the far bank.

A glorious moonlit night; light enough to be able to write by, more subdued but very little difference to daylight and a keen, healthy air. We are all keeping very fit.

All day long our artillery have been ranging on the hills and mountain side, setting fire to a lot of undergrowth which, by now, has spread along the mountain side. As I write, sat on the grass (we are awaiting fresh instructions), we have in front of us the same old range of mountains standing out on the skyline with another phrase of the picturesque made by the fire and capped by the brilliant moon. I think we are all more engrossed in this effect than on the training we have in hand.

Sunday, 24 February 1918

One might have thought that under these war conditions, Sunday might be a day of rest of some sort, but not a bit of it. Back went the battalion to the stinting ground in company with all the other units concerned whilst a few men from each battalion were detailed to attend church parade at Visnadello, a small and adjacent village. I was in charge of our party. The service was held in some open ground and attended by the general officer in command and the brigadier. We were in full view of the Austrians up in the mountains so a fleet of aeroplanes hovered overhead to prevent us being rushed and bombed by enemy planes.

We returned to the battalion in time for lunch and after a blistering hot day, back to billets at 5pm and at the moment of writing, Fritz is overhead, bomb-dropping in the village and our guns kicking up an awful row in reply.

Monday, 25 February 1918

I went to bed with this still continuing. There seemed to be droves of them in the air and unless one went right out of the village and slept in the fields, one place seemed as safe as another. With the reflection of one house well alight in the vicinity, I dozed off about 1am but was suddenly awakened by the house regularly vibrating and rocking. Hopping out of bed, I found that a bomb had dropped in the yard next door amongst some horses. Satisfied by some men shouting that help was available, I got back into bed again.

In the meantime, the planes had passed overhead and in the distance I could hear them dropping another load.

Tuesday, 26 February 1918

I was early astir this morning and could see some of the havoc caused next door. A dead horse lay about. I hear that several were wounded, as were the sentries on duty.

We were on the training ground at 7.30am and carried on till 3pm.

We wonder if we are going to have another dose tonight.

Wednesday, 27 February 1918

[The night] passed very quietly, or at least part of it did. We were on parade at 3am and at 5.30am were supporting the Norfolks in what was to be something like the final formation for going over. We were not the first on parade by any means. As we approached the training ground, we could see through the mist whole rows of men, completely dressed in suits of white moving about the area – they looked very quaint. The object of their dress was to blend with the early-morning conditions.

Ammunition columns and guns still continue to pass along and take up positions. We passed the last convoy for the night as we arrived on the ground.

At 6am the sun rose and the Alps, a never-ending source of delight, looked magnificent as, striking them, it turned the snow and, lower down, the growth into various hues of colour as it rose in the sky.

Back to billets at 10am, we made our preparations and leaving Povegliano at 6.30pm, relieved the Surreys in the line. Taking over the front line invariably leads to some confusion. It was 11.30pm before I got my platoon in position, inspected their sentry posts and was able to report all correct.

Afterwards, a tuck-in and now for a nap before I go on duty again 1am–3am.

Thursday, 28 February 1918

Whilst we have been busy behind the line others have been busy in the line. With the night, all sorts of working parties come up and make preparations for the show. Trench mortars, artillery, engineers and pioneers working for all they are worth whilst the night lasts and, just before daylight, they move back to the rear after covering up any indication of their work.

Piave front: the front line on the banks of the River Piave. Taken in the early hours of the morning by Charles Lacon, the photograph gives some indication of the width of the river when Harry first arrived on this front. The British barbed wire festoons the near river bank while the Austrian line can just be made out on the far side in front of the backdrop of the mountains. When the river suddenly flooded the rifle pits and sentry posts dug into the shingle in the foreground it forced a planned crossing by Harry's battalion to be aborted in early March 1918. (David Griffiths)

Harry's original map – with later annotations – of the sector around the Ponte Priula and held by the 16th Royal Warwicks. (David Griffiths)

During my watch in the night – 1–3am – I went along the line and it represented a veritable rabbit warren.

Trench mortars, of huge capacity and rapid firing ability, are like skittles along one portion. Their sole job is to lay a village flat on the other side of the wall which is occupied by the Austrians.

Wooden bridges have already been sunk under the streams and pegged down so that we shall have some sort of safe foundation and by throwing planks across may make a series of jumps.

Pits are being dug close to our wall and at the last moment, 18-pounders [guns] are to be rushed right on top of the wall to fire point blank at the wall opposite to breach it and so save us using scaling ladders. Their job will be to stand on the wall, exposed to everything and fire like blazes. The teams for these guns are, I understand, all volunteers and have been promised a month's holiday in England immediately after the show is over. I have no doubt decorations will be heaped on them and richly will they gain them.

Pioneers come along, bringing stacks of scaling ladders; engineers with pontoon boats. All these are brought up at night and hidden from observation.

I left all this hive of industry at 3am, McKinnell relieving me. I turned into kip.

With this morning came fresh information. It has been discovered that the stream is too strong and in places too deep to cross in great numbers so we are going across in boats as far as possible. A Company has been taken out of the line during the night and, by lorry, has gone to Treviso to learn punting on the canal there. Men from our warships have been brought up for the purpose from Venice to instruct.

This was a contingent of five sailors plus a number of Venetian gondoliers, bringing with them 16 gondolas under the overall command of Lieutenant Stone RN of HMS Earl of Peterborough.

A little machine-gun fire during the night from the Austrian side but it was wild and inaccurate. They have no idea how to clip the top of a parapet like the Germans or ourselves. We hope their aim will be as erratic when we go over.

It is evident to me, and to us all, that many days will not elapse before we make the plunge. Besides the foregoing account of preparations that are going forward and that have come under my observation, many other things are occurring, both seen and unseen, which gives rise to the conclusion.

There is no other subject we discuss. Do the Austrians have an idea there is something in the wind? Will our artillery be accurate? What are our chances of getting over the river? Will the 18-pounders blow in the wall opposite? These are the questions we ask one another, none of which we are able to answer with any degree of accuracy. We advance several theories but we always come back to the one point. Can we cross the river bed, exposed as we shall be for some 800 yards, without overwhelming casualties? If so, then we have no doubt about the remainder.

There is a current of electricity in the air. Officers, strangers to one another, pass each other in the line and there is always the look in the eyes of 'what are you doing in this show?' Sometimes we have stopped to discuss the problem and then find out the things that are occurring for the success of the show and are, to us, unseen.

It is needless to say that the atmosphere of expectancy has passed on to the men.

Stopping for a few minutes last night in one of my machine-gun posts and viewing, as far as the night would allow, the river bed in front, the sentry on the post turned to me and said in very subdued tones, 'It will be a bit cold getting over if we get dropped into the river. I hope we shall get the rum rations over safe, sir,' which about sums up their outlook upon the whole affair.

Assuming they know well and have confidence in their officers, they are invariably content to follow where they are led and they do follow, reserving to themselves the right to enquire after the rations and always, more particularly the rum. Feeling assured that that part of the programme is in order they assume that their part for the moment is done and are content to leave all other arrangements in other hands, ready to go anywhere when shown the way. Their inward feelings, I do not doubt, are the same as the highest officer going over, wondering whether they will reach the other side but, like the highest down to the lowest officer, they don't express those thoughts and in that way rise equal to the best.

Here, again, one may comment on the extraordinary fortitude of the men. Here is a brigade of them, some 5,000 men, contemplating, almost at leisure, a proposition in which life or death was the gamble and soon to take place and they hadn't a word to say against it, although the odds were so greatly against them.

They are not placid like 'dumb, driven cattle' and unable to put proper constructions on particular conditions that arose, the reverse rather applies. They are able to do so. It is impossible to trace the criss-crossing of the mind on such occasions, discipline has its share. It helps to coordinate the different minds to a common end. Tradition shows what has been done in the past and sets a standard whereby we may be guided. It shows us what is expected. Discipline helps us to do it.

The commissioned officer has much to support him in his outward bearing. There is his uniform, which has to be respected. He is clothed with authority and many occasions may arise when the most junior officer may become a law unto himself. The same may be said of the non-commissioned officer. He, too, is clothed with authority and must be obeyed but the man in the ranks is no more than one of many thousands, yet in circumstances such as this, there must be something whereby he can look with outward calm upon a proposition which is a gamble with death; some factor common to all ranks.

In this instance, he has to contemplate dropping over a wall, racing across shingle and getting into boats to be rowed across a stream of water flowing with great rapidity and some five or six feet deep, or racing across hastily improvised bridges to more shingle, then wading through shallow by-streams until he comes to a wall, a counterpart to the one he had just left. This he has to climb by some method, if our artillery has not been successful in breaching it, and having done all this, he has the contemplation that it was the preliminary only to what he was expected to do.

If the Austrians have any knowledge of our scheme, he knows we are practically doomed. From the mountains on the left, they have a clear view along the river bed and can sweep it with machine guns and artillery and there is not a stick to afford cover. If a man is hit or a boat holed, the men would be drowned before they could be rescued, if it is at all possible to rescue them, which is doubtful, before they are taken away by the current.

These and many other problems, this particular sentry, in common with all, has to contemplate as he stands there watching the night pass. Behind him, only a few yards away and close to the wall, are pits dotted right along the front at intervals of a very short distance and around each of these pits men work like bees around a hive – fixing trench mortars of tremendous destructive powers whose job it is to lay flat a village on the other side of the wall on the Austrian side.

A little to his right is another mass of men, engineers for the most part, digging and shovelling, making a bank to the top of the wall up which, at the last moment, the artillery are going to manhandle an 18-pounder gun. The men who will fire this into the wall opposite and breach it so that we can the more easily scale it, are all volunteers and they will have to stand on the wall, exposed at all time to everything that came over from the Austrian lines in the shape of gunfire.

Along the line, for probably half a mile, men swarm, doing something, bringing up scaling ladders, ammunition, machine guns, whilst all the roads leading to the vicinity of our part of the line are now occupied by artillery.

All this the sentry knows and it may have been because he knows that he is a part of all this movement that gives him the appearance of having a detached mind, or it may be that he was an epitome of that third factor which is ascribed to us as a nation by all those nations who look on – the ability to rise to the occasion, whatever it may be.

He is a soldier, not by profession but for the duration of the war only. He stands there, watching what was to be in a very few hours a battleground on which he would play a part, a battleground fraught with many peculiar difficulties and he hadn't a word to say against it.

Friday, 1 March 1918

Had a little excitement this afternoon. Two enemy planes dropped out of the blue and hovered over our lines. This is the least thing desired at the moment and every available machine gun and rifle was turned on them and in spite of our fire, which was intense, they went along the length of our line, occasionally dropping to so low an altitude that the airmen were clearly visible to the eye. That they have got what they came for – a camera full of photographs – I do not doubt. Their manner of coming, and persistence in hanging so low over the line, indicated they came for a special purpose but we wonder why we were unable to bring them down and suspect that underneath they were covered in sheet steel which we have been unable to penetrate. At any rate, they have got away and left us wondering.

On duty during the night 2–4am. The bright days we have been experiencing in Italy have passed for the moment. A warm, muggy atmosphere has set in with some rain.

After the episode of the aeroplanes, the Austrians started firing on our back areas with long-range guns. This, in conjunction with the aeroplanes and the fact that yesterday, they were ranging along the Piave bed, gives me the impression that they know more about our movements than is pleasant to contemplate. I remarked as such to Major Parry as we happened to meet yesterday in the trench and watched the Austrian shells drop at regular intervals along the river bed. He ventured the idea that it was intentional and was only a coincidence but I have my doubts.

Saturday, 2 March 1918

During all last night and today rain has been falling. There is every indication that the stunt will develop in a day or so at most, although no one appears to know the exact time. Everyone is wondering whether it is going to be a success or whether we shall get it in the neck. It is our only topic of conversation and the air is electric.

Sunday, 3 March 1918

The stunt has had a severe shock. I was on duty at 3am and was sent for by the sentry group on the river bed. (At night, as soon as it was dusk, we had sentry posts along the river bed some 100 yards out from our wall. Their purpose was to spot a raid, supposing the Austrians tried to come over and attempt to catch us napping.)

Dropping over the wall and making my way across the shingle, I was told by the sentry that the river was rising rapidly and soon likely to come up to the sentry post. I stayed for some half an hour and watched the water slowly rising which, by this time, was almost at our feet and appeared to be increasing in velocity as time went on. Withdrawing the sentry group close under the wall, I reported the event to the company commanding officer, Major Parry, and waited his arrival.

He came along a few minutes afterwards and withdrew the whole group back into the line. I went off duty at 6am. The river was then rapidly rising, increasing during the day to a perfect torrent of water. Tonight the whole of the bed, some 800 yards across, is a seething mass of water not unlike a rough sea, pouring down from the mountains and some five feet deep. The trestles which the engineers had placed in the bed for the 'show' have long since been swept away. We watched them go floating down this afternoon.

All this is the result of the recent mild weather and rain melting the snow in the mountains. They have looked weird today, clouds have been whirling around the peaks which, still snow-capped, stand out as each successive cloud passes and exposes them to view.

Monday, 4 March 1918

The wet season appears to have set in. It has been practically pouring with rain for the last 24 hours.

We heard late last night that the show was off and one is conscious of mingled disappointment and relief. The whole scheme seemed to depend upon the surprise element and how great a factor that would be we are unable to gauge. With the incidents mentioned on Friday, I do not think it would have been very great and so, to me, relief is mingled with the disappointment which appears quite general. We were going across tonight and everything was in a state of preparedness even to the white smocks for the first parties whilst 'blue jackets' [sailors] are at our transport lines and were coming up to row us over.

For myself, the aeroplane incident and the ranging on the bed of the river by the Austrian artillery was significant.

Tuesday, 5 March 1918, Arcade

We were relieved last night by the Bedfords and reached here at 9pm.

The same billets as before, we soon had a fire going and sat round this, discussing the pros and cons of the new turn of events.

It was well past midnight before I turned into bed but I was on parade again this morning at 9am and with a fatigue party went road-making. A beastly day, we were able to do this secure from observation and finished at 3pm.

Wednesday, 6 March 1918

Again, as yesterday, road-making. Rumours are strong that the division leaves this area which is going to be taken over again by the Italians. We hope they are not true. Shall be very sorry to leave here.

Taking advantage of the mist, long convoys of lorries have been busy all day bringing back the shells from the front areas. They have been passing all day.

A beastly night outside, raw, cold and pouring with rain.

Thursday, 7 March 1918

The kick has not gone out of our higher command yet. A modified form of operations was issued this morning and D Company has gone off to Treviso to learn more punting.

The Piave appears to have gone down considerably and they think we can get over, but heaven help us if we are not well supported by artillery.

The Austrians have also been busy lobbing 12-inch shells into the village this morning: crumped a few houses but no one injured.

This evening I have been up the line with a fatigue party making machine-gun emplacements. The Bedfords think that to try and get over can only be a forlorn hope. The river is still deep and running strong.

Friday, 8 March 1918

Fatigue work in the line again tonight. Whilst up there I watched Anderson, the brigade major [on the headquarters staff of the 15th Infantry Brigade], try and wade the river. He had not got many feet away from the side when he was nearly swept off his feet and drowned. He got out again very exhausted. On arrival back here I hear that the forlorn hope is cancelled in consequence.

Saturday, 9 March 1918

Back to the line again tonight for fatigues. Nothing happened to disturb a very charming march. The rain of the last few days ceased this evening and as we made our way to the line, the sun came out and striking the mountain tops, turned the whole landscape golden. Occasionally a gun situated somewhere fired. It was the only thing to disturb a very peaceful evening. Handing the men over to the RE, I made my way back here. On the way, I passed droves of Italians working in the back areas so I suppose they are going to take over this part of the line.

Monday, 11 March 1918

After the usual duties attendant to a changeover, we relieved the Bedfords in the line, arriving about 9pm. We followed the Bedfords scheme of sentry posts composed of Lewis guns only and this necessitated re-arranging my platoon in conjunction with other platoon officers and midnight arrived before I was able to leave them.

Crossing the road and coming across to the company headquarters [a farmhouse marked on the maps as 'C Breda'], I have just had a jolly good meal and am turning in to kip – 1am.

Tuesday, 12 March 1918

I awoke to a brilliant morning at 6am and dressing, which in the line consists of putting one's revolver in its holster, left my dugout and 'stood to' till breakfast time, 7am. The duties are very light and consist mainly of keeping out of the way of unnecessary observation.

The company headquarters referred to has, by the efforts of succeeding occupants, become very comfortable. Each time a new company of officers has taken over, something has been brought to add to its comfort. This rule is observed by the men so that dugouts are invariably left in a better state than when taken over. It's a golden, unwritten rule and, as far as circumstances will allow, always observed.

The side of the buildings facing the Austrians has been blown in by shellfire but we have one room intact, sandbagged up to keep out observation and the draught. In this room, we have our meals and are afterwards able to sit in armchairs, though mostly broken, and read the newspaper and listen to a gramophone. As a war experience in the front line, it is unique. The mountains, the never-ending source for scenic effect and which are still snow-capped, stand out very clearly in a rugged line along the sky. Except for the peaks, the snow has all melted and through the glasses we can see pine forests stretching almost to the top. With their various hues of foliage and with the sun shining upon it all, it is very picturesque.

Wednesday, 13 March 1918

We did this till midnight; transport meeting us at a position behind the line and taking [the trench mortar shells] further to the rear.

At midnight, we were relieved by another party and I turned into my dugout to awaken this morning and find the line full of Italian soldiers. Later in the day Nappy Harwood came along from battalion headquarters and told us our departure from this part of the line is imminent and that we are going up into the mountains, or at least a part of them, upon which we have gazed so long.

Thursday, 14 March 1918

This news was confirmed today. We are relieved on the night 17th–18th by the Italians and have to be clear of a ten-mile area by 2pm the following day. The night has set in wet and cold. I am on duty midnight–2am and am turning in for an early sleep.

Friday, 15 March 1918

As if conscious of our early departure, and I think they know far more than we imagine, the Austrians opened out with indirect machine-gun fire, that is firing on a point obscured from view and located on a map. This is done by adjusting the barrel of the machine gun at such an angle as to fire in the air.

The first indication we had of this was the bullets whizzing in the air and so accurate can this indirect fire be in the hands of experienced machine-gunners handling a good machine, that before our men occupying some rear trenches could get under cover, a bullet had gone clean through one man's head. It is our first casualty in Italy and, strangely enough, the man was a recruit. This was his first experience of warfare and his first week in the trenches.

It is a very extraordinary thing and one that we noted many times in France. Some fellows would go up the line time and time again and from the most embarrassing situation would come out without a scratch until eventually they come to the conclusion that they will not meet death in this war; I am beginning to think I am one.

Our only casualty is the other side of the picture. I have known many such cases as these; first time out of England, first time in the line and finished.

The unfortunate soldier was 28-year-old Private Arnold Shaw and in fact he became the battalion's second fatality during its six weeks or so in and out of the line on the Piave up to 15 March 1918. Private Lewis Farrar, 23, had been killed on 7 February 1918 at the end of the 16th Royal Warwicks' first tour of duty in their novel surroundings. These two men were the only ones killed in action. Nobody had been wounded. Compared to six months earlier, or on the Somme in 1916, a casualty list of just two deaths in six weeks was mercifully short.

Saturday, 16 March 1918

Had a useful night's sleep last night finishing duty at midnight. I slept till 'stand to' at 6am. With the remainder I turned out into the line and did what many millions of soldiers were doing at precisely the same moment, watched the breaking of day.

7am – breakfast at company headquarters and then, following custom, everyone lies low from observation.

Everything has been very quiet during the day. This afternoon an Italian colonel came round and inspected the line. They take over tomorrow.

Sunday, 17 March 1918

Relieved by the Italians [the 3rd Battalion, 215th Regiment of the Tevere – Tiber – Brigade].

Monday, 18 March 1918

We were not allowed to leave the line without a parting shot from the Austrians. At 6pm on Sunday they opened up on us with their artillery and we spent the next hour in whatever shelter we were able to get into at the moment the bombardment opened.

I happened to be at company headquarters at the time it opened and an exposed farm building, standing prominently in a field and which is one of the targets being aimed at, is not one of the healthiest places to be situated. Shells dropped very thick in the vicinity of the house so I and others so caught had no alternative but to lie against the best barricade we could find in the house and await events.

The men, we knew, were all right in their dugouts beside the wall, where I wished I was.

After a shell had taken off a corner of the house and several had fallen in the yard, the shelling ceased and on investigation, the only damage that had been caused was a fellow with a broken jaw from a splinter.

At midnight the Italians arrived. Apparently they had also had a dose of shells in the rear areas on the way up and were delayed.

This was the only period of real shelling we had during the whole of our time in Italy and it is not an unnatural assumption to think that the Austrians were fully aware of our movements and knew that we were leaving the line and so sent us a parting gift, saluting the Italians in the same way as they marched up to relieve us. How they got their information is difficult to understand but if the foregoing is correct, then there is very little doubt that they knew all about the plan of ours for crossing the Piave which would have been an affair of some little importance to them and would have been proportionally prepared to receive it.

There then followed, for the next hour, one of the most comic overtures I have experienced. Each British platoon officer in the line had a counterpart in the newly arrived Italian force and we each awaited our respective relief in the shape of an Italian officer with his platoon.

Mine duly arrived. He could not understand English or I Italian, so by the stars, our only light, I took a handful of his men at a time and indicating a machine gun tried to explain that each succeeding post was a machine-gun post and so started to go along the line. We had not gone far when Sergeant Badger, who was following behind, drew my attention to the fact that as soon as I put these Italians in a sentry post, they came out again and followed behind. I drew the Italian officer's attention to this in the best way possible by going back and starting again. On the way I was met by a platoon lance corporal who said one of the Italian soldiers could speak English. Very much relieved, I asked for him to be brought to me.

After listening to him for about ten minutes, I came to the conclusion that if he understood English, I did not.

Meanwhile, Sergeant Badger got my platoon together whilst I dealt with the officer and his platoon. After wasting a further half an hour in trying to explain the various positions and trying also to understand the Italian who said he could speak English, I was eventually able to gather that the Italian officer was more concerned about his own quarters than about getting his men into position.

Fed up with them, I left them to settle the affair themselves and the last I heard of them they were still arguing.

I made my way to my dugout, took an Italian Very light pistol that I had been keeping as a souvenir of the line, picked up my platoon and started for our billets, reporting to the CO on the way 'relief correct'.

Arriving at our billets at 2am, tea and rum were served out and what remained of the night, we made best use of in sleep.

On parade again at 9am. The battalion said 'goodbye' to the locality, leaving at 9.30am en route for the Asiago Plateau [another sector on the Italian front some 37 miles to the north-west].

Marching at first was good but later in the day the sun was almost tropical and we stopped at midday for a lunch. A brook was adjacent and the men, with no great desire for food, were soon stripped and in the water and presented a mass of struggling humanity.

Villanova – we stayed some little time here, giving the men time to dry in the sun. Towards 2am we moved on again arriving at our present billet later in the afternoon. We are here for the night only, I and other officers sleeping in the local hospital.

Harry's misgivings that the Austrians were well aware of their plans turned out to be well founded. He added later, 'I found out that some few years afterwards 'Nappy' Harwood had been in conversation with an Austrian who was in the air force operating on that front and, referring to the attack, asked him if he knew anything of the affair. He replied that they – the Austrians – had every knowledge of it and were waiting for us and as well-prepared as we were. It is possible that the coming of the rain stopped, for us, a tragedy.'

Tuesday, 19 March 1918
Orders changed. We appear to be here for an indefinite period of time.

Wednesday, 20 March 1918
For the next three or four days orders were being constantly altered and we were kept in a perpetual state of unrest, mercifully ignorant of the reason for this apparent indecision and wondering whether at any moment we should have orders to pack and move on.

Friday, 22 March 1918

Definite orders came on Friday evening and the battalion left the village this morning at 8.30am with orders to trek towards the mountains which we have viewed so often, ie, the Venetian Alps – the Asiago Plateau.

Saturday, 23 March 1918, Fossalta

Today we have marched about ten miles, quite enough in an almost blistering heat. A breeze helps things along somewhat.

We have heard that the Germans have started an offensive in France on a large scale (21 March). That it has been developing for some time is common knowledge but at the moment we do not know if they have made any gain.

Three or four of us are billeted for the night in a cottage, or rather the room of a cottage. The usual furniture has been pushed on one side and on the floor space provided, our valises are spread out. The other officers curled up in their sleeping bags are asleep whilst I am paying tribute to my diary and then to follow suit.

Thursday, 28 March 1918, on board boat at Le Havre en route for England

I had barely laid down on Saturday night when I heard someone come clattering up to the cottage on horseback. Silence for a moment and then heard the adjutant yell out my name. I yelled back and he came into the room which only consisted of opening the front door which was on the roadside.

Flourishing some papers, he told me I was for leave the following morning.

Arnold Harwood, whose name was next on the list for leave, was away at Rome for a few days and had not returned. They had given him to the last moment and failing him, I came next. Lieutenant Griffiths was also going and we had to report at Padua Station some 15 miles away at 2pm the following day.

It was already late when the adjutant came. I packed up what things I required for home and lay down again.

6.30 the following morning saw Griffiths and myself along the road. We had got to make our own way to Padua and were taking no chances. A glorious morning, we found some lorries going our way and, jumping on these, arrived in Padua 9am.

With plenty of time on hand, Griffiths and I went and had some breakfast and duly reported at the station 2.30pm.

We met Harwood and his party returning from Rome. Arnold was somewhat vexed when he heard that he had just missed his leave.

Whilst waiting for the train we heard, for the first time, ugly rumours which were brought by officers who, like ourselves were going on leave, to the effect that things in France were not going too well at the moment and we, the 5th Division, were likely to go back there, as reinforcements were being called for.

By the afternoon, some 400–500 officers and men were waiting. We of the 5th Division were not feeling 'too cheery'. The rumours were too persistent to be without foundation.

Eventually the leave train drew in, consisting of carriages for the officers and cattle trucks for the men and we left Padua station at 6pm.

Of the journey, a lot could have been written. Taking the inland route we passed through the Alps – gorgeous scenery – Aix-les-Bains, Lyons, the outskirts of Paris and then on to Le Havre.

At Lyons the train was held up by the railway transport officer who came along the train and informed all officers and men of the 5th Division to hold themselves ready to detrain at any moment and rejoin the division which may be coming back to France. This news was sickening and only tended to confirm the rumours we had heard at Padua.

Arriving at Le Havre last night, we found the last boat had left for England and so had to stay the night in camp. We have lived every moment since arrival expecting to have our leave cancelled and to be told to await the division. This morning, with no news, we were early astir. Snow had been falling during the night and it was bitterly cold. We were on board at 6am and now – 8.30am Thursday, 28 March 1918 – we are waiting for the boat to start.

THE LINE
ON THE LYS

April 1918 – November 1918

'I would sooner be a boot black or crossing sweeper than go into the trenches'

Desperate for his leave boat to slip anchor and get clear of Le Havre, Harry had lived in fear that he might be recalled if the rumours of a crisis developing on the Western Front were to be believed. By 28 March 1918, the reality was even worse than the rumour.

By the spring of 1918, the Germans knew that a time of reckoning was at hand. Bedevilled by economic and political problems on the home front and militarily exhausted by its defensive efforts on the Western Front and the need to conserve its remaining manpower, in early 1917 Germany had voluntarily given ground on the Somme and pulled its line back some 25 miles to a new, shorter, yet deeper and stronger system of defences which the Allies called the Hindenburg Line. The Allies, too, were exhausted. The British desperately needed time to reorganise and train new drafts of men after the severe losses of 1916–1917 and to build up their dilapidated line, but there was one factor which all sides knew would eventually tip the balance. The doughboys were coming; hundreds of thousands of them. The Americans had entered the war in April 1917 and although their troops were not yet on the Western Front in body, their spirit pervaded the battlefield. It was only a matter of time, and time was running out for Germany.

Germany knew it had to strike a knockout blow to the Allies before vast numbers of tall, fit American soldiers stepped off the troopships. The Bolshevik revolution and the collapse of Russia had freed up German units which had been manning the Eastern Front so creating the all-important numerical superiority in the west which the war planners required. The men were now available, so were the guns and so were the methods with which to deploy them. It was now or never – the last throw of the dice – and the Germans chose to cast it against the British. Breaking the backs of the British Tommies would surely lead to a French collapse and the war would be won.

The hammer blow fell on the morning of 21 March 1918. After a meticulously orchestrated and merciless five-hour bombardment, the gathering storm of Operation Michael finally broke and massed German infantry were unleashed to swarm through swirling clouds of fog, smoke and gas to fall on the under-strength, unsettled and inexperienced British battalions holding the line west of St Quentin. The line broke and the British fell back and for day after day, mile after mile, they continued to retreat, re-crossing the sterile battleground of the Somme won at such a high cost 18 months earlier. In four days the Germans drove the British back almost 40 miles until, finally, they were in sight of Amiens.

The situation looked bleak in the extreme; if the great rail nexus of Amiens was taken the British would have to fall back and their army might be split asunder from the French. There could only be one outcome of such a catastrophe and it was too awful to contemplate. Thankfully, the German attack slowed as their supply lines became stretched, and hungry soldiers gorged themselves on the relative riches unearthed in captured British supply dumps. The German offensive in the south had run its course and was called off on 5 April 1918 but a fresh one – Operation Georgette – roared into life on 9 April further north on the Armentières front in the valley of the River Lys and pummelled the British and Portuguese troops holding the line. Yet again, within days, the Allies were sent reeling as the Germans pushed and probed, grasping for the vital rail junction at Hazebrouck and, further north, the main British supply routes from the channel ports of Boulogne and Calais.

Following on so quickly from the disaster which had befallen the British to the south, so serious had the situation on the Lys become by 11 April that no less a person than the Commander-in-Chief himself had issued a Special Order of the Day to be circulated urgently to all ranks of the British Army. Sir Douglas Haig's 'backs to the wall' order achieved lasting military fame. After praising the 'splendid resistance' of his men, he went on to say that victory would belong to the side which held out the longest and his concluding paragraph was calculated to stir the blood:

'There is no other course open to us but to fight it out; every position must be held to the last man; there must be no retirement. With our backs to the wall, and believing in the justice of our cause, each one of us must fight on to the end.'

When Harry arrived back in France from leave on the following day, Haig's words had been trumpeted loudly by a patriotic press, although they often evoked a rather more earthy response from the lowly British Tommy who had to do the actual fighting. Nevertheless, fight on they did. The situation was still fluid, the fighting on the Lys still fierce and Harry had to find his battalion which was already up the line and in the thick of it.

Sunday, 14 April 1918, Le Havre

I have had my fortnight's leave in England undisturbed by any recall, which I expected. With the prospect of France again, it has not been a cheery time.

We left England two days ago, on the 12th, and at Southampton I met the other officers of the 5th Division. Returning from leave is not an inspiring sight at any time, every one looking more or less 'fed up'. It was particularly so on this occasion. With the German offensive going strong, the prospects are not of the rosiest, especially to those of us who know what an 'offensive' means and we are nearly all old campaigners as far as this war is concerned.

We arrived in Le Havre on Friday evening and made our way to the camp here. The camp itself is like a small town and when we reported to the commandant our doubts were at once put to rest. From him, we gathered that the division is on the way back from Italy or are already back and we have to await orders.

They came this afternoon. We leave here tonight 8pm for an unknown destination.

Monday and Tuesday, 15 and 16 April 1918

We left Le Havre at 1.30am on the night of 14/15 April and arrived at Rouen at 6am after a most frightfully cold journey in cattle trucks. The wind came through the floor and kept us stamping up and down to keep warm.

Wednesday, 17 April 1918, Thiennes, three miles from Aire

At Rouen we gathered that we should not be moving again till dark so Griffiths and I went into the town after a breakfast and wash at the officers' club.

At 9pm we returned to the station. Drafts from the camps were already entraining and at 10.15 we drew out of the station under the impression that we were bound for Hazebrouck.

We travelled all night and at 3pm arrived at Lillers. There we learnt that we should not be able to get to Hazebrouck owing to the German advance.

Whilst we were waiting in the train, a couple of long-range shells dropped amongst the station buildings. We were not long in detraining and later in the afternoon, Griffiths and myself made our way to Aire where we heard the divisional headquarters were situated.

At Aire we were redirected to Thiennes, three miles away. Meeting Captain Handford of the 15th Battalion we were able to gather particulars of happenings since we left the division in Italy.

After a coffee at a cottage, we left him and made our way to battalion headquarters and learned in detail all that had happened during our absence. Major Quarry was in charge of the 'dumped' personnel, with Arnold Harwood acting as adjutant. The CO and Sayer were up in the line.

When I left the battalion in Italy on the morning of 24 March, they were making preparations for a march of about 20 miles that day for the Asiago Plateau. It was whilst on this march that they received orders to about turn and make for the nearest railway station en route for France and they eventually entrained at Vicenza.

The transport, with orders to proceed partly by road to France, got lost and did not recover the battalion for some considerable time afterwards. Things were urgent. Arriving in France, the battalion was bound for the north of Arras when they were again stopped, detrained and entrained again for this front, opposite Merville. They were only just in the nick of time. The whole division, dumping their kit on the rail embankment, went into action in open order. With only the knowledge that somewhere in front the Germans had broken through, they streamed across the fields.

The Duke of Cornwall's Light Infantry, the 14th and 15th Warwicks were the first to come into contact with the Germans who, having broken the opposition, were coming forward looking for fresh British forces and they came upon our division advancing. A running fight ensued in which we were successful in driving them back to within a mile of Merville, occupying the line of barricades and slit trenches that the Guards had held.

This was not done without cost to ourselves. One or two brigadier generals have been wounded leading their brigades and the loss of men in killed and wounded has been heavy but we appear to have saved the situation. Had the Germans only known: there were no troops between themselves and Aire and they had broken through completely. We arrived in the nick of time. Portuguese troops, who should have been there in support of the Guards, had run away.

Our battalion, the 16th Royal Warwickshire Regiment acting as support to the division, marched for some distance along a road after detraining and was met by streams of refugees pouring along from the outlying villages and houses. For the most part, the womenfolk were in tears and the men (very old) wheeling a few personal things in perambulators or in anything that could be pushed on wheels. They raised a cheer as the battalion passed them but it was all very pathetic.

The battalion marched on and eventually took up a position alongside the Bedfords, the two battalions acting in support to the Norfolks and Cheshires who are in the front line.

The front line at the moment is difficult to define but consists principally of houses and pits that were hastily dug by the Guards before they were swamped by the Germans. These have been retaken and occupied and, as occasion permits at night, are being joined up, forming another line of trenches across the land.

Here, around the village of Thiennes, every available man is working day and night digging trenches in preparation for another German attack which is expected at any moment.

Everyone is living with their nerves strained almost to the full, lying down to sleep but always fully dressed and ready either to get up and fight or march, either forward or backward. Transport is lined up in the fields, packed, and at night-time, the horses are tied to the wagons ready to harness and move.

At the moment the Germans appear to be concentrating towards the north. Today we have heard that they have taken Bailleul. We can only assume that they will now make for Béthune then there is no doubt that we shall be for it in this direction.

Meanwhile news comes down from the front line by runner at night-time to say how the troops are wearing in the front line. From this we gather that little or no fighting is going on, that the men, making use of the night, are poaching fowls, ducks and so forth for their own consumption and cattle are being rounded up and brought down here and will no doubt be slaughtered and consumed as the best means of dealing with them.

Major Quarry, our second-in-command, who left us yesterday to take over a battalion temporarily, the commanding officer being killed, has, we have just heard, been killed himself, leading an attack upon some farm buildings on our right.

It is a time of thrills, no one knowing from one moment to another what is going to happen. I have just been talking to Captain Handford of the 15th Battalion, Royal Warwickshire Regiment. He led his company to the attack after detraining. At the commencement of the day he was at full strength. By evening, he was reduced to a handful of men; cooks, pioneers, any odd men and a few Portuguese that were in the vicinity. He has himself just been sent down for a night's sleep.

He says the conditions in the line are very nervy, no one having any idea what is going to happen but all prepared for anything, anytime. In daytime the men lie flat on their backs in the slit trenches and as soon as night comes on, dig like fury to deepen and connect up what trenches are in existence.

I expect I shall go up and join them in a day or so. I do not hail the prospects with any great joy. Since I have arrived here, a few shells have dropped in the locality and I find I have that involuntary desire to dive for the nearest cover as I hear them whistling through the air. The months in Italy have not served, as I had hoped, to put my nerves in good working order again and I have that feeling that I had when I first left England, that I would sooner be a boot black or crossing sweeper than go up into the trenches. I do not doubt that there are many such as I in the same frame of mind. The trenches have no joys but many hells, especially when one is getting nervy.

Thursday, 18 April 1918
A great deal of shelling has been going on in the forward areas but today we have only had the echo back here.

A brigade of Portuguese have just arrived for trench digging in the village. It's about all they are good for. The objection to this is that it relieves some of our troops for the front line and they are dog-tired. News has come down from the line that things are quiet for the most part after the shelling this morning and there was no evidence that the Germans were preparing for an attack so tonight I am taking my boots and stockings off for a sleep.

Friday, 19 April 1918

All was quiet this morning so after breakfast I cycled into Aire. The roads were congested with traffic and small drafts of men coming up to join different regiments in the locality. French and Canadian transport was passing through as I arrived, whilst in every street what civilians remained were preparing to move and were stacking their furniture on anything with wheels ready for a trek towards the coast. Very tragic figures they looked, these old men and women pulling their carts of what were probably their most valued possessions and leaving behind them their homes. They have the same information that we have; that the town is going to be attacked. They are sensible and are getting away whilst they are safe.

Fearfully cold wind. I did not stay long in Aire but made my way back to our transport lines.

A heavy bombardment is going on, directed on Merville which is only a few miles from our front line and occupied by the Germans.

Saturday, 20 April 1918

After breakfast this morning, I took a party of men trench-digging in the village and returned this evening to find orders awaiting me to take over a company in the front line. The present officer in charge has cracked up.

Sunday, 21 April 1918, Roussel Farm buildings, battalion headquarters

I left the transport lines after breakfast this morning and, by a series of lorry jumps, arrived on the outskirts of the Nieppe Forest [north-west of the town of Merville in the valley of the River Lys]. Up till then travelling had been easy. The forest, some 40 miles square, very largely hid our movements from the Germans but in the forest itself, things were different. The part which affords us shelter is a spur at the end of the forest going to a point and in this part it is some two miles in depth. It was this two miles I had now to travel.

I was told to have my box respirator ready and be ready for the first signs of gas as the Germans were steadily rendering the wood almost untenable by a constant stream of gas shells that they poured over at intervals night and day.

The forest is bisected by main tracks wide enough for a couple of wagons to pass. These partitions are again bisected by walking tracks.

Having been given my general directions for battalion headquarters, I struck out along one of the main [west-east] tracks, called 'Via Roma' by us in memory of our recent tour in Italy. It was up this road I made my way to emerge at the other end to open fields in the midst of which was situated Roussel Farm.

I had not gone far when I heard the familiar whizz in the air and dropped to the ground whilst a succession of heavy shells crumped in amongst the trees some distance away.

I had walked about a mile. Not a soul was in sight anywhere, I might have been a tourist for what actual signs of war were visible and was beginning to wonder whether I had missed my way when, from around a curve in the distance, I saw a wagon and team of four horses tearing towards me for all they were worth, the driver lashing them and the wagon tossing from side to side in the cart rucks.

It was a fine sight to watch them coming on and I stood aside whilst they dashed past and as they did so the driver yelled 'gas!' and then I knew why they were in a hurry. I could smell nothing in the air myself but got my respirator ready and went forward and eventually reached the other side of the wood and found someone who directed me here, Roussel Farm, a pile of buildings standing out in the middle of a field. I noticed the barns had already been blown down, otherwise the house is as yet untouched.

I found the CO and adjutant occupying what might have been the drawing room of the house. The windows were all shuttered and barricaded up and over a very murky lamp, the CO told me the things of interest since I left them in Italy.

The news of Major Quarry's death had already reached him.

After a drink and some food, I went out to find my platoon. Sergeant Badger welcomed me with one of his big grins. The men were surprisingly jovial and appeared to be enjoying what is undoubtedly a novel situation for us.

All types of poultry are at large and the men, when circumstances permit, creep off and bring back a fowl or duck which is quickly despatched but how it is cooked, I don't know.

Their casualties have been practically nil. All the old faces are there that I got to know so well in Italy. I think they were glad to see me, if one might judge by their faces. They had many woes to tell me; the stopping of leave seemed to be the worst. I told them that they wouldn't get poultry to eat in England. They agreed and I left them very cheery.

Making my way back to battalion headquarters, I learn I take over the company for a few days until Nappy Harwood can take over.

Apparently we are in close support to the front line and move up there tonight, relieving the Cheshires.

Monday, 22 April 1918

This was accomplished about midnight last night and I am back again into real war. Already I am beginning to contrast those few great months in Italy. What a great difference environment makes to one's life.

We carried on sandbagging where the Cheshires had left off. No man was allowed to sleep; officers, NCOs and men, we all turned to. There are no passengers under these circumstances, all are workers and we worked till daybreak, digging deeper into the trenches, joining up those that were still isolated, filling sandbags with the earth we had dug and making a breastwork with the filled bags, useless against shellfire but a protection from observation.

These trenches were dug by the Duke of Cornwall's Light Infantry and the 14th and 15th Warwicks when they detrained on the embankment and after they had pushed the Germans back who had broken through Merville and through the Brigade of Guards.

With the first sign of dawn, all work ceased and we have lain flat in the bottom of the trench all day. They are barely deep enough to sit upright and any movement along the trench is done on the hands and knees. Our rations consist of what we carried up last night. Mine – bread and bully and water – is the same as the men's, who lay stretched out along the trench in varying attitudes and who have tried to spend the day as I have in sleep or trying to sleep.

We shall all be glad when night comes so that we can get up and stretch our legs. Sleep has been difficult for my part and through the periscope I have been trying to see how the land lies in front. The Germans appear to be occupying a hedgerow some hundreds of yards away, their line of trenches taking the line of the hedge which on our right goes at right angles towards their rear area and is lost to sight.

No doubt, like us, they are laid in the bottom of the trench as we are, awaiting the night, then to emerge and dig.

The mixture of dead lying in front is rather strange. There are still some of our fellows of the Guards whom we have not yet been able to get in, some Germans, a horse, cow, calf and pig.

The intention of the Germans is obscure. Since our division drove them back into Merville and after they again attacked and were repulsed, they have done little but artillery work, pasting our rear areas with gas and making everything very uncomfortable but with no signs of movement in their front line.

Headquarters fear an attack. We have orders that if such takes place, no man will leave the trench but fight till we are overrun. It will be a test of cold courage which I think our men will rise to.

Tuesday, 23 April 1918

Nappy Harwood came up last night and took over the company and I am back with my platoon. At dusk last night, or rather at 'stand down' at 9.30pm, we started sandbagging and digging and finished this morning in a sweat at 4.30am as daybreak was beginning.

The night set up a drizzle and we are in a fairly sticky mess today, all of us coated in mud from head to foot.

With the rations last night came up spirit stoves. With these we have been able to have frequent brews of tea during the day. Heathfield is good at this. No doubt frequent cups for me mean frequent cups for himself.

The Germans have been busy all day crumping our rear areas with incendiary shells with the result that several buildings are alight, sending huge columns of smoke into the air.

We are patiently awaiting dark so that we can stretch ourselves. These days seem like a week.

Wednesday, 24 April 1918

We carried on again last night. Bales of sandbags came up soon after dark and by this morning, they were filled and now help to form a very respectable trench.

By filling the bags with earth from the bottom of the trench and placing the filled sandbag on the parapet in front of the trench, two birds are killed with one stone, the trench is made deeper and the head cover higher so today instead of crawling, we have been able, with care, to walk along the trench.

For this last effort in sandbagging, which we have done really well and used some hundreds of sandbags during the last two or three nights, my servant tells me that my platoon now call me the 'Sandbag King'!

King, one of the D Company officers, took out a patrol during the night to reconnoitre the ground and spied a German patrol coming out of a farm house building in no-man's-land and within 100 yards of our front line. They lay and watched them make off towards their own lines and, nothing else occurring, King and company returned. Probably they were a German machine-gun crew or a number of snipers.

Thursday, 25 April 1918

We burnt the buildings down last night; fired Very lights at the thatched roof till one landed right on top. A strong wind was blowing and in less than five minutes, the whole lot was ablaze. The fire spread to adjoining cottages and for a couple of hours, it was rather a fine sight, falling rafters sending up columns of sparks into the night. Only a few charred beams remained this morning standing in the air. The remainder is a black mess on the ground, still giving out volumes of smoke.

Anticipating that the Germans will retaliate on buildings close to our line, I took a small party of choice spirits from my platoon before daybreak and we investigated a farmhouse just opposite here. We ransacked the house, which has been partly blown in by shellfire, and as a result I have a feather bed, some sheets and brass candlesticks and a mirror for my shack which was a hole in the ground at the end of a trench.

Pans of pickled pork that we were unable to carry I sent another party for and they are now on their way to our kitchens to be cooked and returned to us.

Newsom, a young second lieutenant who recently joined the battalion, stopped one in the thigh from a machine gun whilst out on patrol and is probably by this time in one of the rear hospitals and en route for England.

All today I have spent refurnishing my shelter which consists of a sheet of corrugated iron scrounged from an adjoining farm and placed over the top of the trench at a dead end. The feather bed covers the ground and is already caked in mud. Around the sides of the trench which are likewise mud and down which water occasionally trickles, I have hung the sheets. The effect of this, together with the mirror and candlesticks, is to give it the effects of a church altar.

It is evidently a source of admiration to my servant, Heathfield, who has scrounged some wild flowers and they repose in a bottle on an improvised shelf.

The feather bed is great. I have reposed upon it all afternoon. Nappy and Ward crawled along to inspect it and went away full of envy. Its fame has spread. I hope the Germans won't drop a shell on it or the rain come in.

Friday, 26 April 1918

A company of the Cheshires went over last night on our right and took a farmhouse from which snipers and machine guns had been giving them some trouble. They took the whole issue prisoners; about a dozen men with machine guns.

The Germans returned the hate by pasting the whole of our front line with shells, one of which dropped straight into the trench which is under my charge.

As soon as the shelling ceased we concentrated on the crater formed and by daybreak, this morning the trench was its former shape again, I expect I shall be more a Sandbag King than ever.

We are now getting more firmly established in our position. Instead of the long line of slit trenches in the ground we now have one long front line, well-sandbagged in front. No good against artillery, but safe from rifle bullets.

The ground we are occupying was until recently ploughed land, low lying. We have been unable to dig deeply and rely mostly on breastworks of sandbags for protection from bullets.

From overhead observation, we have no cover and to prevent prowling German planes from spotting too much activity, we lie down in the bottom of the trench. So has passed today.

Tomorrow night we are relieved.

Sunday, 28 April 1918

Relief came last night. At 10.30pm, the 14th Royal Warwicks Regiment came up and took over and we made for the rear. Picked up guides at a crossroads and got clear of the line without anything exciting happening and fancied we were clear of the shelled area when suddenly we heard a big brute coming through the air. It passed overhead and another followed. The next fell within 50 yards. By the time it had exploded I was lying flat on the ground and the next moment, we were all doing a double and did not stop for the next 200 yards.

We reached our billets at 1am, situated in the Nieppe Forest.

I saw the men tucked away with a rum ration each and then made my way to where I was told a meal had been prepared for the officers.

I found other officers had already arrived and some came in later and we sat down to a hot meal and hot drinks.

We looked very weird by lamplight. We were covered in mud and dirt and most of us had not had a shave for the last six days.

Dog-tired, we turned in to sleep one by one; I about 3am, and slept like a log till midday. It was the second time I had taken my boots off since leaving Le Havre.

Heathfield awoke me with a bucket of hot water for washing and shaving purposes. I bathed in it.

This afternoon, I inspected my platoon and their kit and then left them to it. I expect most of them went back and had another sleep.

A glorious afternoon. After the inspection I wandered around the wood in the locality of the camp. It's a wonderful spot, we are told that it still teems with game including small deer which can be had for the shooting.

The camp [christened Spresiano in memory of the 5th Division's time in Italy] is situated in a clearing that is clear from undergrowth. We are obscured from aeroplane observation by the huge trees through which the sun percolates. Into this Arcady, our pioneers came yesterday afternoon and, by dint of slogging, erected canvas huts and a mess hut. It was into these we dropped, fagged-out, in the early hours of this morning. It is impossible to describe the feeling of relaxation and safety that comes over one after a period in the front-line trenches, especially under these conditions when, day and night, we expected the Germans to come over *en masse* and given our emphatic orders that we hold the line to the end and, if unable to hold the line, no man was expected to return.

Now for a short time, that is over and we can stroll about the woods. Childish though it may appear, this liberty of action makes life worth living.

Tonight we are sitting around an old brazier in the mess. The gramophone is churning out some old song. Occasionally one of the fellows joins in. It will die down when one of us is too lazy to put on another record. Between the songs we can hear the big guns on the edge of the wood sending over stuff into the German lines. I expect into Merville.

We are in reserve to the 95th Brigade and although here we undress at night-time, we have to be ready to move up the line in one hour's notice in case of attack.

The officer commanding the 15th Brigade, in which Harry's battalion was serving, was eager to provide a tonic for the troops when they came out of the line after the battalion's recent hard graft with 'pick and shovel' in constructing the new front line which skirted the south-eastern fringes of the Nieppe Forest. Keen for all ranks to know that he was 'extremely pleased with the work done by the battalion while in the line' he added that it had 'stood out in the brigade'.

Monday, 29 April 1918

Had a weird time during the night. Our heavy guns continued to fire practically without break till dawn this morning. In the intervals when they ceased fire, the whole wood in our locality was filled by the song of nightingales, in groups. There seemed to be about half a dozen in our locality. Their song simply filled the air. Unable to sleep, I got up and went outside my shack. A brilliant moonlit night – the moon streaming through the trees – threw everything into relief. I stood and listened, so brilliant was the song and so brilliant the night; I was enchanted until our guns started again and I was brought back to earth. I turned into my shack but did not sleep and was glad when breakfast came.

This afternoon, we have been for a short route march, marching on the outskirts of the wood to prevent any risks from observation.

Tonight we are sat around the old brazier. The gramophone is brought in and I suppose will churn out songs again till someone gets too lazy to put on another record.

Tuesday, 30 April 1918

The night passed much as the others. It's no rest cure, lying on the ground whilst heavy guns are firing in the vicinity. At night they seem to have their picnic and the earth vibrates until the early morning.

This afternoon baths. This evening much as last night.

The camp has been made wretched by a heavy rain last night and all the tracks are inches deep in mud and water. Everything is very damp and moist.

Clews turned in to sleep early but has just come back into the mess. He says his shack must be pitched on a bog. He had scarcely laid down when he felt the moisture soaking his clothes and proposes staying in here all night. I expect we shall find the same and do the same.

After baths this afternoon, I went to reconnoitre a line of trenches that are being dug. We take over the work tomorrow. I had to go up and get some idea of what was being done and what had to be done.

Wednesday, 1 May 1918

Today the whole battalion has been out trench-digging in the wood about 1½ miles away. Parade 8am. We reached the locality about 9am and carried on with the work.

It has been rather interesting. Imagine a wood, untouched, into which there has been cut a pathway. From this we have moved forward, cutting away the undergrowth which, in places, grows some six feet high. In positions which offer good observation and are difficult to be observed, we have carried on digging or erecting strong points and trenches. In front of these, barbed wire is pegged to the ground some six feet in breadth.

The weather for the most part has been dull and chilly. We returned to camp at 3pm and after tea those who had got anything to sleep on excepting the ground have gone to get a few hours' sleep before the guns start. Those without beds are sitting around the brazier and here we shall stay until it gets too cold.

Work had begun on constructing two further lines of defences behind what was becoming established as the new front line. Harry was working on the first of these – the Haverskerque–Lamotte Line – one and a half miles back.

Thursday, 2 May 1918

A day off duty and I have been into Aire. Prisoners have been taken at odd intervals and it has been gathered from these that for some days after we came in contact with the Germans and drove them back into Merville, we only held the line by the skin of our teeth. On their repulse, the Germans rushed up another division with orders to attack us at daybreak. They stayed the night in Merville, sacked the town, got drunk (there were vast supplies of ours there) and refused to come on. Another German division was sent for but their opportunity had gone. By the time they arrived, we were digging like fury in the meantime and when they did attack the Duke of Cornwall's Light Infantry and 14th Royal Warwicks Regiment front they were wiped down by our machine guns and rifle fire.

The prisoners also say that our part of the forest was an object of attack from both flanks but for some reason was abandoned.

Friday, 3 May 1918

We moved out of divisional reserve into brigade reserve this morning. Although we have only moved a few hundred yards nearer the line and are still in the wood, it has made all the difference to our conditions. Our valises and the men's blankets have gone back to the transport lines. Now we have to sleep in our clothes and boots and be ready to move out of the camp in ten minutes in case help is required.

Engineers have been busy erecting Nissen huts of corrugated steel situated amongst the undergrowth. It would be very charming if the conditions of life were natural.

Tonight, or rather early morning, I am officer on duty midnight–3am, prowling around the camp.

Saturday, 4 May 1918

I turned in at 3am after my tour of three hours. Time did hang: I thought it would never end as I plodded my way from sentry to sentry and then round again and again. The big guns still keep up their nightly picnics of hate, pouring over shells into the German positions. As yet the Germans have not yet been able to locate them, or have no big guns up. Occasionally we get a shell over but they are wide of the mark and of no account.

3am came at last and with it Ward, who relieved me and carried on till daybreak.

Sunday, 5 May 1918

Saturday passed very uneventfully till 9pm when I took the company trench-digging close up to the front line.

To commence with we lost our way and did not arrive at the place till 10.30pm and got down to work carrying on where others had previously left off. They were digging a communication trench from the edge of the wood to a line of support trenches.

The Germans had evidently spotted this going on for some time and we had barely started when 'crump', 'crump', they began to come over. Their aim was wide and the shells went into the wood but it is an uncomfortable feeling.

From somewhere – I could not locate where – the Germans were switching a machine gun across us. We could hear the bullets whistling through the air. They seemed unpleasantly close. The men dug almost with their backs double and took advantage of any bit of cover that was afforded.

It's an eerie business, digging in the dark. I was not sorry when 3.30am arrived. The men covered up the traces as well as they could and we returned to camp. In strange contrast to all this were the nightingales, singing for all they were worth as we made our way through the wood. The men were impressed and though tired, stopped at intervals to listen. We reached camp as day was breaking and I made straight off to my shack for a sleep.

I awoke about midday to find rain pouring down and apparently it had been doing so for some hours.

Tonight the camp is waterlogged. Rain has been pouring down all day and some of the huts are deep in water and mud. The men are excellent under these conditions. As the conditions become worse so for the most part do [the men] rise to meet them. We have nothing whatever in the camp that will add to their comfort.

Before dark, I went to the shacks occupied by my platoon. I found them quite happy, scraping the wet mud from the bottom of their shack whilst others had been scrounging around and had returned with bits of dry wood which they proposed to light on the ground as soon as dusk came.

Nieppe Forest: A sentry of the 2nd Battalion, King's Own Scottish Borderers in a recently captured German trench close to the village of Arrewage, 4 July 1918. This image was taken a few weeks after Harry had led a raid on the German lines in the very same area south of the Forest of Nieppe. Note the shallow and very rudimentary nature of the trenches at this stage of the war in the valley of the River Lys and the abandoned German kit. (© Imperial War Museums Q 6819)

Leaving them to their own salvation, which I knew they were able to reach without any help from me, I returned to tea, afterwards dinner and now to bed.

Most of the other officers have already gone, glad to put a close to a very murky day.

Monday, 6 May 1918

Up early this morning, I was in charge of a fatigue party.

Breakfast 6.30am, and after a short march through the wood we came to a clearing and carried on with the work already in hand, making barbed-wire entanglements for throwing across the road and pathways in case the Germans break through and attack this part of the forest.

The weather fine overhead, the ground still waterlogged, we finished at 1pm and returned to dinner. This afternoon I have slept.

Some diversion was created early this evening by a German plane coming over. He came too far. One of ours got behind him. We heard the firing of machine guns in the air close overhead and ran to the edge of the wood and were in time to see the final scene; the German plane toppling over somewhere in our rear areas. Such little episodes as this buck our men up wonderfully. It's as good as an issue of rum. I think it makes them think there are compensations in being infantrymen after all.

Tuesday, 7 May 1918

A day of rest or rest as far as the camp provides.

This afternoon I took my boots off and my feet were very swollen and thick with dry mud. With Heathfield's help, I have soaked them in hot water and made things considerably easier. Tonight I take a party trench-digging again.

Wednesday, 8 May 1918

We left camp at 9pm. With my previous experience of losing the way, I made more sure of my route and by 9.30pm the men were hard at work. Prior to leaving the camp, the adjutant told me that information had come to divisional headquarters that the Germans were going to put down a barrage in that vicinity at 1.30am.

After slogging it, I withdrew the men at 1am but I had stayed long enough to have a couple of men sniped or machine-gunned; one through the leg and another through the stomach. I could not locate from which direction the bullets were coming and eventually came to the conclusion that it was indirect fire from machine guns.

I had a very unpleasant experience myself. Standing on top of one of the trenches, a bullet cracked through the air; must have been close to my face. For some few minutes afterwards, my ears were ringing, I was quite deaf.

A vile night; wet and weird, we got the two wounded men away on stretchers and followed ourselves shortly afterwards, arriving in camp 1.15am.

The Germans made some show at 2.15am but a poor effort.

We awoke this morning to a glorious sun and under its influence, have been drying our clothes and boots before going back up into the line tomorrow.

Friday, 17 May 1918

We went up the line on the 9th, distinctly on the nervy side of things. For two days previously we were aware that there was some information in circulation amongst the higher command, the substance of which we were unable to gather. Numerous councils had been held by the divisional general, by the brigadier general and by various units in the division. It put us into a state of nervous expectancy, in view of the precarious entrenchments we had and the general tendency of the Germans to attack now that they are on the aggressive.

A few hours before we left the camp for the line, the CO called the company commanders together and, in a shooting box adjacent to the camp and with a sentry on guard over the door, held another council.

The meeting lasted about an hour and at its conclusion, Arnold Harwood, C Company captain, came along to us, not looking as if he had been left £5,000. We asked him what was in the wind, what was going to happen? At first, he refused to say and so I told him that the position we, the platoon commanders, were placed in was not a fair one. We knew something was likely to happen but were not in a position to guard against it in any way. Such a state of things was not fair to us or to our men.

He agreed with me and, after cautioning us not to say a word to our platoon NCOs – as he and the other company officers were under a pledge not to divulge the information – told us that from information which had come in to general headquarters and had on previous occasions proved accurate, the Germans were going to attack us in force that night at midnight. According to the information, we were going to have an intense bombardment of gas and high explosives for four hours on our trenches. After that they were coming over. Absolute secrecy had been maintained. We knew nothing of what was about to happen and Harwood told us the order still held good that one was not expected to leave the line but fight till captured.

Most of us knew what an 'intense bombardment' meant and when gas is added to the conditions what a perfect taste of hell it is, as with masks on, both breathing and seeing is difficult, which makes quick movement in the dark impossible.

As far as we in the front line were concerned, it amounted to nothing less than a sacrifice but a purpose is gained if, when the bombardment ceases, there are any men left alive who can give the warning at the actual moment when the Germans are in the trenches. The price seems great, and so it is.

All information regarding the movements of our troops in the rear areas had been withheld from us.

With these thoughts in our minds, we started to make preparations for the line. My thoughts were not of the cheeriest. It was almost like waiting to be hanged when, after experiencing these intense bombardments, I knew the chances were all against coming through safely and the most I could reasonably hope was that the good fortune or guardian angel which had carried me so far would see me through this, but how I did not know.

At 5.30pm the battalion fell in, in companies along various paths in the wood, and at 6pm we moved out in platoons at 50 yards intervals. This was necessary so that we should not appear as a large body of men on the move towards the line to any German airman who might come suddenly on the scene.

A Company led the way followed by B, C and D Companies. The CO [still Lieutenant Colonel Grahame Deakin] and adjutant [Captain Alfred Sayer] stood at the gate through which we passed. This was a most unusual procedure on [the CO's] part and seemed to me to confirm what Harwood had said. As each platoon officer took his men through, the CO wished him 'good night'. We who knew the circumstances were quite prepared to believe it was 'goodbye'. As I passed through, in common with the others, he wished me 'good night'. I wondered what was in his mind as platoon after platoon passed out and towards the line and from his control forever if, as expected, the bombardment was going to take place. It may have been my mood but he struck me as looking very pathetic and helpless. Night was closing in, throwing all the trees into relief, therefore the setting of the picture may have been responsible for the effect.

Keeping in touch with those in front, it was quite dark before we left the vicinity of the wood to emerge on to a main road where we joined up and waited for guides to take us up to the front line. The guides arrived at 9.30pm and we moved up to the trenches and relieved the Norfolks.

My first business was to try and gather some information from the platoon officer I was relieving but beyond the fact that he knew something was going to happen and had had orders to get away as soon as possible after relief, he knew nothing and wasted no time in carrying out his orders.

Left to myself, I saw every man had a good firing position, that his gas respirator was ready for any emergency and that he had a supply of rifle oil ready and also his ammunition. Water bottles filled and biscuits we had attended to before coming into the line, so there was nothing now to do but wait. The first half an hour seemed a week. A few shells came over and I wondered if that was the commencement. They stopped and nothing happened. The men, still gazing over the top long after the usual time, wondered what was in the wind.

A couple of hours passed but with the exception of an occasional shell, nothing happened. And so the morning found us still on the fire-step and still looking out into no-man's-land; the men full of disgust for any order that kept them 'standing to' all night for nothing but I was jolly thankful when it came and so I think they would have been had they known the circumstances.

It would be difficult to properly express my thoughts during that six hours before midnight. Here was a different phase. Maricourt during that first month [in the line] was long drawn out, where only the fittest physically survived. The Somme, with its mire and filth, was terrible but in that instance, we were on the move as it were. Here we were going up to meet it and to withstand it, with the full knowledge of what was before us.

Personally, I did not doubt for one moment the accuracy of the information nor did I doubt the fact that after four hours of bombardment there would be little or nothing of us left. It was the ability to visualise myself and for that matter, all of us more or less badly wounded and choking with gas, that appeared to me the horrible part. I had already seen it.

After we had passed the colonel, I thought that this, then, was the end and to me it seemed an inglorious one, that having come through so much I should be knocked out in defence, instead of – if the end had to come at all – in attack.

I recalled those days in Italy only but recently ended; they seemed of another decade and I remembered that when there, I wrote that it was an Arcady from which one day we should awaken to find ourselves in the vortex again, and here we were. It was not a joyous mood but it was one fitting to the occasion.

When the relief had been completed, there had been nothing left then but to await the bombardment and as each shell came over, I wondered if that was the signal for the beginning. Hour after hour had passed and when, towards morning, it was evident that the attack was not going to develop, reaction set in and I experienced the joy of awakening from another nightmare.

With daybreak and no fear of attack, the watch was relaxed except for a single sentry. After breakfast the men lay down in the bottom of the trench for sleep.

I crawled along to the next platoon commander, Lieutenant Ward, but beyond coming to the conclusion that something must have gone wrong somewhere in the German sphere of things he could essay no reason for the failure, so I returned to my men and like them lay down in the trench and slept through the day, waking up at intervals for a drink and a biscuit which constituted our rations for the moment.

With the advent of darkness, we got busy in front, throwing up additional breastworks and laying barbed-wire entanglements. We were still working hard when daylight began to dawn. The men came back into the trench and because there was nothing else to do lay down and slept the day through as the day before, waking up at intervals for a meal from rations which came up during the night.

Nothing eventful happened during the day and at night we sallied out again wiring and throwing up earthworks. We were not so fortunate this time.

Two of my men got pipped by rifle fire, one through the leg and the other through the chest. The latter died before morning. It is impossible to guard against this casual fire which is usually sent over by sentries who, having nothing else to do to pass the time, fire into the night. In this case they were successful in 'finding a billet'.

The German line is some 300 yards away in this particular part but they occupy intervening shell-holes at night with rifles and machine guns. It was from these shell-holes that the damage was caused.

Before daybreak, I sent a report to the colonel and spent some portion of the morning crawling along the trench on my hands and knees and fixing rifles so that we could put over grenades [rifle grenades] at night when they got busy again.

Although we had worked hard on the trenches at night, they were still very fragile, allowing for no unnecessary movement by day, so after a final inspection of my part of the front, which I did on my hands and knees, crawling over some of my men already asleep in the bottom of the trench, I did likewise, one man on sentry being sufficient for daytime.

Night came and with it the CO and Anderson, the brigade major. The CO had received the report of my casualties, passed it on to brigade and they were anxious to see from which direction the fire was coming. What exactly they intended to do I could not quite make out but I volunteered to show them the exact spot.

The night was pitch dark and together we all crawled over the top and I made for the direction in which I thought the fire was coming. It was rather amusing in a way; Anderson, a Scotsman and not much given to jibbing at things, and the colonel keeping level, the three of us pulling ourselves along on our stomachs.

My sense of direction must have been fairly accurate because we had, or so it seemed to me, gone but a few yards when a German machine gun opened fire almost under our noses. We appeared to be almost on top of them. Luckily he was not firing in our direction and we were crawling along on our stomachs but it was unpleasant.

Anderson stopped dead; so did the colonel and so did I. No word was spoken but Anderson began to work himself backwards, so did the colonel.

I was dazed for a moment by the flash of fire but not too dazed to follow the example of Anderson and the colonel. We worked our way backwards on our stomachs until we dropped back into the trench and for the remainder of the night my platoon plastered that vicinity with rifle grenades. It kept [the German] fire down whilst our men went on strengthening our trench.

Anderson seemed quite convinced that he had been near death's door. His remarks were somewhat amusing when he had opportunity for speech.

Daybreak came and with it another weary day of trying to sleep. The weather up to now had been uniformly good. Rations had been got up regularly every night and with them a supply of spirit stoves. These the men made good use of, as soon as it was broad daylight, making tea, toasting bread and warming up bacon that had already been cooked and brought up to us in sandbags. Were the lottery not so great, some scenes in the trenches far surpass, in humour, anything ever put on the stage. It was so this morning. Looking along the trench, each man had his spirit stove alight and was cooking his respective breakfast. Some were kneeling to it; others lay flat on their stomachs, all uniformly covered in dirt and days' growth of beard.

Night came again and with it a party of bombers from the German lines, probably with the intention of retaliation on us for the rifle grenades of the previous night. They were spotted opposite the trenches on my right and were buried half an hour later behind our lines, all three of them.

The supposed attack had not developed so far and, with the passing of days and nothing occurring, I breathed more freely and began to look forward to the relief.

With my name well-established nowadays amongst my platoon as the Sandbag King we slept the day and worked the night, only knocking off when the first suggestion of daylight appeared, then to drop down into the trench and, by the best means we could devise, pass the day and wait for the night which passed uneventfully, we carrying on with our sandbagging, pausing occasionally to send over a rifle grenade to let the Germans know we were awake.

The 16th [May] found us by this time fairly plastered in dirt, mainly from successive nights of perspiration, wiping the face with a hand already caked in dirt. We had no water to spare for washing or shaving and what would not wipe off stopped on, so we all looked forward for the relief to come. They came soon after dusk (King's Own Scottish Borderers). I handed over our portion of the line and with my platoon, made my way to the rear areas only stopping on the way to report to Harwood that we were clear. The alacrity with which I left the line that night and got my platoon of men to the rear and so to camp is still remembered by Harwood. I remember it also and the feeling of mental relief that attended it.

I led the way through the forest and we eventually found our camp in the early hours of the morning. During our absence more huts had been erected into which beds had been placed – wooden frames with wire netting stretched over. Our valises had been brought up and into mine I rolled, dog-tired, but with a sense of relief. I was soon fast asleep and did not awake till midday today.

This afternoon I bathed, Heathfield producing a bucket of hot water for the purpose. After that, a shave and a clean change of clothing. Wonderful the effect of taking off about seven days' growth of beard and with its departure the mud and dirt; add to that a warm bath and afterwards clean underclothes and one feels for the moment that the preceding week was worthwhile to experience the effect of this.

After my ablutions, I went round to the men's hut. They were similarly employed and I left them to it.

Nothing has been said about the expected attack. As we junior officers were supposed not to know anything about it, I have not made any enquiries.

I still seem to require more sleep so I am turning into bed early, 7pm. Fritz is busy overhead, bombing Aire I am told.

Saturday, 18 May 1918

Their planes did not wake me during the night, although they had a Derby going backwards and forwards overhead. This morning I heard that Aire is in flames and it certainly looked like it, huge columns of smoke were going into the sky. I could just see it in the distance.

Have been on fatigue work during the day, digging a line of trenches close by, returning for tea and now as night comes on, so are the Fritz planes coming over. I can hear them purring as they pass to have another shot at Aire.

Sunday, 19 May 1918, Steenbecque

The battalion marched into this village during the afternoon, the reason generally broadcast being so that the men could go to the *estaminets* for a drink, but general headquarters have a wonderful way of combining pleasure and business together and already this evening (we have scarcely settled in the village), rumours are floating around that we are likely to have a night alarm for practice purposes to see how quickly we can turn out and reach a given point, which is a line of trenches to be used in case the Germans break through.

Monday, 20 May 1918

At 5.30am the alarm went. There was a general shuffle, the troops turning up on parade with their boots half tied up and their equipment somewhere in the vicinity of their neck but it was dark. We moved off, occupied the line and returned to the village again by midday, in a boiling hot sun and bathed in a mass of perspiration.

This afternoon I slept. After tea I sat at my bedroom window (I am billeted in a cottage in the main street), watching the passing of time and a few of our fellows at an *estaminet* opposite. They were getting well oiled and apparently were discussing amongst themselves the shortcomings of the Portuguese troops in general and particularly a small party of Portuguese sitting close by, which they went up to and accused of running away and being the cause of our recall from Italy. Soon there were chairs and arms and legs flying in all directions. I withdrew into my room and watched the fight. It soon ended with the arrival of the military police.

Tuesday, 21 May 1918

Up at 4.30am for a brigade scheme. After tearing about the locality doing nothing in particular, we returned to the village at midday, as yesterday, bathed in perspiration from a very hot sun and fed up to the teeth.

Thursday, 23 May 1918

We relieved the 12th Gloucesters in support last night after a dickens of a march up here. We left Steenbecque at 8.30pm. The night was muggy and stuffy; the men carrying their heavy packs were very irritable and full of complaints. Towards 11pm we were close on our destination and ran into a barrage that the Germans suddenly put over. We had several casualties before the shelling stopped and it was gone midnight when we finally reached the line and relieved the Gloucesters there.

With daybreak, I was able to see how the land lay. We are situated in what was once a cornfield; the stubble still stands. Our trenches are mere slits in the ground, dotted right across the field. The position is about 250 yards from the German front line and we are likely to be gassed at any moment of the day or night, which is not cheery. We had a dose of it last night when we were barely settled.

Today I have slept. It seems the best thing to do if one can, leaving a sentry on duty in case a dose comes over.

Friday, 24 May 1918

We followed what is now old custom; working all through the night, every available man digging and strengthening the trench. Nothing happened to break the monotony. Occasionally I crept out to the screen of men who lay out in front of us as sentries. They reported that occasionally they could hear spades striking stones in the German lines so I supposed they were also digging. Before the approach of dawn, I called the screen of men in. They were nearly stiff with the raw, cold night and lying on the ground. The working party came in and the rum issue went round: wonderful drink, rum on these occasions. It seems to percolate every blood vessel of the body, penetrating where any hot drink does not seem to go. Before its influence had worn off, the men had had breakfast and those not on sentry duty were asleep in the bottom of the trench.

Cold and dull all morning and rain this afternoon, we have no sort of cover in these slit trenches and I have been very cold in consequence. Sleep has passed away some of the day but I think the men will be glad when night comes so that they can get up and stretch themselves and work and get warm. They are wonderfully cheery under these circumstances, no doubt finding comfort in the fact that we are all in the same boat together.

Looking along the trench now (I am sat at one end), it presents nothing but a mass of arms and legs in the bottom of the trench. They are mostly asleep with their overcoats drawn over their bodies and faces. One or two are sat up, making preparations for tea. These are very simple, boiling some water in their mug and adding dry tea. If they have eaten their rations, they go without, if not they produce a piece of bread and some jam and the meal is soon finished.

Heathfield, my servant, tells me of a very amusing incident that occurred on the way up to the line Wednesday night.

Someone in the rear of the company gave the gas alarm and there was a scramble to put on masks. At the same moment, a wagon came dashing along. Several of the men stood aside to let it pass and stepped into a fairly large roadside brook. They were pulled out soaked to the neck, their rifles and steel helmets sank and they were unable to recover them.

After writing the foregoing and after dusk, I have been round some of the farm buildings in our vicinity. When we first came up to this part about a month ago, they were intact for the most part, complete with furniture then. Now they are practically laid flat: burnt to the ground.

Everything is beginning to look very desolate here. Artillery soon leaves its mark. Burnt-out houses, trees broken down and charred and the ground pitted and scarred by shells soon changes the atmosphere of one's surroundings. At night when the mist rises, it brings with it the acrid smell of gas and burst explosives. We have not yet the smell of the dead to mix with it but if we stay long enough, we shall get that; both German and our own.

These slit trenches were part of those occupied by the Brigade of Guards when they fought in small knots of men on 14 and 15 April. Their graves lay scattered in odd corners of the field, mingled with those of the Germans. The Irish Guards appear to have held this bit of ground and held it, as their graves indicate, to the end when our division, the 5th, came up and pushed the Germans back some 700 yards from here.

3.30am. My platoon is working on a communication trench to connect us with the front line. In this position we are situated some distance from the Germans and dead quiet is not so essential. I am sitting in a cubbyhole in the trench with a candle stuck in the side and a ground-sheet overhead to keep down the light and am writing to pass the time.

Occasionally I hear one of my stalwarts enquire where the Sandbag King is, as he unearths something – probably a piece of rock – and enquires in subdued tones to the one next to him, how I would like to sandbag that.

Occasionally I take a pick and shovel myself to keep warm. It helps to pass the time waiting for the first signs of daybreak.

Saturday, 25 May 1918

Daybreak came at last, finding us all very tired and, in turn, glad of the rest to be obtained in the trench, with all our supplies brought up during the night by troops in the rear. Our water supply, in particular, is very scarce. Washing is out of the question and I am getting fairly muddy again. Dirt and dust is clinging to what becomes a very respectable beard.

The day has passed much as yesterday. At 10pm, the men went on digging. They had not been on long before the Germans opened up machine-gun fire from somewhere, firing indirectly. The bullets began to fall amongst my platoon and one of them has joined the 'great majority' with one through the head. They are chance shots fired from a distance overhead and one has found a billet.

2.30am. We have sent our casualty to the rear and carry on digging till the beginning of daybreak, about 4am.

3.30am. Have just been having a dig with the men. They are decidedly on the nervy side. The Germans, no doubt, have spotted this trench in daytime and are making things uncomfortable for us with their machine guns. Soon day will break and we shall be able to retire into the trench and, probably under the influence of rum and a meal, get to sleep and forget it.

Sunday, 26 May 1918

We finished without any further casualties and prepared to settle down for the day. Towards midday, I was awakened by a runner who brought through a message to say we were to move back to a rear position tonight.

Monday, 27 May 1918

At 1.30am we were relieved and half an hour later I took over some Nissen huts erected some distance in the rear of the trench we had been occupying. A quick scrutiny of the huts soon found weak places so my platoon, in conjunction with another platoon which had been similarly placed, started sandbagging and did not leave off till daybreak at 4.30am. We had had an occasional shell over but they appeared to go well over and did not prevent us from working.

I had barely dozed off when I was awakened by the colonel of a battalion which was apparently situated close by, saying he was being burnt out. I got up and, crawling out of the hut, saw some 300 yards away, a couple of houses and farm buildings well in flames with a whole battalion pouring out from the farm buildings and streaming in all directions from the flames. The action of the men was not unobserved. Away in the distance, almost on the skyline, a German plane was hovering. I pointed this out to the colonel and also the danger of the men streaming across the field. He had not spotted the aeroplane but at once sent orders for the men to take cover from observation along the nearest hedge but by this time no doubt, the Germans had seen all they required and would inform their artillery accordingly, as without a doubt, the plane and artillery which was shelling us were working together.

However, the burden of the colonel's visit was that he required our two Nissen huts that we had only occupied at 2am and on which we had spent the remainder of the night in making them more safe.

Our hopes for sleep had gone. We turned out and the colonel and his staff moved in and Lieutenant Clews, the other platoon commander, and myself scoured round for some other cover. We found a couple of huts half-finished in the wood adjacent (a corner of Nieppe Forest), and throughout the day we have been sweating, building up the outside with sandbags and finishing the work commenced by someone else.

The day has not been without its adventures. The German plane that we had seen this morning had also seen us and we have been pasted all day by shells dropping, in some cases, well away from us and occasionally too close to be anything like pleasant. During one of these last salvos, I saw what is quite an unusual sight – that of shells actually falling.

We have had a brilliant sun all day and with this at my back and my eyes focused on a spot where they all appeared to be directed, I saw each shell immediately before it reached the ground some 500 yards away. One after another, they fell in quick succession; great heavy brutes, they shook the ground as they exploded.

Occasionally, we have had one in the wood but the Germans do not appear to be quite certain where our troops are situated and appear to be searching the locality rather than one particular spot.

Midnight, the men have just finished sandbagging and Clews and myself have settled down in one of the huts. We wonder who is going to turn us out this time, probably the Germans with gas.

Tuesday, 28 May 1918

I slept the night through and was awakened soon after daybreak by a curious itching all over my face and hands, distinguishable by little red spots; mosquitoes. I was itching all over. I got up and went outside. Some of the men were already walking about in the wood and with the same complaint as myself. Too dog-tired to feel them biting during sleep, we were now having the full benefit of their endeavours.

We had scarcely finished breakfast (mine was a piece of cold bacon, bread and a mug of tea, same as the men), when the Germans started shelling again. We were not so lucky this time. A shell dropped into a trench that my platoon were taking shelter in. One man joined the realms above, another wounded, while another man, considerably shaken by the concussion, we put right with a stiff glass of whisky borrowed from the colonel in the hut.

After that we have had no rest all day. Practically all the time shells have been falling and, as they searched one locality, so we moved back to the one they had just shelled, hoping to escape any more casualties by doing so.

The men stand the strain very well in spite of the lack of sleep, washing facilities, cooked food and the general strain of the conditions we are under. They are quite cheery and so long as the shells do not fall too close, greet its coming and passing overhead with a joke and sometimes a cheer.

At tea-time, I had orders to take them up the line for wiring and now at 2am we have just returned. Sleep will probably be out of the question, the wood swarms with mosquitoes. Before settling down, I went and saw the men. They are getting down to it with their faces wrapped up in their greatcoats, quite cheery in spite of the previous days and finishing up with tonight, wiring in the front line, which has been no picnic.

Tomorrow we go back up the line; C Company in support to the remainder of the battalion.

Wednesday, 29 May 1918

We left the wood last night after dark and joined the remainder of C Company in this support line and in support of A, B, D Companies who are in the front line and so far we have had a comparatively easy time.

Thursday, 30 May 1918

Raids are apparently being developed. Report says that our intelligence department requires some prisoners for identification purposes and apparently the Germans are equally anxious that we shall not take any. Several parties have been over without success, finding in most cases that the front line has been deserted for the night. One party went over last night on our right and brought back a man who, on investigation, was found to be a native of one of the Balkan states. He knew nothing of German, neither language nor anything about their movements and for information purposes is useless.

Rumour says that our battalion is providing a raiding party and going over.

Today I have lain in my shack all day, the same with us all. As in the front line, no movement is allowed here during daylight. At dusk, we shall be busy no doubt. One of the companies in the front line will find us something to do.

Friday, 31 May 1918

At dusk last night the company was split up into working parties, some going to each company in the line and those that remained spent the night working in our own line. Occasionally we had doses of gas over, of the sneezing type. Then all work was stopped, masks were put on and we had to wait till the wind took it away.

Arnold Harwood had a near shave. He and I were going along the line to make sure no men were gassed and helpless. On returning we were conscious that bullets were coming over in great rapidity from German machine guns. Whistling through the air, they appeared too close to be pleasant so we knelt on the ground till it finished. We had barely got on our knees when one struck Harwood's steel helmet. No doubt the helmet saved him. On investigation there was a very fair dent where the bullet made contact but apart from giving him a headache, no harm was done.

With daybreak, the Germans started to shell our line with gas shells. We have lived in our masks most of the day. This ceased towards dusk. A glorious moonlit night, outside my shack the men are busy sandbagging. The keen night air seems to put new life into them. They are laughing amongst themselves as they fill and pile up bag after bag.

Saturday, 1 June 1918

After writing the above, or rather I had scarcely finished writing, when 'thud', a shell dropped uncommonly close to my shack, making the corrugated iron rattle overhead and almost at the same moment, the gas alarm was again given. I emerged from my shack to find clouds of gas floating over the line. A breeze was blowing and it soon passed but we were kept in a state of expectancy all the night which has continued all today. The men have slept in batches at a time whilst those awake were responsible for their safety.

Harwood went down to battalion headquarters during the day and we are awaiting his return. Rumour says that this company has to carry out a raid that, rumour says, our battalion is responsible for. Everything is always rumoured, so we await Harwood's return for definite news. Clews, Beeteson and myself are sitting around a brazier in one of the shacks. Outside, a biting wind is blowing in spite of the month and there appears only one way of keeping warm; that is with the aid of a pick and shovel and plenty of earth to dig at. The men are very busy. We can hear them lumping filled sandbags of earth one on top of another to form a better protection. We have sergeants who remind them of their work should they lapse into too long a rest so, for the moment, our presence is not required.

Evening passed and with its passing, night came and also Harwood. At a commanding officers' conference of company commanders this afternoon, C Company was chosen as being the company in reserve to carry out the raid and I the officer to lead the party. We were still round the brazier when Harwood came creeping in and we gathered around him to hear the news.

I was not too cheery when he told us that the choice had fallen on me. Raids are not things in which one is able to cover oneself in glory; all the odds are against a safe return, besides which there are other officers who have not had half the service in the trenches I have had and are consequently far fitter than myself as far as nerves are concerned. It savours of the 'willing horse' I think. Harwood, I think, caught my thoughts and when Clews and Beeteson had gone out, asked my opinion on the prospects of success. I told him my views. He quite agreed with me. He had volunteered himself, he said, as soon as it was decided his company had to do the show but the CO was not agreeable from the point of view that he was a company commander. However, it does not become a private to quibble when there is a job to be done, much less an officer, so I take them over on the night of the 3rd with one intention – to bring back prisoners.

During tours of duty in the front-line trenches, every battalion had to do its fair share of patrolling in no-man's-land, in order to build up a picture of the strength of the German defences opposite. Although intelligence gathering was the fundamental objective of this constant patrolling, it was also seen as a means of developing tactical awareness and leadership skills on the part of junior officers and NCOs whilst at the same time inculcating the necessary 'offensive spirit'. The declared aim of the British was to dominate no-man's-land so denying it to the Germans; the mantra of higher command being that the German wire was to be regarded as the British front line.

The trench raid was an altogether larger enterprise, although the numbers of participants varied. A form of 'trench terrorism', the raid – as the name implies – was planned with the explicit purpose of getting British soldiers, often with faces blackened by burnt cork and armed to the teeth with fearsome clubs, revolvers and bags full of bombs, into the German trenches to destroy as many dugouts and weapons, grab as many papers and documents and kill and capture as many Germans as possible, hauling hapless prisoners back across no-man's-land in order to interrogate them to gain valuable information. The larger and more sophisticated a trench raid became, so it involved the close cooperation and coordination of several arms, including artillery and often, by 1918, specialist machine-gun units.

The raid planned under Harry's command would involve him leading 38 men divided into six parties across no-man's-land in the dead of night to cause as much mayhem as possible amongst several German-held enclosures and houses along the road between the villages of Arrewage and Les Puresbecques, north of Merville. His specific orders were brief and unequivocal: 'to kill and capture as many of the enemy as possible, and secure identification'.

Friday, 7 June 1918, the Hatfield Anglo-American Hospital, Wimereux, near Boulogne

It was known that new German divisions were occupying the trenches opposite. Our aeroplanes had seen eight trains pass through Estaires station during the latter part of May and it was assumed that the occupants were then in the line and we had to capture some for identification. Having tried every means of silent raid without success, this one was to be [on a large scale] so that we should have every chance of bringing something back dead, if not alive.

Nearly every type of raid had been tried without success. The Germans, it is to be assumed, were fully aware of our wishes and so withdrew their front line men to a safer distance at night from raids.

It was in consequence of our lack of success that this raid was to be a more highly organised affair with a 'box barrage' [a bombardment which sealed the German defenders in the target area in a 'box', allowing no one out and no reinforcements in] consisting of artillery, trench mortars and machine guns. The intelligence department was so keen to get a prisoner that on the night of the raid, the telephone wires were cleared between brigade and army headquarters so that in case of success, the information could be got through without loss of time.

Harwood and myself set about making our own arrangements whilst the artillery got on with theirs. Part of ours included investigating the ground over which we had to travel. One night, Harwood, myself and the corporal of the battalion scouts, crept out stealthily on all fours into no-man's-land. Ahead of us was a mobile fowl house, now apparently derelict. Stealthily we crawled up to this and passed it and then I was conscious that there were only two of us; one was missing – the scout corporal. Harwood and I lay flat, cautiously looking in all directions for an explanation and it was soon forthcoming. An awful cackling arose from the fowl house and almost immediately a shower of bullets came from the German lines. I pressed closer to the ground. A few minutes elapsed and we were joined by the scout. 'I've got one,' he whispered and produced a bantam from under his tunic. We made our way back to our lines. To proceed was useless with the Germans now wide awake. The scout corporal had some little reputation for his unorthodox methods, of which this was a sample.

Raids are not things to raise one's enthusiasm and the problem was the choice of men. Harwood, like a great sportsman, put the whole of the company at my disposal. With Sergeant Hewlings as my second-in-command [Arthur Hewlings had crossed to France with the Birmingham Pals on 21 November 1915, the same day as Harry] and a corporal, we picked out the 30 best men of the company. Whilst the CO and adjutant got out the plan of attack and Harwood scouted the front line for the best 'jumping off' position, I tried to raise the enthusiasm of my party and instil into them a 'desire to raid' – which I certainly did not feel myself – and impressed on them the importance of our not returning without some good means of identification; alive if possible.

On the night of Sunday, 2 June, operation orders came up from battalion headquarters and, on paper at least, it looked as if no German could possibly live under such [a barrage], completely enclosed by fire from artillery, trench mortars, machine guns and rifles whilst we advanced.

At 3am, before daylight on the morning of Monday, 3 June, Harwood and myself took the party down to battalion headquarters situated in Nieppe Forest with the idea of showing them the actual distance from obstacle to obstacle we had to encounter on the way. We slept till lunch and, after tea, went over the course as mapped out on the ground of a clearing in the forest.

We had got to jump over a couple of German trenches, turn sharp right behind some farm buildings, cross a main road, come back again and attack a German trench in the rear. As we were finishing, the brigadier rode up. He shook hands with me and wished us all success.

Returning to the battalion headquarters hut in the wood, bombs and armlets were issued (we all wore white bands around our arms to avoid mistakes in the dark) and whilst the men rested, I went into the hut to make final preparations. Various units came in from the locality to wish us good luck, amongst which was the officer in charge of the artillery that was covering us whilst we were in the German lines. He was very uncertain of the accuracy of his guns he told me. They were very worn. According to army regulations, a gun can only be fired so many times with accuracy, owing to the fact that each shell as it passes along the barrel tends to wear the hard steel lining. When this occurs the shell, instead of being forced direct to its object, wobbles on its flight and loses its impetus – in effect, it falls short.

I pointed out to him that such a thing was fatal as we proposed to creep up within a few yards of his barrage, advancing as the barrage advanced. He agreed that that was risky but promised to pitch the muzzles of the guns up, a proposition that I had to agree to but it left me very uneasy.

At 10pm the men fell in and Sergeant Hewlings took them back up the line. Harwood and I stayed and had dinner with the colonel and then followed them on.

It was a glorious night for the occasion, clear and starlit. The colonel came some short distance with us and then, wishing us the best of luck, turned back.

Fritz was lobbing some heavy shells over so we got going and arrived shortly afterwards in the front line. The men were ready and waiting and at 11.20pm Hewlings took the first party out to the jumping-off ground, a line some 30 yards in front of 'Hun' Sayer's front line.

Harwood and myself took the remainder out and, after a few more instructions to the men, we were all in position by 11.40pm, lying in the grass and waiting to go forward. Harwood, who had worked like a brick for the success of the show, stayed to the last moment and then slipped back to our front line.

In its way, this was quite a little episode of war life; the night bright and clear helping towards that end. The men, only a couple of yards in front, lay in a long line ready for the signal to advance, each grasping his rifle, the bayonets of which I could see at odd intervals and whilst Harwood and myself stood whispering, occasionally our artillery would send over a shell which we knew to be the calm before the storm. Ever thoughtless of himself, he told me how he wished that it was himself going over and not me. Wishing me good luck, he slipped back into the trench and I took my place amongst the men.

(Some long time afterwards, he told me that he had had only one premonition in his life and it was on that occasion – that I should not return alive.)

How that last five minutes hung. It seemed like a week. At last a solitary gun fired. It was the signal for the artillery and the next moment for 1,000 yards, there was a terrific crash along the German lines of shells, trench mortars and machine-gun and rifle fire. This remained on their front line for three minutes before it lifted and crept slowly towards their rear areas.

After lying in the grass for 1½ minutes, I gave the order to advance and up we sprang and went forward. The noise was deafening, the flashes from shrapnel livid as they burst in air, heavy shells as they exploded further forward, the continual crash as trench mortar after trench mortar screeched through the air and crashed on the German lines and the rattle of our machine guns all helped to set up a perfect inferno. Conscious that they were for us and not against us, I felt perfectly cool myself.

Taking the lead and leaving Sergeant Hewlings to keep the men in line as far as possible, we advanced at a very slow double. A few shells began to fall short. I had not gone far when I felt a terrific clout at the back of my right knee which let me down but I was quickly up again and looking back, was surprised to find the men almost at a standstill. Hewlings came up, said we were advancing too quickly and were getting into our own barrage and I remembered what the artillery officer had said and I visualised for a moment standing before the colonel and telling him I was sorry 'but the raid was a failure'. I imagined [the colonel] was standing at the door of a hut situated in a wood and I was standing before him. He had a look of surprise mingled with regret and somehow I felt I was to blame and was proportionally ashamed.

It was gone in a second and so was I, back to the men. Under the circumstances, they were quite justified in hesitating. Our artillery was dropping shells short all around us and already casualties had occurred from that source. Hewlings and I pulled them together and we went forward again. We originally started off as an organised force but as we pushed forward, we became a seething mass of men with rifles, bayonets and bombs.

We crossed over the first German trench and found it empty, crossed the second trench and dropped some of our party to guard our left flank and pushing forward, turned sharply to the right, crossed a main road and around some farm buildings and turned sharply right again to face our own lines. With Hewlings and I leading the way, we should now be close on the line we were attacking.

Shrapnel was still exploding in the air, setting out everything in relief. By one of these flashes, we both saw what looked like a trench and dashed towards it, revolvers ready and followed by the men. Reaching it, we found it was what looked like a long mound of potatoes with a covering of earth.

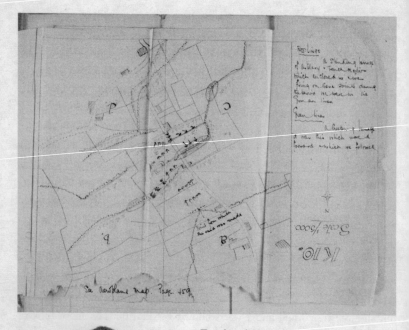

Trench raid: Harry's original map for the raid he led on the German lines on the night of 4 June 1918, for which he was awarded the Military Cross. He later annotated it and added arrows to indicate his journey across no-man's-land and over the German trenches. He turned it upside down to orientate it in the direction he actually travelled. (David Griffiths)

Identification: The epaulette torn from the shoulder of the German greatcoat as Harry raced along the German trenches during the raid. Although the two prisoners captured belonged to the German 103rd Infantry Regiment the epaulette was proof that the 177th Infantry Regiment was also in the area. British commanders were 'frightfully bucked' on learning that the line opposite was manned by the generally less aggressive Saxon soldiery.

(David Griffiths)

We dashed forward again and as we ran, I saw, by the aid of the shell flashes, Germans running from the direction in which the trench ought then to be. Hewlings and I, firing at them as we ran, dashed madly for the trench. It was a shallow affair and I dropped into it. The men, now well in the soup, were as eager as myself and we swarmed along the trench, I taking with me a German overcoat that I had picked up and pulling off the shoulder strap as I went along, in case we could not find anything alive. This I retained and still have as a souvenir of the episode. On it is worked the number of the German regiment, which would have been useful for identification.

We had barely gone a dozen yards when a commotion in front told me something was occurring a few steps forward and I saw our fellows pulling up a German from the bottom of the trench by the scruff of his neck followed by another a few moments afterwards. Having got what we had set out for, ie, Germans for identification purposes, I blew the rally – two short blasts of a whistle was the prearranged signal for everyone to get back to our trench – and we all made for our front line. At the same time, I signalled two flashes by torch to a signaller waiting in our front line. He phoned battalion headquarters and so on to brigade headquarters and so on to divisional headquarters and so on to army headquarters who probably knew the result before we arrived back to our trench.

From start to finish, we had been away about 20 minutes and one lives every moment during such times. I dropped into our trench. Some of the party I found were already back, others followed me soon after, dropping into the trench in twos and threes.

The prisoners I had sent on and were in the safe keeping of 'Hun' Sayer. Shells were still going over, the fag end of the bombardment. It was unfortunate for us that these particular guns kept on firing so long, as apparently it was this battery that had been firing short and were now dropping them amongst us in our own front line, causing unnecessary casualties.

The clout on the knee began to materialise. My breeches were fairly covered in blood, my leg was stiff and knee swollen to a large degree. When things had quietened down, I made my way back to company headquarters and found Harwood awaiting me. Together we made a report of the show, stopping to thank all the party who had remained intact for their efforts and also to have my leg dressed. (Not sure if all our party had returned,

Harwood, later on in the early hours, made some attempt to scour no-man's-land over the part where we had been. He crawled up to the German front line which had in the meantime been re-occupied by the Germans, who, hearing some noise in front of their trench slung a bomb out and he stopped a splinter from it.)

I wished goodbye to Harwood, Beeteson and Clews and followed down to the dressing station those of the men who had been hit and had gone on down. Our battalion dressing station was in the cellar of one of the houses in the vicinity and there I went. On arrival I found that most of the casualties had preceded me and were now in the course of having their wounds dressed. The cellar was thick with the smell of iodine and within its limited space the men were sitting or lying. There was a fair amount of blood and rum about, the latter to compensate for the loss of the former. There was no daylight: candles took its place and by their light, the doctor was patching up the men, prior to their removal to hospital.

At the field ambulance in Nieppe Forest, my leg was dressed and I was put on a light railway running through the forest to the stationary field ambulance. On arrival, I had a meal and was inoculated and then by canal to Aire Stationary Hospital where I was X-rayed. A bullet was found in the back of my knee. The bullet had caught me in the seat and, having travelled down the leg, was taken out from the back of the kneecap.

I was told afterwards by the surgeon that on its course, it passed within the merest fraction of an inch of one of the main arteries and also the sciatic nerve. Had it caught the former, I should quickly have bled to death and in the latter case, it would have meant a shortened leg, after a period of excruciating pain. I was operated on at once and put back to bed. By midday I was awake again and consuming a good meal.

So in 12 hours from the time we went over on the raid, I had been hit, finished the raid, walked down to the first and passed through two other dressing stations. At each place, I was examined and the wound redressed and I was inoculated at the third port of call, had been operated on at the fourth hospital, had had a sleep and was awake again and eating a good meal.

With the afternoon came my valise from the battalion, also a letter from the colonel and from Harwood. After congratulations, they said the raid had been a great success in spite of our casualties (14 wounded caused by our own artillery using worn guns) and valuable information had been gained. The brigadier general had sent his congratulations to the colonel on the result.

At a subsequent inquiry by the brigadier, it was stated the bad firing of the artillery was caused by faulty ammunition but those there must have known that any guns at fault should not have been used.

When I had read the letters and it dawned on me that, for some considerable time at least, I should have no more trench duty to do: no more smells of acrid fumes from shell bursts and of gas and of the dead, no more all-night duty and sleeping when and where I could in the daytime and meals of anything at any time, but that I should have a bed to sleep in and meals at regular times, I burst out crying – no doubt the anti-climax – and cried myself off to sleep again. Whilst I was in the process of doing so, I remember faintly hearing the fellow in the next bed ask the sister if I was crying or dying.

During the night I awoke again. The sister was sitting by my bedside. The bright, cheery girl I had known in the daytime had altered to one who looked tired and ill. I heard her mutter to herself 'will it never cease', repeating it again and again, then I heard a series of detonations. The Germans were dropping bombs on the town and so I went off to sleep again whilst she kept what must have been a very wearying vigil.

I stayed two days in the hospital at Aire and yesterday, the 6th, I was put aboard a train and brought down to Boulogne. It was a great sensation to lie comfortably on the bed of the hospital train, to speed along and know that every minute was taking me further from it all for a rest under civilised conditions and now today, the 7th, I am waiting for the next move, which will probably be England.

The letters of congratulation from Arnold Harwood, Harry's C Company commander, and Lieutenant Colonel Grahame Deakin, his commanding officer, were effusive in their praise of his work during the raid, but neither man pulled any punches with regard to what they saw as a 'botched job' on the night by the artillery.

Arnold Harwood wrote first to Harry:

My dear old Drinks,

I am most awfully sorry that you have had to go down but I hope you will have the best of times in England.

The CO was very sorry not to see you, and much admires all that you did.

Despite the artillery the show was a great success and the identification has proved most valuable, for no one had the least suspicion that these troops were here and at first Brigade could hardly believe it.

The CO sent up his congratulations through [the] Coy and the Brigadier wired, 'congratulate all ranks most heartily on their excellent raid; I very much regret their unnecessary losses'.

Our total casualties were yourself, me and 10 O[ther]R[anks], some serious. The M[achine] G[uns] had a man killed and others wounded and A Company had several L[ewis] G[unners] wounded, so mine was the only casualty inflicted by the enemy.

The men are very much 'tails up' and we're the company just now but we owe it nearly all to you!

I'll write again when I get your address, meanwhile my very best good wishes.

Lieutenant Colonel Grahame Deakin's letter came next:

My Dear Drinks,

First let me congratulate you on your extremely stout work in the raid and secondly how awfully sorry I am that you were hit. I can't tell you how sorry I am to lose you but I hope you will roll up again after a well-deserved rest in England.

The raid was an undoubted success but was prevented from being an even greater one by our bloody guns.

The identification was extremely valuable and everyone from brigade down to the army is frightfully bucked at finding the Saxons here.

Let me know your address and movements as you go on as I hope to have an interesting bit of news for you.

Again many thanks for all you did and the very best of luck.

The 'interesting bit of news' to which Deakin referred was that he had put several names forward for gallantry awards, including Harry's, and if, in due course, the recommendations were accepted, Harry would become a decorated war hero.

On 1 July 1918, word came through that Sergeant Arthur Hewlings, Harry's trusted lieutenant on the night of 3/4 June, had been awarded the Military Medal for gallantry during the raid, along with Private Michael Murphy.

It took almost another three months but the interesting bit of news for Harry, hinted at by Lieutenant Colonel Deakin in his letter, finally appeared in the London Gazette on Monday, 16 September 1918. Harry had been awarded the Military Cross. His citation read:

> For conspicuous gallantry and devotion to duty when in charge of a raiding party on hostile trenches. Two minutes after zero he was badly wounded in the leg, but in spite of great pain and difficulty in moving, he carried on in charge of the party which he handled with the greatest dash and initiative. It was largely due to his courage and ability that the raid was a success and valuable identification secured.

It was a proud moment for Harry but while he could celebrate, his achievement had led to shame for some on the 'other side of the wire'.

An account of Harry's raid from the German perspective appeared in the history of the Saxon 103rd Infantry Regiment, written by Hauptmann Rudolf Monse in 1930:

> During the night of 3 to 4 June, at 12.45am, the enemy abruptly opened up heavy artillery and machine-gun fire against our front line; an especially dense Feuerglocke [literally 'bell fire'– the German term for a 'box barrage'] was put over the boundary line between Infantry Regiment 103 and Infantry Regiment 177, which was holding the position to our right. Before the reserve units could grasp the situation, a strong English patrol overran a picket-guard of Infantry Regiment 177 on the road between Arrewage–Caudescure and moreover captured Unteroffizier Bauer and one more man of 1st Battalion, Infantry Regiment 103, who had been deployed for trench duty at that point.

The shoulder strap Harry tore from the German greatcoat as he raced along the German trench was embroidered with red stitching which formed the number 177. This indicated that it belonged to a soldier of the Saxon 177th Infantry Regiment, the unit to the right of that from which prisoners had been taken. Remarkably, the history of the 177th Regiment does not refer to the raid at all. Only in the Ehrentafel – Roll of Honour – are the following casualties listed:

4th June 1918 near Neuf Berquin: Soldat Edwin Öhler, born 19.12.1899 Trünzig (Zwickau); Soldat Oskar Kühne, born 17.4.1895 Nieder-Lössnitz (Dresden); Soldat Karl Berger, born 21.1.1884 Reichenhain (Chemnitz).

All three of these Saxon soldiers lie buried side-by-side today in Sailly-sur-la-Lys Kriegsgräberstätte in Block 8, graves 507 (Kühne), 508 (Berger) and 509 (Öhler). There can be no doubt that these men were killed either as a result of the British bombardment or due to the actions of Harry and the men of his raiding party.

Monday, 10 June 1918, Queen Alexandra's Hospital for Officers, Highgate, London

I was awakened yesterday morning before 5am and after a wash and breakfast was placed on a stretcher and a few minutes later was on the way to a hospital boat. Ambulances were arriving from all directions from hospitals and ours joined in the procession.

We left the harbour at nine o'clock reaching Dover at 11am. Trains were waiting to take us to London. There, we were split up according to our case and about half an hour afterwards, I found myself at the above [hospital].

For bed patients, all hospitals seem to have the same idea about our treatment. I was awakened at 5.30am with a cup of tea and shortly afterwards water to wash and shave. The nurse on duty has the next turn at us. Breakfast follows shortly afterwards, followed by inspections by the matron and medical officer. The day is passed according to the mood. My mood for the moment is to sleep.

Less than a week separated Harry's mad dash across no-man's-land and his helter-skelter charge through the German trenches from his lying dozing in a hospital bed in London.

Whether some of his lethargy was due to the after-effects of surgery or the ordered sanctuary of hospital routine is unclear, but there can be no doubt that after his years of exertion in the trenches, Harry's final diary entry also betrayed a body overwhelmed by sheer physical exhaustion and a mind bathed in a deep pool of relief. He believed he had, for a time at least, escaped the war. In the event

Harry would never have to fight again but as he embarked on his path towards recovery he was not to know that, and accordingly had to face the possibility of a return to France. His thoughts and reflections on the period covering the many months of his hospitalisation, recovery and convalescence written after the war shows a stark honesty.

Armistice

Whilst I was in hospital, things on the battle fronts went on apace. The German advance which had started in March 1918 and which had brought us back from Italy had been finally arrested and we, in our turn, had taken up the initiative and began to hammer back with the help of American troops who made a belated entry into the war. The Central Powers, suffering from exhaustion from the result of the terrific drives they made from March 1918 onwards, were unable to withstand the counter-attacks developed by the Allied powers.

First one country and then another of those comprising the Central Powers asked for peace, eventually leaving only Germany to fight, and Germany, weakened by our blockade and suffering from internal trouble amongst its civil population, sued for peace and the war came to a close on 11 November 1918 at 11am.

Meanwhile, in hospital, I was content to watch events as chronicled in the daily papers and read with interest some three weeks after arrival that, with the knowledge gained from the results of the raid, our division attacked the German troops opposite, taking ground, prisoners and guns, and retaining the ground which was eventually used as a jumping-off [point] for one of the final pushes on our part.

I stayed in the London hospital some two months. My wound, which was of no real account and had caused no permanent injury, soon began to heal and I was transferred to a convalescent hospital near Farnham [in Surrey]. The hospital was in reality a large private house, belonging to a lady who at the commencement of the war had put it at the service of the government, being responsible herself for its maintenance, she sleeping in the servants' quarters so that she could provide another bedroom.

At the end of the month of August, I duly reported to a medical board for an examination and was marked 'Al' and fit for duty.

I was somewhat surprised at their decision but the war was still on and I could only conclude that the need was great. There is a vast difference between being 'fit' and being 'fit for duty', as duty is understood in France. That I was not fit for the latter I was quite sure, as after events proved.

I almost shrank from going back to France and back to that most awful mire and felt somewhat sick when at the end of the medical board, the colonel got up and congratulated me on my quick recovery. I thanked him but did not feel it and left with very mixed feelings.

I reported to our service depot at Dover on 31 October, there to await orders for overseas but things in France had been moving apace and before draft orders came, peace was signed on the morning of 11 November 1918.

At a few minutes to 11 o'clock on that morning, I was standing on the edge of the cliff overlooking the sea and awaiting any sign that would tell us that the war was at an end. Precisely to the minute of 11, maroons blew and coloured lights were fired from the boats in the harbour. Looking down on the town, I could see flags going up in all directions.

On the barrack square, the 'fall in' blew and we all assembled and, with band playing, marched round the building. Meanwhile in Dover, sailors were coming in off the boats. All the troops stationed in the locality went down into the town and the remainder of the day was given over to celebration.

So peace had come at last.

AFTERWORD

Harry's war was over but, as a serving officer, now passed A1 and fit for duty, the signing of the Armistice did not signal an end to his military career.

From Dover he was posted to Salisbury Plain, where many battalions were still training and although not needed now to fight, Harry helped prepare the men for garrison duty abroad. Harry was struck by the extreme youth of these soldiers; 'mere boys' he called them. 'To see them on parade,' he remarked, 'brought forcibly to one how short we were getting of men.'

Harry's accommodation in the barracks was filthy; sleeping on the floor in a dirty room with equally dirty blankets he quickly developed a rash while his wound, still not completely healed, flared up. News of a posting to Italy two weeks later to join the 1/5th Battalion of the Royal Warwickshire Regiment, which had remained to fight on in Italy after Harry's battalion had been recalled to France, was greeted with joy. His previous experience of Italy, especially the climate, had been so good that he felt it was just what he needed in order to recover. But his health deteriorated markedly as he was jammed into a carriage with several fellow officers to reprise his long rail journey through France. Long before Harry reached Italy a severe infection had set in down his leg along the track the bullet had taken and he was also plagued with scabies and impetigo. Little wonder that on arrival at the base in Arquata he was transferred immediately to hospital in Genoa.

Harry stayed in hospital until the end of January 1919, having 'a thoroughly enjoyable time'. Cured of all his ailments he finally joined his new battalion – a unit, like many others, still suffering from the after effects of a long and wearying war. Although the climate was excellent almost every military duty, it seemed, was an effort. Parades were only held in the morning, with afternoons devoted to sports. Rumour had it that the battalion was bound for Army of Occupation duty in Austria but instead Harry only moved down to the British base at Arquata. Here he received a gift of a brass shell case artistically worked by three prisoners of war from the Austrian prisoner of war camp close by and made the most of his time by visiting Rome, Florence, Venice, Milan and Verona.

Towards the beginning of May 1919, Harry was posted to Egypt to be greeted by the intense heat of a scirocco wind and a simmering cauldron of revolution against British rule.

Moving to Helmiah, a camp on the desert five miles from Cairo, Harry initially wondered why he was there. Cairo itself was relatively quiet, although a strong undercurrent of revolt was evident. Several Westerners and army personnel had already been murdered when they had become lost in the maze of Cairo's narrow alleys and thoroughfares and Harry was told to keep his eyes and ears open as he walked the capital's streets.

A few weeks after arrival in Egypt he was posted, first as adjutant and then as commandant, to Ghamrah camp housing 500 Indian troops on leave from Palestine. Many were the weird and wonderful experiences he had as he set to industriously re-organising the camp to his satisfaction and liaising with the local villagers.

Ghamrah was only a short distance beyond the outskirts of Cairo, but given the then current state of civil unrest its location was particularly unpleasant – only a single, unlit track across a narrow neck of land linked it to the Egyptian capital – and the area beyond the boundary fence was dangerous after dark. Harry was convinced that he and his staff had been marked out as targets by local youths and although he brought his suspicions to the attention of his superiors they were brushed aside, as was his request to be issued with a gun for self defence.

Several weeks passed where Harry, now promoted to temporary major, was constantly on the alert, but nothing untoward occurred.

When danger finally confronted him on the evening of 3 December 1919 it exploded with a startling suddenness and when he least expected it. Harry and his adjutant had just reached the main station square during one of his forays into Cairo when, according to his account written after the war, 'we heard a revolver report and guessed the rest. I felt a sting in the foot and looking round quickly saw a native holding a smoking revolver not more than 15 yards away. We had the sense to part and the native did not know which to fire at and the succeeding bullets went wide of the mark. I saw them kicking up the road in front of us as I parted from the adjutant.'

A passing car scooped him up and whisked him to the military hospital and the following morning he was operated on and the bullet extracted. One of his visitors was none other than Lady Allenby, the wife of the Great War British Army commander Field Marshal Viscount Edmund Allenby, then serving as Special High Commissioner to Egypt.

Towards the end of 1919, after less than a month of treatment, news reached Harry that his father had been taken ill. Applying to return to England, he left Egypt early in the New Year of 1920 but he was too late. He arrived in Dover on the day of David Drinkwater's funeral in Stratford-upon-Avon.

Admitted yet again to hospital, this time in Aldershot, Harry stayed until the end of March when he was finally discharged and given two months' holiday before transfer to the Royal Warwickshire Regimental depot at Budbrooke Barracks, Warwick. Here, he joined men who were going through the final phases of demobilisation from the army; a process which, with the war finally over, the victory won and the peace secured, should have been a cause for rejoicing, yet many felt a sense of anticlimax. Certainly for Harry there appeared to be no sense of elation; on the contrary, his comment 'So peace had come at last' on the day of the Armistice is heavy with resignation.

In a little over four years the war had literally changed the course of world history; old orders had been swept away, empires had been toppled, new economic powers had emerged. More important, however, was the immediate and enduring effects it had had on the lives of individuals and their families and here the figures are truly staggering in their enormity: ten million soldiers dead, a further 21 million more or less physically or mentally scarred, a little short of a million civilians killed as a direct result of military action and almost six million more killed as a result of disease or severe malnutrition. In the years which followed, many of those who remained, their immunities sapped by so many years of emotional stress, privation and exhaustion, succumbed to the widespread and virulent epidemic of 'Spanish flu' which, by the time it had run its deadly course, had claimed even more lives than had the war itself.

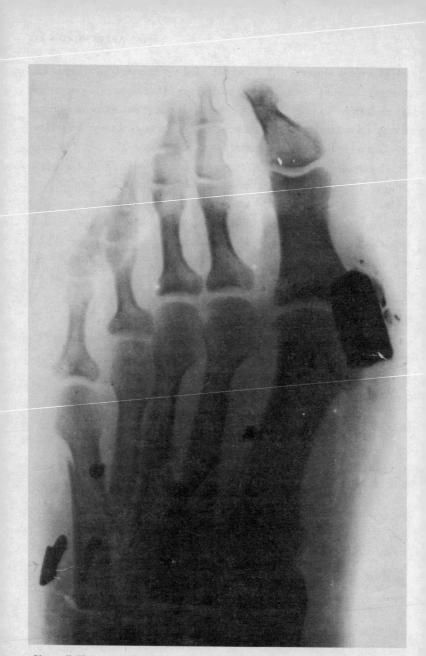

Close call. This remarkable image is the actual X-ray of Harry's left foot after the attempt on his life in Cairo in December 1919. At the time the use of X-rays was still a relatively new technology but here the image is crystal clear, showing the bullet lodged near his big toe and several fragments from the pavement that were driven into his foot as a result of the impact.

Harry's final thoughts and reflections were written in 1928 at a time when harsh reminders of the fighting in the trenches were still visible on relatively young men with eye patches, empty jacket sleeves or who were hunched in wheelchairs. Then there were those whose war wounds ran just as deep but were invisible, those whose mental anguish would blight their lives and whose case Harry felt compelled to champion, lest at best they be misunderstood, or at worst, forgotten.

'Writing now, some eight years after the foregoing, another aspect of this point arises, and that is the attitude of the civilian of today, who knew no war service, towards the halt and lame of the war. According to official returns, there are still some 14,000 men in hospital, requiring medical and surgical attention, but it would be difficult to estimate the number of those who, having no wounds to show as an outward sign, nevertheless require the care and attention of a hospital. One refers to the mental case; the man who, to all intents and purposes, presents an outwardly healthy appearance but who is broken internally by the effects of gas, concussion or mental strain – mentally wounded. Speaking to such a fellow a short time ago, he expressed the opinion that the people, generally, little understand the after-effects of war, after-effects which medicine does not always cure.

'The general attitude towards the man who is disfigured is "poor man"; they don't understand any other aspect. With this opinion, one is inclined to agree.

'That one's senses may have become impaired to a degree by the continued usages of the war is reasonable to expect, also that time will put them right again, but that there are many whose senses are injured beyond repair, is equally true. The papers chronicle their decease with regularity; died usually by their own action, after prolonged depression.'

In May 1920 Harry came before his final medical board. Mischievously noting that the medical profession was 'unable to cure me anymore' he was finally discharged with a pension, after an army service of five and a half years full of thrills and pathos and which, he concluded, had taken him, 'from the north to the south of England, to France, Belgium, Ireland, Italy and Egypt and through it all had brought me, with the exception of a few broken bones in the foot, safe home at last.'

It is a fact, often overlooked, that many more men who fought in the trenches survived than died. Like Harry, most came home to their families or got married and started families and although many struggled to cope with debilitating physical or mental trauma there were many more went back to their jobs, if they could get them. Yet the war had left its mark on every one of those who fought. They were not the same men who had left Britain's shores a few years earlier. While thousands of his contemporaries either could not talk or chose to remain silent, Harry Drinkwater was able to summon the words which might serve to speak for them all.

'I had been scarcely able to appreciate the fact that there would be no more war, but by degrees I began to realise the fact that I should not have to fight any more in trenches and smell the acrid fumes. I did not feel that elation and relief that possibly one might think would follow the strain of so long a time.

'With the idea of getting at my senses, I tried to imagine that I had been left vast wealth and I found the thoughts of that left me quite cold. Discussing this with other fellows, I found them very much the same. For those who had done any great amount of service in the fighting area, the war had left one, as a legacy, with dulled senses and a lack of ability to appreciate the conditions which one might be in for the moment, good, bad or indifferent.

'When I contemplated the many incidents that had taken place since November 1915 when I first crossed to France, I was inclined to believe Shakespeare when he wrote:

"There's a divinity that shapes our ends,
Rough-hew them how we will."'

ACKNOWLEDGEMENTS

The quest to bring Harry Drinkwater's words to life and present them to a wider audience has entailed a great deal of collaboration and coordination on the part of many people over many months. It was literary agent David Luxton who instantly agreed with the assessment of the potential of Harry Drinkwater's diary, based on a few sheets of his writing pulled out of a briefcase; just days after Jon had first set eyes on it at the home of David Griffiths. His advice and encouragement, along with that of his colleague Rebecca Winfield, is greatly appreciated.

Liz Marvin, our editor at Ebury Press, has acted as a welcome critical friend throughout the editing process. Her efficiency, eagle-eye and plain good sense have undoubtedly spared many blushes and improved the final work immeasurably. Thanks also to our talented publicist, Ellie Rankine.

We are indebted to the late Rod Suddaby of the Imperial War Museum for his sage advice and to Mrs Jean Drinkwater – the wife of Harry's late nephew William Wilson Drinkwater – for her support in the initial stages of the project.

If we have missed anyone else who has been kind enough to help in any way, please be assured that this has not been intentional. To those so affected please accept our sincere apologies.

Finally Jon and David would like to thank Harry Drinkwater. If he had not had the will, the strength or the perseverance to pick up his pencil – every day, often amid the most horrific conditions – and commit his thoughts to paper, none of this would have been possible. Thank you Harry.

Jon Cooksey's Acknowledgements

Little did I know, when I picked up the phone one afternoon in early December 2012 that it would lead here; to the publication of *Harry's War*. The voice on the other end of the line that day belonged to David Griffiths, owner of Harry Drinkwater's war diary. His desire to see Harry's words in print after living with them for over thirty years and following in Harry's footsteps was palpable. When he spoke of Harry's remarkable life, written in his own words, I was persuaded to read it for myself. When at last I set eyes on the war diary, it took minutes to fall under Harry's spell. *Harry's War* is the result.

Thanks then are due to David Griffiths for having the foresight to contact me and for his enthusiasm and support in the development of the book. I am grateful too to his wife Patricia who has, during several visits to their home, fed and watered me most royally. Thank you Patricia for understanding that it is not just armies that march on their stomachs and that some authors do too!

Although I knew immediately that Harry's diary was a remarkable and unique document I also knew that in order to bring it to life I required the support, help, advice, and encouragement of a great many people with a deep knowledge of and expertise in their particular field. I would like to record my gratitude then to the following – in no particular order – who, during the course of my research, provided valuable assistance or commented on early drafts: Richard Pearson, archivist at King Edward VI School, Stratford-upon-Avon; the late Alan Tucker, who kindly supplied the results of his exhaustive research into the men of the Royal Warwickshire Regiment; the unfailingly helpful staff at the Shakespeare Birthplace Trust in Stratford-upon-Avon; Sebastian Laudan in Berlin and Jack Sheldon in France, both experts on digging out the stories of the men on 'the other side of the wire' and Graham McKechnie, BBC journalist, sometime off-spinner and great friend who, as always, has served as a critical sounding board for all my theories.

At home my wife Heather and daughter Georgia have continued to indulge my often anti-social working habits as they fought some difficult battles themselves. I could not do what I do without them and I thank them for their encouragement and their seemingly limitless patience and understanding.

David Griffiths' Acknowledgements

Thanks must first go, as always, to my wife Patricia who patiently checked Harry's diary against the first draft of the book alongside me.

I am indebted to my former secretary, Samantha Rose, who, many years ago, painstakingly typed out Harry's words to produce the transcript that formed the first step in the long process to bring his diary into print.

I would also like to thank the staff at the Royal Regiment of Fusiliers Museum (Royal Warwickshire) in Warwick, who, several years ago now, kindly copied the regimental war diaries for various key periods, which allowed Harry's experiences to be set in the wider context of the war in which he was engaged.

I should also like to thank my collaborator Jon Cooksey, whose drive, enthusiasm and desire to see Harry's diary finally published matched my own.

INDEX

Page numbers in italics indicate photographs

ABOUT THE EDITORS

Jon Cooksey is a leading military historian who has written a number of books about both World Wars and the Falklands conflict. He is often asked to write articles about battlefield history for the national press, and has co-written and co-produced several radio documentaries for the BBC on the subject of war.

David Griffiths is a collector of military artefacts and acquired Harry's diary in 1980. He became fascinated with Harry's story and has long hoped to see it in print.